Celestial India

Celestial India
Madame Blavatsky and the Birth of Indian Nationalism

Isaac Lubelsky

Translated by Yael Lotan

SHEFFIELD UK   BRISTOL CT

Published by Equinox Publishing Ltd
UK: Unit S3, Kelham House, 3 Lancaster Street, Sheffield S3 8AF
USA: DBBC, 28 Main Street, Oakville, CT 06779

www.equinoxpub.com

First published 2012

© Isaac Lubelsky 2012

This translation © Equinox Publishing Ltd 2012

All rights reserved. No part of this publication may be reproduced or transmitted in any form or by any means, electronic or mechanical, including photocopying, recording or any information storage or retrieval system, without prior permission in writing from the publishers.

British Library Cataloguing-in-Publication Data

A catalogue record for this book is available from the British Library.

ISBN   978-1-84553-922-1 (hardback)
          978-1-84553-923-8 (paperback)

Library of Congress Cataloging-in-Publication Data

Lubelsky, Isaac.
Celestial India : Madame Blavatsky and the birth of Indian nationalism / Isaac Lubelsky; translated by Yael Lotan.
   p. cm.
 English translation of an unpublished manuscript in Hebrew.
 Includes bibliographical references and index.
   ISBN 978-1-84553-922-1 (hb) – ISBN 978-1-84553-923-8 (pb)
  1. Theosophy – History. 2. Theosophy – Influence. 3. India – History. 4. Nationalism – India – History. I. Lotan, Yael, 1935- II. Title.
BP530.L83 2011
299'.9340954 – dc22
                          2010020070

Typeset by S.J.I. Services, New Delhi
Printed and bound by Lightning Source UK Ltd., Milton Keynes

To Rita

The *Sanscrit* language, whatever be its antiquity, is of a wonderful structure; more perfect than the *Greek,* more copious than the *Latin,* and more exquisitely refined than either, yet bearing to both of them a stronger affinity... than could possibly have been produced by accident; so strong indeed, that no philologer could examine them all three, without believing them to have sprung from some common source, which, perhaps, no longer exists.
 – Sir William Jones (1746–1794), The Third Anniversary Discourse, Calcutta, 1786

We all come from the East – all that we value the most has come to us from the East, and in going to the East... everybody... ought to feel that he is going to his "old home"...
 – Friedrich Max Müller, Lecture I, *India: What Can It Teach Us?* Cambridge, 1882

India was the *Alma-Mater,* not only of the civilization, arts, and sciences, but also of all the great religions of antiquity...

...whenever the subject of magic is discussed, that of India has rarely suggested itself to any one, for of its general practice in that country less is known than among any other ancient people. With the Hindus it was and is more esoteric, if possible, than it was even among the Egyptian priests...
 – Helena Petrovna Blavatsky, *Isis Unveiled,* New York, 1877

As many scores of rivers
Enter into the sea,
So the understanding of the world
Has come unto me...
I am thy Lover,
I am thy Teacher,
Renounce all
And follow me,
For my way
Is the way of Liberation.
 The World-Teacher, Jiddu Krishnamurti (1895–1986), 'Come Away', Eerde-Ommen, 1927

Contents

	List of Illustrations	xii
	Introduction and Author's Acknowledgements	xv
1.	Following the Steps of the Orientalists – The Quest for the Linguistic Origins	1
2.	Friedrich Max Müller – Orientalism at the Zenith	39
3.	The Theosophical Society – The Quest for the Spiritual Source	77
4.	The Theosophical Doctrine	118
5.	The Sources of the Theosophical Doctrine	147
6.	Annie Besant: Her Pre-Theosophical Career	190
7.	The Struggle Over the Leadership of the Theosophical Society, 1889–1907	214
8.	The Struggle for the Leadership of the Indian National Movement, 1907–1919	247
9.	Theosophy and the World Teacher: The Esoteric Alternative	285
	Postscript	319
	Bibliography	323
	Index	341

List of Illustrations

Sir William Jones, Founder of the Asiatick Society of Bengal. A Portrait by Sir Joshua Reynolds (reproduced by Yanai Zeltzer).   9

F. Max Müller (aged 40, sitting), 'Friedrich Max Müller, 1863,' by Hills & Saunders, reproduced by Yanai Zeltzer from *The Life and Letters of the Right Honourable Friedrich Max Müller*, ed. Georgina Max Müller (2 vols., New York, 1902).   44

Madame Blavatsky, founder of the Theosophical Society (reproduced by Yanai Zeltzer).   85

Colonel Henry Steel Olcott, President of the Theosophical Society, 1875–1907. Olcott's bust stands opposite the library at the Theosophical Society Headquarters in Adyar. Photograph by Isaac Lubelsky.   92

Annie Besant, President of the Theosophical Society, 1907–1933, wearing Blavatsky's signet ring (reproduced by Yanai Zeltzer).   116

Charles Webster Leadbeater, 1914 (reproduced by Yanai Zeltzer).   140

Jiddu Krishnamurti, the Theosophical World Teacher, 1935, USA, photograph courtesy of the Krishnamurti Foundation Trust.   296

Jiddu Krishnamurti, 1976, New Delhi, photograph by Sunil Janah, courtesy of the Krishnamurti Foundation Trust.   308

A memorial statue, the gardens, Theosophical Society Headquarters, Adyar. Photograph by Isaac Lubelsky.   316

she is not here to see the book in print. I was lucky to have had the chance to know and work with Yael, and benefit from her deep interest in India.

This book could not have become real without the endless care, love, and support of my parents, Masha and Dov Lubelsky. Thank you!

Finally, I wish to express my thanks, love, and appreciation to my wife, Rita, without whom none of these words would have been written, and to my three bandits, Michael, Shira, and David, whom I love much more than anything else, celestial or earthly.

Isaac Lubelsky

and I was considering the various possible research paths before me. I had been reading several Hermetic texts by Marsilio Ficino and Giordano Bruno, determined to immerse myself in research of their vast corpus of writings. One day one of my professors asked me to read a short article by Madame Blavatsky. Realizing that Blavatsky belonged to a centuries-old line of occultists marked a turning point in my studies, and the history of East/West encounters in general, and the Theosophical Society in particular, captured my imagination to a point of no return. I quickly learned of the 'historian's paradise', awaiting in the relatively unexplored body of Theosophical writings, and in the personal stories of the Society's leaders, which often seemed as colourful as the brightest fantastic Oriental tale. Later, my PhD dissertation was dedicated to these same themes, as were several of my research projects during the past five years, first and foremost this book.

Many good people have helped me in bringing this book to its final stage, in directing me, supporting me both financially and morally, and contributing their original insights and offering feedback when needed.

I would like to thank the Israeli Theosophical Society, especially its chairman, Mr. Avraham Oron, for generously letting me use their library in Tel Aviv. I would like to thank the librarians both at the Theosophical Society Headquarters in Adyar, India, and the Theosophical Society in England, especially Mr. Barry Thompson, who introduced me to several genuine treasures in the magnificent London Lodge's library collection.

I am grateful to Mr. and Mrs. Gottesmann, whose financial support allowed me to conduct my research in Israel, England and India.

I would like to thank Ms. Tammy Yannay, of the Open University of Israel, for all the hours spent reading my manuscript, and for all her wise advice, support, and her good sense of humour.

I am indebted to Professor David S. Katz, who, apart from acting as my advisor for several years, has often opened my eyes and helped me become aware of the multiple connections co-existing between the various protagonists in this 'Oriental Fantasy', particularly regarding 'Mad Max', whom we both cherish.

I would like to thank the late Yael Lotan, whose translation admirably succeeded in ameliorating the original Hebrew text. The translation of this book was one of Yael's last projects. Unfortunately,

in a manner which vividly illustrates the way ideas can seep in and influence political bodies, alongside the usual forces affecting them.

This book deals with the contribution of the Theosophical Society to the rise of Indian nationalism and seeks to restore it to its proper place in the history of ideas, both with regard to its 'theology' and the sources on which it drew, as well as its role in giving rise to the New Age movement of the twentieth century. The book is perhaps the first to show how nineteenth century Orientalist study dramatically affected the rise of the Theosophical ideology, and demonstrate the impact of the work of Friedrich Max Müller (1833–1900) on Mme Blavatsky, the founder of the Theosophical Society. Max Müller was an Anglo-German scholar who, in the second half of the nineteenth century, made a brilliant career at Oxford University as a leading philologist and the founder of the field of Comparative Religion. As the successor of the Orientalist Sir William Jones (1746–1794), Max Müller promoted the Aryan Myth (the belief in the racial relationship and common cultural sources between Europeans and the ancient Indians). His numerous books and articles helped to improve the image of India in the Western mind, and somewhat paradoxically led Blavatsky to the conclusion that the cradle of occultism was to be found in India and in Hinduism. This led to her decision to move to India and help its people to free themselves from British rule, both spiritually (by reviving the Hindu philosophy), and practically (by creating an Indian national movement).

Advancing these aims became the principal activity of the Theosophical Society in India for many years, and produced substantial results for the Indian national movement. This movement was in fact launched by a British Theosophist named Allan Octavian Hume (1829–1912), who was instrumental in founding the Indian National Congress in 1885. The Congress maintained strong links with the Theosophical Society, which in various ways steered Indian national ideology for many years, at least until 1919. In that year, following the trauma of the massacre at Amritsar, Gandhi became the dominant leader of the national leadership, and as noted above, severed the connection between the Congress and the Theosophical Society, and caused Besant's removal from the center of active Indian politics.

I first came to learn of the Theosophical Society in 1999. I have just begun my postgraduate studies in history at Tel Aviv University,

Introduction and Author's Acknowledgements

In 1917 Annie Besant (1847–1933), a white Englishwoman, was elected president of the Indian National Congress, the body which, under the guidance of Mohandas Gandhi (1869–1948), would lead India to independence. Besant – in her earlier career an active atheist and a socialist journalist – was from 1907 until her death the president of the Theosophical Society, an international spiritual movement whose center in Adyar (a suburb of the southern Indian city of Madras, now Chennai,) symbolized her belief in India as the world's spiritual heart.

The Theosophical Society was founded in New York in 1875, by Helena Petrovna Blavatsky (1831–1891) and Henry Steel Olcott (1832–1907). The two moved to India in 1879, and in 1882 settled in Adyar, where the Society maintains its global headquarters to this day. Besant was initiated into Theosophy in 1889. She became involved in Indian politics, and in 1916 founded the India Home Rule League, which included in its leadership such influential local figures as Jawaharlal Nehru (1889–1964), India's future first Prime Minister, who had also been initiated into Theosophy in his youth. Besant's position in the League led her to be elected to the presidency of the Indian National Congress in 1917, but her relations with the Indian leadership soon deteriorated. In 1919 she was obliged to resign from the presidency of the League in favour of Gandhi, who ended the close association between the Congress and the Theosophists. Thereafter Besant concentrated on cultivating her Hindu protégé, Jiddu Krishnamurti (1895–1986), whom she promoted as a would-be World Teacher or messiah.

The contribution of the Theosophical Society to India's national movement rested on two elements – an ideology legitimizing India's right to independence, and the practical experience of helping to build an organized national structure. The Theosophical Society progressively turned its focus from the theoretical to the practical,

Chapter 1

Following the Steps of the Orientalists – The Quest for the Linguistic Origins

The Birth of the Orientalist Study

The common image of India in the Western imagination is characterized by high values of spirituality, religiosity and a philosophical way of life. The origins of this image appear obvious – primarily, the differences between ancient Indian philosophy and Western Christianity, and the success of Indian spiritual doctrines in the West. Both have led to a perception of India as having an ancient spiritual tradition, much earlier than the Western. Yet the image has a relatively short history, and is largely a European 'invention', stemming from the West's re-encounter with India. The history of this image corresponds to the process of colonizing the Orient, which began in the sixteenth century and reached its apogee in the empire of British India. The image of India, which during most of the colonial period was considered primitive, was re-cast as possessing a dominant spiritual element, in a process that ended in the early decades of the twentieth century. Sir William Jones created this image in the late eighteenth century, and in the latter half of the nineteenth century Friedrich Max Müller developed it into a vision of a spiritual partnership of East and West. In the late nineteenth century and early twentieth century the leaders of the Theosophical Society – Madame Blavatsky, Colonel Olcott and Annie Besant – sought to apply this vision in practice.

Prior to the encounter with India, the European self-image resembled that of the ancient Greeks and Romans – as the centre of the world and the basis for comparison with any other part of it. This concept underlay the distinction between 'West' and 'East' – a distinction dating from the Classical Period, which already then meant a qualitative distinction between cultures as well as continents.[1] The age of exploration changed this perception and gave rise to new European thinking, involving the need to meet and confront new cultures and unfamiliar races. The fresh Western awareness of the existence of a developed culture outside Europe grew stronger as contact with India deepened. It grew to a significant extent from the study of Sanskrit and the dating of Hindu sacred texts as earlier than the Bible. It produced a need to re-examine human history, which suddenly appeared to stretch backwards beyond the familiar, accepted limits. The new interest in Sanskrit contributed to the creation of new areas of scientific research, such as comparative philology and the study of religions. These fields, which acquired their methodologies in parallel with the translation of the corpus of Sanskrit writings into European languages, were energized by the exciting discoveries about the ancient Indian culture, above all by the surprising discovery of the affinity between Sanskrit and classical European languages. From this kinship sprang historical and pseudo-historical theories reconstructing the history of human civilization and attempts at explaining the assumed relationship between the brown-skinned Indians and the peoples of Europe.

By 1868, when Max Müller was appointed to the chair of comparative philology at Oxford University, the methodical-academic study of Sanskrit and Indian philosophy had been going on for 90 years. The starting-point of Oriental study may be defined as 1784, the year in which William Jones launched the Asiatic Society of Bengal, and Charles Wilkins (1750–1836) completed the first English translation of the *Bhagavad-Gītā*, regarded in the West as one of the principal Hindu holy texts.[2] The two events signalled the birth of the new interest the English conquerors took in the ancient Indian culture, and led to a real intellectual revolution with regard to Sanskrit writings, not only in England but in other academic centres in Europe, notably in Germany and France.

Western interest in India and her culture began when the Portuguese landed in Goa. Until then, the general ignorance about the Subcontinent rested mainly on travellers' tales, some going back to Classical Greece. The Portuguese, who throughout the first half of the sixteenth century dominated the trade in the Indian Ocean

1. Raymond Schwab, *The Oriental Renaissance, Europe's Rediscovery of India and the East, 1680–1880* (New York, 1984), p. 1, first published in French 1950.
2. *The Bhagavad-Gītā, or, Sacred Song* (trans. Charles Wilkins; London, 1902), first published 1785.

Calcutta Council, and in 1769 joined the Madras Council. Before the Madras appointment he spent some time in England, and on board ship on the way back he met Baron Imhoff and his wife, who were going to India to seek their fortune. Hastings and the Baroness fell in love and after her divorce, in 1777, she became his second wife (the first had died in 1759). In 1772 Hastings was appointed governor of Bengal, the British Parliament having authorized him to implement an extensive administrative reform in the region.

Becoming Governor General of India in 1774, Hastings headed the Supreme Council of India, which had four members, one of whom was Sir Philip Francis (1740–1818). The relations between the two men were bad and deteriorated to the point when, in 1780, they fought a duel in which Francis was wounded.[9] Shortly afterwards Francis returned to England and became a Member of Parliament in 1784. He helped the prominent politician and essayist Edmund Burke (1729–1797) to conduct a persistent campaign against Hastings, claiming he was failing in his post. Driven by the Burke-Francis campaign, Hastings resigned his post in 1784 and returned to England, where he fought a prolonged legal battle, which began in 1788 and ended only in 1795. He was charged with a serious crime against the realm, based on claims of irregular conduct of military campaigns during his rule in India, and collaboration with local rulers. He was accused, among other things, of receiving a bribe of 20,000 pounds from the Rajah Cheyte Singh, without reporting it to the Council of Bengal or to the directors of the East India Company in London. In reality, Hastings had delivered the entire sum to the Company's treasury, but what galled the Company's directors and the anti-Hastings opposition in Parliament was the freedom he assumed in conducting the affairs of India, rather than the financial issue. He was eventually acquitted, and in 1811 even became a Privy Councillor.[10]

It was during the decade in which Hastings was India's Governor General that the future nature of the study of Indian culture was determined, along with the ground-rules of governance that would eventually lead England to full control over the entire Subcontinent.

9. Penderel Moon, *Warren Hastings and British India* (London, 1947), pp. 11, 30, 43, 62–64, 85, 246–48.

10. Thomas Babington Macaulay, 'Warren Hastings', in Hugh Trevor-Roper (ed.), *Critical and Historical Essays* (New York, 1965), pp. 460–61, 484, 511, first published 1841.

of accommodation; a firm peace is concluded greatly to the honour and advantage of the Company, and the Nabob has entered into an alliance and is returned to his Capital.'[8]

Clive's victory marked the change in the function of the East India Company. The Company, which until then had been dependent on the goodwill of local rulers – first the Moghul sovereign, then local governors – became an active partner in the struggle for political hegemony in the crumbling empire. In the battle of Wandiwash near Madras in 1760 the British triumphed over the French. The conclusion of this campaign – the Asian reflection of the Seven Years War in Europe – removed the last Western presence that could still challenge the British.

The final significant effort by a local ruler to reunite the empire took place in 1764, when Shuja-ud-Daula, the governor of the state of Oudh in northern India, fought against the British forces, lost the battle and was taken captive. Consequently, the Moghul emperor was exiled from the capital Delhi to the city of Allahabad, where he lived under close British supervision. His successors, the remaining Moghul emperors, were rulers in name only. The last one was Bahdur Shah II, crowned emperor during the Great Rebellion in 1857.

The relative speed in which India was conquered seems surprising, particularly since most of it was achieved under the aegis of a trading company, in fairly small battles and at a very low cost to the British exchequer. The East India Company conducted its business meticulously, took pains to avoid deficits and employed first-rate personnel that served it loyally and efficiently. The prospects of young officers serving the Company were excellent – the ones who proved themselves rose swiftly through the ranks, regardless of their social class and economic circumstances back home. This was the case of Clive, the victor of Calcutta, who was raised to the peerage after the end of his service, as well as of Warren Hastings (1732–1818), who became the first Governor General of British India in 1774.

Hastings, a 17-year-old orphan of poor background, sailed in 1750 to Calcutta, where he became a minor official of the East India Company. He rose rapidly – in 1761 he became a member of the

---

8. Robert Clive, 'Battle at Calcutta', *Yorke's Hardwicke Papers*, II: 385 (23 February 1757).

Thus, in the course of the sixteenth to seventeenth centuries India became a lively hub of European activity which spread from the areas of commerce, culture and religion. The European nations, reinforced by the missionary organizations, functioned in India almost undisturbed, according to their relative power and influence in Europe, and scarcely competed with one another in India itself. This state of affairs changed in the middle of the eighteenth century, with the expansion of British presence in India and the rise of the British East India Company as the dominant political factor in the Subcontinent. The relative ease with which the Company seized control over large parts of India was due to the collapse of the power structure of the Moghul empire. At this time the empire was already profoundly decadent, and was in reality run by local regional governors (Nawabs), though officially subject to a central ruler.[7]

In 1756, the Nawab of Bengal resolved to restrict the British presence in his region and to drive the British out of Calcutta, the regional seat of the East India Company. Robert Clive (1725–1774), a young officer in the Company's service, re-captured Calcutta in February 1757, having defeated the Nawab's large force of some 50,000 troops with the help of a renegade local officer. Clive's report reflects the self-confidence characteristic of the British in relation to the native populace:

> '...At three in the morning (Feb. 4) our little army, consisting of 600 Europeans, 800 Blacks, seven field pieces and the sailors set out for the attack ... We returned safe to our camp, having killed, by the best accounts, 1,300 men. The loss on our side amounted to 200 men killed and wounded. This blow had its effect; for the next day the army decamped, and the Nabob sent me a letter offering terms

Special Reference to Caste, Conversion, and Colonialism, ed. Robert Eric Frykenberg and Alaine Low (London, 2003), pp. 62–69; Muhammad Kasim Ibn Hindu Shah Firishtah, *The History of Hindostan, from the Earliest Account of Time to the Death of Akbar* (trans. A Dow; 3 vols., London, 1768–1772); O.P. Kejariwal, *The Asiatic Society of Bengal, and the Discovery of India's Past, 1784–1838* (New Delhi, 1988), pp. 17–18; Garland Cannon, *The Life and Mind of Oriental Jones, Sir William Jones, the Father of Modern Linguistics* (Cambridge, 1990), p. 243.

7. The Mughal dynasty, which ruled India for some 270 years, was founded by the Uzbek Babur (1483–1530), who Invaded India in 1519. His heirs, Akbar (1542–1605), and Aurangzeb (1618–1707) expanded the empire's borders, but soon after the latter's death the empire began to degenerate, as the emperors lost their power to ministers and local rulers: John F. Richards, *The Mughal Empire* (Cambridge, 1993); Douglas E. Streusand, *The Formation of the Mughal Empire* (Delhi, 1999).

and established emporia in Goa and several cities in the state of Gujarat in western India, soon dispelled this ignorance with true information about Indian customs and beliefs. The Portuguese economic activity, principally in the spice trade, also bore fruit in the cultural field, with the publication of a series of books on India's geography, economy and culture.[3]

In the course of the seventeenth century other European countries joined the effort to obtain power and influence in India, principally Holland, England and France. The three formed trading companies that functioned concurrently with the establishment of power centres in the Subcontinent.[4] The competition between their companies, which also expressed their underlying national interests, accelerated the study of Indian culture. At this time the first translations of passages from Sanskrit literature and from Persian sacred writings began to appear as appendices to various works about India.[5] The corpus of European translations of sacred Hindu writings also kept growing with the spread of Christian missionary activities in India. Its expansion was also due to the efforts of individuals whose interest in the local culture stemmed from intellectual curiosity, rather than from a desire to convert the local populace.[6]

3. A fine example to the Portuguese contribution was Goa's second viceroy's large composition: Alfonso de Albuqurque, *The Commentaries of the Great Alfonso de Albuquerque, Second Viceroy of India* (ed. & trans. T.F. Earle and John Villiers (4 vols., New York, 1970), first published in Portuguese, 1774. For further discussion on the Portuguese involvement in India, see, M.N. Pearson, *The Portuguese in India* (Cambridge, 1987).

4. The Dutch East India Company was established in 1602 as a private enterprise, and was granted a monopoly on spice trade in the Indian Ocean. Its main competitor, the British East India Company, was also a private enterprise, established in 1600. In order to improve profits from textile trade, the British founded several fortified settlements in India, such as Madras, Bombay, and Calcutta. The French joined the Indian profit race in 1664, with the establishment of the French East India Company. For further details on the history of these companies, see, Anthony Wild, *The East India Company: Trade and Conquest from 1600* (London, 2000); Philip Lawson, *The East India Company: A History* (London, 1993).

5. See, for example, Henry Lord, *A Discovery of the Banian Religion and the Religion of the Persees: A Critical Edition of Two Early English Works on Indian Religions*, ed. Will Sweetman (Lewiston, 1999), first published as *A Display of Two Forraigne Sects in the East Indies: The Sect of the Banians and the Sect of the Persees* (London, 1630); Abraham Roger, *Abraham Rogers Offne Thür zu dem verborgenen Heydenthum: oder Warhaftige Vorweisung dess Lebens, und Sittens, samt der Religion und Gottesdienst der Bramines auf der Cust Chormandel, und herumliegenden Ländern* (Nürnberg, 1663), first published in Dutch, 1651.

6. Iwona Milewska, 'First European Missionaries on Sanskrit Grammar', in *Christians and Missionaries in India: Cross-Cultural Communication Since 1500, with*

When Hastings was first appointed there was no coordination among the arms of the British rule in the various provinces, but by the time he quit it the system was better organized and subject to the power of the Governor General in Calcutta. The noted historian Thomas Babington Macaulay (1800-1859) stated that Hastings showed greater capacity as ruler than had the Cardinal Richelieu.[11] Such a statement, coming from one of the persons who later actually designed the system of British rule in India, indicated the great appreciation Hastings won posthumously.

Hastings was a learned man who knew Bengali, Urdu, Persian and Arabic.[12] His appointment as the first Governor General led to a dramatic change in the attitude of the British rule to the local culture, because he maintained that the key to efficient government was understanding the local culture, its laws and religious and social traditions. He sought to partially reconstruct the Moghul government system in order to create a ruling hierarchy familiar to the inhabitants. He also cultivated contacts with the Brahmins of Bengal. According to Macaulay, Hastings was the first to persuade the Brahmins to disclose to English scholars the secrets of ancient Hindu theology and law. This may be overstating the case, but there is no doubt that these contacts led to a small number of Brahmins being willing for the first time to help Englishmen learn Sanskrit, a project Hastings regarded as enormously important. He maintained that the British power should rule the country by means of the ancient Hindu laws, notably the ancient codex called the Laws of Manu, hitherto known in the West only in its Persian translation.

To advance this vision Hastings recruited English philologists and brought them to India as employees of the East India Company. The three most prominent of these were Charles Wilkins, Henry Thomas Colebrooke (1765-1837), and Sir William Jones who is regarded as the most influential figure in the early days of the new research of India – favourably as a scientist and discoverer, unfavourably as the father of Orientalism in its condescending sense.[13] Working as a team under Jones, these scholars produced rapid results, translating large segments of ancient Sanskrit literature. Their translation project

11. Macaulay, 'Warren Hastings,' p. 512.
12. David Kopf, 'The Historiography of British Orientalism, 1772-1992', in Garland Cannon and Kevin R. Brine (eds), *Objects of Enquiry, The Life, Contributions, and Influences of Sir William Jones 1746-1794* (New York, 1995), pp. 141-42.
13. Edward Said, *Orientalism* (New York, 1978), p. 78.

created the basis for the dramatic and positive change in the Western attitude towards Indian literature. The conclusions drawn from reading these ancient texts gave rise to a completely new Western concept of human history as a whole, and of the Aryan race in particular. Thus the person who led the work in its inception, Sir William Jones, made a dramatic impact on the ideological trend of the scholars of Indian culture for the next 100 years, in Britain, France and above all in Germany. His own work, impelled in part by pure intellectual curiosity, in part by the need to understand ancient Hindu laws, and in part by the desire to locate the mother-lode of human civilization, left a clear imprint on the field of Indian scholarship and opened a new era in its history. His intellectual inheritance was almost forgotten in his homeland for many decades, until its rediscovery and development by Max Müller.

Sir William Jones, Founder of the Field

In April 1783, William Jones and his bride, Anna Maria Shipley, boarded the frigate 'Crocodile' and set out for a five-month journey to India, where he was to head the supreme court of Bengal. Jones, who had been called to the bar ten years earlier, was known as an authority on Oriental languages thanks to his book, *A Grammar of the Persian Language*, published in 1771, and reprinted nine times by 1812. Another of his books, *The Moallakat*, a translation of seven Arabic poems, appeared in 1782, reprinted the following year and acclaimed throughout Europe. Jones was a polymath and an expert on Classical culture and before travelling to India was already fluent in a dozen languages, including Arabic, Persian, Hebrew and Turkish. His legal qualification strengthened his association with Hastings, given his interest in promoting the study of ancient Hindu law.[14] The two soon became close friends, as did their wives. His association with the Governor General was useful to Jones in the early stage of his work in India. He soon joined the circle of learned Englishmen who worked for the East India Company, and became a good friend of Charles Wilkins, a senior Company merchant. Wilkins had arrived in Calcutta in 1770, grew enthusiastic about Indian culture and had begun studying Sanskrit back in 1778.

---

14. Hans Aarsleff, *The Study of Language in England, 1780–1860* (Princeton, NJ, 1967), pp. 116-18; A.J. Arberry, *Oriental Essays, Portraits of Seven Scholars* (Chippenham, 1997), pp. 64-65, first published 1960.

> *Persia* on our left, whilst a breeze from *Arabia* blew nearly on our stern... It gave me inexpressible pleasure to find myself in the midst of so noble an amphitheatre, almost encircled by the vast regions of Asia, which has ever been esteemed the nurse of Sciences, the inventress of delightful and useful arts...'

This romantic picture expresses Jones' Oriental imagery, which had evidently crystallized in his mind before he ever set foot in Asia. This imagery would shape and nurture the emerging Western conception of India and of the Orient as a whole. Approaching the shores of India, Jones saw himself as standing centre stage amid the magnificent civilizations of the ancient world. The central position he felt he was occupying in relation to those civilizations – corresponding to his real geographic or imaginary location – reflected the place and self-perception of subsequent European students of the Orient. As a rule, they saw themselves as the dominant and superior representatives of the modern Western world, able to observe the civilizations of the East from above, with a precise perspective, as if they stood in the centre-stage of human history. This image has another important significance, reflected in the function of the Orient in the new historical narrative begun by Jones. The East in general, and India in particular, would metamorphose in the European mind and become the Europeans' lost home, indeed their ancient homeland, to which they were returning with a sense of doing it historical justice and closing a circle.

In Cambridge, in 1882, Max Müller gave a series of lectures to young cadets preparing to go to India. Müller concluded the first lecture of the series, entitled, 'India: What Can It Teach Us?', by quoting the above passage from Jones. Then he added, 'India wants more such dreamers as that young Mr. Jones, standing alone on the deck of his vessel and watching the sun diving into the sea – with the memories of England behind and the hopes of India before him... Such dreamers know how to make their dreams come true, and how to change their visions into realities.'[15]

Jones' Oriental imagery was the idea that Max Müller sought to imprint in the minds of the British Empire's civil servants. Thus the image with which Jones set out to form the Asiatic Society from its inception was conveyed directly a century later to India's English rulers.

15. F. Max Müller, *India: What Can It Teach Us?* (Escondido, 1999), pp. 49–50, first published 1882.

Sir William Jones, Founder of the Asiatick Society of Bengal. A Portrait by Sir Joshua Reynolds (reproduced by Yanai Zeltzer).

Early in 1784, a few months after Jones' arrival in Calcutta and a little before Wilkins published his translation of the *Bhagavad-Gītā*, the two decided to found The Asiatick Society of Bengal, to promote the study of the ancient culture of the Orient in general and of India in particular. The Asiatic Society functioned until 1839, publishing an influential periodical entitled '*Asiatick Researches*'. It supported unbiased research, promoted an innovative scholarly approach, independent of past studies, and served as the publishing venue for researchers of India in the early days of the new subject.

The first meeting of the Asiatic Society took place on 15 January 1784, in the courtroom of the Calcutta Supreme Court. Jones gave the founding lecture, describing the Society's nature, aims and future plans. He began it with impressions of his recent sea voyage from England:

> 'When I was at sea last August, on my voyage to this country which I had long and ardently desired to visit, I found one evening, on inspecting the observations of the day, that *India* lay before us, and

towards the material in the Sanskrit texts changed as he grew more proficient in the language. His view of India and her culture before he learned Sanskrit was expressed in a lecture he gave to the Asiatic Society on 24 February 1785, marking a year since the society's founding: 'Whoever travels in *Asia,* especially if he be conversant with the literature of the countries through which he passes, must naturally remark the superiority of *European* talents'. He continued in the same vein further on: 'but we may decide on the whole, that reason and taste are the grand prerogatives of *European* minds, while the *Asiaticks* have soared to loftier heights in the sphere of imagination.'[19]

This low opinion of Indian culture changed rapidly, as shown in the lecture he gave a year later, on 2 February 1786, marking the society's second anniversary. By then he had sufficient command of Sanskrit, and his impressions from reading and translating the ancient manuscripts he had come across are evident in the lecture, which contained most of the elements of his mature perception of India, her culture and affinity to the cultures of Europe. Indeed, the opinions he expressed on this occasion would soon influence a number of European thinkers who followed him in viewing India as a 'lost relative'.

'Nor can we reasonably doubt,' he affirmed, 'how degenerate and abased so ever the *Hindus* may now appear, that in some early age they were splendid in arts and arms, happy in government, wise in legislation, and eminent in various knowledge.'

He proceeded to define the areas whose study enabled scholars to know the ancient culture of the Indians – their languages and writings, their philosophy and religion, the remains of their sculptures and architecture and the written evidence of their science and art. The following passage in this lecture became the most widely known and quoted of his statements:

> The *Sanscrit* language, whatever be its antiquity, is of a wonderful structure; more perfect than the *Greek,* more copious than the *Latin,* and more exquisitely refined than either, yet bearing to both of them a stronger affinity, both in the roots of verbs and in the forms of grammar, than could possibly have been produced by accident; so strong indeed, that no philologer could examine them all three,

---

19. Jones, 'The Second Anniversary Discourse', in Cannon, *The Collected Works of Sir William Jones*, III, pp. 12–13.

In the rest of his Asiatic Society founding lecture Jones stated that the Society's goal was the study of man and nature, via the three principal areas of knowledge – history, science and art. The most efficient research tool in his view was the study of Oriental languages:

> 'The attainment of them is, however, indispensably necessary; and if to the Persian, Armenian, Turkish, and Arabick, could be added not only the Sanscrit, the treasures of which we may now hope to see unlocked, but even the Chinese, Tartarian, Japanese, and the various insular dialects, an immense mine would then be open, in which we might labour with equal delight and advantage.'[16]

The second meeting of the Asiatic Society petitioned the Supreme Council for sponsorship. Hastings and the others responded favourably, which meant financial resources and a patron that would help promote the society.[17] Although Hastings had to leave India that year, 1784, to defend himself from the accusations levelled against him in London, the Supreme Council continued its patronage of the Asiatic Society. Jones foresaw a broad cooperation among all educated Englishmen who lived in India and were interested in her ancient language and in uncovering her history. The bulletin of the Asiatic Society was the venue for publishing their findings. Thus in a short space of time, without the aegis of an academic institution and relying exclusively on the personal abilities of the membership, Jones in effect launched a new field of research and defined the methodology which would be practiced by future students of India, as Orientalist research became established in European universities.

Jones began to study Sanskrit in 1785, about a year after the founding of the Asiatic Society. According to Jawaharlal Nehru (1889–1964), Jones found Brahmins reluctant to teach him the sacred language, for fear of sacrilege, but eventually persuaded a local doctor to do so.[18] It did not take him long to learn it, and his attitude

---

16. Sir William Jones, 'A Discourse on the Institution of a Society, for Inquiring into the History, Civil and Natural, the Antiquities, Arts, Sciences, and Literature, of Asia', in Garland Cannon (ed.), *The Collected Works of Sir William Jones*, III (New York, 1993), pp. 1-2, 5-7, first published 1807.

17. The first volume of the periodical was dedicated to Hastings, who himself contributed an article: Warren Hastings, 'Trial by Ordeal, among the Hindus,' *Asiatick Researches*, I (Calcutta, 1788), pp. 389–401.

18. Jawaharlal Nehru, *The Discovery of India* (New York, 1946), p. 317.

without believing them to have sprung from some common source, which, perhaps, no longer exists.

His changed approach was also evident in the following statement:

... nor is it possible to read the *Vedânta*, or the many fine compositions in illustration of it, without believing, that Pythagoras and Plato derived their sublime theories from the same fountain with the sages of India.

Jones proceeded to state his belief in the common racial origin of Indians and Greeks, and argued that the Indians were related to the ancient Persians, Ethiopians, Phoenicians, Greeks, Scythians and Goth, Celts, Chinese, Japanese and Peruvians. He noted that there was no reason to assume that they had ever been colonized by any of the above nations, or that they colonized any of them. Therefore, he concluded, they probably all derived from a single land of origin.[20]

Thus in one short lecture before a small audience, far from Europe and based on intuition and recently acquired knowledge of Sanskrit, Jones reviewed the tenets of his theory, which would in the nineteenth century form the basis for the Aryan ideology. His revolutionary idea about a cultural and racial affinity between the Indians and the ancient Greeks led to a major change in Western historical concept, and gave European thinkers an opening for an intellectual alternative to the usual cultural sources that had hitherto been accepted. Jones' principal contribution to his successors was not necessarily his map of cultural and racial affinities, comprising many nations which were quite unrelated, but the way in which he proposed their assumed connections. He was responsible for coining the term 'Aryan' – Sanskrit for 'noble'. Moreover, he was the first to describe the territory of Iran as the geographic origin of the Aryan race (one of the three original races, according to Jones), which he associated with Ham, the son of biblical Noah. Hence, in his ninth annual lecture to the Asiatic Society, on 23 February 1792, Jones argued that 'those three races, how variously soever they may at present be dispersed and intermixed, must... have migrated originally from a central country.' The Indians, in his view, were

---

20. Jones, 'The Third Anniversary Discourse, On the Hindus,' in Cannon, *Collected Works*, pp. 32, 34–35, 37, 45–46.

racially related to Ham, as the direct ancestor of the Indian race was Kush, described in Sanskrit as the son of Brahma.[21]

The reasons and justifications – or proofs – Jones claimed for his assumptions strike a modern reader as quaint. For example, in 1786 he argued that the archaeological findings in Egypt and India show that they had been associated in antiquity. He claimed that some of the letters carved on Indian monuments were Ethiopian. He went so far as to assert that there were marked physiological similarities between Indians and Ethiopians, such as their respective complexion, the form of their lips and their hair. It was the Indian climate that caused the hair of Indians to be straight, unlike that of their Ethiopian relatives. The decisive proof of the ancient relationship between the two nations was the frequent portrayal of the Buddha with 'woolly' hair, the statues 'apparently designed for a representation of it in its natural state.'[22]

The imagined connection between the Indians and Ethiopians continued to preoccupy Jones for years. It is likely that his interest was aroused by the fact that the Ethiopians were Christian and supposedly descended from King Solomon. He did, however, maintain that it was necessary to produce concrete evidence for these assumptions. In 1792, for example, *Asiatic Researches* published an exceptionally long article (taking up 167 pages) by Francis Wilford, arguing that ancient Indian mythology was full of references to the Nile and to ancient Egypt. Jones responded critically to the article's claims, emphasizing the importance of scientific proofs.[23]

Nevertheless, it seems that the absence of serious proof did not overly trouble Jones with regard to his own researches. He accounted for the supposed link between the ancient Indians and distant nations with a 'historical' argument:

> 'That the first race of *Persians* and *Indians*, to whom we may add the *Romans* and *Greeks*, the *Goths*, and the old *Egyptians* or *Ethiops*,

---

21. Jones, 'Discourse the Ninth, On the Origin and Families of Nations,' in Cannon, *Collected Works*, pp. 189–201.

22. Jones, 'The Third Anniversary Discourse,' p. 42. This ridiculous assumption echoes in later Orientalist literature. Edward Moor wrote in 1810 that 'there is something mysterious, and still unexplained, connected with the hair of this, and only of this, *Indian* deity,' Edward Moor, *The Hindu Pantheon* (London, 1810), p. 231.

23. Francis Wilford, 'On Egypt and other Countries adjacent to the Ca'li' River, or Nile of Ethiopia, from the Ancient Books of the Hindus', *Asiatick Researches*, III (Calcutta, 1792), pp. 295–462, 467.

originally spoke the same language and professed the same popular faith, is capable, in my humble opinion, of incontestable proof; that the *Jews* and *Arabs*, the *Assyrians*, or second *Persian* race, the people who spoke *Syriack*, and a numerous tribe of *Abyssinians*, used one primitive dialect wholly distinct from the idiom just mentioned, is, I believe, undisputed, and, I am sure, indisputable.'

He explained the geographic division of the Aryan race, which he claimed inhabited Iran 4,000 years ago, as follows:

the children of HAM, who founded in *Iràn* itself the monarchy of the first *Chaldeans*, invented letters, observed and named the luminaries of the firmament, calculated the known Indian period of four hundred and thirty two thousand years... and contrived the old system of Mythology, partly allegorical, and partly grounded on idolatrous veneration for their sages and lawgivers; that they were dispersed at various intervals and in various colonies over land and ocean; that the tribes of MISR, CUSH, and RAMA settled in *Africk* and *India*; while some of them, having improved the art of sailing, passed from *Egypt*, *Phenice*, and *Phrygia*, into *Italy* and *Greece*...; whilst a swarm from the same hive moved by a northerly course into *Scandinavia*... ; nor is it unreasonable to believe, that some of them found their way from the eastern isles into *Mexico* and *Peru*, where traces were discovered of rude literature and Mythology analogous to those of Egypt and India.[24]

This 1792 lecture contained the elements of what came to be known as the 'Aryan myth'. The connections between a number of ancient peoples, which Jones attributed to their belonging to a single race that had sprouted numerous branches, became the standard explanation in the following century. His dating of the division of the Aryan nation was likewise adopted with variations of a few hundred years. The method of retracing the ancient routes taken by the ancient Aryans by studying their languages would be the dominant research tool until the last quarter of the nineteenth century. Moreover, Jones declared that the linguistic study was the ultimate and almost sole proof of the affinity of the diverse Aryan peoples. This position stressed the significance of language as the predominant Orientalist research tool, and thereafter the Orientalist scholar was seen as the researcher who discerns the underlying meaning of phenomena through the study of the local language.

24. Jones, 'Discourse the Ninth', in Cannon, *The Collected Works*, pp. 185–86, 202–203.

Language became the tool that made possible the understanding and description of the research subjects, and thus the source of the scholar's authority. Jones' pseudo-scientific theory about the origins of the Aryan race, so popular during the nineteenth century, reached its highest standing with Max Müller's philological theses, which sought to prove by means of comparative philology and comparative religion the common Aryan descent of the Indo-European peoples.

Yet the impetus for Jones' great efforts to advance his research was not racial theory, but his desire to locate the earliest traces of human civilization and the sources of the 'historical' biblical narrative.[25] This is well illustrated by the preoccupation of *Asiatick Researches* with the origins of the Afghans. In 1789 the periodical published an article by Henry Vansittart, arguing that the Afghans were of Jewish origin. Jones responded to the article, stating that the Afghans' Jewish origin could indeed be demonstrated by a number of Persian manuscripts and the affinity between the Afghan language Pushto and ancient Chaldaic. He recommended studying the Afghans' literature and history, as they were probably descendants of the ten lost tribes of Israel.[26]

It seems then that Jones' philological endeavours were meant not only to increase scientific knowledge, but to demonstrate the validity of biblical historiography. He hoped to find Noah's antedeluvian language, or the language spoken by Adam, the first man. This aspiration did not conflict with his wish to master Sanskrit and reconstruct the relationship he believed prevailed in antiquity between the Indians and other nations. Jones unwittingly founded the philological study of Indo-European languages, when in reality his aim was to discover humanity's original language. The aspiration to discover this 'Ursprache' – as the later German scholars called it – became one of the principal motives for the efforts of European Sanskrit scholars in the following years.

The theory arising from Jones' study, namely, that there was an actual kinship between the Indian and European Aryans, became highly influential. It gave India and her culture a chronological seniority over the younger European culture, and set India at the heart of the European discourse, as a challenge to be deciphered.

25. Thomas Trautmann, *Aryans and British India* (Berkeley, CA, 1997), pp. 34, 40–41, 51–52.

26. Henry Vansittart, 'On the Descent of the Afghans from the Jews', *Asiatick Researches*, II (Calcutta, 1790), pp. 69–76.

The research it launched in Europe produced positive results even for its subjects – namely, the Indians themselves – because without these Europeans India might not have recovered her lost culture. Nehru himself, independent India's first Prime Minister, argued that India owed much to Jones for his discovery of her ancient riches.[27] On the other hand, as Edward Said argued, this view of India presented it as a set of information to be catalogued in an orderly, hermetical way, to facilitate the work of the colonial power. This critique views Jones as aiming 'to rule and to learn, then to compare Orient with Occident', in order to domesticate the Orient and turn it into a province of European learning, which he, as the father of modern Orientalism, the inventor of the method of Western rule in the Orient, reorganized and assumed authority over it.[28] Thus Jones' ideas appear to lead to a conclusion seen clearly from the European viewpoint, that Europe was the height of modernism whereas India was the primitive mirror which reflects it and defines it as modern.

An analysis of Jones' contribution to this subject serves to sharpen this issue and to evaluate his responsibility for the subjugation of India. Through his 11 years in India, until his death in 1794, he spent most of his time working as a judge in the supreme court of Calcutta. In addition to the study of Sanskrit, he also devoted much time to researching other fields, such as India's endemic flora. Hence his achievements in the study of Sanskrit and Indian culture are all the more impressive, yet they must not be separated from the ideas he developed in the service of the East India Company.

One of his contributions to the British power was a document entitled 'The Best Practicable System of Judicature for India', composed shortly after his arrival in Calcutta. The document adopted Hastings' idea, which as mentioned above, favoured a local legal system based on ancient Hindu law. 'A system of liberty,' he wrote, 'forced upon a people invincibly attached to opposite habits, would in truth be a system of cruel tyranny.' Having determined the pointlessness of imposing the British system of justice upon the Indians, Jones went on to say, 'Any system of judicature affecting the natives in Bengal, and not having for its basis the old Mogul constitution, would be dangerous and impracticable.' Further on he noted, 'The natives must have an effective tribunal for their protection against

---

27. Jawaharlal Nehru, *The Discovery of India* (New York, 1946), p. 317.
28. Said, *Orientalism*, p. 78.

the English, or the country will be rendered worse than useless to Britain.' Finally he stated, 'A system like this, consisting of reciprocal checks and balances of power, would give satisfaction and security to the natives, the government and the English subjects in India.'[29]

Plainly, then, Jones' goal as a judge in the service of the East India Company was the creation of a legal system that would make for efficient government and contribute to the establishment of a harmonic society in which both the rulers and the ruled would be content. To advance this purpose, Jones began to translate from Sanskrit into English the ancient Hindu codex, the Laws of Manu. This ambitious project was finally accomplished shortly after Jones' death, with the publication of his book, *Institutes of Hindu Law*.[30] The book – which was translated into German in 1797 and into French in 1833 – depicted the British attempt to govern the local population by means of its own laws. This attempt continued, if only partially, until 1833, when the British Parliament limited the franchise of the East India Company and the government of India rapidly influenced by utilitarian thought which despised the local tradition and sought to suppress its memory and replace it with modern British law.

In retrospect, Jones' endeavour appears almost absurd, because while the Moghul rulers did consider the ancient traditions of their Hindu subjects, their own legal system derived partly from Islam and partly from Hindu tradition as interpreted by the Brahmins. The Brahmin judges relied mainly on the oral tradition that they applied and adapted to the spirit of the time, as evolved during the millennia that passed between the promulgation of the Laws of Manu and the end of the eighteenth century. The flexibility of the local judicial system conflicted with the Western rationale applied by Jones, who sought to institute a system based on a written, inflexible law. Hence the Laws of Manu were no more relevant to the Hindus of the time than the British law. Yet Jones' attitude, which evinced respect for the local tradition, was without doubt less condescending than that of the later British rulers. Jones the jurist was prompted by the wish to institute a better, more orderly, world than the existing one, rather than by a domineering and patronizing attitude.

29. Jones, 'The Best Practicable System of Judicature for India,' in Cannon, *The Collected Works*, pp. cxxxiii–cxxxv.

30. *Institutes of Hindu Law, or, the Ordinances of Menu, According to the Gloss of Culluca, Comprising the Indian System of Duties, Religious and Civil* (trans. Sir W. Jones; Calcutta and London, 1796).

Jones made another important contribution to the study of Indian culture with his 1789 translation of the drama *Sacontala* (usual spelling: *Śākuntalā*) by Kālidāsa, the great Indian author of the late fourth century CE.[31] He had planned to do a series of translations of Indian legal and literary texts, but his illness and death at the age of 48 cut the project short. After his death, members of the Asiatic Society carried out some of these plans, and promoted the academic recognition of the Indian research. The first indication of this recognition came in 1833, when the Boden Chair of Sanskrit was created at Oxford University – the first of its kind in the UK. The man chosen to lead it, Horace Hayman Wilson (1786–1860), was a former president of the Asiatic Society, a post he had assumed in 1816.

Jones' view of the history of England, a country which had been conquered repeatedly before becoming a conqueror, expressed the sense of mission that characterized him and his associates. In his lecture to the tenth annual conference of the Asiatic Society, on 28 February 1793, he said:

> the *Greeks* overrun the land of their forefathers, invade *India*, conquer *Egypt*, and aim at universal dominion; but the *Romans* appropriate to themselves the whole empire of Greece, and carry their arms into *Britain*... by this time the *Americans* and *Peruvians*...have peopled the continent and isles of *America*, which the *Spaniards*... discover and in part overcome: but a colony from *Britain*, of which CICERO ignorantly declared, that it *contained nothing valuable,* obtain the possession, and finally the sovereign dominion, of extensive *American* districts; whilst other *British* subjects acquire a subordinate empire in the finest provinces *of India*, which the victorious troops of ALEXANDER were unwilling to attack.[32]

This description of the British Empire placed it on a historical sequence of empires from the distant past to the present, and appears to legitimize the English conquest of India. Given an almost deterministic conception of history, implying that there was always one or another empire in the world, Jones concluded that Britain's historic role, as the leading empire of its time, permitted her to

---

31. Kālidāsa, *Sacontala; or, the Fatal Ring; an Indian Drama* (trans. Sir W. Jones; London, 1902), first published 1789.

32. Jones, 'The Tenth Anniversary Discourse, On Asiatick History, Civil and Natural', in Cannon, *The Collected Works,*, pp. 209-10.

emulate the earliest Western empire, namely the Greek, and exceed its example by a wider conquest of India.

Jones' effort to legitimate the British Empire and his contribution to the construction of an effective judicature in British India, have been interpreted in recent decades as evidence of his condescension towards the Indian subjects.[33] Indeed, his early expressions clearly support this view – before he learned Sanskrit his view of India and her culture was patronizing and domineering. But as soon as he began to study Sanskrit and to translate the ancient texts, his views changed quickly to appreciation, going so far as to include the Indians in the family of European nations. Regardless of the lack of accuracy or scientific value of his ideas, it seems that their overall tendency was far from negative in the Western perception of India – on the contrary, it showed a genuine interest in Indian culture and a sincere desire to find ways of ensuring an 'enlightened conquest', recognizing the importance of the local culture and seeking to harmonize it with that of the conqueror. The way Jones is depicted by his critics is very far from his actual record. While conquest is always objectionable, there is nevertheless a great difference between a conquest that seeks to annihilate the local culture and one that seeks not only to preserve it, but actually cultivate it as a legitimate field of academic study.

However, the criticism is certainly applicable to the next generation of British rulers in India, those who were predominant in the 1830s. Especially prominent among these was Macaulay, who as a member of the Supreme Council of India (1834–1838), launched an educational reform designed to westernize India, impose the English language upon it and defeat the Orientalist approach. The criticism is inappropriate with regard to Jones and his successors, who viewed Indian culture as a serious subject of study and were therefore the ideological opposite of Macaulay and his supporters. Jones' thinking, followed by Colebrooke, Wilson and Max Müller, was that India could teach the West an important lesson, since it harboured vital knowledge that the West had not yet acquired. Jones' approach led directly to Max Müller, who determined, based on the principles set by the founder of the field, that the discovery of this knowledge was not mere scientific categorizing, but the acquisition of a mental alternative to problems that beset the West.

33. Said, *Orientalism*, p. 43; Ronald Inden, *Imagining India* (Oxford, 1990), pp. 37-38, 55, 263-64.

The English Successors

The Asiatic Society remained fully active after the death of its founder on 27 April 1794. Four days later, on 1 May 1794, its members elected as their new president the Governor General of India, John Shore (1751–1834), who had been a close associate of Jones' and later his first biographer.[34] The son of a senior merchant in the East India Company, Shore became a member of the Supreme Council of India in 1787, and in 1793 succeeded the Governor General Lord Cornwallis (1738–1805), who arrived in India after his defeat in the American War of Independence. The Asiatic Society was much strengthened when its president was the holder of the highest political position in India.[35] This move prevented its collapse after the demise of its founder and ensured its continued existence. Wilkins and Colebrooke, and later Wilson, were the most notable members of the society who carried on Jones' enterprise into the nineteenth century in both India and England.

In 1784 Charles Wilkins, Jones' co-founder of the Asiatic Society, published his important translation of the *Bhagavad-Gītā* – the very first full version of an Hindu sacred text translated from Sanskrit into a European language. The *Bhagavad-Gītā* became the most familiar and influential Hindu scripture in the West until the present time. As his health deteriorated, Wilkins returned to England in 1786 and continued working on ancient Hindu texts. In 1787 he finished his translation of the *Hitôpadeśa*, a collection of ancient Indian fables. This book, which had been translated earlier by Jones (but published posthumously in 1807), became popular in Europe and aroused special interest in Germany. Max Müller's first published work, in 1844, was a German translation of the *Hitôpadeśa*, an indication of Wilkins' influence over the later researchers of India.[36] In 1805 Wilkins was appointed examiner at Haileybury College, established

---

34. G.F.R.B., 'Shore, John, First Baron Teignmouth (1751–1834)', *The Dictionary of National Biography* (Oxford, 1921–1922), pp. 149–51; John Shore, Baron Teignmouth, *Memoirs of the Life, Writings and Correspondence of Sir William Jones* (London, 1804).

35. Shore was a regular contributor to the Asiatic Society's periodical before his appointment. See, for example, 'An Account of the Kingdom of Nepal, by Father Giuseppe, Prefect of the Roman Mission – Communicated by John Shore', *Asiatick Researches*, II, pp. 307-21.

36. *Hitôpadeśa: Fables and Proverbs from the Sanskrit* (trans. Charles Wilkins; Gainesville, FL, 1968), first published 1787; *Hitôpadeśa of Vishnu Sarman* (trans. Sir William Jones; Calcutta, 1851), first published 1807; Max Müller, *Hitôpadeśa: Eine alte Indische Fabelsammlung aus dem Sanskrit* (Leipzig, 1844).

that year by the East India Company to train its staff in foreign languages. Not long afterwards, in 1808, he published a Sanskrit Grammar.[37] Colebrooke said of Wilkins, 'That gentleman was Sanskrit mad, and has more materials and more general knowledge respecting the Hindus than any other foreigner ever acquired since the days of Pythagoras.'[38]

Colebrooke, a mathematician and philologist, was unquestionably Jones' heir. Max Müller regarded him as no less important and protested that whereas Jones' name was known in England, no one had a word to say about Colebrooke – in Germany, he maintained, they would have erected a statue of him. Described by Max Müller as the father of Sanskrit studies in Europe, Colebrooke was the son of a wealthy London banker who became the chairman of the East India Company in 1769, and while in that position supported the appointment of Warren Hastings as India's Governor General. Using his association with the latter, Colebrooke Senior got his son a position in the Company. Colebrooke Junior arrived in Calcutta in 1783, the same year as Jones, and remained unemployed for a long time. His father's relations with Hastings turned out to be useless, as the Governor General was preoccupied with defending himself against his enemies in London. He was finally given a minor post in 1786, began researching Indian culture and studied Sanskrit between 1791 and 1793. He was especially interested in the ancient Indian sciences, primarily astronomy.

His first paper, entitled 'On the Duties of a Faithful Hindu Widow', was presented to the Asiatic Society in 1794, soon after Jones' death. Not long after, *Asiatick Researches* published two of his short scientific articles. The success of these publications led to his appointment as translator and editor of a collection of Hindu laws that Jones had been working on before his death. Colebrooke worked hard and in 1798 published *A Digest of Hindu Law on Contracts and Successions*. Printed in Calcutta, it ushered in a new era in the British administration of the country, as it spared the British judges the trouble of consulting local pundits. The book made Colebrooke famous as a Sanskrit scholar.[39]

37. Sir Charles Wilkins, *A Grammar of the Sanskrita Language* (London, 1808).
38. F. Max Müller, 'Life of Colebrooke', in *Chips from a German Workshop*, IV (New York, 1895), p. 368, first published 1875.
39. H.T. Colebrooke, 'On the Duties of a Faithful Hindu Widow,' *Asiatick Researches*, IV (Calcutta, 1795), pp. 209-19; Colebrooke, 'Astronomical Observations

Colebrooke rose through the ranks of the East India Company, becoming president of the court of Calcutta in 1805 and a member of the Supreme Council of India in 1807. He was elected president of the Asiatic Society in 1806, and remained in that position until 1815, when he returned to England, withdrew from public life and devoted his time to research. In 1822 he was elected president of the Astronomical Society of London, succeeding Sir John Herschel, and later that year founded the Royal Asiatic Society in London. Four years earlier he had donated his vast collection of manuscripts to the library of the East India Company in London, launching what gradually grew into the richest Sanskrit library in Europe. Max Müller, who spent much time in the library when working on a translation of the *Rig Veda*, noted that without this collection the most important Sanskrit researches in the nineteenth century could not have been written – presumably including the research that brought him his own fame.[40] He held that Colebrooke's most important achievement was his book, *A Grammar of the Sanskrit Language*. The first volume of this book, which Colebrooke never finished, appeared in 1805. Another work of his, *Essays on the Religion and Philosophy of the Hindus*, would later lead to the friendship between Max Müller and the philosopher Friedrich Wilhelm Joseph Schelling (1775–1854), which began with their discussion of it.[41]

Horace Hayman Wilson reached Calcutta in 1803, when he was 22. He had studied medicine in London and joined the East India Company as a surgeon. He was soon drawn into the research activity of the Asiatic Society, studied Sanskrit and in 1813 published in Calcutta his first translation from Sanskrit of Kālidāsa's drama, *Meghaduta*. The translation was a success, because Kālidāsa's name was already known thanks to Jones' famous 1789 translation of

---

made on a Voyage to the Andaman and Nicobar Islands' and 'Astronomical Observations made on a Survey through the Carnatic,' *Asiatick Researches*, IV, pp. 317-20, 321-24; Jagannatha Tarkapanchanana, *A Digest of Hindu Law on Contracts and Successions, With a Commentary* [the whole called Vivababhangrnava] (trans. H.T. Colebrooke; 4 vols., Calcutta, 1798).

40. Max Müller, *Life of Colebrooke*, pp. 381-82, 391-93. *The Life and Letters of the Right Honourable Friedrich Max Müller*, ed. Georgina Max Müller, I (New York, 1902), p. 25.

41. Henry Thomas Colebrooke, *A Grammar of the Sanskrit Language*, I (Calcutta, 1805); Henry Thomas Colebrooke, *Essays on the Religion and Philosophy of the Hindus, By the Late H.T. Colebrooke, Esq.*, a New Edition (London, 1858), first published 1837; Georgina Max Müller, *The Life and Letters*, p. 25.

Śākuntalā. Wilson drew very close to Colebrooke, the president of the Asiatic Society, who regarded him as Jones' successor and took pains to advance him and get him appointed president of the Society after him in 1816.

In 1819 Wilson published the very first Sanskrit-English dictionary, which held over 1,000 pages and made him the most respected Sanskrit scholar of his time. Between 1826–1827, towards the end of his stay in India, he published *Select Specimens of the Theatre of the Hindus*, based on translations of ancient Indian dramas. Colebrooke welcomed the publication:

> I rejoice to learn that your great work on the Indian drama may be soon expected by us… you and I may derive some complacent feelings from the reflection that, following the footsteps of Sir W. Jones, we have, with so little aid of collaborators, and so little encouragement, opened nearly every avenue, and left it to foreigners, who are taking up the clue we have furnished, to complete the outline of what we have sketched.[42]

Colebrooke's despondent tone reveals the atmosphere of isolation and neglect which increasingly enveloped British Sanskrit research at that time. The two ideological camps which contended over the best way to rule India – the Orientalist versus the Utilitarians – had reached a crossroads, after which the Utilitarian approach predominated. The opening shot in the struggle was the publication of *A History of British India*, by James Mill (1773–1836), in 1817.[43] Mill, the father of the famous philosopher John Stuart Mill (1806–1873), together with his friend Jeremy Bentham (1748–1832), founded in 1824 a periodical called '*The Westminster Review*', which served until the beginning of the twentieth century as the main venue for radical and progressive ideas. Mill never visited India and did not know any Indian language. His book described the British as rationalists and the Indians as non-rationalists, people who had never understood the concept of history in its Western sense, but only in terms of sacred traditions. He was sharply critical of the way India was being governed, and called for a widespread reform of the British administration. The conclusion drawn from his book was that the Indians

---

42. Kālidāsa, *Meghaduta; or, The Cloud Messenger* (trans. H.H. Wilson; London, 1902), first published 1813; Horace Hayman Wilson, *A Dictionary, Sanscrit and English* (Calcutta, 1819); Horace Hayman Wilson, *Select Specimens of the Theatre of the Hindus* (3 vols., Calcutta, 1826–1827); Max Müller, *Life of Colebrooke*, p. 393.

43. James Mill, *The History of British India* (3 vols., London, 1817).

were inferior to the British, and this may have been one reason for its success. Lord Bentinck (1774–1839), Governor General of India between 1828 and 1835, was quoted as saying to Mill that he would be the real Governor General of India.[44] In 1819, Mill was appointed to senior position in the East India Company and by 1830 reached the position of head of its examining board, a position second only to the company's directors. In the course of his career in the Company he advocated an extensive reform of the ruling administration of India in keeping with his Utilitarian philosophy. In his view, India was a fund of resources to be economically exploited; its culture was of secondary importance.

This attitude, represented by Mill and followed by Macaulay, displaced Wilson and Colebrooke from the decision-making centre in India.[45] Wilson had to be content with an academic career and the presentation of his views on the importance of Indian cultural research to a limited audience of colleagues and readers. Nevertheless, as noted, in 1833, though by then the Utilitarian approach predominated, Oxford University established its first chair of Sanskrit and invited Wilson to hold it. In addition to this post, Wilson also served as the chief librarian for the East India Company. In this dual position he was able to help Max Müller in his first years in England and was chiefly responsible for his appointment as lecturer in European languages at Oxford in 1850. In 1841 Wilson published his study *Ariana Antiqua*, a pioneering study of Afghan archaeological findings and ancient coins. His book, *Sketch of the Religious Sects of the Hindus*, appeared in 1846. At this time he also supervised the issuing of a new edition of Mill's *A History of British India*, attempting, 30 years too late, to change its original message and promote a liberal approach to the Indians and a less condescending attitude towards their culture.[46]

Although he was German, Max Müller was viewed as Wilson's spiritual heir and the man who preserved the superiority of British

---

44. A.J.A., 'Bentinck, Lord William Cavendish (1774–1839),' *The Dictionary of National Biography* (Oxford, 1921–1922), pp. 292–97; Kopf, *Historiography*, p. 146.

45. David Kopf, *British Orientalism and the Bengal Renaissance* (Berkeley, CA, 1969), pp. 217–72.

46. Horace Hayman Wilson, *Ariana Antiqua: A Description Account of the Antiquities and Coins of Afghanistan* (London, 1841); Horace Hayman Wilson, *Sketch of the Religious Sects of the Hindus* (Calcutta, 1846); James Mill and Horace Hayman Wilson, *History of British India, from 1805 to 1835* (3 vols., London, 1845–1848).

research over its Continental rivals. He himself said Wilson had prepared the ground for future research, had engaged only in original work and never presented himself as a great scholar. He noted that Wilson had said to him on more than one occasion, 'You see, I am not a scholar, I am a gentleman who likes Sanskrit, and that is all.'[47]

Nevertheless, by the time Max Müller arrived in Oxford there was already a serious gap between the knowledge and interest in Indian culture in England and in the centres of study in Europe. Up until the second decade of the nineteenth century, under interested Governors General, considerable energy was invested in encouraging cultural research in India, but then the economic interests of Britain in the Subcontinent became central in London's policy considerations. The cultural research had served Britain's interests in the early stages of her domination of India, when it needed to find solutions to the immediate problems that arose in the encounter with the alien culture. As the conquest advanced towards completion, the administration grew more power-oriented and exploitative. Thus as political control developed, the cultural interest waned. At the same time, significant aspects of the research passed to European scholars, in France and mainly in Germany, Max Müller's native land. These scholars continued in Jones' footsteps and extended his suppositions, while developing the science of philology and turning it into the principal cultural research tool of the first half of the nineteenth century.

The German Successors

The German intellectuals' profound involvement with India and her culture arose from Germany's particular circumstances in the latter half of the eighteenth century, when German poets and dramatists were resisting the dominance of the French literary manner and looking for new sources of inspiration. This trend grew stronger in the early nineteenth century, with Napoleon's conquests, when the academic and cultural interest in the Orient grew concurrently with the rise of the new German national identity. This trend was markedly affected by the opposition to the cultural values of the

---

47. F. Max Müller, *My Autobiography, a Fragment* (New York, 1901), p. 158.

French conqueror, and hence the search for alternative cultural sources.⁴⁸

To start with, the German involvement in researching Indian culture was motivated by the philosophical interest that would later advance Sanskrit philology, which was especially cultivated in Germany and quickly developed a tradition and rules of its own. The philological research made India an inseparable part of German intellectual life, and a landmark in the study of the mental evolution of humanity as a whole and of the Aryan race in particular. The ideas that emerged from the German philological study heightened the interest in the common origin of Indians and Germans, and defined the aim of the philological research as the reconstruction of the birthplace of the Aryan race and of the primal Aryan language, the Ursprache. These ideas were embraced in the course of the nineteenth century by German Romanticists, whose aspirations for a unified Germany were reinforced by the supposedly scientific evidence that there existed in the past a unified Aryan nation which spoke the ancient mother-language of German.

The German interest in Indian culture was further strengthened in 1791, when Georg Forster (1754-1794) published his German translation of Jones' English translation of Śākuntalā, only two years after its publication in Calcutta. It received greater attention in Germany than Jones' translation had received in England. It launched a new era in German literature, philology and thought, as generations of philosophers and philologists plunged into the world of Indian culture in search of similarities between German language and thought and those of Sanskrit.⁴⁹

---

48. Dietmar Rothermund, *The German Intellectual Quest for India* (New Delhi, 1986), p. vii; Isaiah Berlin, 'The Counter-Enlightenment', in Henry Hardy (ed.), *Against the Current, Essays in the History of Ideas* (New York, 1980), p. 24.

49. Forster's translation influenced famous intellectuals, such as Herder (1744-1803), Schiller (1759-1805), and Goethe (1749-1832), who have deepened their knowledge of India by reading other translations by Wilson, Wilkins and Jones. Forster died in 1794 in Paris, where he studied Oriental languages, while preparing himself for a journey to India. In Paris, he had a love affair with Caroline, the daughter of the German Orientalist Michaelis (1717-1791). In 1796 Caroline married Wilhelm Schlegel (1767-1845), Friedrich Schlegel's (1772-1829) elder brother. In 1803 she divorced him and married the philosopher Schelling, who became one of Max Müller's early patrons. It seems that Sanskrit study at that time went hand in hand with a complicated love life. That was the case with Friedrich Schlegel, whose wife, Dorothea (1763-1839), Moses Mendelssohn's daughter, divorced her first husband and converted to Christianity in order to marry him: Schwab, *The*

The Indian obsession which gripped a large number of German intellectuals in the early nineteenth century was clearly illustrated in the lives of the brothers Wilhelm and Friedrich Schlegel. Their eldest brother, Karl August Schlegel, had died in Madras in 1789, while on a visit with a military expedition from Hanover. His younger brothers proposed to approach India with different tools. Friedrich Schlegel studied law, philology and philosophy in 1790-1794 in Gottingen and Leipzig, and in 1798 arrived in Jena, where his brother Wilhelm taught. The latter then moved to Berlin, where he became famous for his translations of Shakespeare, and in 1818 was appointed to the very first Sanskrit chair in Germany, in Bonn.[50]

Friedrich Schlegel left Germany in the spring of 1802 and went to Paris to study Oriental languages. He made a special study of Sanskrit, which he began learning in May 1803 from Alexander Hamilton (1762-1824). Hamilton, the first person to teach Sanskrit in France, had been an officer in the British navy who had spent a long time in India and was one of the first members of Jones' Asiatic Society. He was captivated by Indian culture, studied Sanskrit and even married a Bengali woman. It is very likely that, as well as Sanskrit, Schlegel also absorbed Jones' ideas from his studies with Hamilton.[51]

These ideas, which had travelled from Calcutta to Paris through the intermediacy of a British officer, would be the basis of Schlegel's *On the Language and Wisdom of the Indians*, whose effect upon European thought was described by Max Müller as 'a touch of a magician's wand'.[52]

The opening lines of this book, which appeared a few days before Schlegel and his wife were received into the Catholic Church, bear a strong resemblance to Jones' lecture on 2 February 1786:

> The Old Indic Sanskrito... has a very close relationship with the Roman and Greek, as with the Germanic and Persian languages. The similarity consists not only in a great number of roots, which it shares

Oriental Renaissance, pp. 57-59, first published in French 1950; Rothermund, *The German Intellectual Quest for India*, pp. 33-34.

50. Winfred P. Lehmann, 'The Impact of Jones in German-Speaking Areas,' in Garland Cannon and Kevin R. Brine (eds), *Objects of Enquiry, the Life, Contributions, and Influences of Sir William Jones*, p. 134.

51. Aarslef, *The Study of Language in England, 1780-1860*, p. 155; Schwab, *The Oriental Renaissance*, p. 67.

52. Max Müller, *Lectures on the Science of Language, I* (London, 1994), pp. 157-58, first published 1861.

with them, but it extends to the innermost structure and grammar. The agreement is accordingly not one of chance which might be explained by mixture, but rather an essential one which points to common descent. Comparison yields the further result that the Indic language is the older, the others however later and derived from it.

Schlegel further argued that,

> In Hebrew and related dialects, as well as in Coptic, a goodly number of Indic roots may possibly be found still. But this does not prove an original relationship since it can be the result of simple mixture. The grammar of these languages like that of Basque is basically different from that of Indic.

He may have been conscious of the ideological implications of his research, and therefore stated: 'The important results of this linguistic comparison for the oldest history of the origin of peoples and their earliest migrations will be the subject of investigation in the future.'

On the Language and Wisdom of the Indians concerned the philological comparison between Sanskrit and European languages, stressing that Sanskrit was the most ancient of them, as well as possessing the purest philosophical clarity. The idea that ran throughout the book was that the original and most ancient divine manifestation echoed in the later cultures, though its original significance had been forgotten. In order to understand the original manifestation, it is necessary to eliminate the later interpretations, until we reach the original, namely the Sanskrit writings, which Schlegel regarded as the earliest expression of divine manifestation. In this connection, he proposed conducting a comparative investigation between the Sanskrit texts and the Bible, following the ideas of Jones, 'who first brought light into the knowledge of language through the relationship and derivation he demonstrated of Roman, Greek, Germanic and Persian from the Indic.'[53] The revolutionary implication of this proposition was that the Jewish scriptures were not exclusive, as evidence of divine manifestations appears in other sacred writings as well.

In making this point Schlegel was decades ahead of Max Müller, who built his theory on the assumption that divine manifestation

---

53. Friedrich Von Schlegel, *Über die Sprache und Weisheit der Indier: ein Beitrag zur Begründung der Alterthumskunde* (London, 1995), pp. 1-3, 85-86, first published 1808.

had occurred in many nations and took place in various periods. Max Müller argued that religion was essentially an expression of human needs shared by all mankind.[54] Hence claims of exclusivity concerning divine manifestation reflected narrow-mindedness and incomprehension of history.

After 1808, Schlegel's interest in India waned, as he became increasingly preoccupied with universal philosophical questions. Between 1815 and 1818, he and his wife moved between Austria – where he served as court secretary in the imperial palace – and Germany, where he became a member of the German assembly in Frankfurt. Until his death in 1829, he lectured in various institutions but, unlike his older brother, never obtained a regular professorial post. The Indian subject occasionally came up in his lectures, though not in the concentrated form it had taken in 1808. In one of his later series of lectures, 'The Philosophy of Life', given in Vienna in 1827, the subject of India came up anew, but this time from a conservative position designed to affirm the validity of the Reich system of justice, by comparing it to the ancient Brahmin judicial system.[55] This use of an Indian image in 1827 suggests primarily that Oriental imagery had become integrated in the German intellectual discourse at that time.

Max Müller stated that Schlegel's prominent heirs in Germany were Franz Bopp (1791–1867), the brothers Wilhelm and Jakob Grimm (1786–1859, 1785–1863 respectively), and Wilhelm von Humboldt (1767–1835).[56] To these might be added Alexander von Humboldt (1769–1859) and Arthur Schopenhauer (1788–1860). The world outlook of the latter, who took a great interest in the Hindu sacred texts, influenced a whole generation of German thinkers, including Max Müller himself. The following is a brief summary of the contributions of these thinkers to the research of Indian culture.

Bopp studied Sanskrit in Paris between 1812 and 1816, returned briefly to Germany and published his book, *On the Conjugational System of the Sanskrit Language*, comprising his conclusions from his four years of study in France and opening a new era in the study of Sanskrit. He was the first to develop a methodology which at once

---

54. F. Max Müller, *Chips from a German Workshop*, I (Chico, CA, 1985), p. x, first published 1867.
55. Friedrich Von Schlegel, *The Philosophy of Life, and Philosophy of Language* (trans. A.J.W. Morrison; New York, 1973), p. 312, first English edition 1847.
56. Max Müller, *Lectures on the Science of Language*, I, p. 160.

raised the field of Sanskrit philology and made it into an orderly, rational scientific discipline. He determined that 'Among all the languages known to us, the sacred language of the Indians shows itself to be one of the most capable of expressing the most varied relations and connections in a truly organic manner through inner modification and forming of the stem syllable.' He maintained that in the ideal language the root is inflected in an organic, natural form. He argued that Sanskrit was characterized by a more organic structure than any other language, with Greek resembling it, Latin somewhat less, and so on to the Germanic languages. The conclusion arising from this argument suggests that the family of languages reveals an historical process of degeneration:

> In order to show in its full light the truth of these principles which are extremely important for the history of languages, it is necessary to become acquainted above all with the conjugational system of the Old Indic languages, then to survey and compare the conjugations of the Greek and the Roman, the Germanic and Persian languages, whereby we will see their identity, but will also recognise the gradual and graded destruction of the simple speech organism and observe the striving to replace it by mechanical combinations, from which an appearance of a new organism arose when their elements were no longer recognised.[57]

The idea that a language may degenerate, combined with the statement that a language cannot develop new organic motifs, but only to lose them to mechanical components, led to the conclusion that languages may be arranged in chronological order, and also explained the changes they underwent. Bopp's assertion confirmed the position of Sanskrit as the oldest language, which best preserved the mother-dialect of the Ursprache. These ideas would form the basis of Max Müller's later theories, which as we shall see, presented the same concept with the term 'the disease of language'.

Bopp won recognition with his book, and using a grant from the king of Bavaria travelled to London, where he continued to study Sanskrit with Wilkins and Colebrooke and translate ancient Hindu manuscripts. In 1820 he returned to Germany, where the following year he was appointed to a chair of Sanskrit, Oriental Literature and General Philology at Berlin University. Between 1833 and 1852

---

57. Franz Bopp, *Über das Conjugationssystem der Sanskritsprache in Vergleichnung mit jenem der griechischen, lateinischen, persischen und germanischen Sprache* (London, 1995), pp. 7, 10, first published 1816.

he published the six volumes of his great oeuvre, *A Comparative Grammar of the Sanskrit*, which were translated between 1845 and 1854 into English, under Wilson's supervision. This book series fixed the term 'Indo-European languages', propounded by Bopp, in the European mind.[58]

Jakob Grimm is remembered mainly as a collector of German folk-tales, which he and his brother Wilhelm gathered in a lengthy project, with the added participation of the poet Wilhelm Müller (1794–1827), the father of Max Müller. Grimm also worked on medieval literature, law, mythology and philology. He worked for years in parallel with Bopp, and was one of the leading contributors to the establishment of the new field of philology. He studied law at Marburg, and held a number of minor government posts, until in 1817 he was made professor and librarian at the University of Gottingen. Two years later, the first volume of his book, *German Grammar*, was published, the remaining three volumes appearing by 1837. This was the first book to contain a thorough and comprehensive study of an ancient language, here a Germanic one, and proposed the rule that came to be known as Grimm's Law, concerning phonetic changes in spoken languages.[59]

Grimm sought to define the fixed rules according to which words having the same meaning in different languages and a common source in a mother-dialect, change phonetically from language to language. In the course of the nineteenth century Grimm's Law, originally devised as a tool in the etymological analysis of ancient German, became used as a popular philological proof, especially in showing the affinity of Sanskrit to European languages. In 1837 Grimm was sacked from his post at Gottingen University because of his protest against the abolition of the constitution by the king of Hanover. Not long after, in 1840, he and his brother were appointed professors at Berlin University and members of the Royal Prussian Academy.[60]

---

58. Franz Bopp, *A Comparative Grammar of the Sanskrit, Zend, Greek, Latin, Lithuanian, Gothic, German and Slavonic Languages* (trans. principally by Lieutenant Eastwick, conducted through the press by H.H, Wilson; 3 vols., London, 1856), first published in German 1833–1852.

59. Winfred P. Lehmann, *A Reader in Nineteenth-Century Historical Indo-European Linguistics* (Bloomington, IL, 1967), p. 48; Jacob Grimm, *Deutsche Grammatik* (4 vols., Göttingen, 1819–1837); Aarsleff, *The Study of Language in England, 1780–1860*, p. 161.

60. For further discussion on the brothers Grimm, see, Jack David Zipes, *The Brothers Grimm: From Enchanted Forests to the Modern World* (New York, 1989).

The brothers Wilhelm and Alexander von Humboldt belonged to the Prussian aristocracy and they both contributed, each in his own field, to the modernization of their country and the development of the new science of philology. Wilhelm Humboldt headed the department of education and the arts in the Ministry of the Interior in Berlin, where he instituted a comprehensive reform in the Prussian educational system. Berlin University, which bears his name, was established in 1810 as part of this reform. Earlier, in the years 1802-1808, he was Prussia's ambassador to the Vatican, and after finishing his work in Berlin he returned to the diplomatic service as Prussia's ambassador to Vienna and later to London, until 1819. In London he met Franz Bopp, who was studying Sanskrit with Colebrooke. Bopp taught him and awakened his interest in the subject of India. The two were joined by Wilhelm Schlegel, who was also in London to perfect his knowledge of Sanskrit. Wilhelm von Humboldt's senior position enabled him to reward the two scholars for their friendliness. He was responsible for the appointment of Wilhelm Schlegel to the new chair of Sanskrit created at Bonn in 1818, and Bopp's appointment to the Sanskrit chair created specifically for him in Berlin in 1821.[61]

Wilhelm's younger brother Alexander von Humboldt became known for his research in the natural sciences. He travelled in Asia and in South America and contributed to the study of geography and meteorology. Between 1845 and 1862 he published in Berlin the scientific encyclopedia *Cosmos*, which was the first to give methodological definitions to Natural Sciences (Naturwissenschaften) and the Sciences of the Humanities (Geisteswissenschaften). It was he who categorized philology as belonging to the Natural Sciences, a definition that was later developed further by Max Müller.[62]

---

61. Schwab, *The Oriental Renaissance*, p. 179.

62. Humboldt paved the way for the young Max Müller, when he introduced him to the Prussian ambassador in London, Baron Christian von Bunsen (1791-1860), who became Max Müller's patron in his first years in England: Max Müller, *My Autobiography*, p. 167; Max Müller, *Lectures on the Science of Language*, I, pp. 2-3; *The Life and letters of the Right Honourable Friedrich Max Müller*, I, p. 30; Alexander von Humboldt, *Kosmos: Entwurf einer physischen Weltbeschreibung* (5 vols., Stuttgart, 1845-1858). For further discussion on the brothers Humboldt, see, Paul R. Sweet, *Wilhelm von Humboldt: A Biography* (2 vols., Columbus, OH, 1978-1980); Helmut De Terra, *Humboldt: The Life and Times of Alexander von Humboldt, 1769-1859* (New York, 1955).

Arthur Schopenhauer, one of the great thinkers of the nineteenth century, first encountered the Hindu thought in the Vedânta texts, particularly the Upanishads, which he read in a German translation from Persian. His great work, *The World as Will and Idea*, was published in 1818, when he was 30. It had a mighty influence over German metaphysical philosophy, largely because of its juxtaposition of Christianity and Hinduism. Schopenhauer stated, 'I believe that the influence of the Sanskrit literature will penetrate not less deeply than did the revival of Greek literature in the fifteenth century,' and argued that philosophical knowledge was found in its richest and finest form in the Upanishads. He was powerfully influenced by this literature, finding in it an answer to what he defined the defects of Jewish culture, which he claimed had distorted original Christianity. He sought to separate the New Testament from the Old – in other words, to separate between Jewish thought and the original Aryan spirit.

Schopenhauer believed in the Indian idea of Karma, and adopted the terminology of the Vedas in this matter: 'It is the Maya of Brahminism... I believe that at the moment of death we become conscious that it is a mere illusion that has limited our existence to our person.' He compared the Vedas with Christianity and found a resemblance between their concepts of salvation, which is achieved by the knowledge that the Hindus attain through repeated rebirths, until their union with Brahman. This idea struck him as conclusive proof that the origin of the New Testament lay in Hindu thought.[63]

Schopenhauer accounted for what he claimed were Hindu motifs in Christianity by pointing to the story of Christ's family's flight into Egypt from fear of Herod, as described in the New Testament. According to Schopenhauer, Jesus received in Egypt spiritual knowledge derived from Pythagoras and Plato, which had its origins in India. This theory became an essential part of the Aryan myth. These ideas, expressed in *The World as Will and Idea* in 1818, reverberated later in Max Müller's lectures in Glasgow in 1892, when he argued that,

> Christianity is not a mere continuation or even reform of Judaism, but that... it represents a synthesis of Semitic and Aryan thought... It has been my chief object to show that this reaction was produced or at

---

63. Arthur Schopenhauer, *The World as Will and Idea* (trans. R.B. Haldane and J. Kemp; London, 1964), I, p. xiii, III, pp. 281, 418, 426-27, 431-32, 445-46, first published 1883.

least accelerated by the historical contact between Semitic and Aryan thought, chiefly at Alexandria.[64]

Max Müller was strongly influenced by Schopenhauer's ideas. He quoted him in two of his books – 'In the world there is no study so beneficial and so elevating as that of the Upanishads. It has been the solace of my life – it will be the solace of my death' – and often referred to him as a philosophical authority.[65] He met him in Berlin and spoke with him, and stated that although he understood but a small part of his thought, its inspiration 'led me far away beyond the historical foundations of Christianity.'[66]

The French Successors

The early years of the study of Indian culture made an impact not only in England and Germany, but also in France, which, as noted above, had some political aspirations in the early stages of colonial rivalry in India. The French scholar and translator who was most influential at this time was Abraham Anquetil-Duperron (1731-1805), who spent a long time in India, beginning in 1754. Anquetil was the first European to translate the entire Zoroastrian *Zend-Avesta*, in 1771. He was also the first to translate the Upanishads from their Persian version into Latin. The first translation, of four Upanishads, appeared in 1787. A more comprehensive translation, of 50 Upanishads, was published in 1801, with the title *Oupnek'hat*. This was the name by which Schopenhauer first encountered the work he so admired.[67]

France was a leading centre of Oriental studies, especially in the first half of the nineteenth century. In Paris could be found large collections of Oriental manuscripts, gathered by French Jesuit missionaries who worked in South Asia in the eighteenth century. These collections made Paris a lodestone for the leading German students of the Orient, who travelled there in hopes of gaining international recognition. Another aspect of the attraction of France as

64. F. Max Müller, *Theosophy or Psychological Religion* (London, 1893), p. ix.
65. F. Max Müller, *India: What Can It Teach Us?* p. 274; F. Max Müller,*The Sacred Books of the East*, I (New York, 1962), p. lxi, first published 1879.
66. F.M. Müller, *My Autobiography*, p. 289.
67. Abraham Hyacinthe Anquetil-Duperron, *Zend-Avesta*, reprint of the 1771 edition (3 vols., New York, 1984); *Oupnek'hat, id est, secretum tegendum* (trans. Anquetil Duperron; Paris, 1801). For further discussion of Anquetil, see, Schwab, *The Oriental Renaissance*, pp. 18, 57, 66, 158, 427.

a research centre at that time was its reputation as being free from prejudice and open-minded in relation to alien cultures. Possibly this openness followed the loss of France's imperial standing after the fall of Napoleon and during the monarchist restoration in Europe.

Yet it was Napoleon himself who was responsible for laying the foundation for a new Orientalist research methodology, unlike that which characterized Jones and his associates in India. Napoleon made a cultural-scientific plan for his campaign of conquest in Egypt in 1798-1799, utilizing all the contemporary knowledge about Egypt, and took with him in his ships a company of academics and specialists in the Orient. It may be said that he developed his information about the object of the conquest without any physical acquaintance with it, unlike the British Orientalists in India, who acquired their knowledge of the Orient during their sojourn there.[68]

Needless to say, the tangible research fruits of this military campaign also helped to make Paris a leading centre of Orientalist research. The scholars who travelled with Napoleon documented their findings, published them upon their return to France, and kindled Europe's imagination about the wonders of ancient Egypt. Some time later, it was also thanks to this campaign that in 1822 Jean-François Champollion (1790-1832) deciphered the ancient Egyptian hieroglyphics, by means of the Rosetta Stone, found by Napoleon's troops in 1799. The decipherment of the hieroglyphics and the technique used by Champollion to achieve it influenced an entire generation of language scholars in France and the rest of Europe, excited the imagination and contributed to the growing popularity of philology.

Silvestre de Sacy (Baron Antoine Isaac, 1758-1838), regarded as one of the leading Oriental philologist in France, had already attempted, with scant success, in 1802 to decipher the hieroglyphics by means of the Rosetta Stone. Yet, De Sacy had the greatest influence over Oriental research in France, leading to the creation of the first European chair of Sanskrit, at the College de France in 1814, and he founded the Societe Asiatique on 1 April 1822. It was his name which drew the German scholars to Paris.[69]

A student of Sacy's, Antoine Leonard de Chézy (1774-1832), held the chair of Sanskrit from its establishment in 1814 until his death

68. Said, *Orientalism*, pp. 81-83.
69. For a sample of his philological contribution, see, Silvestre de Sacy, *Principles of General Grammar* (trans. D. Fosdick Jr.; Andover, 1834), first published in French 1799. For further discussion, see, Schwab, *The Oriental Renaissance*, pp. 82, 295-97.

of cholera in 1832. Two years before he died he published the first French translation of *Śākuntalā* from Sanskrit, following the translations made by Jones in 1789 and Forster in 1791.[70] The successor of Sacy and Chézy was the philologist Eugène Burnouf (1801–1852), regarded as the leading Orientalist in France during the 1830s and 1840s. Occupying the chair of Sanskrit in the College de France from 1833, Burnouf was chiefly interested in Buddhism.[71] It was he who persuaded Max Müller to dedicate his life to translating the Rig-Veda, thus launching him on his great career.

Max Müller arrived in Paris in 1845, following the footsteps of German Orientalists who saw Paris as the main station on the itinerary of travel and study that took shape in the early nineteenth century. This itinerary, which included London, served the German scholars who wished to qualify and win a reputation. Most of them returned to Germany, and some, like Max Müller, obtained teaching posts in England, the only place where it was possible to apply the theoretical research in practice.

It should be noted that at that time staying in France for several years was not a simple matter. The German scholars who stayed there in the early nineteenth century were exposed to the repeated political upheavals that shook France. Among them was Friedrich Schlegel, who remained in Paris at the height of Napoleon's conquests in Germany, and Bopp, who while studying in France, witnessed the fall of Napoleon's empire. It seems that the Oriental research was subject to its own laws, and its practitioners were able to keep out of the political scene and maintain a professional association even with scholars in enemy states. Paris continued to attract German scholars during the period of restoration and after, and they generally returned to their country after studying Sanskrit in Paris. They then applied their acquired knowledge in Germany, which became the foremost centre of Sanskrit philology in the nineteenth century.[72]

******

70. Kālidāsa, *La Reconnaissance de Sakountala, drame sanscrit et pracrit de Calidase* (trans. A.L. Chézy, Paris, 1830).

71. Eugène Burnouf, *Legends of Indian Buddhism* (trans. Winifred Stephens; London, 1911), first published in French 1844.

72. However, some stayed in France, as did Julius von Mohl (1800–1876), who came to Paris in 1823. Mohl was a professor at the Collège de France, and was later

This was the beginning of Orientalist research in Europe. The powerful appeal of the Orient influenced many scholars, who made the field a central element in the European mind in the nineteenth century. The importance of India in the European mind as the birthplace of Aryan culture gave rise to a historical problem whose resolution concerns the effects of colonialism upon its actors. Opening the boundaries of Europe, the discovery of the traces of the ancient cultures of Egypt and India (and later of Mesopotamia), and above all the identification of Sanskrit as the eldest sister of the European languages, provide the means for resolving the problem.

Another problem concerns the ambivalence of the European attitude towards India, which was perceived as primitive while its past was glorified. How and what can one learn from a civilization which has degenerated? – That was the crucial question with which Max Müller contended. His work served to develop the Aryan narrative, which culminated in the latter half of the nineteenth century:

> We all come from the East – all that we value most has come to us from the East, and in going to the East, not only those who have received a special Oriental training, but everybody who had enjoyed the advantages of a liberal, that is, of a truly historical education, ought to feel that he is going to his "old home", full of memories, if only he can read them.[73]

Thus in 1882, Max Müller brought to perfection the idea first formulated 100 years earlier by Sir William Jones.

---

elected president of the French Asiatic Society. He married an Englishwoman, who made their house the central Oriental salon in Paris. Max Müller and his wife, Georgina, spent an evening at the Mohl salon in June 1863. The main attraction that evening, as Max Müller cynically described, was 'Madame Mohl, who amused her guests by parading all the bonnets she had provided for her expedition, and trying them on, one after another': *The Life and Letters of the Right Honourable Friedrich Max Müller*, I, p. 293; Schwab, *The Oriental Renaissance*, p. 313.

73. Max Müller, *India: What Can It Teach Us?*, p. 49.

Chapter 2

Friedrich Max Müller – Orientalism at the Zenith

This chapter deals with the best-known Orientalist in the second half of the nineteenth century – Friedrich Max Müller, heir to England's Jones, Wilson and Colebrooke, and Germany's Schlegel and Bopp. Max Müller developed his predecessors' ideas into a coherent whole, which called for East and West to collaborate and learn from each other. Perhaps more than any other contemporary factor, it was his thought which gave rise to the new spiritual image of India. In this sense, he was the inadvertent link between the seemingly disparate spheres –the academic and the esoteric – and also had a direct effect on the Theosophical Society. As we shall see, this movement became the outstanding practitioner of the ideas he had originated. The following is a summary of his biography and his Orientalist ideology, which reached its peak in his Aryan vision.

Max Müller: A Biographical Summary

Friedrich Max Müller was born on 6 December 1823 in Dessau, in the independent duchy of Anhalt-Dessau in eastern Germany. His father, the poet Wilhelm Müller, wrote the poem cycles 'The Pretty Miller Maid' and 'A Winter Voyage', which were put to music by Schubert. His godfather was the famous composer Karl Maria von Weber (1786–1826), and it was he who gave him his middle name Max (which he later adopted as his last name), the name of the hero of his opera 'The Free Shooter', which he had recently composed.[1] Friedrich was only four when his father died, so naturally had only dim memories of him, but he recalled vividly being seated with

---

1. Müller made his middle name a part of his last name only after having settled in England: F. Max Müller, *My Autobiography, A Fragment* (New York, 1901), p. 119; F. Max Müller, *Auld Lang Syne* , I (New York, 1898), p. 10; *The Life and Letters of the Right Honourable Friedrich Max Müller*, ed. Georgina Max Müller, I (New York, 1902), p. 2.

his sister on his father's knees, and being told amusing and scary stories from the tales of the Brothers Grimm, with whom his father collaborated.[2]

Max Müller began to attend the University of Leipzig in 1841, majoring in Oriental languages, including Sanskrit.[3] He passed the test for the doctorate of philosophy before his twentieth birthday. Soon afterwards he published his first book, a German translation of the ancient Indian collection of fables, *Hitôpadeśa*. Having obtained his doctorate, Max Müller went to Berlin, to hear the lectures of Bopp and Schelling and examine a large collection of Sanskrit manuscripts, which the King of Prussia had recently acquired in England. Bopp, though only 53, struck Max Müller as an old man with a feeble memory. He was bored by his lectures and felt they did not add to his knowledge. His request to read the Sanskrit manuscripts ran into bureaucratic problems. He asked to be allowed to take them home, to read in reasonable comfort, but was refused repeatedly, and permission was only given a little before he left the city. Nevertheless, he managed to contact Alexander von Humboldt, who recommended him to Baron Bunsen, Prussia's ambassador to London. He also made friends with the philosopher Schelling, who enjoyed discussing Indian and Western philosophies with him. Schelling had read Colebrooke's *Essays on the Religion and the Philosophy of the Hindus*, and took an interest in Max Müller's interpretation of Sanskrit texts.

After about a year in Berlin, Max Müller decided to continue his study of Sanskrit in Paris, Europe's main centre of Orientalist research. At this time, the dominant figure in his life was Eugène Burnouf, whose course was attended by a number of select scholars.[4] Max Müller's view of his research subjects changed under

2. This childhood memory reflects his later interest with fables and fairytales, which led him to deal with myths and their origins: Max Müller, *My Autobiography*, pp. 48–52.

3. Max Müller became fascinated with Sanskrit after reading Schlegel's 'On the Language and Wisdom of the Indians': Friedrich Von Schlegel, *Über die Sprache und Weisheit der Indier: ein Beitrag zur Begründung der Alterthumskunde* (London, 1995), first published 1808. Another reason for that was his wish to study 'something which his friends and fellow-students did not know,' see G.M. Müller, *The Life and Letters*, I, pp. 17–18; Max Müller, *My Autobiography*, p. 146.

4. Bournof taught some of Europe's leading Orientalists, among them Ernest Renan (1823–1892) and Theodore Goldstücker (1821–1872), who later followed Max Müller to England, was appointed as a Sanskrit lecturer in University College London, and in 1856 published in Berlin a revised edition of Wilson's English-

the influence of Burnouf, who helped him to focus the direction of his research. Burnouf told him, 'Don't publish extracts from the commentary only... If you do, you will publish what is easy to read and leave out what is difficult.' When Max Müller expressed concern that he might not find a publisher to issue his full translation of the *Rig Veda*, Burnouf replied, 'The commentary must be published, depend upon it, and it will be.'[5]

The search for a publisher for the translation of the *Rig Veda* was not a simple matter. The cost of printing the monumental work was considerable for its time (Max Müller estimated it at 4000 pounds sterling). Moreover, it would be necessary to maintain the translator and the editor for the duration of the work, which would take years. Max Müller tried to get academic institutions in various countries to take an interest in the project, and received serious offers from Russia and from England. The Russian proposal came from Otto Böhtlingk (1815-1904), a well-known Sanskrit scholar and a member of the Imperial Russian Academy. He suggested that Max Müller would come to St Petersburg and there print the Rig Veda in collaboration with him.[6] Burnouf opposed this proposal, because Böhtlingk made no commitment regarding the funding of the project. In the end, Max Müller decided not to go to Russia, and acquired an enemy with a very long memory.[7]

In June 1846 Max Müller went to London for a fortnight's visit, to examine the Sanskrit manuscripts in the library of the East India Company. He had corresponded with Wilson the Orientalist, who

Sanskrit dictionary: Rosemary Ashton, *Little Germany, Exile and Asylum in Victorian England* (Oxford, 1986), pp. 38-39; Horace Hayman Wilson, *A Dictionary, Sanskrit and English*, extended and improved from the Second Edition of the Dictionary of H.H.W., together with a Supplement, Grammatical Appendices, and an Index, serving as an English-Sanskrit Vocabulary, by T. Goldstücker (Berlin, 1856).

5. Max Müller, *My Autobiography*, pp. 178-79. In a letter he wrote to his mother dated 11 June 1845, Max Müller described the translation of the *Rig-Veda* - 'the oldest and the most important book in India'. His intensive efforts, which made him work day and night, worried his portier, who spread odd rumours about 'Monsieur Max... who drinks no coffee early, eats till evening only two dry rolls, and writes *Hebrew* the whole day', G.M. Müller, *The Life and Letters*, I, p. 38.

6. Böhtlingk was of Dutch origin and was educated at German universities. He specialized in Sanskrit and later published a German-Sanskrit lexicon: Otto von Böhtlingk und Rudolph Roth, *Sanskrit-Wörterbuch herausgegeben von der Kaiserlichen Akademie der Wissenschaften* (7 vols., Delhi, 1990), first published 1853-1875.

7. Böhtlingk published in 1891 a malicious article, which claimed that Max Müller based his work on imaginary myths, see G.M. Müller, *The Life and Letters of the Right Honourable Friedrich Max Müller*, II, p. 296.

occupied the chair of Sanskrit at Oxford and was in charge of the East India Company's library. Wilson expressed willingness to publish the *Rig Veda* in Oxford, on condition that he was credited with the translation of the work, and Max Müller with the translation of the commentaries, which in fact constituted the bulk of the project. Max Müller might have accepted this offer, but his trip made him change his plans, as his meeting with Bunsen, the Prussian ambassador to London, produced a happier outcome than he had dreamed of. Eventually Max Müller would work with Wilson but was able to take exclusive credit for the translation of the *Rig Veda*.

After working for a fortnight at the East India Company's library, Max Müller decided to extend his stay in England. Before long he had his first meeting with Bunsen, who became his patron and great benefactor.[8] He persuaded the board of directors of the East India Company to approve the great cost of the *Rig Veda* translation, thereby paving the way for Max Müller's academic success in England. Bunsen's argument, that it would be a disgrace if the *Rig Veda* were to be published in any country other than England, convinced the directors, who were practical businessmen, to devote a large amount of money to publishing an ancient book that 'none of them could understand and many of them had perhaps never even heard of.'[9] Thus did a Prussian ambassador cause a German scholar to publish the legendary *Rig Veda* in England.

Bunsen promoted Max Müller's interests not only on the social scene in London, but also in England's academic circles. For instance, he invited Max Müller to accompany him to Oxford, where he was to attend an academic conference. This was Max Müller's first visit to Oxford, and on his return to London he wrote his mother, 'I have been staying in Oxford, working in the library there, and have thus seen the most interesting and beautiful city

---

8. Bunsen was a romantic Egyptologist, whose diplomatic career did not prevent him from publishing several wide-scale books: Christian Carl Josias von Bunsen, *Egypt's Place in Universal History: An Historical Investigation* (trans. C.H. Cottrell; 5 vols., London, 1848–1867), first published in German 1845; Christian Carl Josias von Bunsen, *God in History; or, The Progress of Man's Faith in the Moral Order of the World* (trans. Susanna Winkworth; 3 vols., London, 1868–1870), first published in German 1857; Max Müller, 'Bunsen', in *Chips from a German Workshop*, III (New York, 1892), pp. 357-69: first published 1870; Raymond Schwab, *The Oriental Renaissance, Europe's Rediscovery of India and the East, 1680–1880* (New York, 1984), first published in French 1950, pp. 464-65.

9. Max Müller, *My Autobiography*, pp. 201-202.

in Europe.'[10] This first impression led to his decision to move to Oxford in May 1848, and there supervise the printing of the *Rig Veda* at the University's publishing house. Two years later, in April 1850, he began to teach modern literature and languages. One of the scholars who recommended him for the appointment was Wilson, who had collaborated with him for the past two years on editing the *Rig Veda*. The university appointment, four years after his arrival in England, was the start of one of the most brilliant academic careers in nineteenth century Europe. Oxford remained Max Müller's home for the rest of his life, during which he became known as the world's leading authority on India. At the same time, Oxford University became the leading centre for the study of religions and Sanskrit philology.[11]

Max Müller became a member of All Souls College in May 1858, and remained there until the end of his teaching career. In August 1859 he married Georgina Grenfell (1835-1916), an Englishwoman who would bear him three daughters and a son. The following year he experienced the worst crisis of his life. Following Wilson's death in May 1860, Max Müller applied to succeed him in the chair of Sanskrit. He was the leading candidate and enjoyed the support of influential persons, such as Edward Bouverie Pusey (1800-1882).[12] In November Max Müller was informed of the death of his patron Bunsen (who had left England in 1854). About a month later, on 7 December 1860, elections to the chair of Sanskrit took place, with 4,000 voters participating. Pusey's recommendation proved insufficient – Max Müller's friendship with Liberal elements and his German nationality militated against him, and the post was given to Monier Monier-Williams (1819-1899), an Oxford graduate who had spent several years in India in the service of the East India Company. Monier-Williams, doubtless a fine scholar, had the advantage of his national origin, but it appears that the University also preferred his religious views, which supported the absolute superiority of

10. G.M. Müller, *The Life and Letters* I, p. 63.
11. The conservative mentality which characterized the atmosphere at Oxford University began to change in 1854, due to a thorough reform that was maintained throughout the next two decades. However, the change was still shadowed by minor xenophobia, of which Max Müller suffered for some time: Max Müller, *My Autobiography*, pp. 243-44; Christopher Harvey, 'Reform and Expansion, 1854-1871', in M.G. Brock and M.C. Curtyhoys (eds), *The History of the University of Oxford*, VI: Nineteenth-Century Oxford, Part 1 (Oxford, 1997), pp. 697-730.
12. G.M. Müller, *The Life and Letters*, I, pp. 248-49.

F. Max Müller (aged 40, sitting). 'Friedrich Max Müller, 1863,' by Hills & Saunders, reproduced by Yanai Zeltzer from *The Life and Letters of the Right Honourable Friedrich Max Müller*, 1902.

Christianity over all other religions. This conviction underpinned his belief in the complete superiority of Western civilization over the Oriental civilization he was studying.[13]

13. For samples of his scholarly contribution, see, Monier Monier-Williams, *Religious Thought and Life in India: Vedism, Brahmanism and Hinduism* (New Delhi, 1974), first published 1883; Monier Monier-Williams, *Dictionary, English and Sanscrit*, published under the patronage of the East-India Company (London, 1851). For further discussion on his tensed relations with Max Müller, see, Lourens P. van den Bosch, *Friedrich Max Müller, A Life Devoted to the Humanities* (Leiden, 2002), p. 366.

Max Müller, deeply disappointed, would wait eight years for a university chair of his own. Finally, in May 1868, Oxford University announced a new chair of Comparative Philology, created especially for him. Thereafter he could devote most of his time to researching his favourite subjects. Nevertheless, seven years later, in 1875, he decided to leave Oxford and return to Germany. When it became known, it provoked a public outcry. The issue became so fraught, that on 15 February 1876, Max Müller was informed by the University that it would allocate a large enough remuneration to maintain him even if he did not teach but only engaged in research.[14]

From that time until his death, Max Müller gave a series of lectures at Oxford, Cambridge, Birmingham, Edinburgh and Glasgow, but devoted most of his time to writing. Full of energy, he began to publish the 50-volume series, *The Sacred Books of the East*, which began to appear in Oxford in 1879. The series included translations of the Qur'an, the Brahmin and Buddhist scriptures from India, the texts of the Zoroastrian religion from Persia, and the writings of Kung-fu-tse and Lao-tse from China. Some of these texts he translated and others were done under his editorial supervision. The immense project set out to present the Western reader for the first time with complete translations of a vast literature which, in Max Müller's opinion, had hitherto been translated either partially or amateurishly. The production of this series kept him busy until the end of his life. It is considered by many to be, at least in part, an authoritative translation, and it was certainly the crowning achievement of his life's work.

The cultural and political relations between England and Germany in the latter half of the nineteenth century, especially after Germany's unification in 1871, also affected Max Müller's life. England's concern about Prussia's growing strength intensified in the 1860s, and with it a general antagonism towards Germans who had won a high social position in England. Nevertheless, England continued to offer a haven to many expatriate Germans, to both political exiles like Marx and Engels and scholars and authors like Max Müller, who had achieved a respected position in British ruling circles.[15]

14. Tomoko Masuzawa, *In Search of Dreamtime, the Quest for the Origin of Religion* (Chicago, IL, 1993), p. 65; G.M. Müller, *The Life and Letters*, I, pp. 133, 452, 473, 527, II, p. 7.
15. This is evidenced in his friendship with Queen Victoria, who invited him as her personal guest several times at Windsor Palace, where they conversed in fluent German. Moreover, in 1896, Max Müller was appointed privy chancellor,

Max Müller's association with Gladstone demonstrates his closeness to power. The two men first met in Oxford in 1853, and remained in contact when Gladstone became Prime Minister. In his four terms in the post (1868–1874, 1880–1885, 1886, 1892–1894) Gladstone became one of England's most outstanding statesmen, and Max Müller's association with him suggests he was an influential advisor to the government.[16] Max Müller unquestionably had a significant influence on the empire's policies, especially in India. His connection to the government was created by the assistant secretary of the Treasury, Sir Charles Trevelyan (1807–1886), whom he met at Bunsen's. Trevelyan spent much of his career in India, at first in the East India Company, later as governor of Madras (in 1858) and minister of finance in the government of India (1862–1865). He carried out a reform in the British Civil Service, which made it into a professional organization requiring its members to abide by high standards and to pass entrance examinations. Trevelyan was interested in philology, which led him (without success) in the 1850s to found an Oriental institute in London. He married the sister of the historian and statesman Macaulay, to whom he introduced Max Müller in 1855.

Macaulay, one of the proponents of the utilitarian approach to India, was a member of the Supreme Council of India between 1834 and 1838, designing the British policy on education and law. In 1855 he invited Max Müller to join a discussion on the question of the appropriate study for members of the Civil Service. At this meeting Max Müller discovered how conservative the older generation of British rulers were with regard to the Indians. Macaulay was repulsed by the culture of India and sought to replace it with the English. He maintained imperiously that it was easier for Indians to learn English than for Englishmen to learn Sanskrit, and that the ancient Hindu law was inferior to the advanced British law. His

---

G.M. Müller, *The Life and Letters*, I, pp. 300, 517-18, and G.M. Müller, *The Life and Letters*, II, pp. 196, 198-99 and 363.

16. G.M. Müller, *The Life and Letters*, I, pp. 409-12; Erich Eyck, *Gladstone* (London, 1966), p. 220, first published in Dutch 1938. It is worth noticing that his relations with the Imperial authorities began as early as 1854, when during the Crimean War he was asked to teach army officers Albanian, Romanian and Bulgarian. Several months later, he published a short book, in which he summarized the leading philological theories of his time: Max Müller, *Suggestions for the Assistance of Officers in Learning the Languages of the Seat of War in the East* (London, 1854).

views on the religious issues were much the same – like many of his generation, he wished to convert the Hindus to Christianity.[17]

Max Müller's contacts with Trevelyan and Macaulay helped his appointment in 1855 to the Civil Service Commission's examination board. The appointment demonstrated his excellent contacts with the ruling circles from early in his career in England. He saw it not as a national loyalty, but as an honourable service to his hosts.[18] In any event, over the years he acquired a position of influence not only in the academic sphere, but also in the political one, especially with reference to India – a distinguished position achieved by few academics. His researches into India's ancient culture served as the basis for his Aryan vision and his dream of unifying the two principal branches of the ancient Aryan nation, the Indian and the European. His influential position facilitated the promotion of this vision beyond the limits of academic life. As we shall see, this vision provided scientific legitimacy for Britain's rule over India.

As well as his association with central figures in England, Max Müller's long career also led to contacts with a number of European royal houses. In addition, honours of various kinds were lavished on him, such as the French Légion d'honneur, bestowed on him by the President of France in 1896, and honorary doctorates from the universities of Cambridge, Edinburgh, Bologna, Budapest and Princeton. He was a member of the Institut Français, the royal academies of Vienna, Berlin, Amsterdam, Hungary, Belgium and Romania, of the American Academy of Sciences and Arts, and other respected bodies the world over. His social connections encompassed the pillars of European culture.[19] Moreover, his reputation spread

17. G.M. Müller, *The Life and Letters*, I, p. 170; Max Müller, *Chips from a German Workshop*, I, pp. 185–86, first published 1867.

18. The question of Max Müller's nationalistic identity might be confusing. His first biography curiously declares that 'the fact that Max Müller was German by birth and spent his early life in Germany, has quite unnecessarily fixed the idea that he was a German scholar writing in German.' It is difficult to understand this statement, since Max Müller himself declared many times his German patriotism, and explained that his choice to live in Oxford was of a purely financial character, Nirad C. Chaudhuri, *Scholar Extraordinary, The Life of Friedrich Max Müller* (New Delhi, 1996), pp. 1–2, first published 1974; Masuzawa, *In Search of Dreamtime*, p. 62; Bosch, *Friedrich Max Müller*, p. xv; F. Max Müller, 'On the Language and Poetry of Schleswig-Holstein', in *Chips From a German Workshop*, III, pp. 116–50; G.M. Müller, *The Life and Letters*, I, pp. 402, 445, and G.M. Müller, *The Life and Letters* II, pp. 218–19.

19. Max Müller kept close connections with the Romanian king and queen, and was well acquainted with the queen of Holland and the king of Italy. Oscar, the

beyond Europe, especially to India, where he became known as the great friend of the local culture. When his translation of the *Rig Veda* arrived in India, local pundits dubbed him Moksha Mulara. In India he remained known for many years by this sobriquet, with its phonetic resemblance to his name.[20]

This brief summary of Max Müller's connections with numerous prominent political, cultural and scientific figures, illustrates his central position in England's cultural life in the second half of the nineteenth century. His reputation and standing as a major key figure in the country's social scene as well, add an important aspect to the assessment of his influence. This, of course, rested primarily on his standing as a scholar and his scores of academic publications. Max Müller was an unusually prolific writer. From his translation of the *Hitôpadeśa* until his death, hardly a year went by without at least one book of his appearing, if only a collection of his papers or lectures. In addition, he published numerous articles in newspapers and periodicals. And throughout his career he promoted his main idea – the common source of all the religions, above all Christianity and the religion of the *Vedas*. The methodology of philological research, in which he first won fame, became the tool with which he sought to substantiate this idea. It led him to found a new academic field, that of Comparative Religion. In this way Max Müller, the son of the poet from Dessau, came to link the Orientalist thought in Germany, France and imperial England, and became one of the most renowned scholars in the world.

From the Study of Language to that of Religions

Max Müller's Theory

'Die Weltgeschichte ist das Weltgericht' – 'The history of the world is the law of the world' – with this aphorism of Schiller's, Max Müller

---

Swedish king, made him a member of the Polar Star Order in 1889, and in 1900 took tea with him in Oxford. Another guest at the tea table was the crown prince of Siam. Many famous artists and scientists visited his Oxford home at 7 Norham Gardens. Among those were the legendary Swedish singer Jenny Lind (1820-1887), the violinist Joachim (1831-1907) and the inventor Alexander Graham Bell (1847-1922), who in 1878 demonstrated to Müller his telephone, microphone and phonograph: G.M. Müller, *The Life and Letters* I, pp. 322, 375, 474, 493 and G.M. Müller, *The Life and Letters*, II, pp. 50, 59, 206, 258, 272-73, 283, 348, 362, 431-32; Max Müller, *Auld Lang Syne*, I, p. 35.

20. G.M. Müller, *The Life and Letters*, I, p. 236.

summarized his historical world view at the start of his Gifford Lectures at Glasgow University in 1892. He was saying that the holistic view of history presumes the existence of universal wisdom and justice which direct its course, even if not always visibly. This Romantic concept might amuse the modern scholar, who has seen many conventional research methods crumble to dust, including those that served the Romantic scholars of the nineteenth century. Yet Max Müller was also aware of the arguments proposed by new progressive scholars, which threatened to make his views obsolete. He therefore went on to state, in this connection: 'No doubt such a view of the history of the world requires faith.'[21]

This comment reflects the dual function that characterized his research. He was simultaneously a rationalist and a believer, if not in the conventional Christian sense, who regarded the ancient religions of the Orient as relating to the same deity as worshipped in the West. Indeed, he valued the Oriental expressions of faith as more sublime than those of the West, for being simpler and closer to the truth.[22] This idea rested on his conviction that India's ancient civilization was in some ways no less advanced than Western civilization in the late nineteenth century. This led to his clash with the Darwinists, who believed in the idea of progress. They fought against him and gradually succeeded in edging him out of the scientific world until, not long after his death, most of his assumptions were discarded and he was dropped from the academic discourse.

Understanding the way in which Max Müller's personality combined the two elements, the rationalist and the religious, helps shed light on his research ideas and his Romantic vision, which contributed so significantly to the new Western image of India. Using rationalist comparative analysis, he helped to develop the academic fields of Sanskrit philology, the study of Indian culture and of religions. On the Romantic-religious side, he was one of the leading exponents of the Aryan Myth. Yet his belief in the racial kinship between the European Aryans and the ancient Aryans of India was not a racist one. Max Müller was a liberal in the true sense of the word, and perceived the affinity between the two Aryan families as a spiritual one, rather than as a shared inheritance of blood. Below I summarize Max Müller's scientific endeavour and analyse some of his studies which represent his contribution to the

21. F. Max Müller, *Theosophy or Psychological Religion* (London, 1893), pp. 1–2.
22. F. Max Müller, *Chips from a German Workshop*, I, p. 24.

fields of philology and comparative theology. I also try to restore him to his proper place in the academic discourse of his time, while examining the arguments brought against him by his principal opponents.

His ground-breaking article, 'Comparative Mythology', which marked the birth of the field of comparative theology, appeared in April 1856.[23] It contained most of the working assumptions that would serve him in future, and its stylistic blend of scientific materials with a Romantic approach would characterize his writing for the rest of his life. It was this blend which gave his work its ideological content with implications far beyond the conclusions of the scientific research.

In 'Comparative Mythology' Max Müller argued that the study of the origins of language was the most reliable tool for researching human history. He divided the history of language into three phases. In the first phase there was an Ur-language from which sprang all the known languages. The second phase saw the rise of the two main language families, the Aryan and the Semitic. He dubbed the third phase 'the mythological era', in which all the Aryan peoples had similar mythologies. He maintained that in pre-history there had been an ancient Aryan nation, whose culture gave birth to the original myths. These migrated far from their geographical source as the primary nation broke up into secondary ones, and the primary language sprouted various secondary Aryan languages. He asserted that comparative philology made it possible to identify and isolate the elements of the original Aryan language from the myths preserved in the languages which sprang from it. The mother-language was the source of Sanskrit, Greek, Latin and German, in the same way as French, Spanish and Italian sprang from Latin. Max Müller, like Jones before him, believed that the origins of the Aryan race lay in Central Asia. Before the ancient Aryan nation became divided, there was a time when every word had a central signification, but the original significations of these words was forgotten, until they became myths.

23. Some of the more esteemed scholars in the field of Comparative Religion (including Joachim Wach, Mircea Elieade, and Eric Sharpe), described the article's publication as the birth moment of the field: Masuzawa, *In Search of Dreamtime*, p. 58; Joachim Wach, *Comparative Study of Religion* (New York, 1958), p. 3; Mircea Eliade, *The Sacred and the Profane, the Nature of Religion* (New York, 1959), p. 229; Eric J. Sharpe, *Comparative Religion, A History* (La Salle, 1987), p. 35, first published 1975.

To explain this historical process, Max Müller coined a new term, 'the Disease of Language', which he used to narrate the way the original ancient Aryan ideas degenerated until they became myths. He claimed that in order for an idea to become a myth, it should be forgotten in the original language in which it was first phrased. Hence, a comparative examination of various Aryan languages, and especially the Sanskrit, might help us expose the original ideas that gave birth to the later Aryan myths.

The apex of 'Comparative Mythology' was the formulation of the Solar Myth – an idea that would become most closely associated with Max Müller. The Solar Myth rested on the assumption that the source of all religions, especially the Aryan ones, lay in the interpretation given by ancient people to natural phenomena, in particular to the sun and the dawn (for example, in Aryan mythology the sun symbolized immortality, and the dawn the life of mortal man). Thus words which originally signified 'sun', 'dawn', 'sky' and the like, underwent a process of identification with divine or mythological entities, and as a result lost their original signification.[24]

The hypotheses proposed in 'Comparative Mythology' provided the foundation for Max Müller's subsequent main theories, also in relation to the study of religion. His ideas reverberated widely and brought him fame, both in the academic world and in the general public. His fame increased further with the two series of *Lectures on the Science of Language*, which he delivered in 1861 and 1863 at the Royal Institute in London. They were innovative in placing language research among the exact sciences, by defining the methodology of philological investigation as scientific-empirical, subject to the demand for verification and proof, and in their formulation of the principles of the Aryan Myth.

The first series, in 1861, mainly surveyed the family of Aryan languages and its affinity with Sanskrit. The second series, in 1863, also discussed the methodology of the science of language and the way in which languages can be sorted into families and broken into component elements, and the definition of the principles that reveal their origins, their growth and their degeneration. But this series also held a sharper ideological message, namely, that a late phase in the development of a language is characterized by confusion and

---

24. Max Müller, 'Comparative Mythology', in *Chips from a German Workshop*, II, pp. 3, 7-10, 15-16, 18-19, 40-41, 46-47, 52, 54-56, 74, 76, 98, 125-26, first published 1856.

disarray, in contrast to the clarity that characterized it in its early development. This idea was compatible with Max Müller's recommendation to learn the ancient languages in a Christian spirit, without disparaging the languages of the pagans as representing faulty values.

This advice stemmed from his religious belief which bordered on blasphemy. He held that the common origin of all the religions arose from spiritual needs shared by all humanity, and from a single ancient truth. He posited that perhaps the deity manifested himself to various persons before revealing himself to the founders of Judaism, and did so in various places other than those described in the Scriptures. The methodology he proposed for the study of religion was based on philology, the two disciplines having the same purpose. Thereafter these would not be mere investigations of the histories of religions and language with the aim of enriching the corpus of human knowledge, but the attainment of spiritual materials to enhance the future of humanity. According to Max Müller, we need to know the ancient eras, so that the two great currents of mankind – the Semites and the Aryans – would blend and proceed to flow together towards a new course.[25]

Clearly, Max Müller was not anti-Semitic. The vision he proposed entailed blending the two races, the Aryan and the Semitic, in a process aimed at creating a single human current that would draw on their shared heritage. However, he did believe that the original Aryan culture and language were 'untainted' by Semitic influence, especially in their Indian manifestation. Arguing that the Semitic family of languages differed entirely from the European, he asserted that the Aryan faith, whose purest expression was found in the *Vedas*, had, unlike Judaism, developed free from any external influence. This pronouncement was the basis of his Aryan vision, which would become one of the driving forces that changed the European attitude towards India. Whereas in 1863 Max Müller emphasized the importance of the two main cultural currents, the Aryan and the Semitic, as time went on he concentrated on the effort to unify the two main streams of the Aryan race, namely the Indo-Oriental and the Western-Teutonic. The discovery of the spiritual sources of

25. Max Müller, *Lectures on the Science of Language*, II (London, 1994), pp. 1, 299, 423–24, first published 1864; Eric J. Sharpe, *The Universal Gita, Western Images of the Bhagavad Gītā, a Bicentenary Survey* (La Salle, 1985), p. 56.

the Oriental stream and their adoption by the Western would, he asserted, lead to a better future for the entire Aryan race. In order to realize this vision, it was essential to learn what India could offer the West: 'Whatever sphere of the human mind you may select for your special study... you have to go to India... because some of the most valuable and most instructive materials in the history of man are treasured up in India, and in India only.' Accordingly, as we shall see further on, he saw India as an unmistakable kin of the Aryan Europeans, as the source of their culture and the place where their future would be fulfilled.[26]

Some 30 years passed between *Lectures on the Science of Language* and the four Gifford Lectures Max Müller gave in Glasgow in 1892. The latter, which were published the following year in a book entitled *Theosophy, or Psychological Religion*, represented his spiritual convictions towards the end of his life. They may therefore be seen as his summary of the field of research to which he had devoted his life. They defined all religions as attempts to conceive of infinity. He argued that all 'natural' religions (those that derive from a belief in the forces of nature) shared two indispensable characteristics – belief in the eternal deity and in the immortal soul. The religion he called Psychological comprised both characteristics in such a way that they seem to correspond – the deity is perceived as linked to the soul and the soul is perceived as divine. The belief in the infinite soul and deity inevitably leads to the recognition of their unity, since there cannot be two simultaneous infinities.

The term 'psychological religion' served Max Müller as a substitute for the terms 'mystical religion' and 'theosophical religion', which he felt had been misused to the point of distortion. He stated that 'theosophical religion' engaged in wild speculations about the deity's unknown nature, while the term 'mystical' gives a vague and arcane impression. By contrast, the study of psychological religion analyses the relations between man's soul and the divine as something clear and logical. He contended that by means of this methodology one finds that Christianity is not a reform or continuation of Judaism, but a synthesis between the Aryan and the Semitic thoughts:

> What interests the historian is to understand how the belief of a small brotherhood of Galilean fishermen and their devotion to their Master

26. Max Müller, *India, What Can It Teach Us?* pp. 33, 144–45.

> could have influenced... the whole of the ancient world. The key to that riddle should be sought for, I believe, at Alexandria rather then at Jerusalem.

The fact that other religions had ideas resembling those of Christianity did not detract from its standing, he said, because the widespread notion that pagan religions were not as profound as Christianity was mistaken. In fact, he claimed, religious faith in general and the belief in miracles in particular spring everywhere from the same source.

The concluding idea of *Theosophy, or Psychological Religion* was that, as some of the oldest religious literature was lost, comparative philology could be used to discover the mutual influences of the various religious texts.[27] Max Müller maintained that, unlike the other religions, which had influenced one another, Hindu philosophy had grown spontaneously and had never been affected by external factors – in contrast to other Aryan cultures which had been subjected to alien influences after the original mother-nation had split up. The conclusion proposed to his modern English readers was therefore plain to see – be the blood in our veins Saxon or Norman, the common source of our intellect lies in India – there was found the oldest evidence of our ancient culture in its purest form.

These were the principal ideas that Max Müller developed during his career at Oxford, via philology to comparative theology. His research led him to develop far-reaching hypotheses which started by seeking to identify the common denominator of European cultures, and ended by concluding that the ancient Indian culture was the best representative of the ancient Aryan mother-culture.

The Academic Criticism of Max Müller

Max Müller's working method made extensive use of imagination and speculation. This was due to his being one of the first to work in philology as a regular discipline, and the fact that his main interest was in Sanskrit and in the reconstruction, practically *ab nihilo*, the culture which created it. This method attracted constant criticism for its excessive use of imagination.[28] In the course of his

---

27. Max Müller, *Theosophy or Psychological Religion*, pp. vi-vii, ix-x, xiv, 8-9, 11-25, 31-34, 47-49, 52, 67, 71-72, 89, 91-94.

28. Kurt Jankowsky, 'F. Max Müller and the Development of Linguistic Science,' *Historiographia Linguistica* (1979), p. 340.

career he acquired numerous academic opponents, in England and elsewhere.[29] Among the best known were Charles Darwin (1809-1882), Edward Burnett Tylor (1832-1917) and Andrew Lang (1844-1912), who for years conducted a dialogue with him – the first two in a courteous manner, the third with fierce attacks.

Darwin published *The Origin of Species* in 1859, three years after Max Müller's influential article 'Comparative Mythology'. Although they were working in quite disparate fields, over time a serious dispute arose between them and between their supporters. The principal bone of contention was the heart of Darwin's theory about human evolution, especially in reference to the development of language, which Max Müller regarded as the conclusive proof of Man's superiority over the animal world. The indirect argument between them began soon after the publication of *The Origin of Species*. While the book itself discussed the natural world, the ideas in it were adopted by philologists, anthropologists and students of mythologies, who proposed new theories about the rise of human language. At the centre of these theories was the idea that language evolved from low-grade noises, and that its development could be analysed in the same way as the evolutionary processes in the natural world. The two leading new theories were Onomatopoeia (the development of language through the imitation of sounds in nature) and Interjection (that words developed from primitive cries). Max Müller derided them as 'the theory of Bow-wow' and 'the theory of Pooh-pooh'. In his lectures he said that the theory of onomatopoeia was a good description of the language of ducks and chickens, but certainly not of human speech. Accordingly, he protested that it took greater boldness to criticize Darwin than to express doubt about Hebrew being the mother of all languages.[30]

Nevertheless, the direct confrontation between Darwin and Max Müller grew heated fairly late, in the early 1870s, when Darwin's theory of evolution had become predominant. The dispute grew

---

29. His first academic opponent was Bournof's other famous student, Renan, who attacked his 1854 'The Classification of the Turanian Languages'. Max Müller reacted with an attack on Renan's 1855 book on Semitic grammar, but years later admitted that Renan was right: F. Max Müller, *The Classification of the Turanian Languages* (London, 1854); Ernest Renan, *Histoire Générale et Système Comparé des Langues Sémitique* (Paris, 1855); G.M. Müller, *The Life and Letters*, I, pp. 148, 181-82.

30. Max Müller, *Lectures on the Science of Language*, II, p. 91; Max Müller, *Auld Lang Syne*, I, p. 193.

stormy and engaged more individuals in England and across the Atlantic, among them William Dwight Whitney (1827–1894), a professor of Sanskrit and Comparative Philology at Yale University, and Charles Darwin's son George (1845–1912). It broke out in 1871, following the publication of Darwin's *The Descent of Man*, which argued that the historical development of human speech could be analysed with the tools of evolution theory.[31]

In 1873, Max Müller gave a series of three lectures, entitled 'On Darwin's Philosophy of Language', which discussed 'language as the barrier between man and brute'. In these lectures he propounded his ideas about the rise of language, along with a fairly moderate criticism of Darwin's theory. The main points of his argument remained unchanged in the following years. Max Müller sent Darwin a copy of these lectures. In the accompanying letter (dated 29 June 1873) he remarked that,

> 'the interjectional and mimetic theories of the origin of language are no doubt very attractive and plausible, but if they were more than that, one at least of the great authorities on the science of language... would have adopted them. However, it matters very little who is right and who is wrong; but it matters a great deal what is right and what is wrong...'

Darwin replied elegantly (3 July 1873):

> I feel quite sure from what I have read in your works that you would never say anything of an honest adversary to which he would have any just right to object... as far as language is concerned I am not worthy to be your adversary, as I know extremely little about it... He who is fully convinced, as I am, that man is descended from some lower animal, is almost forced to believe *a priori* that articulate language has been developed from inarticulate cries; and he is therefore hardly a fair judge of the arguments opposed to this belief.[32]

Max Müller visited Darwin at his home in Kent in October 1874. This was the only time the two adversaries met. According to Müller, he was warned that Darwin was incapable of carrying on a serious discussion for more than a quarter of an hour before he started complaining of sickness. Therefore, he put his arguments before Darwin 'in the shortest way possible.' After having finished,

---

31. Charles Darwin, 'The Descent of Man, and Selection in Relation to Sex', in *The Complete Works of Charles Darwin*, ed. Paul H. Barrett and R. B. Freeman, XXI (London, 1989), pp. 84–92, first published 1870.

he shook hands with Darwin, who told him: 'You are a dangerous man.' Darwin's sophisticated sense of humor may reflect his perception of Max Müller as belonging to the old school he had fought 15 years earlier. Max Müller's reply to this remark – 'There can be no danger in our search for truth' – reflects his graveness and lack of humor, compared to his respected rival.

A short while later (7 November 1874), Max Müller wrote to Darwin:

> I can assure you I feel, as strongly as any mere layman in natural history can feel it, the impulsive force of your arguments. If I hesitate in following you... it is not because I am afraid, but simply because I see certain elements in human nature which would remain unexplained... You know better than anybody how infinitely great is the difference between man and animal: what I want to know is the first small and hardly perceptible cause of that difference, and I believe I find it in language and what is implied by language.

In another letter (13 October 1875), Max Müller wrote:

> In the higher animals the potential traces of language are smaller than in some of the lower, but even when the phonetic organs are most perfect, there has never been the slightest attempt at language in the true sense of the word. Why should natural science be unwilling to admit this?... more facts and fewer theories is what we want, at least in the Science of Language.

Replying two days later, Darwin wrote:

> With respect to our differences, though some of your remarks have been stinging, they have all been made so gracefully, I declare that I am like the man in the story who boasted that he had been soundly horsewhipped by a duke.[33]

But the courtly antagonism between Max Müller and Darwin grew more intolerant when it widened to include Whitney, Max Müller's leading opponent in the United States, and George Darwin (a scientist in his own right, and since 1883 a professor of Astronomy at Cambridge University). Young Darwin attacked Max Müller with

---

32. *More Letters of Charles Darwin: A Record of His Work in a Series of hitherto Unpublished Letters*, ed. Francis Darwin, vol. 2 (New York, 1972), p. 45, first published in 1903; Max Müller, *Auld Lang Syne*, I, pp. 194–195, 197–201.

33. Max Müller, *Auld Lang Syne*, I, pp. 202–204; *The Life and Letters of the Right Honourable Friedrich Max Müller*, I, pp. 503–504, 523–24.

the arguments brought by Whitney against his working methods.[34] Max Müller hastened to respond. In January 1875 his article, 'My Reply to Mr. Darwin', appeared in the periodical *Contemporary Review*, in which he referred to Whitney for the first time and elegantly dismissed his American opponent's research, originality and attack: 'It is both interesting and instructive in the study of Dialectic Growth, to see how words which would be considered offensive in England have ceased to be so on the other side of the Atlantic, and are admitted into the most respectable of American reviews.'[35]

In September 1875, at the height of his dispute with Darwin and his supporters, Max Müller published an article entitled 'In Self-Defense', which was entirely devoted to a robust attack on Whitney and the Darwinist schools of philosophy.[36] Whitney responded ferociously, and in 1876 attacked Max Müller: 'To me he is simply, with all his ability, one of the great humbugs of the century... He has always been rated at full ten times his value as a scholar.'[37]

The strong language employed by both Whitney and Max Müller in their confrontation was due not only to personal animosity, but also to a genuine disagreement about the history of language, in particular the degree of mutual influence between the Aryan and Semitic languages. As we shall see, there was a lively debate about this issue in the final decades of the nineteenth century, when various scholars argued against Max Müller and sought to prove the existence of Semitic influence over the Aryan language and culture. While Max Müller argued for the purity of the Aryan

---

34. G.H. Darwin, 'Professor Whitney on the Origin of Language', *Contemporary Review* 139 (Oxford, 1874), 894.

35. Max Müller, 'My Reply to Mr. Darwin', *Chips From a German Workshop*, IV (New York, 1895), pp. 432, 453, 455, first published in *Contemporary Review*, 25 (1875), pp. 305-26.

36. Max Müller, 'In Self Defense', *Chips from a German Workshop*, IV, pp. 456-531.

37. *The Life and Letters of the Right Honourable Friedrich Max Müller*, II, p. 23. Whitney was not the only American who criticized Max Müller, who was frequently mocked in American periodicals. On December 1868, The '*Atlantic Monthly*' published a harsh review of Max Müller's article, 'On the Stratification of Language'. Many years later, the New York '*Nation*' claimed that the real credit for translating the *Rig Veda* ought to be given to another German scholar: *The Life and Letters of the Right Honourable Friedrich Max Müller*, I, p. 499; Max Müller, 'On the Stratification of Language', *Chips from a German Workshop*, IV, pp. 63-110; 'Muller's On the Stratification of Language', *The Atlantic Monthly*, 22 (December, 1868), pp. 761-762.

languages, above all Sanskrit, his opponents based their theses on a completely different historical conception, according to which the Semitic languages had a decisive effect on the formation of European languages.

Max Müller also conducted a prolonged, though not heated, dispute with Tylor, the father of modern anthropology.[38] It began in 1866, a year after the publication of Tylor's book, *Researches into the Early History of Mankind*, which Max Müller reviewed favourably in April 1865.[39] In March 1866, Tylor criticized Max Müller's *Lectures on the Science of Language*, attacking the author as an alien, and for his method that entailed belief in a divine power. In response, Max Müller wrote Tylor (16 April 1866), thanking him for his fair review, which he said 'was exciting the interest and allaying the fears of that large and important class of Englishmen who are, more or less, led by *The Quarterly Review*.'[40]

Not long afterwards, Tylor published another article in the *Fortnightly Review*, criticizing Max Müller's objections to the theories of Interjection and Onomatopoeia.[41] He continued to criticize him in the following years. In 1871 he argued in his book *Primitive Cultures*, that in contrast to Max Müller, he believed that the mythology of the inferior races derived from the analogy of reality and the senses, whereas the widespread infusion of verbal metaphors into the ancient mythology characterized more highly developed cultures. Thus the material myth was the primary source, and the verbal myth was secondary and later.[42] In this connection, he further criticized

38. For further discussion on Tylor, his concept of 'Animism' and support of Darwin's evolution theory, see, George Ward Stocking, *Victorian Anthropology* (New York, 1987); George Ward Stocking, *Race, Culture, and Evolution: Essays in the History of Anthropology* (New York, 1968); Peter J. Bowler, *The Invention of Progress: the Victorians and the Past* (Oxford, 1989).

39. Edward Burnett Tylor, *Researches into the Early History of Mankind and the Development of Civilization* (London, 1865); F. Max Müller, 'On Manners and Customs', in *Chips from a German Workshop*, II, pp. 248-83.

40. E.B. Tylor, 'Lectures on the Science of Language', in *The Collected Works of Edward Burnett Tylor*, VII (London, 1994), pp. 394, 400-401, 423, 427; 431-33, first published in *Quarterly Review*, 119 (London, 1866); *The Life and Letters of the Right Honourable Friedrich Max Müller*, I, p. 332.

41. E.B. Tylor, 'On the Origin of Languages', in *The Collected Works of Edward Burnett Tylor*, VI (London, 1994), p. 545: first published in *Fortnightly Review*, 4 (London, 1866); *The Life and Letters of the Right Honourable Friedrich Max Müller*, I, p. 332.

42. E.B. Tylor, 'Primitive Culture: Researches into the Development of Mythology, Philosophy, Religion, Art, and Custom', I, in *The Collected Works of Edward Burnett Tylor*, III, p. 271, first published 1871.

Max Müller in his book *Anthropology*, published in 1881, disparaging the idea of the 'disease of language' as a principal contributor to the formation of myth.[43]

Tylor also attacked Max Müller's belief in the advanced state of the ancient Vedic religion and the culture from which it sprang. In 1880, in the Presidential Address at a conference of the Anthropological Institute, Tylor said:

> If we could admit Prof. Müller's starting-point of theology in a state like that of the Aryans of the Veda, his consequence would no doubt follow. But I am bound to stand up for the opinion that the Vedic deities represent not a primitive, but a high and late state of religion.[44]

This challenge to Max Müller derived from Tylor's belief in the Darwinist theory, that Man arose from animal elements, and led to his assumption that there still existed some human races which were less developed than others. Max Müller rejected this argument, and maintained that what distinguished ancient Man from the animals – i.e., human speech – had not changed in the past thousands of years, and thus there was no great difference between him and modern humanity.[45]

The prolonged dispute with Tylor was a contributing factor that led to Max Müller's ideas on the degeneration that spread through the ancient cultures becoming outdated even in his lifetime. His position was anti-progressive, suggesting that the ancient era was not as primitive as his opponents maintained. Max Müller held that the ancient Hindu mythology was the spiritual source of the Aryan civilization. He therefore conceived of the Sanskrit texts as a spiritual challenge for modern Western man, who could draw inspiration from them. These Romantic ideas became outdated and unfashionable, primarily because they were the opposite of the concepts of Tylor and his associates in the Progressive-Darwinist

---

43. E.B. Tylor, 'Anthropology: An Introduction to the Study of Man and Civilization', *The Collected Works of Edward Burnett Tylor*, V, p. 395, first published 1881.

44. E.B. Tylor, 'The President's Address', *The Collected Works of Edward Burnett Tylor*, VI, pp. 456–57: first published in *Journal of the Anthropological Institute*, 9 (1880).

45. It is worthwhile to note that Max Müller was not a racist, but a true liberal, regarding racial issues:'...we mean by Aryans no more than speakers of Aryan languages, whatever their skulls or their hair may have been': Gregory Schremp, 'The Re-Education of Friedrich Max Müller: Intellectual Appropriation and Epistemological Antinomy in Mid-Victorian Evolutionary Thought', *Man*, New Series, 18 (1983), 97; Max Müller, *My Autobiography*, pp. 32–34.

current which kept growing stronger at the expense of Max Müller and his supporters. Tylor may therefore be seen as one of the main individuals responsible for the decline of Max Müller's popularity after his death.

Another person notably responsible for the reduction of Max Müller's place in Europe's intellectual history was Andrew Lang.[46] The rivalry between the two men went beyond the good manners that characterized Max Müller's relations with Darwin and Tylor. Lang used harsh terms in attacking his opponent, and cast doubt on his basic assumptions. The dispute between the two men grew increasingly rancorous, since Lang saw himself as representing the anthropological school and conducted a crusade against Max Müller, whom he viewed as the representative of the rival, philological school.

Lang challenged Max Müller's Aryan motifs, and sought to show that his belief in the Aryan languages being 'untainted' rested on his imagination. He maintained that the existence among non-Aryan nations of stories identical to those of the Aryan ones disproved Max Müller's theory. He also attacked Max Müller's belief in the cultural perfection of the ancient Aryans, arguing that Max Müller believed that man had appeared on earth in a state of perfection and has been degenerating ever since. Furthermore, Lang attacked the philological method used by Max Müller, accusing him of inaccurately interpreting the etymology of many words, and of inability to comprehend the extent of Semitic influence over the Aryan languages. He sought to show, *inter alia*, the Semitic influence on the creation of Greek deities like Aphrodite, thereby disproving Max Müller's Solar Myth.[47] Lang's criticism hit its target, when in 1892, Max Müller declared that 'we can account... for the grafting of Semitic ideas on Greek deities, as in the case of Aphrodite or Heracles.' However, it seems that Max Müller was offended by his younger rival's style, as evidenced in a letter he sent him on 8 July 1897: 'Still less could I understand why you should have attacked me, or rather my masters, without learning Sanskrit... You must

---

46. Lang's fame was based primarily on his Fairy tales compilations, as well as on his translation to The Iliad: Andrew Lang, *Blue Fairy Book*, ed. Brian Alderson (New York, 1987), first published 1889; Homer, *The Iliad*, trans. Andrew Lang, Walter Leaf and Ernest Myers (London, 1914), first published 1883.

47. Andrew Lang, *Myth, Ritual and Religion*, I (New York, 1968), pp. 26–27, 30–31; 61–62; II, II, pp. 274, 305, 315–16; 336, first published 1887.

have a rapier to fight a man who has a rapier, otherwise it becomes a row.'[48]

The rivalry between the two reached its climax with the publication, in 1897, of Lang's book *Modern Mythology*, which was wholly devoted to an attack on Max Müller and his book, published that year, *Contributions to the Science of Mythology*. In it Lang undertook the advocacy of the discipline of Anthropology in its battle against Philology. He attacked Max Müller who, he said, 'never comes to grips with his opponents, and his large volumes shine rather in erudition and style than in method and system.' He defined thus the dispute with his opponent: Was language, especially in a state of 'disease', the source of mythology, or did mythology represent an early phase of thought (unconnected to language), from which culture arose? According to Lang, Max Müller believed that language caused the kind of thinking behind mythology, whereas the anthropologists maintained that language was merely the means by which mythological thinking could express itself.[49]

This was, in fact, the essential difference between the two opposing approaches. The solution which both proposed for it contained the seed of Anthropology's triumph over Max Müller and his disciples. It led to the obsolescence of Max Müller's dogmatic assertions regarding the Aryan languages and their purity. Lang's argument that the common source of myths was human nature, rather than shared cultural roots, became dominant, as evident in contemporary publications.[50] Nevertheless, there is no disputing Max Müller's contribution to scientific research, which consisted of infusing a system of ideals and creating a terminology, framework and impetus to the field of comparative religion, which had previously been inchoate. By the end of Max Müller's career, and resulting directly from his work, this was a scientifically organized discipline, subject to research methodology. In addition, Max Müller was principally responsible for attracting a whole generation of scholars to the new discipline of comparative religion, and for stimulating the intense

48. Max Müller, *Theosophy or Psychological Religion*, p. 63; *The Life and Letters of the Right Honourable Friedrich Max Müller*, II, p. 381.
49. Max Müller, *Contributions to the Science of Mythology* (2 vols., London, 1897); Andrew Lang, *Modern Mythology* (New York, 1968), pp. ix-x, first published 1897.
50. See, for example, Robert Brown, *Semitic Influence in Hellenic Mythology, with Special Reference to the Recent Mythological Works of the Rt. Hon. Prof. F. Max Müller and Mr. Andrew Lang* (Oxford, 1898).

research activity which led, paradoxically and ungratefully, to the development of the very schools that brought him down.

Furthermore, Max Müller was principally responsible for opening the minds to the dialogue between Christianity and the religions of the Orient, and between intellectual circles in Britain and their opposite numbers in India. His view of the history of religions gave a new dimension to the discussion about the origins of Christianity and European civilization. By depicting them as arising from the ancient Aryan thought, from which Oriental cultures had likewise arisen, he made the European Aryan a kinsman in the Orient and reduced the gulf between East and West to its geographic sense. His great contribution, therefore, was to bring the Hindu civilization into the Victorian academic discourse, and beyond it – to heighten the spiritual interest in India among Western people in general. To understand this contribution we need to analyse his views on India, her civilization and the roots of its connection with European culture. As we shall see, the analysis reveals a Romantic who sought to weave a joint dream between the two principal cultures of his life – the English culture, in which his career flourished, and the Indian, which he regarded as the cradle of wisdom and the source of spirituality that would enable humanity to thrive in the future.

Max Müller and the Creation of the New Image of India

Max Müller and India

Max Müller never visited India. Nevertheless, it was the centre of his intellectual interest throughout his life. He said that his interest in India began when he was a schoolboy – one of his schoolbooks bore a picture of men and women bathing in the Ganges. They struck him as beautiful. The mosques and temples on the river banks looked more regal and impressive than the churches and palaces in Dessau. The picture fired his imagination and caused his mind to wander in the classroom. When the teacher noticed, he made him copy many pages from that book, which were filled with the motifs of Benares, the Ganges and India in general. In this original way were engraved in his mind the landscapes of the country which would preoccupy it throughout his adult life, though he never once set foot in it.[51]

---

51. F. Max Müller, *Auld Lang Syne, Second Series, My Indian Friends* (New York, 1899), pp. vi–vii, 1–3; 162.

This story helps to illustrate Max Müller's conception of India. His imagination retained the picture of a land of magical landscapes and a wondrous atmosphere, even when he had grown and become a well-known scholar. India's exotic-looking inhabitants, which despite their dark complexion seemed to his child's eyes to differ from the black races, became in his adult writings the 'kinsmen' of his own race, the European Aryans. This childish image of India, essentially a part of an Oriental fantasy, was developed in his adult life into his Aryan vision, which did not have much connection with reality. Max Müller's books on Indian subjects were widely distributed and helped to implant this fantastic image in the general public.

Beyond his influence in England, Max Müller played an important role in encouraging the national movement in India, which arose in the late nineteenth century. His research legitimized its demand for a national recovery by helping to reveal India's glorious past and placing it at the centre of public and academic debate in both Britain and India. That Max Müller himself was at the intellectual heart of the colonial power, namely, at Oxford, enhanced his influence over the Indians, which was further reinforced as the younger leadership received a British education. The clear contrast between the liberal values imbued in that education and the rule of a foreign power over their country led them to seek support for their cause in Britain itself, and found it in the person of Max Müller. His ideas fell on willing ears in India, where he gained an almost legendary stature and was seen as the Indians' best friend in the West. This may account for the fantastic explanation given in India for the fact that Max Müller himself never visited their country – namely, that he had been a Hindu in a previous life and feared that if he saw his land of origin the excess of happiness would kill him. The American transcendentalist, Moncure Daniel Conway (1832–1907), echoes this impression in his memoirs: 'Wherever I went in India I usually met the students and the pundits... and all of these, of whatever caste or sect, regarded Max Müller as the greatest of mankind.'[52]

The problems that arise from Max Müller's Indian research material involve two main areas – his Aryan ideas with their implications for the racial theories of his time, and his views about the

---

52. Chaudhuri, *Scholar Extraordinary*, p. 271; Moncure Daniel Conway, *Autobiography, Memories and Experiences*, II (Boston, 1905), p. 309.

Indians and the attitude due to them from Western people. With regard to the first, there is no doubt that Max Müller helped to disseminate the Aryan Myth, and was therefore perceived by many as the person responsible for the rise of modern European racism, even for the Aryan terminology used by the Nazis.[53] Yet a critical and comprehensive reading of his work shows that his conception of the Aryan issue was based principally on romantic rather than racist motifs. For example, in a letter to the Oxford history professor Edward Freeman (1823-1892), he remarked:

> I believe the confusion in the popular mind arises chiefly from a confusion of terminology which was meant for linguistic purposes, for historical or physiological work. Let people classify blood as much as they like, only let them use their own bottles for that, and not bottles that were labeled for the purpose of holding languages.[54]

Nevertheless, his responsibility for the spread of the Aryan Myth cannot be dismissed. He did, in fact, promote the idea that India and her culture were the source from which sprang the roots of Aryan Europe, thereby advancing the use of the Aryan racial terminology, as well as legitimizing British imperialism. Yet it is necessary to note that he expressed tolerance towards alien cultures, and argued that kernels of wisdom could be found in every religion.[55] This idea, which he proposed in 1879, was not at all prevalent at that time, two years after Queen Victoria became Empress of India, and England formally changed from a kingdom into an empire.

As we have seen, British interest in India waned, somewhat paradoxically, in the course of the nineteenth century, as its power over the Subcontinent consolidated. The interest that its administration showed in Indian culture in the time of Warren Hastings stemmed from the need to make its rule more effective. As noted before, it was the main impetus for recruiting students of the local language and culture that brought about the breakthrough in the study of Sanskrit. In the last quarter of the nineteenth century, about 100 years after that wave of eager English research, India had become an integral part of the British Empire, which the government had no interest in favouring as a source of cultural inspiration – rather the

---

53. Thomas R. Trautmann, *Aryans and British India* (Berkeley, 1997), pp. 172, 194-97; Bosch, *Friedrich Max Müller*, p. 203.
54. *The Life and Letters of the Right Honourable Friedrich Max Müller*, I, p. 396.
55. Max Müller, *The Sacred Books of the East*, I, p. xxxviii.

contrary. The imperial interest was opposed to the view of India as a singular case, both because it wished to make her an integral component of the empire, and for fear that demands for self-rule and independence would be based on local history.

The imperial interest also affected the treatment of the local inhabitants. India had indeed become 'the jewel in the crown', but the supercilious view of the jewel's inhabitants was of 'natives', or at best 'subjects'. This attitude became problematic in relation to the study of Indian culture. Was it possible to rule over another nation, emphasizing its inferiority (to justify that rule), while at the same time lauding its culture and attributing to it such high qualities as you attribute to your own? This would have been an impossible quandary even if the British were willing to resolve it. It was therefore natural that the preparation for the administration of India was, as Max Müller argued, sadly deficient in serious information about India's culture. The deficiency was not due to the general training – which was very good by European standards – but because information about India was regarded as superfluous.

Such complaints characterized Max Müller's views of the British administration in India from his early days in England. His meeting with Macaulay, when the latter declared that Indian culture was inferior, Trevelyan's failed attempt in those days to found an Oriental institute in London, his familiarity with leading figures in the British administration, and his encounters with students all over the United Kingdom – all these revealed to Max Müller the extent of English prejudice about the Indians. Further on, I shall try to show how he himself viewed the Indians, how he battled against the prejudices about them, and what led him to act as the advocate for a nation he knew chiefly through its writings.

Max Müller's Indian crusade occupied him almost to the end of his life, its outstanding expression being two of his works. The first was *India: What Can It Teach Us?* – a collection of lectures he gave in Cambridge in 1882. The second appeared in 1899 (as volume II of his autobiographical notes, entitled *Auld Lang Syne*), headed 'My Indian Friends'. I shall now discuss these two works, which mainly sought to dispel the prejudices about the Indians. The earlier volume, written when Max Müller's career was at its height, is especially interesting to a researcher wishing to examine his influence over the modern image of the Indian in the West. I follow it with a discussion about the later work, with its sober consciousness of an ageing man writing a kind of spiritual testament on the issue of India.

India: What Can It Teach Us?

In May 1882 Max Müller was invited to lecture at Cambridge University, to an audience consisting of candidates for employment by the Indian Civil Service. These lectures were published in December of that year under the title, *India: What Can It Teach Us?* The lectures and book summarized Max Müller's ideas about ancient India's culture and religion, focusing mainly on the Sanskrit texts and on the connection with the Aryan languages. The book reinforced Max Müller's status in India as the person who, more than any other Westerner, helped to improve the relations between the Indian subjects and their rulers.[56]

These lectures are especially interesting not only because of their contents, but because their audience was preparing to leave for India a short while later, to take up practical government posts. The way Max Müller presented his opinions was directly relevant to this fact, both in his attempt to correct the widespread English errors and prejudices concerning India, and in his choice of subjects for discussion – raising the status of India in the minds of his audience, a re-examination of the Indians' questionable integrity, modern man's interest in ancient Sanskrit, the uniqueness of Indian culture by comparison with other known cultures, its antiquity and seniority over European culture, and the Aryan roots common to India and Europe.

These lectures were given at a time when Max Müller's standing was stronger than ever, at any rate in the field of Oriental studies. He had recently retired from regular teaching, and was engaged in the project *The Sacred Books of the East*, whose volumes were then appearing one after the other. This made him an authoritative speaker to his audience of trainees for the Indian Civil Service, destined to administer the affairs of the empire in India. His impact upon them, and indirectly on the quality of the governance of India, was therefore significant also on the practical political level.

In his first lecture of the series, Max Müller defined the main problems besetting the British attitudes towards the Indians, and

---

56. Jawaharlal Nehru, who quoted a full paragraph from that book in his *The Discovery of India*, told his readers how Max Müller influenced his interest in his own culture: Jawaharlal Nehru, *The Discovery of India* (New York, 1946), pp. 78-79.

surveyed the main elements of his thought as crystallized since the days of 'Comparative Mythology'. He explained that India was the birthplace of the 'natural religion', which sprang from belief in the forces of Nature. In addition, it was the source of Buddhism and Brahminism, and the refuge of the Zoroastrians. His Aryan vision of India, as Europe's unmistakable 'kin', embodying Europe's destiny, was clearly spelled out: India's historical role was not confined to being the cradle of the Aryan religions. Moreover, the integration of the Eastern with the Western Aryan traditions would ultimately give rise to a new religion that would rest on the kernels of truth inherent in both.

Max Müller stated that the culture of India was insufficiently appreciated by those who were about to manage its governance. Their approach was doomed to be problematic, because they viewed the place as alien. His suggested solution was to acknowledge the kinship between the ancient Indian civilization and modern English culture, a kinship which rested on a historical investigation that has recognized India's seniority in the family of Aryan nations. The lecture concluded with a reference to Sir William Jones and an idealized description of his romantic concept of India and of the Orient as a whole. To Max Müller, Jones was the archetype whom the Indian Civil Service trainees should emulate. Like Jones, Max Müller viewed the Orient as the source of European civilization. He called on his hearers to view the East and India as their 'old home', as 'the port whence Man started, the course he has followed, and the port towards which he has to steer.'

This metaphor gives Max Müller's Aryan Myth in a nutshell. The conclusion his listeners were to draw from his lectures was unequivocal – India was not a foreign country. Its conquest did not mean ruling over an alien culture. The English, India's present rulers, were in reality returning to their ancient homeland![57]

It is hard to say what Max Müller sought to achieve by these assertions. Did he seek to serve the imperial objectives by deepening the interest of the future administrators of India so as to make them more effective? Or was he offering a liberal alternative to the existing reality, one that ultimately emphasized the study of Indian culture as not inferior to that of the West? There is no simple answer to these questions, and as we shall see, the answer could be surprising.

57. Max Müller, *India: What Can It Teach Us?*, pp. 19–21, 25–31, 33–43, 49.

An analysis of the rest of the lectures in the series *India: What Can It Teach Us?* may provide a solution to the seeming contradiction in Max Müller's theory.

The second lecture in the series, entitled 'The Truthful Character of the Hindus', was a head-on assault on the British prejudice which held that all Hindus were liars and untrustworthy witnesses in a court of law. Max Müller stressed that in all his contacts with Hindu scholars he sensed that these were people who greatly valued truth. He quoted a statement from the *Mahābhārata*, asserting that Truth is the highest value. He stressed that while he did not claim that all Hindus are truth-seekers, the argument that they are all liars was false, and certainly inapplicable to their ancient culture.[58]

The third, and possibly most significant, lecture in the series sought to explain why the study of Sanskrit was important, although the language had ceased to be a spoken language 2000 years ago. Max Müller divided the Sanskrit texts into two chronological periods – the time before the first century BCE, and the time after. The first period was also, in his view, divisible in two: the time when the 'natural' literature was written, mainly the Vedic writings and the Buddhist *Tripiṭaka*, and the later time, when 'artificial' literature, such as the *Bhagavad-Gītā*, was written. While the works produced during the 'artificial' period might be interesting and aesthetically pleasing, they could not be compared to the Vedic literature, which dealt with the spirit of the human race and comprised all the elements of modern thought. Unfortunately, he said, Europe was introduced to Sanskrit via texts dating from the 'artificial' period, such as the *Bhagavad-Gītā* or the plays of Kālidāsa. These are valued because of their antiquity, but objectively-speaking, they were not superior to ancient European writings. On the other hand, in the really ancient Hindu writings we find the true spirit of Aryan man, who developed his meditative side to perfection in the *Vedas*.

Max Müller regarded the Vedic literature as the source of the modern Europeans' Aryan roots. He claimed that the *Vedas* contained evidence showing how the ancient Aryans took control over India. They describe how the conquerors defended their new home, and how they invented the caste system, which was designed to preserve

58. Chaudhuri, Max Müller's Indian biographer, indicated that 'among us the notion of verbal truthfulness was never very highly developed', a notion worth noticing in regard to that lecture: Chaudhuri, *Scholar Extraordinary*, p. 292; Max Müller, *India: What Can It Teach Us?*, pp. 53-55, 64, 71, 80-81, 90.

the peace and tranquillity by creating an aristocratic stratum to rule over the masses. The *Vedas*, he argued, expressed the Aryan ideals of these rulers in a different form from the European Aryan ideal. It was a passive, meditative ideal, the opposite of the European active and materialistic ideal. The Indian ideal could teach us something not to be obtained from any other source:

> Instead of simply despising this Indian view of life, might we not pause for a moment and consider whether their philosophy of life is entirely wrong, and ours entirely right... or whether we, sturdy Northern Aryans, might not have been satisfied with a little less of work, and a little less of so-called pleasure, but with a little more of thought and a little more of rest.

This Indian wisdom consisted chiefly in the exploration of the inner 'self', the heart of the Vedic philosophy, which Max Müller viewed as expressing the 'childish age' in the history of religions, that might teach us what was lacking in the wisdom of Greece and Rome. Given that the Vedic hymns were dated to between 1500 and 1000 BCE, this called, according to Max Müller, for a reappraisal of the supposedly savage image of the Indian, whose culture had created such advanced ideas as early as 3000 years ago.[59]

The fourth lecture focused on Max Müller's assertion that the Indian culture evolved in isolation, with no other culture touching or influencing it. The fifth lecture discussed the Hindu pantheon, and the sixth described extensively the theory of the Solar Myth, explaining how the names of Hindu deities testified to their origins as forces of nature. He exemplified the phonetic resemblance of various Aryan gods in remote cultures, as was the case with Vata and the Nordic god Wotan, Bhaga and the Slavonic god Bogu, or Pavana and the Greek god Pan.[60] The seventh lecture examined the philosophy of the Vedânta and the Upanishads, which Max Müller defined as the concentration of sublime wisdom and the climax of the process of coalescence of the diverse deities into a unitary one – the Atman, the self. He held, as did Schopenhauer, that the corpus of Hindu wisdom writings could enrich the student of philosophy no less than the works of Spinoza or Plato, and contribute to the general education of all Westerners:

59. Max Müller, *India: What Can It Teach Us?*, pp. 98–100, 105–11, 116–18, 121–22, 125, 130, 132–33.
60. Max Müller, *India: What Can It Teach Us?*, pp. 198, 201, 212–13.

Friedrich Max Müller

I do not mean to say that everybody who wishes to know how the human race came to be what it is... must learn Sanskrit... But I *do* believe that not to know what a study of Sanskrit... has already done for illuminating the darkest passages in the history of the human mind... is a misfortune... just as I should count it a loss to have passed through life without knowing something, however little, of the geological formation of the earth, or of the sun, and the moon, and the stars – and of the thought, or the will, or the law, that govern their movements.[61]

My Indian Friends

In the second volume of *Auld Lang Syne* Max Müller described some of his Indian acquaintances. The description of their noble qualities was meant to dispel the prejudices against their nation, and show the British reader that there lived in India people of a high standard that would not shame English society. Max Müller also wished for friendly relations between the Indian subjects and their rulers. The basis for establishing trust between the sides, he maintained, required mutual awareness of the cultural kinship between them. He thought that the reason Europeans viewed Hindu philosophy as strange and inferior was due also to the Indians' dark skin, which made them seem alien. To this he offered a magic cure:

> from my own limited experience, I can truly say that there is behind that warm and almost Italian colour of the Aryas of India the same warm heart, the same trust, and the same love as under the white skin of the Europeans.

His aim was to provide a favourable description of the cultivated members of the Indian elite and thereby change the attitude towards them, based on Western criteria of honesty, openness and tolerance. But the book also included a sharp criticism of the English government in India and of the Christian Mission. Max Müller argued that the mission was insensitive to the spiritual needs of the local people, notably among those who had already become Christians.[62]

---

61. Max Müller, *India: What Can It Teach Us?*, pp. 267, 274–75.
62. Max Müller's criticism was directed at the methods of the Mission, and not against its purpose. All in all, it seems that he was indeed right, since the Mission in India has failed to convert large numbers of Hindus. The local and successful reaction against the Missionary attempts was evident first and foremost in the foundation of several Hindu reform movements (known collectively as Neo-Hinduism movements), during the nineteenth century. The first was Raja

He was also critical of the faulty communication between Englishmen and Indians. This problem was aggravated as more students arrived in England from India, having been permitted to join the Indian Civil Service. Max Müller stated that these students received a distorted impression of the British rule, due to the English press, which freely attacked the government. It led them to lose respect for the empire, with a negative effect on their attitude towards the ruling power when they returned to their homeland. It should, however, be noted that Max Müller approved the integration of Indians in the Indian Civil Service and the legal system. He maintained that the method had proved itself as an alternative to other imperial systems, notably the Russian, which believed in the total subjugation of its subjects as the only way to deal with Orientals. He rejected this approach, because he believed that India could teach the West more than Greece or Rome, and therefore her inhabitants ought to be allowed relative liberty.[63]

Celestial India: Max Müller's Aryan Vision

These humanist messages make Max Müller look like a liberal whose only wish was to enhance human civilization, regardless if it originated in the East or in the West. Yet they do not solve the problems, mentioned earlier, about the nature of his aspirations in the Indian connection. The views expressed in his books on India – about the antiquity and superiority of Sanskrit, the honesty of the Indians and the religious tolerance required of the West – were not consistent with the promotion of the conquered country as the ancient homeland of the conquerors, with its implied approval of British imperialism. What then were his motives? Did he seek to promote the Indians for liberal reasons, or did his dream of India's

Rammohan Roy's (1772-1833) Brahmo Samaj (the Brahman society), which was founded in 1828. Other movements followed Roy's society, including Diananda Saraswati's (1824-1883) Arya Samaj (the Arian Society), and Vivekananda's (1863-1902) Ramakrishna Mission. For further discussion of Neo-Hinduism and its prominent leaders, see, Bosch, *Friedrich Max Müller*, pp. 203, 361-62; Rammohun Roy, *The English Works of Raja Rammohun Roy*, ed. Jogendra Chunder Ghose (New Delhi, 1982); *The Essential Writings of Raja Rammohan Ray*, ed. Brice Carlisle Robertson (Delhi, 1999); Kesavachandra Sena, *Keshub Chunder Sen's Lectures in India* (2 vols., London, 1901-1904); P.C. Mozoomdar, *The Life and Teachings of Keshub Chunder Sen* (Calcutta, 1891).

63. Max Müller, *Auld Lang Syne*, II, pp. viii-ix, 8, 25, 60, 63, 86, 93-95, 109-10, 155-58, 178-79.

future have a different character, of far-reaching romantic significance? Was he a man who devoted himself to dry research in order to broaden human knowledge, or a thinker searching for a spiritual goal that would be an alternative to the Western way of life?

The answer to these questions can be found running like a thread through his writings, from his earliest attempts to define comparative religion to his last writings, which summed up his life's work of theory and thought. There is no doubt that he regarded the ancient Indian civilization as the source of Western civilization, including the aspect of Christianity that he saw as significant. As he put it: 'I have tried to show that the doctrine of the Logos, the very life-blood of Christianity, is exclusively Aryan.'[64]

Reconstructing the history of the Aryan faith and the influence of India on the West, using the method of comparative theology, led Max Müller to call for a new path in which the religions of the East and the West would advance towards a better future. He did not outline an exact political or geographic nature of that path, but we can examine his utterances to find out what he aspired. He evidently thought that the human condition would be improved by a synthesis of the religions and the ancient ways of thinking, by searching for similarities rather than rejecting the differences: 'It is a perfect misery not to be happy in this world, and much of the misery which there is, is the work of men, or could be removed by men, if they would but work together for each other's good.'[65]

Max Müller's Aryan vision, which began to take shape with the publication of 'Comparative Mythology' in 1856, and continued to engage his mind to his dying day, defined Sanskrit as the eldest sister in the Aryan family of languages, and the Vedic literature as the oldest and purest historical expression of Aryan thought. His belief in the unique way that Indian civilization developed, untainted by any outside influence, was another major building-block of this vision. The combination of the two – the concept of the Vedic literature as the most ancient Aryan literature, with the belief in its independent development – led to the conclusion that the knowledge preserved in India was not only the oldest but the purest extant knowledge. A person who believed that there were in ancient times cultural systems which in certain aspects were not

64. Max Müller, *Theosophy or Psychological Religion*, p. x.
65. *Life and Religion: An Aftermath from the Writings of the Right Honourable Professor Friedrich Max Müller*, ed. Georgina Max Müller (New York, 1905), p. 237.

inferior to modern civilization, could hardly fail to regard India as the ideal place in which to search for the pure, authentic spirit. This might help heal the ailments of Western Aryan culture, which had been driven by environmental circumstances in a materialistic direction and hence discarded the spiritual option that was cultivated in the Orient. Thus a synthesis of Western activism with the ancient Indian spirituality could produce the best in both Aryan worlds, enabling the Aryan race and humanity in general to rise towards a better future.

Such was the spiritual aspect of Max Müller's Aryan vision. On the face of it, it looks like a humanist philosophical idea, seeing India as a higher entity worthy of instructing the West. This was why his ideas were embraced so enthusiastically in India itself, and why he was so highly regarded by its people. Yet, in the historical and political context of his time, a question arises about the role his vision assigned to the masses of Indian subjects. Were they included in the picture of the ideal future world that he was promoting? The question is crucial in view of the British policy in India and the way its administration perceived the role of the masses in the general imperial framework. For example, the resources invested in the Christian mission, testified to the desire to create some kind of cultural and religious unity to the empire's inhabitants. Such a move, even though it left the Indians in an inferior position compared to white Englishmen, would still have granted them formally a higher status than to idolatrous aliens. Did Max Müller favour such a development? Did he truly believe that the Hindu masses were the kinsmen of Englishmen and Germans?

The answer may be found in Max Müller's description of ancient India's social stratification. In his opinion, this stratification, being an ideal example of a society based on calm, tranquillity and peace, might serve as a model for modern Western society. He painted an idyllic picture of ancient Indian society, comprising two principal classes – the masses and a separate aristocratic elite. The elite was made up of the Aryan conquerors who had seized power over the original inhabitants of India in ancient times. This form of government, which Max Müller regarded as the origin of the existing caste system, is described in the Vedic literature, and in his view could be most instructive if only we discarded our prejudices.[66]

66. Max Müller, India: *What Can It Teach Us?*, p. 117.

Max Müller saw the Aryan Indian, the aristocratic conqueror, as a person who spent his entire life in an inward search for the eternal truths of life – in contrast to his Western brother, who was obsessed with the pursuit of external glory and wealth. He maintained that what characterized the ruling class in ancient India was not eagerness for honour and titles of nobility, but the search for enlightenment. This was the aspiration of the rulers, including the women, the priests and the nobles, who all perceived earthly existence as unreal. They valued those whom they saw as 'enlightened' higher than kings and princes.[67] This image clearly enchanted Max Müller, who like many academics must have detached from 'real' life, and saw the purpose of life as study and the quest after truth.

The search for the self, for enlightenment and truth, which according to Max Müller characterized the Aryan elite of ancient India, was the ideal he sought. He believed that this ideal, attained in India by the ancient Oriental Aryans, was still maintained by the Brahmin caste, which was responsible for preserving the ancient knowledge and transmitting it through the ages.[68]

The Brahmin caste was still India's elite in the nineteenth century, and Max Müller was referring to it when discussing Aryan elements in contemporary India. This fact negates the possibility that he was a liberal concerned with the welfare of the Indian subjects as a whole. His enthusiastic description of the narrow Aryan aristocracy which had ruled over the Indian masses in ancient times underlines this negation. This observation ought to resolve the seeming inconsistency between his encouragement of the English rulers' return to their ancient homeland, India, and his promotion of a humanist and tolerant approach to Indian culture. His tolerance was meant primarily for the elites, both the English and the Brahmin. His idea of a synthesis between East and West was a synthesis between elites, certainly not between the people of India and all Englishmen. His Romantic approach was clearly elitist, and his vision of the future of humanity required a spiritual-aristocratic leadership – resembling perhaps the Platonic ideal, but certainly not the ideals of national liberation movements.

We may conclude that Max Müller's vision entailed an imaginary India which existed only in dreams about the glorious past and

---

67. Max Müller, *Theosophy or Psychological Religion*, p. 71.
68. Max Müller, *India: What Can It Teach Us?*, p. 232; *Life and Religion*, p. 100.

'historical' echoes arising from her ancient literature. There was no real connection between that imaginary country – which I suggest to refer to as 'Celestial India' – and the actual geopolitical entity. It was this imaginary concept which animated Max Müller when he urged modern man to change his attitude towards that wretched India which was suddenly shown in glorious raiment as the homeland of the Aryan race. Similarly, the proposed alternative for the future of humanity –the synthesis between East and West, with India as the purest marvel and the land in which true knowledge is preserved in its chastest form – arose in his mind in an abstract fashion, almost without any connection to the physical reality of India, which in any event he only knew from secondary sources, certainly not from first-hand experience.

Given his high standing, both in England and in India, it can be assumed that his ideas were widely received. It is possible that the young trainees of the Indian Civil Service, who heard his Cambridge lectures, set out to the Orient with a somewhat different mental luggage than their predecessors. In this way, Max Müller contributed to a more positive attitude on their part towards the new Indian national awakening. Likewise, British public opinion, which had been accustomed to looking down on India, was slightly changed thanks to his efforts, and began to see a certain glitter in 'the jewel in the crown'. Celestial India – the image of India as the mother-lode of the Aryan and of human civilization – began to take shape in the collective minds of Indians, English people and Europeans in general, who regarded the earthly India as a place in which the marvel might be re-discovered, here and now, even in the modern age.

The subject of India remained the area in which Max Müller's influence was more significant than any other in which he engaged. His responsibility for the new Indian image overshadowed all his academic achievements, his splendid translations and highly-developed theses in comparative religion and philology. Most of his great achievements in these fields, except possibly *The Sacred Books of the East*, fell into oblivion soon after his death. In contrast, his efforts to change the Western perception of India made a major contribution towards the view of India as a matchless cultural and spiritual source, a wondrous land holding secrets waiting to be discovered – Celestial India.

Chapter 3

The Theosophical Society – The Quest for the Spiritual Source

The Founders

In July 1874, several American spiritualist newspapers reported the appearance of supernatural phenomena at the farm of the Eddy family in Chittenden, Vermont. The mother Mary Eddy and her children William, Mary and Horatio, claimed to have supernatural gifts, which enabled them to summon to their house a large number of ghosts. The ghosts materialized, moved objects and conversed with the family and guests.[1]

Henry Steel Olcott, a New York attorney, a retired colonel, who was interested in spiritualism, was so intrigued by the stories about the Eddy family that he decided to go to Vermont and see things for himself. He went to Chittenden in August, visited the farm and was convinced by what he saw. On his return to New York he published his impressions in a series of reports in *The New York Sun*. These led to an offer from another New York newspaper, *The Daily Graphic*, to return to the Eddy farm accompanied by an illustrator. He went there on 17 September 1874 and spent 12 weeks at the farm, during which, he reported, he witnessed daily contacts with the world beyond. While he was there, the paper ran his reports with illustrations showing the ghosts that he and the illustrator witnessed.

One day a new visitor showed up at the farm, a Ukrainian spiritualist named Helena Petrovna Blavatsky. Olcott was struck by her piercing gaze, and noticed that she was a complusive eater and smoker. In his journal he described their first encounter: 'I said: "Permettez moi, Madame," and gave her a light for her cigarette;

---

1. Peter Washington, *Madame Blavatsky's Baboon: A History of the Mystics, Mediums, and Misfits Who Brought Spiritualism to America* (New York, 1995), pp. 27-28: first published 1993.

our acquaintance began in smoke, but it stirred up a great and permanent fire.'²

Though dramatic, the description was accurate enough. The encounter engendered the creation of an esoteric movement called The Theosophical Society, which was destined to have a distinctive influence over Western spiritualism, as well as on modern Indian nationalism.

Helena Petrovna Blavatsky, the founder of the Theosophical Society, was born in 1831. Her father, the Baron von Hahn, was an army officer of German-Russian origin, a member of the minor aristocracy which constituted the upper echelons of the Czar's officer class. Blavatsky's mother came from the higher aristocracy, the Dolgorouky family. She died in 1842, when Blavatsky was 11 years old. The young Helena passed her adolescence between the house of her maternal grandparents and the army bases in various parts of the Czarist empire where her father was stationed. While staying with her father, who was stationed mainly in the Caucasus, she met Tatars, Georgians and Armenians. These experiences were given a spiritualist expression at the Eddy farm. As Olcott described it, prior to Blavatsky's arrival the spirits which manifested themselves at the farm were Europeans, Americans or Native Americans, identities familiar to the visitors. From the moment of her arrival, spirits from Russia and the Caucasus began to appear.³ When Olcott and Blavatsky returned to New York, she wrote a series of letters to *The Daily Graphic*, describing her experiences in Vermont and fiercely rebutting accusations which had appeared in the paper charging the Eddy family with trickery. She maintained that she had personally seen there ghosts of people she had known as a child manifest themselves: 'The first was a Georgian boy... Second – a little old man appears... It is "Hassan Aga", an old man whom I and my family have known for twenty years in Tiflis.'⁴

Blavatsky's widowed father, the Baron von Hahn, was presumably anxious to find her a suitable match. In 1848 he married her to the 40-year-old Nikifor Blavatsky, the deputy military governor

---

2. Henry Steel Olcott, *Old Diary Leaves, America, 1874–1878* (Adyar, 1941), pp. 1–3, 449, 452–53, first published 1895 (Hereafter Old Diary Leaves, I).

3. Olcott, *Old Diary Leaves*, I, p. 8.

4. H.P. Blavatsky, 'The Eddy Manifestations', *The Daily Graphic* (New York, 27 October 1784).

of Erevan in Armenia.[5] The age gap between them might explain why after only three months Blavatsky ran away from her husband to Constantinople, and began a new phase in her life. Thereafter, according to her account, she wandered for years before arriving in America. Her travel tales, covering several continents, cannot all be verified. She claimed that she was guided by her longing for the ancient esoteric lore which had been preserved in countries with a rich magical tradition. Egypt, which existing esoteric tradition saw as the oldest source of arcane knowledge, was her first major stop. But her most significant sojourn was in Tibet, where she claimed to have spent more than seven years, during which time she was instructed by spiritual teachers, whom she called Mahatmas or Masters. They taught her their esoteric secrets and brought her to the highest level of initiation accessible to a mortal being.

Information from other sources conflicts with some of Blavatsky's stories. For example, Olcott stated that after her death, he was told that prior to coming to America, Blavatsky had been a professional pianist and travelled about Russia and Italy under the name Madame Laura. Another testimony suggests that during the period when she was supposedly in Tibet, she was seen in other places.[6] These contradictions are not important in themselves, though they undermine Blavatsky's credibility, but as we shall see, her own writings contained material much more dubious than the questionable veracity of her various travel stories.

According to Blavatsky, the Masters who mentored her in Tibet, and kept in touch with her throughout her life, were human beings who had succeeded in evolving to a higher level of existence than that of ordinary mortals. They were members of a body called The Great Brotherhood, consisting of a succession of spiritual teachers who had influenced human history. The members of The Great Brotherhood were always engaged in a struggle against the forces of darkness (whom Blavatsky called the Brothers of the Shadow),

---

5. Blavatsky's most detailed biography observes her marriage differently, claiming that young Helena proposed to Nikifor Blavatsky, after having said that she would marry the most repulsive man she has ever met, Sylvia Cranston, *HPB, The Extraordinary Life and Influence of Helena Blavatsky, Founder of the Modern Theosophical Movement* (New York, 1993), p. 36.

6. Olcott, *Old Diary Leaves*, I, p. 458; *World Religions, Eastern Traditions*, ed. Willard G. Oxtoby (Oxford, 1996), p. 79.

who sought to hold back humanity's development.[7] From time to time these Masters approached evolved individuals who aspired to be their apprentices during their spiritual development. Such a disciple was called a 'chela'. As the chela advanced, he became an 'adept', able to apply his acquired magical knowledge to himself and to his surroundings. Next came the highest stage of development, when the adept became an 'initiate'. Such a person was freed from the constraints of time and his consciousness contained the past, present and future.

Blavatsky especially venerated two particular members of the Great Brotherhood – Koot-Hoomi (who in one of his renowned incarnations was named Pythagoras)[8] and Morya. These two Masters cultivated and initiated Blavatsky in Tibet, instructed her to create the Theosophical Society and remained in contact with her successors after her death. Communication with them took two forms. The first was by means of visions, which was rare and accessible only to sufficiently advanced Theosophists. The second and more common method entailed more earthly means – the messages from the Masters arrived in the form of written and sealed messages, which miraculously dropped from the ceiling or appeared out of nowhere. Many members of the Society were granted such marvellous missives. Actual visions were granted to very few other than Blavatsky.[9]

According to Blavatsky, it was the duty of the members of the Great Brotherhood to watch over the human race and guide its spiritual development. She claimed that they intensified their efforts in the final quarter of every century, when one of them

---

7. *The Mahatma Letters to A.P. Sinnett*, from the Mahatmas M. & K.H., transcribed and compiled by A.T. Barker, Letter no. 9 (K.H. to Sinnett), 8 July 1881 (Adyar, 1972), p. 40, first published 1923.

8. C.W. Leadbeater, *How Theosophy Came to Me* (Adyar, 1986), p. 3, first published 1930.

9. Olcott tells of a rare encounter with Koot-Hoomi in Lahore in 1883. Annie Besant experienced her first encounter with Master Morya in 1889. Leadbeater, who considered himself as Blavatsky's heir, had frequent conversations with the Masters. Krishnamurti wrote his first book under direct guidance from Koot-Hoomi: *Lucifer* (June, 1891); Leadbeater, *How Theosophy Came to Me*, pp. 126-33; Alcyone, *At the Feet of the Master* (Adyar, 1974), first published 1910; Henry Steel Olcott, *Old Diary Leaves, Third Series, 1883-87* (Adyar, 1929), pp. 36-37, first published 1904 (Hereafter *Old Diary Leaves*, III).

would appear to communicate esoteric lore to humanity.[10] This idea was developed further by Blavatsky's successor, Annie Besant, who called this Master a World Teacher, identified him with the Buddhist term Bodhisattva, and maintained that Krishnamurti was the World Teacher of our time.[11]

Blavatsky located her Masters in the mountains of Tibet, probably chosen for two reasons. One, that mountains are generally thought of as sacred, or as the home of the gods; two, Tibet's geographic and cultural isolation at that time made it a suitable venue for stories of the mystical sort.[12] For these reasons, Tibet and her version of Buddhism have been favourites of the Western imagination for the past 200 years. Although during the nineteenth century a good number of Western adventurers, military men and mystics attempted to reach Tibet, few actually succeeded. Regular contact with Tibet began only in 1904, when a British military mission arrived in Lhasa. It was led by the explorer and mystic Francis Younghusband (1863–1942), who was born in India, and who forced the current Dalai Lama to approve a trade agreement with Britain.[13]

The Tibetan mystique grew in the West to an exceptional degree as the country became more accessible. Today this mystique seems to be at its height, with the widespread Western support for the Tibetan national struggle and the popularity of Tibetan Buddhism, as shown in a number of films and the spread of religious material. It seems that Blavatsky contributed to the glorification of Tibet's image in the world, by locating the Masters on the roof of the world and linking her spiritual movement to the Himalaya. She claimed that it was the Masters who instructed her to go to America and visit Chittenden in order to meet Olcott, 'whose Karma linked him to her as the co-agent to set this social wave in motion.'[14]

10. H.P. Blavatsky, *The Key to Theosophy* (London, 1938), pp. 152-53: first published 1889.

11. Annie Besant, 'Saviours of the World, or World-Teachers', in *Superhuman Men in History and in Religion* (London, 1913), pp. 37-55.

12. Tibet and its surroundings were considered mysterious and mystical in that time, thus giving birth to myths, such as the myth of Shangri-La. The romantic view of Tibet was evidenced in popular literature as well. For example, Arthur Conan Doyle sent Sherlock Holmes to hide in Tibet, after his final struggle with Moriarty, Peter Bishop, *Dreams of Power, Tibetan Buddhism and the Western Imagination* (London, 1993), p. 13.

13. Peter Fleming, *Bayonets to Lhasa: The First Full Account of the British Invasion of Tibet in 1904* (London, 1962), pp. 15-31, 276-84.

14. Olcott, *Old Diary Leaves*, I, pp. 20-22.

Olcott was born in New Jersey in 1832. As a young man he engaged in agriculture and in 1859 became editor of the agricultural section of the daily *The New York Tribune*. When the civil war broke out he joined the army of the North, reached the rank of Colonel, and served first as a signals officer then as military interrogator. He was successful in his main task of questioning war profiteers, and after the war was one of the three-member commission appointed by the US Congress to investigate Lincoln's assassination.[15] After his discharge he studied Law, specialized in naval law and insurance, and opened his own practice in New York in the late 1860s. Having married in 1860, he fathered four children, two of whom died in their infancy. He was divorced in 1874, in parallel with his awakened interest in spiritualism. Presumably his encounter with Blavatsky that year, close to his divorce and not long after he began to take an interest in the occult, seemed like the fulfillment of a wish, as frequently happens to people who seek answers in religious mysticism. In Blavatsky he found a teacher and a friend who could provide answers to his questions. She, for her part, found an eager adherent who supported her morally and financially.[16]

In October 1874 Blavatsky returned from Vermont to New York, and Olcott joined her in November. Her apartment at 46 Irving Place soon became a lively meeting-place that attracted various more-or-less dubious spiritual types. The two friends, imbued with a sense of mission, attempted to launch a spiritual society, named 'The Miracle Club', in May 1875. When this failed, they formed the Theosophical Society. In his journal Olcott described the occasion of its foundation. It is especially noteworthy because of the powerful contrast between the somewhat pathetic scene in Blavatsky's apartment that evening and the great success of the Society further on.

On 7 September 1875, 17 guests came to Blavatsky's apartment to hear a lecture by a certain Mr. Felt about the magicians of ancient Egypt. Olcott was deeply stirred by the lecture. 'It would be a good thing to form a society to pursue and promote such occult research,' he wrote on a note, which he passed to Blavatsky, asking for her

---

15. Stephen Prothero, *The White Buddhist: The Asian Odyssey of Henry Steel Olcott* (Bloomington, 1996), pp. 34–35.

16. Their relations lacked any sexual tension. They referred to each other as 'chums'. Olcott nicknamed her 'Jack', and this was the name she used in their future correspondence, Olcott, *Old Diary Leaves*, I, pp. 6, 10.

opinion. She read it and nodded. Then Olcott took the floor and proposed to all those present to join the new Society. According to him, the response was enthusiastic, and was followed by a vote. Olcott was voted President of the Society, and two other positions were created at the start – Blavatsky was elected Corresponding Secretary and William Quan Judge (1851–1896), a junior advocate in Olcott's law office, was chosen to be the Secretary of the Society.

The name of the new Society was decided at the third meeting held by the small membership on 18 September. Various suggestions were declined, among them the Hermetic, the Rosicrucian and the Egyptological Society. According to Olcott, the sought-for name came up when one of the people present leafed through a dictionary and came across the word 'Theosophy', which struck everyone as most appropriate. On this occasion they also drew up the Society's rules, modelled on the rules of the American Geographical and Statistical Society and the American Institute. They strenuously sought features that would distinguish them from other secret societies. At their meeting on 12 January 1876, they resolved to adopt some secret signs, among them a seal designed for Blavatsky and the symbol of the Society.[17] Such were the early days of the Theosophical Society, which was created almost casually and in a manner that bore no hint of its brilliant future. That preliminary phase in New York did not arouse great hopes of expansion, but nevertheless, valuable experience was gained in recruiting new members and conducting public relations. Blavatsky and Olcott were determined to achieve fame, and did all they could to achieve it. Their efforts bore fruit, and before long they won the fame they desired.

The Beginning of Public Activity, 1876–1879

Once the Theosophical Society was founded, Blavatsky and Olcott rented two suites of rooms at 433 West 34th Street, one above the other. Blavatsky lived on the first floor and Olcott on the second. It is not easy to reconstruct the atmosphere that characterized their close relations. Olcott's description claimed to be 'The true story of the Theosophical Society' (as the title of his journal proclaims), as opposed to other people's descriptions of those early days. Olcott's perception of his role in the Society's annals differs from the

---

17. Olcott, *Old Diary Leaves*, I, pp. 114–18, 132–33, 146.

impression given by other Theosophical sources, who, he claimed, were seeking 'to deify Mme Blavatsky and so give her commonest literary productions a quasi-inspirational character.'[18]

Blavatsky is usually seen as the central figure in the history of the Theosophical Society, while Olcott, its President, is regarded at best as an efficient bureaucrat, and in less favourable accounts as little more than a loyal aide de camp. This must not be accepted uncritically. As we shall see, his share in the Society's success was no smaller than hers. While in the West, Blavatsky's charismatic personality and the spiritual powers attributed to her were the Society's chief appeal, it was thanks to Olcott that the Society became established in India and formed the political ties that assured its future. In the final analysis, they complemented each other, even in the geographical sense. Blavatsky was the focus of attraction for the followers of Theosophy in America and Europe, while Olcott was mainly responsible for the Society's growth in India and the surrounding region.

Two main factors gave the Theosophical Society its early publicity. The first was Blavatsky's and Olcott's skill in utilizing the press for self-promotion. Blavatsky wrote for New York newspapers the whole time she was in the United States, winning a reputation for herself and the Society. Olcott also contributed to the press coverage of the Society's activities. The most intriguing example of his use of the press was a cremation ceremony, the first in the United States, that he conducted in 1876. The ceremony was extensively covered in the press and spread the name of the new Society.[19]

The other and more significant factor contributing to the success of the Society was Blavatsky's impressive writing ability. Though self-taught, she was evidently familiar with the academic publications of Comparative Religion studies. This familiarity, as well as her long interest in the occult, led her to conclude that Theosophy, like any new religion or faith, needed a broad theological basis to allow for future exegesis and give it a long-term vitality.

---

18. Those 'other sources' referred to Judge and his supporters, who, as we shall see, later split from the Society and founded the American Theosophical Society, existing to this day, Olcott, *Old Diary Leaves*, I, pp. Vii, 141; Olcott, *Old Diary Leaves*, III, p. 62.

19. Olcott, *Old Diary Leaves*, I, pp. 148–67; Stephen Prothero, *Purified by Fire: A History of Cremation in America* (Berkeley, 2001), pp. 24–34; H.P. Blavatsky, 'My Books', *Lucifer* (May, 1891).

Madame Blavatsky, Founder of the Theosophical Society (reproduced by Yanai Zeltzer).

From this insight was born *Isis Unveiled*, published in 1877 – a massive, 1,200-page work in two volumes, which took Blavatsky six months' labour to produce. She claimed that large parts of it were supernaturally dictated to her by the Masters, making her the transmitter of the revealed knowledge rather than its author. Her primary motive in writing the book was to answer two questions which had preoccupied her when she was travelling in the East – who and what was the Deity and where He dwelt, and was there any evidence of the immortality of the human soul?[20] The book surveyed the histories of various religions in antiquity, and attempted to trace the roots of the magical arts in biblical, Vedic and Hermetic literature. The survey, which concluded that India was the cradle of arcane lore, purported to use the methodology of comparative research. The various subjects were approached through questions concerning the mysterious phenomena in our world, though without offering substantial answers. Blavatsky contented herself with describing the phenomena, and left their solutions to her readers' imagination.[21]

The Oriental insights in *Isis Unveiled* did not go unchallenged. *The New York World*, for example, argued that Blavatsky showed ignorance about Indian history. Her furious response betrays her extremely high self-esteem: '... a pretty wide reading of European "authorities" has given me a very poor opinion on them, since no two agree. Sir William Jones himself, whose shoe-strings few Orientalists are worthy to unite, made very grave mistakes, which

---

20. H.P. Blavatsky, *Isis Unveiled: A Master-Key to the Mysteries of Ancient and Modern Science and Theology*, I (Pasadena, 1998), p. vi, first published 1877.

21. *Isis Unveiled* is a difficult to read, confusingly written, and loosely narrated book, which makes one wonder about the actual number of people who have read it from its first page to the last. Nonetheless, it is certainly impressive, regarding Blavatsky's exceptional imagination, and her acquaintance with her contemporary scientific publications, and particularly those of Friedrich Max Müller's. Its importance, academically speaking, lies with Blavatsky's change of orientation, regarding the origins of the occult. Until then, occultists considered ancient Egypt as the source of esoteric wisdom. As shown in the previous chapters, the advancement of philology and religion studies during the nineteenth century helped to widely spread the Aryan myth and the belief that India treasured the oldest spiritual wisdom. Thus, the academic research, headed by Müller, unintentionally influenced the esoteric arena. Blavatsky, who admired Müller, adopted his views with a little twist, and replaced Egypt with India as the source of occultism. This sharp curve was about to influence the Western image of India, and make it an ongoing focal point for spiritualists worldwide.

are now been corrected by Max Müller... I did not invite the visits of reporters... If I reply to your criticism... it is because I... cannot sit quiet and be made to appear alike devoid of experience, knowledge and truthfulness.'[22]

Such negative criticisms in the press did not overly impress Olcott, who thought of *Isis Unveiled* as a reflection of his associate's personality. In his view, 'Her personality, not the Theosophical Society, was the magnet of attraction, and she reveled in the excitement of the entourage. So miscellaneous was it, such a mixture of music, metaphysics, Orientalism, and local gossip, that I cannot give a better idea of it than by saying it was like the contents of *Isis Unveiled*, than which no literary product is a greater conglomerate.' Indeed, he maintained that Blavatsky's writing ability equalled that of philosophers like Aristotle or Leibniz.[23]

Strangely, the operation of the Theosophical Society declined after the publication of *Isis Unveiled*. Few people joined during this period, the most prominent of them being Thomas Alva Edison (1847-1931), who sent Olcott his membership forms on 4 April 1878. He added a note, saying, 'I herewith return signed, the forms of the Theosophical Society... Please say to Madame Blavatsky that I have received her very curious work and I thank her for the same. I SHALL READ BETWEEN THE LINES.' (Edison's emphasis.)

Blavatsky replied to Edison on 30 April, informing him that she had finished translating into Russian his article on the phonograph, and would try to use her contacts with the newspapers in Odessa and St Petersburg to get it published.[24] In 1885, Edison denied any connection with the Theosophists, following the publication of a report by the Society for Psychical Research (SPR), which denounced Blavatsky as a fraud. Yet his own records, as well as the attitude of Blavatsky and Olcott towards him, confirm that he was, if only for a while, a member of the Theosophical Society. Blavatsky's regard for him is evident in her references to him in a number of articles she published in India and England.[25]

---

22. H.P. Blavatsky, 'A Protest', *The New York World* (6 April 1877).

23. Olcott, *Old Diary Leaves*, I, pp. 277, 341-42.

24. *Thomas A. Edison Papers*, Document 8912 (4 April 1878); and Document 7802 (30 April 1878), republished online by Rutgers University, see, http://edison.rutgers.edu/

25. H.P. Blavatsky, 'Magic', *The Deccan Star* (30 March 1879); 'Nizida', 'Edison', *Lucifer* (October, 1888).

Blavatsky and Olcott were dissatisfied with the Society's slow progress. Most esoteric movements devoted to the search for gnosis are selective and elitist, but not the Theosophists, who definitely hankered for the widest publicity. The slowness of the process seemed to the movement's leaders to reflect the materialistic degeneration of American society. Blavatsky maintained that a vast struggle between spirituality and materialism was taking place in her lifetime, and suggested that the success of the materialistic approach resulted from the French Revolution and the decline of the Church.[26] American materialism was impeding the reception of the Theosophist message, and led Blavatsky and Olcott to the conclusion that they ought to propagate the tenets of their new faith in a different geographical setting, one less tainted with materialism. And since the ideological transition Blavatsky underwent at that time led her to conclude that India was the cradle of esoteric wisdom, she naturally looked to India as the lodestone of her dreams and plans. However, in the 1870s a journey to India entailed considerable financial and physical efforts. Moreover, it was an unknown land for Blavatsky and Olcott, neither of whom was young.

Their main hope in 1877-78, therefore, lay in the contacts they established with a number of Indian correspondents who showed interest in the new esoteric movement. The connection began in 1877, when Olcott wrote to Moolji Thackersey, whom he had met in 1870 on board ship returning to America from England. Olcott informed his Indian acquaintance about the Theosophical Society and its dream of blending the wisdom of the East with that of the West, and invited him to join. According to Olcott, Thackersey responded enthusiastically, and put him in touch with Hurrychund Chintamon, president of the Bombay Arya Samaj.[27] The Arya Samaj ('Aryan Association') had been founded two years earlier by Swami Dayananda Saraswati, a purist who agitated for Indian national revival, in the belief that this would be made possible by a religious reformation and a return to the ancient Vedic religion. Chintamon responded to Olcott's letters, was granted an honorary membership

---

Neil Baldwin, *Edison, Inventing the Century* (Chicago, 2001), pp. 92-93, 96, first published 1995; Paul Israel, *Edison, a Life of Invention* (New York, 1998), pp. 111-12.

26. Blavatsky, *Isis Unveiled*, I, pp. xliv-xlv; see also Vol. 2, pp. 1-2.

27. Olcott, *Old Diary Leaves*, I, p. 395.

of the Theosophical Society, and put Olcott in touch with Dayananda Saraswati.[28]

One of the interesting aspects of the spiritual-national awakening in India at this time was the local drive to forge links with the West, especially with the United States. This initiative was, to begin with, a protest against the coercive methods of the Christian missions in India, which were backed by the imperial British rulers. As we have seen, the rulers' attitude towards the Hindu religion from the 1830s on became less tolerant, from a conviction that it was necessary to import English culture into the Subcontinent and as much as possible suppress the study of the local culture. Indian counter-action soon spread beyond England to reach the United States, where Hindu reformers sought to win material and political support for their cause, as well as to propagate their faith. The Neo-Hinduism movement, which arose in 1828 with Rammohan Roy's Brahmo Samaj, reached its apogee towards the end of the century, with the movement of Dayananda Saraswati and the spiritual reform of Ramakrishna, its most prominent exponent. In 1896, Ramakrishna's disciple Vivekananda visited Oxford, where he met Max Müller.[29] Prior to this meeting, he had already become an active Hindu missionary in America, where he established centres for the study of Hinduism, which are still thriving.[30]

Dayananda Saraswati had similar ambitions 20 years before Vivekananda. This accounts for his association, beginning in 1877, with Olcott and Blavatsky. He must have hoped that the connection with the Western Theosophists would provide him with material and propagandistic advantages. For their part, Blavatsky and Olcott viewed the connection in terms of their own goals – acquaintance with local Hindus, in preparation for their journey to India and a rare opportunity to expand the membership of their movement, which at this time was declining in America.

The correpondence of Olcott and Blavatsky with Chintamon and Dayananda Saraswati led to the proposal to merge the Theosophical

28. Chintamon became Blavatsky and Olcott's close companion on their arrival in India. However, their friendship ended after Dayananda Saraswati publicly renounced Theosophy. Later, Blavatsky described Chintamon as a liar, see, *The Mahatma Letters*, Letter No. 54 (K.H. to Sinnett), October 1882, pp. 303–304, 308.

29. *The Life and Letters of the Right Honourable Friedrich Max Müller*, ed. Georgina Max Müller, II (New York, 1902), p. 369.

30. Timothy Miller, *The Quest for Utopia, Vol. 1: 1900–1960* (Syracuse, 1998), pp. 91–94.

Society with the Arya Samaj. Olcott agreed to become, as he put it, number two under Dayananda Saraswati. Blavatsky helped this move by telling Olcott that Dayananda Saraswati was actually a member of the Great Brotherhood, who inhabited the body of the Indian personage. This helped Olcott to accept the Hindu reformer as a spiritual mentor. A motion to merge the two movements was put to the vote by the membership of the Theosophical Society. In May 1878 they voted to approve it, and resolved to change the name of the Society – henceforth to be called The Theosophical Society of the Arya Samaj. Shortly after this Olcott received an English translation of the Hindu movement's principles. These caught him by surprise, as he realized that there was a certain distance between the Theosophical faith and Dayananda Saraswati's ideas. Consequently, in September 1878 the Theosophical Society reverted to its original name.[31]

The ups and downs in the relations with the leadership of the Arya Samaj led to a refinement of the Theosophist programme, and the formulation of the Society's three main principles, which remained the basis for the Theosophical operations in the following years:
1. The study of occult science.
2. The formation of a nucleus of universal brotherhood.
3. The revival of Oriental literature and philosophy.

The second half of 1878 looked more promising than the first. In addition to strengthening the contacts with India, Blavatsky and Olcott were heartened by the news from London, where on 27 June the British Theosophical Society was formally founded, the first branch of the Society outside the United States. The birth of the British Society was due to Olcott's initiative in sending to London the treasurer of the New York Society, John Storer Cobb. Cobb gathered a number of British individuals who were excited by the Theosophical ideas. They elected as their first president Charles Carlton Massey (1838–1905).[32] Later, in 1884, under the presidency

---

31. Olcott, *Old Diary Leaves*, I, pp. 396-97, 401.
32. Massey, a wealthy barrister, whose father was MP for more than 20 years, was well acquainted with Olcott and Blavatsky, whom he met several years earlier, first with the Eddies at Chittenden, and then in New York, where he became one of the Society's founders: Olcott, *Old Diary Leaves*, I, pp. 121, 473-75. Janet Oppenhiem, *The Other World, Spiritualism and Psychical Research in England, 1850-1914* (New York, 1985), p. 31.

of Anna Kingsford (1846–1888), the British branch changed its title to The London Lodge of the Theosophical Society.

Late in 1878 Blavatsky and Olcott decided to go to India and join up with their new friends. A few months earlier, on 8 July 1878, Blavatsky had become a citizen of the United States. The two used the autumn months to prepare for the trip to India, and perhaps Blavatsky's newly-sworn status helped Olcott to activate his old associations and win an official appointment for the journey. On 13 December he received two important documents – the first was a personal letter of introduction signed by the President of the United States, Rutherford Birchard Hayes (1822–1893), and the other a State Department appointment of Olcott as an official emissary of the US Administration. Armed with these documents, the pair constituted an official American delegation empowered to look into the possibility of expanding the commercial interests of the United States in Asia.[33] On 15 December Olcott and Blavatsky threw a farewell party, to which Olcott invited Edison by telegram, though the latter finally did not come.[34] Nevertheless, Olcott used a phonograph of the first series produced by Edison to record greetings from the New York Society to their friends in India.

Two days later, at midnight, the pair left home and boarded the British steamer the *Canada*. Olcott described in his journal how moved he was, when unlike the rest of the passengers who stood on deck to watch the American shore receding from sight, he remained in his cabin and located Bombay on a map of India.[35] Thus ended the first chapter in the history of the Theosophical Society, when its founders sailed from its birthplace towards the unknown.

Passage to India

On 24 January 1879, the London paper *The Spiritualist* published a letter by Charles Massey, the president of the British Theosophical Society, informing the readers that the founders of the Theosophical Society had stayed in England for two weeks en route from New York to Bombay. He noted that Blavatsky and Olcott had left guidelines for their followers in England and made clear the nature of the association between the Theosophical Society and the Arya

---

33. Olcott, *Old Diary Leaves*, I, pp. 473–79.
34. *Thomas A. Edison Papers*, Document 7802 (14 December 1878).
35. Olcott, *Old Diary Leaves*, I, pp. 183, 483.

Colonel Henry Steel Olcott, President of the Theosophical Society, 1875–1907. Olcott's bust stands opposite the library at the TS Headquarters in Adyar. Photograph by Isaac Lubelsky.

Samaj. They explained that the primary aim of the ties between the two societies was to eliminate the racial and religious divisions between East and West by obliterating prejudices and discarding theological and materialistic restrictions. Massey explained Olcott and Blavatsky's view of the hierarchy created by joining the two societies – the Indian centre of the Arya Samaj was defined as senior to the Western Theosophical centres; moreover, they regarded the Indian movement as responsible, in the missionary sense, for developing Western centres of the Theosophical Society. This hierarchy was based on the assumption that all the religions of the world were essentially distortions of the original true religion, whose earliest and purest expression was the Vedic religion.[36]

Though the love-affair between the Theosophists and Dayananda Saraswati came to an end in 1882, the leaders of the Theosophical Society continued for the rest of their lives to argue the superiority of the Indian religions over the Western ones. This message, which in the early days was associated with the call for India's spiritual liberation, and later with concrete efforts to achieve her national liberation, decisively helped to change the image of India in the West, and prepare the ground for India's national independence. As we shall see, Blavatsky and Olcott's early work laid the foundations of the great transformation effected by their successor Annie Besant who, perhaps more than any other Westerner, contributed to India's national liberation. Thus the Theosophical Society became the foremost instrument implementing the ideas promoted by Max Müller from 1856, when he published his article 'Comparative Mythology', to his dying day.

Blavatsky and Olcott disembarked in Bombay at the end of January 1879, about seven weeks after they had left New York. The letter of accreditation by the State Department helped them to integrate rapidly in the Anglo-Indian community in Bombay. Ten months after their arrival, they launched the monthly publication of the Theosophical Society, *The Theosophist*, which soon became profitable and acquired hundreds of subscribers in a matter of months. *The Theosophist* served as a platform for discussing diverse subjects, from supernatural phenomena to India's national question. The periodical promoted the aims of the Society and reflected the range of subject matter that preoccupied its founders. The subheading of the first issue, October 1879, spelled this out: 'A Monthly Journal Devoted to Oriental Philosophy, Art, Literature and Occultism: Embracing Mesmerism, Spiritualism, and Other Secret Sciences.' The titles of the articles in that first issue also indicated their diverse topics: What is Theosophy? Antiquity of the Vedas, The Learning Among Indian Ladies, the Inner God, Aryan Trigonometry, Magnetism in Ancient China, and others. Yet from the start, *The Theosophist* also dealt with more earthly issues. For example, its second issue ran an article denouncing the destruction of Indian forests by the British

---

36. C.C. Massey, 'Madame Blavatsky and Col. Olcott in England', *The Spiritualist* (London, 24 January 1879), 41–42.

rulers.[37] The magazine was distributed throughout India, but also in England and the United States, and was a principal instrument in spreading the Theosophical message.

At this time Blavatsky and Olcott began to give lectures to local audiences, both Indian and English, expounding their theory about India's major historical role and how the Indian masses should wake up and return to the ways of their ancestors. These intensive efforts brought immediate reactions. The subject-matter of their lectures was a thrilling novelty for the Indian public, and that these Western people were praising their ancient religion and urging them to form a local leadership was even more radically new. Blavatsky and Olcott travelled around India, visited the holy places, reported their impressions to the New York press, and met a large number of Hindu and English people. Two of the latter, Allan Octavian Hume (1829–1912), and Alfred Percy Sinnett (1840–1921), would be their nearest allies in the coming years.

Hume was a retired colonel with a senior position in the Indian Civil Service, who was interested in spiritualism. He was very sympathetic to the Indian subjects of the crown, and as we shall see, was the moving spirit behind the formation of the Indian National Congress, which was first convened in 1885. He was fascinated by Blavatsky and became her follower, until 1883, when he broke away from her and the Theosophical Society, claiming that the supernatural phenomena attributed to Blavatsky were mere charlatanry. He did, however, remain a faithful admirer of the Mahatmas, even after he broke off with their apostle. His accusations would later lead to the great attack on Blavatsky, which climaxed in 1885, with the SPR's publication of the Hodgson Report.

Sinnett was a respected journalist who met Blavatsky in December 1879 at his house in Simla. He became her admirer and remained one of her outstanding supporters even after the publication of the Hodgson Report, when she quit India for Europe. Sinnett was perhaps Blavatsky's most ardent disciple. In 1881, soon after they met, he published his first book, *The Occult World*, which contained letters sent to Blavatsky by her Masters.[38] His second book, *Esoteric Buddhism* – esoteric commentary on the Buddhist religion – appeared in 1883, and is supposed to have introduced the term 'esoteria' into

37. *The Theosophist* (Bombay, October and November 1879).
38. A.P. Sinnett, *The Occult World* (London, 1882), first published 1881.

the English language.[39] Structurally, this book closely resembled *Isis Unveiled*. Sinnett, like Blavatsky, wished to create a synthesis between Oriental and Western beliefs, and his book sought to provide extensive information about the 'secret' history of the world, to serve students of the occult, as his book proclaimed: 'The great end and purpose of adeptship is the achievement of spiritual development.'[40]

Esoteric Buddhism, like *Isis Unveiled*, reviewed the history of human races, the structure of the universe and human evolution, with the emphasis on the supposed occult aspect of Brahmin and Buddhist theology, and focused on such ideas as nirvana and karma. The book was so popular that its title became a common phrase, as shown by Max Müller's article by that name in 1893, which he published after *Theosophy, or Psychological Religion*, to continue his resolute attack on the Theosophical Society that reached its climax at this time.[41]

A belated product of the friendship between Blavatsky and Sinnett was the publication in 1923 of *The Mahatma Letters*, comprising letters supposedly sent by the Masters Koot-Hoomi and Morya, mainly to Sinnett. These letters, written between 1880 and 1884, contain a great deal of information about the early development of Theosophical theological doctrine. Assuming that Blavatsky composed those letters, one may therefore regard them as the intellectual laboratory in which she developed the ideas expressed in *Isis Unveiled*, in preparation for her second large book, published in 1888, *The Secret Doctrine*. The letters of the patron Mahatmas contained, beside the 'theological' material, many references to the social and personal contacts that marked the early activities of the Theosophical Society in India. For example, after Allan Hume began to distance himself from the Theosophical Society because of his doubts regarding Blavatsky's honesty, Sinnett received a letter from the Master Koot-Hoomi, saying that Hume 'is pushed and half maddened by evil powers, which he has attracted to himself and come under subjection to by his innate moral turbulence.'

---

39. Wouter J. Hanegraaff, *New Age Religion and Western Culture, Esotericism in the Mirror of Secular Thought* (New York, 1998), p. 384, first published 1996.

40. A.P. Sinnett, *Esoteric Buddhism* (London, 1883), p. 13.

41. F. Max Müller, 'Esoteric Buddhism', *The Nineteenth Century* (London, May, 1893), pp. 767-88.

The Master then strongly advised Sinnet, 'Avoid him, but do not madden him still more.'[42]

It is difficult, looking at it rationally and critically, to understand the effect this correspondence had on Sinnett. On the face of it, it would seem plain to any clear-minded person, that Blavatsky herself had penned the letters. Yet her success in convincing her disciple of their authenticity demonstrates her charisma and the impact of her imagination upon other people. *The Mahatma Letters* comprised 145 letters, some short and some very long, altogether a volume hundreds of pages long. As their belated publication shows, they were not meant for the general public. This too demonstrates the extraordinary writing capability of Mme Blavatsky, who at the same time was editing *The Theosophist*, starting to write *The Secret Doctrine*, keeping up an extensive correspondence, and sending articles to newspapers in India and America.

Two of these articles provide an interesting background for the short but intense relationship between the Theosophical Society and Dayananda Saraswati. The first appeared in the Indian newspaper *The Deccan Star*, on 30 March 1879, in response to a letter from a member of Arya Samaj in the newspaper *The Indian Tribune*, wondering at the importance placed by the Theosophists on the practice of magic. In it, Blavatsky explained that she believed only in natural phenomena, and justified her position by arguing that the Vedic literature is rich in magic. The Hindu writer's criticism had actually touched on the very connection between Arya Samaj and Theosophy. Blavatsky responded sharply, arguing that if the Theosophical Society were rejected by the Arya Samaj, the former would continue to exist in its own right. Here she brought up an interesting argument in support of the Theosophical preoccupation with the *Vedas*:

> Neglect this study, and we, in common with all Europe, would have to set Max Müller's interpretations of the *Vedas* far above those of Svami Dyanand Sarasvati... And would have to let the Anglo-German Sanskritist go uncontradicted, when he says that with the exception of the *Rik*, none other of the four sacred books is deserving of the name of *Veda*, especially the *Atharva Veda*, which is absurd, magical nonsense, composed of sacrificial formulas, charms and incantations.[43]

42. *The Mahatma Letters*, Letter No. 56 (K.H. to Sinnett), January 1883, pp. 320–21.
43. Blavatsky, *Magic*.

Another article, which appeared in the American publication *The Banner of Light* in October 1879, described the encounter with Dayananda Saraswati. Blavatsky revealed that she and Olcott had travelled to India for the purpose of meeting him and examining at first-hand the phenomena associated with his knowledge of occult sciences. The acquaintance with him and his associates had led Blavatsky to the startling discovery that there was no spiritualism in India – the Indians had never heard of spiritualism and knew next to nothing about America, which seemed to them as remote as the North Pole. However, she wrote, recently Dayananda Saraswati had discovered in the testimonies of the sacred writings that the ancient Aryans had known America, and it was that which led to his present interest in Theosophy.[44]

The first meeting between Dayananda Saraswati, Blavatsky and Olcott took place on 2 May 1879. The Hindu leader's impression was that his guests were gentle, kind and amiable people. He thought that the union between his movement and the Theosophist sahibs, as he called them, would help the advancement of the Hindus. His next meeting with the sahibs took place on 4 July, in Meerut, and they talked for four or five days, at which time his name was recorded in the membership list of the Theosophical Society. Significantly, Dayananda Saraswati wrote that he expected the money from America to help propagate the religion of the *Vedas*.

Dayananda Saraswati's descriptions can shed light on his interest in the two Westerners, who must have struck him as quite eccentric. It seems that Blavatsky and Olcott promised the Hindu leader to obtain American finance for his movement – or, at any rate, that was what he wished to hear. No doubt he did not acquiesce with the status that the two visitors soon claimed for themselves as commentators on Vedic literature – a role reserved exclusively to senior Brahmins. Dayananda Saraswati, who did not hesitate to criticize a famous scholar like Max Müller (he claimed that his translations of the Vedic commentaries were inaccurate), disparaged the Theosophists' pretensions to interpret the Hindu scriptures.

Indeed, his tone towards the Theosophists soon changed. He wrote Blavatsky on 23 November 1880 that her current activities were not in keeping with her past promises. He complained that

---

44. Blavatsky, 'Echoes from India, What is Hindu Spiritualism?', *The Banner of Light* (18 October 1879).

Blavatsky and Olcott, who had come to India to be his students, were now seeking to be teachers. He was sharper still in another letter to Blavatsky, written on 19 March 1881, in which he stated brusquely that he was not interested in any honour or position in the Theosophical Society. As time passed, Dayananda Saraswati distanced himself more and more from the Theosophists, until he broke off with them completely and announced publicly, on 28 March 1882, that the Theosophical Society and its instructions were not worthy of interest.[45]

What was it that infuriated Dayananda Saraswati, a respected figure and religious leader who is still highly regarded in India? The disappointed anticipation of American money to finance the operations of Arya Samaj – whether the money had been promised or not – cannot account for it. The main element was the pretension of Blavatsky and Olcott to understand and interpret the ancient Vedic scriptures, before they could even read Sanskrit well, if at all. The manner in which they propagated their ideas, the liberties they took in involving themselves with spiritual matters that he regarded as purely Hindu – these must have seemed to him intolerable.

Olcott's version of the events is somewhat different. He maintained that their misunderstanding was due to language barriers. According to him, they communicated through interpreters who were unable to transmit their messages correctly, and this was the reason the swami publicly denounced the Theosophists as charlatans. Olcott tried to give the impression that he felt no rancour for Dayananda Saraswati, whom he described as undoubtedly a great man, a Sanskrit scholar, possessing will power, a natural leader of impressive good looks, height and dignified appearance.[46]

In the early stage of the relationship with Dayananda Saraswati, in 1879–1880, *The Theosophist* published installments of the first part of his autobiography, with footnotes and commentary by Blavatsky. The footnotes to the first chapter, which appeared in the first issue of the periodical, October 1879, seem to contain the seeds

---

45. *The Autobiography of Dayanand Saraswati*, ed. K.C. Yadav (New Delhi, 1978), pp. 60, 64; see also, 68–72.

46. However, a few years later, Olcott described the swami as a fat, short, and earthly man. One could observe Olcott's plastic impressions as reflections of the change he had gone through in his first years in India, when transforming himself from a modest foreign disciple to a spiritual leader in his own right, Olcott, *Old Diary Leaves*, I, pp. 404–407.

of their future disagreement. For example, Dayananda Saraswati's description of the yogi's highest initiation prompted the following commentary by Blavatsky:

> A religious "magician", practically. One who can embrace the past and the future in one *present*; a man who has reached the most perfect state of clairvoyance, and has a thorough knowledge of what is now known as mesmerism, and the occult properties of nature, which sciences help the student to perform the greatest phenomena.[47]

This minor footnote clearly illustrates the problem of communication between the Theosophists and the local Hindus. Blavatsky and Olcott's understanding of the corpus of Hindu wisdom was fundamentally different from the way the Hindu pundits interpreted their own religion. The essentially-Western interpretation which Blavatsky put on Dayananda Saraswati's writing stemmed from her perception of the Hindu scriptures as belonging to the same tradition as Western esoteric writings. Blavatsky and Olcott (and later Besant) viewed the Hindu scriptures as ancient Gnostic writings, which gave rise to the subsequent Hermetic philosophy. Given the Theosophists' original interest in Hermetic philosophy, Kabala and Western occult sciences, they saw the Hindu texts as cryptic and laden with hidden significance, to be viewed in a Gnostic light and interpreted by means of Gnostic terms.[48]

This was also evident in Blavatsky's reaction at the end of the Dayananda Saraswati affair. In October 1882 the Master Koot-Hoomi sent Sinnett a letter:

> And if *my* word of honour has any weight with you, then know that D. Swami *was* an initiated Yogi, a very high Chela... endowed some years back with great powers and a knowledge he has since forfeited... And now see what has become of this truly great man, whom we all knew and placed our hopes in him. There he is - a moral wreck, ruined by his ambition and panting for breath in his last struggle for supremacy, which *he knows* we will *not* leave in his hands.[49]

Henceforth, this was how Dayananda Saraswati was depicted by Blavatsky - he and his movement were viewed as belonging to the

---

47. 'Arya Prakash, The Autobiography of Dayanund Saraswati Swami', *The Theosophist* (October 1879).

48. Eric J. Sharpe, *The Universal Gita, Western Images of the Bhagavad Gītā, a Bicentenary Survey* (La Salle, 1985), pp. 89-92.

49. *The Mahatma Letters*, Letter No. 54 (K.H. to Sinnett), October 1882, p. 304.

forces of evil. The Theosophical Society had confronted him successfully, playing an historical role on behalf of the Great Brotherhood.

In faraway England, the affair intrigued Max Müller, who stated that Dayananda Saraswati 'was still more unfortunate in falling, for a time, an easy prey to Madame Blavatsky's spiritual fascinations. For some time he understood her as little as she understood him... But when at last they came to understand each other, there followed a breach that could never be healed.' Max Müller explained this breach thus:

> Poor Dayananda Saraswati had no idea of what Madame Blavatsky was thinking of; but, though bewildered for a time by the unaccustomed adulation poured on him and the extravagant veneration paid to him by Europeans, he soon recovered, and declined to have anything to do with the Polish prophetess and her vagaries.

But Max Müller was as condescending about Dayananda Saraswati as about Blavatsky: 'His ignorance of English deprived him of much that would have been helpful to him, and would have kept him from some of his wild ideas about the Veda.'[50]

Thus ended this curious affair, which clearly demonstrated the discrepancy between the Theosophists' claim to understand Hinduism and the reality on the ground. Blavatsky and Olcott, whose journey to India was originally predicated on their connection with Dayananda Saraswati, soon wrecked their relations with him. While alienating the leader of one of India's great spiritual-national movements, they continued to offer their followers their own doctrine as a spiritual alternative to his.[51] These differences would continue to bedevil the complex relationship between the leading Western Theosophists and the local Indian community. As we shall see, it was precisely these differences which led ultimately, at the height of Annie Besant's career, to the greatest crisis in the history of the Theosophical Society, and to its expulsion from the Indian political scene, at the very moment when it seemed as if the synthesis between Theosophy and Hinduism had been accomplished.

In December 1882, as the Dayananda Saraswati affair was drawing to a close, Blavatsky and Olcott's economic situation improved,

---

50. F. Max Müller, *Auld Lang Syne, Second Series, My Indian Friends* (New York, 1899), pp. 105-106, 164.

51. For further discussion on the affair, see, J.T.F. Jordens, *Dayananda Sarasvati, Essays on his Life and Ideas* (New Delhi, 1998), p. 91.

thanks mainly to the increased circulation of *The Theosophist*. The movement's two founders could afford to leave Bombay and purchase a large estate in Adyar in south Madras. The estate became the headquarters of the international Theosophical Society. From it were sent the guidelines to the Theosophical lodges, which began to spring up all over the world through the 1880s. The movement's work is still directed from the same place.

On 12 September 1883 the Theosophical Society and the government of Madras signed an agreement regulating the Society's civil status. The agreement ratified a declaration by the government of India's foreign office, issued on 2 October 1880, guaranteeing the members of the Society freedom from any hindrance, so long as they confined their activity to philosophy and the sciences. The government of Madras affirmed its obligation to that declaration, provided the Theosophical work refrained completely from politics.[52] This agreement assured the Theosophists relative freedom and peace for their work among the local populace, but it shows that the British administration was already at that early stage concerned about the potential political risks of the Theosophical activities.

By 1885, about a decade after the founding of the Theosophical Society, it already had 121 lodges worldwide. Alongside the early lodges in the United States and England, new branches were being launched in Australia. However, most of the lodges at this time were in India, Burma (which Olcott visited several times) and Ceylon (today Sri Lanka). The last-named became an important Theosophical centre and a kind of living laboratory, where Theosophical techniques combining spirituality with national aspiration were tried successfully.

Olcott and Blavatsky first went to Ceylon in 1880 and stayed for two months, during which Olcott was captivated by the local Buddhism, and adopted a new costume (thereafter he favoured the garb of a Buddhist priest). It was on this visit that Olcott and Blavatsky publicly converted to Buddhism, probably the first Westerners to do so.[53] Ceylon became the focus of the Theosophical struggle against the spiritual repression practised by the British rulers. At this time the religious life of the islanders, most of them Buddhist Sinhalese, was ruled by the Christian mission, so totally that only Christian

---

52. Olcott, *Old Diary Leaves*, III, pp. 7–8.
53. Prothero, *The White Buddhist*, pp. 85–116.

marriage was permitted. Schooling was essentially Christian, and scholarships were contingent on Bible study. Olcott and Blavatsky, and later Besant, realized the significance of white Europeans lauding local religions and philosophies, which the British looked down on. This was one of the reasons for the success of Theosophy in Ceylon and later in India, with the growing popularity of the Society's leaders, who became national heroes precisely because of their Western origins.

Though Olcott did not initiate the Buddhist uprising in Ceylon, he certainly contributed to the organization of the Buddhist monks and advised them in their struggle against discrimination. His activity began as early as 1880, with the publication of his book, *A Buddhist Catechism*.[54] He befriended Anagarika Dharmapala (1864–1933), a Ceylonese boy who was trained in Theosophy and would later become the most prominent reformer of Sinhalese Buddhism. Their prolonged association led to the formation of the Maha Bodhi Society in 1891. The goal of this society, which still has branches worldwide, was to take over the sacred sites of Buddhism. Dharmapala was the society's president, and Olcott was its director and chief advisor.[55]

Already in his first stay in Ceylon, Olcott had founded seven branches of the Theosophical Society there. In the following years he founded the Buddhist Theosophical Society in Ceylon, and a network of Buddhist schools, which influenced the local population far more than implied by the size of its pupil population. In 1880, when Olcott first arrived in the island, there were only four Buddhist schools there. By 1907, shortly after his death, there were 183 Buddhist schools all over the island, teaching 20,000 pupils.[56] The struggle against the Christian missionaries was conducted by adopting their techniques – Olcott created a network of Buddhist

---

54. The book, which contained some 170 questions and answers in regard to Buddhism, was soon translated to various languages, including German (1887) and Swedish (1889), Henry S. Olcott, *A Buddhist Catechism, According to the Canon of the Southern Church* (Colombo and London, 1882), first published 1880; Olcott, *Old Diary leaves, Fifth Series, 1893–1896* (Adyar, 1932), p. 434; Carl T. Jackson, *The Oriental Religions and American Thought* (Westport, 1981), p. 164.

55. Thomas A. Tweed, *The American Encounter with Buddhism, 1844–1912: Victorian Culture & the Limits of Dissent* (Chapel Hill, 2000), p. 53, first published 1992.

56. These figures appear in the formal report of the Director of Public Instruction in Ceylon, quoted by *The Theosophist* (Madras, January, 1908).

Sunday schools, and even composed Buddhist carols, to counter the mission's hymns.[57]

The Theosophists' project in the island reached its height in 1884, with Olcott's founding of the Buddhist Defence Committee of Ceylon. That year he travelled to London on behalf of that committee, to persuade the British government to recognize the standing of the Buddhists in Ceylon, appoint a Buddhist marriage-registrar, restore the rights of the Buddhist monasteries and declare the Buddha's birthday – Wesak, the full-moon night in May – an official holiday in Ceylon. His efforts were successful, and on 28 April 1885, Wesak became an official holiday in the island.[58] Thanks to his efforts on behalf of the local population, Olcott became an honoured figure in Ceylon, where he is remembered as a national hero, and a major street in Colombo is named after him. The Theosophist work in the island did not pass away with him, but continued to thrive with local support.

It was during this first trip of Blavatsky and Olcott to Ceylon that the first disagreements arose between them, which would later intensify. On this trip Olcott showed his superb organizing abilities, overshadowing Blavatsky by his political activity. His new adherence to Buddhism did not conflict with her beliefs, as she maintained that there were kernels of truth in every religion, but it seems that the old spiritualist was unimpressed by her good friend's political aspirations. Her own regard for the Indian national cause was less combative than his. Her perception of their passage to India was not as emotionally-charged as Olcott's, to whom it seemed like the fulfilment of his destiny. Blavatsky, by contrast, hoped to create 'a nucleus of universal brotherhood' – not necessarily a national liberation movement.

The disagreements between the leaders of the Theosophical Society grew sharper as public criticism against Blavatsky increased. She was accustomed to such attacks, which mainly consisted of accusing her of being a charlatan and of attempts to disprove the supernatural phenomena which supposedly occurred around her. In 1885 these repeated accusations built up into a veritable storm which threatened to bring down the Theosophical Society. The furore angered Olcott, who sought to project a respectable image

---

57. E.F.C. Ludowyk, *The Modern History of Ceylon* (London, 1966), p. 116.
58. Olcott, *Old Diary Leaves*, III, p. 72; Prothero, *The White Buddhist*, p. 114, f. 71.

and probably believed wholeheartedly in his spiritual-political mission. When the storm subsided, the two founders separated. Only one of them, Olcott, remained in Adyar. Blavatsky left India for Europe, never to return. Unexpectedly, it was in Europe that her activity would determine the future course of the Theosophical Society.

Crises and New Beginnings

On 5 February 1894, three years after Blavatsky's death, *The Times* of London published a leading article, stating that India had become a playing-field for everything that commonsense rejected in England. It asserted that, in the final analysis, Blavatsky's phenomena consisted of tricks with teacups and letters dropping from the ceiling instead of being delivered at the door.[59]

This sharp criticism represented the way conservative circles in England viewed the Theosophical efforts in India following the Blavatsky era. Their hardened position was due mainly to the report about Blavatsky issued by the Society for Psychical Research (SPR) almost ten years before, in 1885. The report, written by a young researcher, Dr. Richard Hodgson (1855-1905), condemned Blavatsky, who would thereafter be dismissed as an outright charlatan by the establishment. The relations between the SPR and the Theosophical Society merit a brief summary to explain why that distinguished English Society was interested in blackening the reputation of the latter, with which it had been on cordial terms until 1885.

The SPR was founded in 1882 by a group of respected academics, led by Henry Sidgwick (1838-1900), a Philosophy professor at Cambridge University. Sidgwick was the president of the Society almost continually until 1892, with the two Balfour brothers and their sister among his most noted associates. Arthur James Balfour (later Lord Balfour, 1848-1930, British Prime Minister between 1902 and 1905), was the Society's president in 1893-1894; his younger brother Gerald (Earl Balfour, 1853-1945) was appointed president in 1906; their elder sister, Eleanor (1845-1936), who married Sidgwick in 1876, was the Society's president in the 1930s. Other presidents of the SPR included well-known figures from the contemporary spheres of science and politics, among them Andrew Lang, the

---

59. *The Times* (London, 5 February 1894).

mythologist and Max Müller's opponent, and the former Prime Minister Gladstone.

The purpose of the Society was the scientific examination of the spiritual phenomena which occurred in séances, and to try and determine scientifically and objectively whether the soul persisted after death. The need for such a society arose from the proliferation of spiritualist movements and the almost obsessive preoccupation with the supernatural that markedly characterized the late Victorian period. During the 1880s spiritualist interest reached unprecedented flowering in England. A variety of esoteric societies mushroomed, interest in the Kabala was revived, as well as in Hermetic lore and reincarnation, the number of astrologers and practitioners of palmistry increased, and books on magic and the occult were extremely popular. The founding of the British Theosophical Society and the SPR stemmed from this spiritualist burgeoning. This great interest in the occult and spiritualism at that time is usually attributed to the Victorian crisis of faith, and the numerous individuals who engaged in these subjects are commonly described as fugitives from the Christian church.[60]

This was a period rife with contradictions, when religion, belief in progress and spiritualism cohabited in relative harmony. The Theosophical Society fitted in with the spirit of the time. Its call for a scientific investigation of the occult, its reservations about the supernatural, and its claim that phenomena which were seen as mysterious would in future be found to belong in the natural sciences, accorded with the tendency towards spiritualism widespread in England at the time. As a result, the SPR in its early years maintained close relations with the Theosophical Society. Statements made by representatives of the two Societies created the impression that they were pursuing the same goals. Moreover, some of the leading English Theosophists were also members of the SPR, among them Charles Massey, and Blavatsky's disciple Alfred Sinnett, who returned to England from India in 1883.[61]

60. Oppenheim, *The Other World*, pp. 159-60.
61. The SPR's council included in its early days the Theosophist Francesca Arundale, alongside Anna Kingsford's companion, Edward Maitland (1824-1897). Another prominent Theosophist, the Countess of Caithness (1830-1895), joined the SPR in 1884, 'List of Members', *Journal of the Society for Psychical Research*, 9 (London, October, 1884), p. 155; 'Constitution and Rules' (20 February 1882), see also 'List of Members' (September, 1882 and July, 1883), *Proceedings of the Society for Psychical*

Olcott and Blavatsky went to England in 1884, Olcott's objective being to promote the cause of Ceylon's Buddhist Defence Committee. On 16 April, soon after his arrival in London, Olcott dined with some members of the SPR, including the chemist and physicist William Crookes (1832–1919), who would be president of the Society in 1913–1915,[62] the scientist William Fletcher Barrett (1844–1925), a founding member, and Alfred Sinnett. The following day Olcott attended Crookes' laboratory, where he observed scientific experiments.

Perhaps the impression made by Olcott on his hosts was more peculiar than he anticipated, because shortly after their encounter the SPR decided to investigate the work of the Theosophical Society. On 30 April Olcott first met the SPR investigators, bringing with him his young Indian associate, Mohini Mohandas Chatterjee (1858–1936).[63] Among other matters, the discussion dealt with evidence for the existence of the Mahatmas and the phenomenal delivery of their letters.[64] This meeting was the first move in a lengthy investigation which went on until the end of 1885, and constituted the principal work of the SPR during that time.[65] Another high point in the investigation took place in August 1884, after Blavatsky's visit to the president of the SPR in Cambridge. Sidgwick's impressions were not unequivocal. 'On the whole,' he wrote, 'I was favourably impressed

---

Research, I, 1882–1883 (London, 1883). Accordingly, the SPR library purchased Theosophical books, and proudly announced the acquisitions in its Journal. See, for example, the acquisition list of October 1884, 'Library Catalogue', *Journal of the Society for Psychical Research*, 9 (London, October, 1884).

62. Crookes was then a member of the Theosophical Society, which he joined with his wife in December 1883, Gregory Tillett, *The Elder Brother: A Biography of Charles Webster Leadbeater* (London, 1982), p. 30.

63. Mohini was a young and handsome Hindu, who accompanied Blavatsky and Olcott to Europe. His exotic appearance had its effect on several English ladies, but not only on them. Oscar Wilde, who attended a reception for Olcott and Blavatsky (held in Prince's Hall, Piccadilly), was reported to have said the following after meeting Mohini: 'I never realised before what a mistake we make in being white'. After having scandalously seduced several Theosophist ladies, Mohini was forced by Blavatsky to leave the society. Eventually, he returned to India, where he ran a home for fallen women, *The Theosophist* (October, 1884); *Lucifer* (February, 1888); Olcott, *Old Diary Leaves*, III, p. 90; Leadbeater, *How Theosophy Came to Me*, pp. 23–24, 36–37; Arthur H. Nethercot, *The First Five Lives of Annie Besant* (Chicago, 1960), p. 300; Washington, *Madame Blavatsky's Baboon*, pp. 88–89.

64. *Journal of the Society for Psychical Research*, 4 (May, 1884), p. 50.

65. *Journal of the Society for Psychical Research*, 5 (June, 1884), pp. 72–75, 6 (July, 1884), p. 93, 9 (October, 1884), pp. 156–57; and 10 (November, 1884), pp. 170, 179.

with Mme. B. No doubt the *stuff* of her answers resembled *Isis Unveiled* in some of its worst characteristics; but her manner was certainly frank and straightforward – it was hard to imagine her the elaborate impostor that she must be if the whole thing is a trick.'[66]

Since the leaders of the SPR felt that the interviews with Olcott and Blavatsky were insufficient, Sidgwick decided to hire Dr Hodgson, who had graduated in Philosophy from Cambridge in 1881, and send him to Adyar to conduct a proper investigation. Hodgson arrived in Adyar on 18 December 1884, and stayed there for several months, during which the heads of the Theosophical Society enabled him to conduct his investigation in relative freedom. They did not imagine that his work would all but destroy their enterprise.

Several factors combined at this time to launch a mighty assault on the Theosophical Society. The leading element in it was the Christian mission in Madras, which ever since the Society established its headquarters in the city had been attacking it and seeking proof that its leaders were frauds. The Anglican mission in India was not doing particularly well during the nineteenth century, which led it to view the Theosophists as serious rivals, particularly in view of the Society's rapid growth and the sympathy it won from the local population. Anti-Christian expressions uttered by Blavatsky and Olcott stoked the mission's hostility against the Theosophical Society. Another factor was Allan Octavian Hume, who as early as 1882 began to suspect Blavatsky and expressed his doubts in public. The third factor, without which Hodgson would have been unable to reach his conclusions, was the betrayal of the Theosophical Society by the Coulomb couple, who worked at the Adyar headquarters.

Emma Cutting was a Briton married to a Frenchman by the name of Alexis Coulomb. She had met Blavatsky in 1872 in Cairo, before Blavatsky set sail for America. During the 1870s the Coulombs were involved in a number of failing business enterprises, and in the early 1880s they reached Ceylon, where they met Blavatsky and Olcott, who invited them to come to Adyar and run the household of the Society's new headquarters. Blavatsky must have placed too much faith in her old friend, who repaid her with an exposure that forced Blavatsky to leave India for good. In 1884, while Blavatsky and Olcott were away in England, Emma Coulomb sold to the

---

66. Arthur Sidgwick and Eleanor Mildred Sidgwick, *Henry Sidgwick: A Memoir* (London, 1906), pp. 384–85.

head of the Madras Christian College a number of letters, allegedly written by Blavatsky. The letters contained explicit instructions for acts of trickery designed by Blavatsky, to be presented as miracles performed by the Masters. The mission published these letters in its organ, *The Christian College Magazine*, precisely when Hodgson arrived in Adyar, and his report was clearly influenced by them.

Hodgson investigated several incidents in which alleged miracles took place. He interviewed people who witnessed them, cross-referenced them, and concluded that behind the supposed Theosophical supernatural phenomena was a systematic fraud invented by Blavatsky. The most outstanding of these so-called miracles took place in August 1883, when Blavatsky and Olcott were away from Adyar. Some members of the Society who were staying in Adyar reported a miracle that had taken place in the 'Occult Room' at the Theosophical Society headquarters, the room which contained the shrine of Master Koot-Hoomi. A china saucer placed in the shrine – a doubled-doored cabinet – fell on the floor and was smashed to bits. The pieces were placed for a few moments inside the shrine, and were miraculously restored by Koot-Hoomi as an unbroken saucer. With the help of Mme. Coulomb, Hodgson discovered that the broken saucer was one of an identical pair which had been bought in a Madras shop the previous month, and that Blavatsky had instructed Mme. Coulomb to smash one and replace it with the other identical piece while she herself was away from Adyar, to heighten the impact of the miracle performed by Koot-Hoomi despite her absence. The deceit was further exposed when a double door leading to Blavatsky's bedroom was discovered behind the shrine.

Hodgson sent progress reports about his work to England in the course of 1885. They were published extensively in the SPR journal, building up expectation for his final report.[67] When he finished his investigation he returned to England and reported to the general assembly of the SPR on 29 May and 26 June 1885.[68] His final report was published in December that year. It stated that Blavatsky was not the mouthpiece of occult forces, neither was she 'a mere vulgar

---

67. The journal reported in April 1885 that Hodgson was rapidly bringing his investigation to an end, assisted by the Coloumbs, who were eager to expose Blavatsky's frauds, see, *Journal of the Society for Psychical Research*, 15 (April, 1885), pp. 323–24.

68. *Journal of the Society for Psychical Research*, 17 (June, 1885), pp. 420–24, 18 (July 1885), pp. 451–60; 461–64.

adventuress'. Hodgson's coup de grace was his assertion that she was 'one of the most accomplished, ingenious and interesting impostors in history.'[69]

The campaign against Blavatsky also challenged her morals. Emma Coulomb maintained that Blavatsky had abandoned a baby she bore during her stay in Cairo. Blavatsky was maligned as immoral, both for conceiving a child outside marriage, and for the alleged way she treated it. Another curious aspect of this story was that it contradicted her claim that she abjured sex – conforming with the Theosophical tenet that spirituality requires chastity. In response to these accusations, Blavatsky was examined in November 1885 by a German physician, who affirmed that she had never given birth.[70] Another accusation, brought by Allan Octavian Hume, was that Blavatsky forged *The Mahatma Letters*, having in fact written them herself. Hume maintained that from a certain time the Masters' letters which reached him were written on a type of paper manufactured exclusively in the Darjeeling region. He stated that previously, the Mahatma letters had been written on paper manufactured elsewhere, but the Darjeeling paper made its appearance only after Blavatsky had been to that region. Blavatsky responded by sending Sinnett a letter from the Masters which she claimed had been written in 1879, on Darjeeling paper.

Another awkward element in the Hodgson report was a suspicion that Blavatsky was a Russian spy, and that she was using a false identity. To rebut it, Blavatsky sent Sinnett a letter from her Russian uncle, confirming her identity. She described Hodgson as 'the most excellent, truthful, expert young man. But how can he recognise truth from a lie, when there is a thick net of conspiracy around him?' She responded to his accusations sarcastically: 'An old and dying woman, confined to her room... a spy, a dangerous character!'[71]

It is not difficult to imagine the outcome of the Hodgson report, which denounced the Theosophical Society as based on fraud and led

---

69. 'Report of the Committee Appointed to Investigate Phenomena Connected with the Theosophical Society', *Proceedings of the Society for Psychical Research*, 3 (December, 1885), pp. 201–400. Adlai E. Waterman, The *'Hodgson Report' on Madame Blavatsky, 1885–1960: Re-examination Discredits the Major Charges Against H.P. Blavatsky* (Adyar, 1963).

70. Olcott, *Old Diary Leaves*, III, pp. 319–20.

71. *The Mahatma Letters*, Letter No. 140 (Blavatsky to Sinnett), 6 January 1886, p. 474, Letter No. 134 (Blavatsky to Sinnet), undated, p. 456, and Letter No. 138 (Blavatsky to Sinnett), 17 March 1885, pp. 465–66.

by a clever charlatan. The SPR succeeded in damaging the reputation of the Theosophical Society almost beyond repair. It is interesting to observe how the respected SPR, with its highly-regarded members and a power-base at Cambridge, succeeded in denigrating the Theosophists, when a close look at its own areas of interest raises many questions about the belief of its leading members in equally absurd ideas.[72] It seems that 'truth' and 'science' are relative terms, and those who claim them are not necessarily free from the faults they decry in others. The method used by the SPR against Blavatsky clearly demonstrates the fluctuating value of the term 'scientific' at different times. In the end, even if one takes into account other considerations regarding the operation of the SPR,[73] it appears that the main objective of Sidgwick and his associates was to eliminate ambitious rivals and preserve their own Society's scientific standing. The goal even justified the loss of several members of the SPR, including Sinnett, who resigned from the Society on 18 September 1885, preferring to remain faithful to Theosophy.

Blavatsky began to feel the sword hanging over her head following the betrayal of the Coulombs and the arrival of Hodgson's report in England. She was very ill, and her relations with Olcott deteriorated, until the final rupture between them. On 21 March 1885 she resigned her position as corresponding secretary of the Theosophical Society. Soon afterwards she left the Theosophical Society headquarters in Adyar for the last time, and sailed to Europe. This was the sour ending of the friendship between the two founders.

Olcott, who probably urged Blavatsky to leave India, wrote disingenuously in his memoirs that Blavatsky's departure for Europe was due only to her ill health. Soon after the crisis in 1885, he wrote in his journal that malicious people hinted to Blavatsky that he was planning to remove her from all the work of the centre in Adyar, and even meant to drop her name from the front page of *The Theosophist*, which she had founded and was still editing.[74] He denied that he'd had any such intentions at that time, and claimed

---

72. Such was the case of Arthur Balfour, who for many years attended séances, in which he communicated with the spirit of his lover, who died in 1875: Oppenheim, *The Other World*, pp. 132-33.

73. Dixon gives a feminist interpretation to what she describes as a misogynist attack on behalf of the SPR (whose members were almost exclusively male) on the Theosophical Society (Who had a majority of women members), Joy Dixon, *Divine Feminine: Theosophy and Feminism in England* (Baltimore, 2001), p. 20.

74. Olcott, *Old Diary Leaves*, III, p. 313.

that his relations with Blavatsky remained quite normal, even after she moved to London, where she stayed until she died. It seems that they had agreed to avoid attacking each other in public in the coming years. Olcott abided by this understanding until she died, and only later, presumably due to the struggle over her legacy, did he grow increasingly critical about his deceased associate.[75]

But for all his tolerant references to Blavatsky, her departure from Adyar must have caused Olcott considerable relief. From this moment on he could devote himself energetically to promoting the Theosophical Society, without the fear that had always haunted him that it would be seen as a mountebank operation. Indeed, in the following years, under Olcott's presidency, the Society was taken seriously by the local population and continued to thrive. Curiously, the Hodgson Report served to revive the Theosophical vigour in India, as though it were a surgical operation that removed a malignancy from a body and enabled it to recover its health. Olcott's plans for the Society entailed two principal activities – the cultivation of the Buddhist elements in the Theosophical programme, and the call for Indian Home Rule. He could not have imagined that in faraway London the activities of his former associate would lead to the finding and cultivation of a successor, who would eventually occupy his seat as well. As we shall see, the distinctive contribution of Annie Besant was her clever combination of Blavatsky's esoteric ideas with Olcott's political ones. Her achievements in both areas would surpass those of her predecessors.

Blavatsky arrived in Naples on 23 April 1885. After three months in Italy, she decided to move to Würzburg, Bavaria, arriving there in mid-August. She took a suite of rooms and settled down to work on her second magnum opus, *The Secret Doctrine*. At this time she became friends with the Countess Constance Wachtmeister (1838–1919), the widow of a Swedish ambassador to London, who had joined the Theosophical Society in 1880. Wachtmeister became her inseparable companion for the rest of her life, and would even

---

75. Olcott's diaries express an ambivalent perception of Blavatsky, sometimes in the harshest manner, 'H.P.B. made numberless friends, but often lost them again and saw them turned into personal enemies... We were to her, I believe, nothing more than pawns in a game of chess... But she was loyal to the last degree to her aunt, her other relatives, and to the Masters; for whose work she would have sacrificed not only one, but twenty lives, and calmly seen the whole human race consumed with fire, if needs be', Olcott, *Old Diary Leaves*, I, pp. 462-63.

maintain close relations with Annie Besant. In the early summer of 1886 the two women travelled to Ostend in Belgium, hoping that the sea air would help Blavatsky to regain her health, but after a few months she decided to move to England, which she did on 1 May 1887.[76] The four years she lived in England, up to 1891, were Blavatsky's final years, and it seems she was invigorated and recovered her creativity. The Indian summer of her life left a lasting impact on the Theosophical Society – by the end, she had bequeathed the Society a number of books which joined *Isis Unveiled* on the Theosophical bookcase, primarily *The Secret Doctrine* and *The Key to Theosophy*. Moreover, it was in London that she found a successor, Annie Besant, whom she discovered, developed and groomed.

The history of the London branch of the Theosophical Society up to Blavatsky's arrival was stormy. A short while after its foundation back in 1879, it was joined by one of the outstanding British spiritualists of the time, Dr Anna Kingsford. Kingsford had studied medicine at the Sorbonne between 1874 and 1880, having been unable, as a woman, to do so at an English university. She returned to London after graduation, promoted vegetarianism as a way of life, and developed a great interest in the study of the occult. She had earlier married a priest, who had little influence over her. The dominant male in her life was Edward Maitland (1824–1897), her faithful friend and biographer.

Kingsford was elected president of the British Theosophical Society in January 1883. It was during her leadership that it changed its name to the London Lodge of the Theosophical Society, but this was not the only change she implemented. Her theological programme was quite different from that of Blavatsky, who as we have seen regarded India as the fountainhead of esoteric wisdom. Kingsford remained faithful to the old Hermetic belief, which held that Egypt was the cradle of secret knowledge. Into this concept she interpolated obvious Christian elements, arguing that early Christianity derived its kernel of wisdom from Egyptian knowledge and from the Hellenistic world.[77] She also differed from the Theosophists in

---

76. Cranston, *HPB*, pp. 287–322.

77. For Kingsford's main fields of interest, see, Anna Kingsford, *The Perfect Way in Diet: A Treatise Advocating a Return to the Natural and Ancient Food of our Race* (London, 1881); Anna Bonus Kingsford and Edward Maitland, *The Perfect Way, or, Finding of Christ* (London, 1882).

her attitude towards Christianity. Whereas Blavatsky regarded the Church as the embodiment of evil, Kingsford's attitude towards it was far more positive. This is attested in a letter she wrote Olcott in October 1883, expressing displeasure about the antagonism which had grown between the Theosophical Society (which she called the Oriental Church) and the Christian mission in India. She argued that the two should be reconciled, since they both engaged in the search for esoteric and Gnostic knowledge. Olcott was clearly unenthusiastic about her tolerant ideas. Kingsford was ejected from the Society a few months after writing that letter.

Kingsford's views sowed discord among the London Theosophists soon after they elected her as their president. Sinnett, the author of the popular *Esoteric Buddhism*, had recently returned from India. His views conflicted with those of Kingsford, who regarded Oriental esotericism as inferior to the Hermetic-Christian kind. The two soon became outright enemies. By the end of 1883 their clash came out into the open, as a series of letters distributed among the members of the London Lodge made plain. The principal letter, written by Kingsford, attacked Sinnett, arguing that his *Esoteric Buddhism* was not original, that the doctrine it expounded was far older than Buddhism, and that students of metaphysics were thoroughly familiar with it through the *Vedas* and Buddhist, Hermetic and Christian texts.

'Pure Buddhism,' she wrote, 'is in no radical aspect different from pure Christianity, because esoteric religion is identical throughout all time and conditions, being eternal in its truth and immanent in the human spirit.' Maitland backed his friend and attacked *Esoteric Buddhism* with similar arguments. Sinnett, for his part, responded to the attack in a letter which was also distributed among the members of the London Lodge in March 1884.[78]

---

78. Anna Kingsford, 'To the President of the Theosophical Society, Madras' (31 October 1883), Edward Maitland, 'Remarks and Propositions Suggested by the Perusal of Esoteric Buddhism' (undated); A.P. Sinnett, 'Theosophy and Esoteric Buddhism, Some Comments on the Recent Pamphlets by the President and Vice-President of the London Lodge, T.S., and especially on the Reply to the Observations of Mr. T. Subba Row' (March, 1884). A copy of these letters, bound for private circulation among the members of the London Lodge, is held by the British Library, under the title: Anna Kingsford and Edward Maitland, a Letter addressed to the Fellows of the London Lodge of the Theosophical Society: by the President and Vice-President of the Lodge, Private and Confidential.

Before long, the dispute between Sinnett and Kingsford led to a major rift in the London Lodge, reaching its climax just when Olcott and Blavatsky were in England. It is not clear who actually settled the row and found the solution for Kingsford. Certainly the result of the crisis was that Kingsford and Maitland withdrew from the Theosophical Society and founded The Hermetic Society, which Kingsford led until her death in 1888. Sinnett became the dominant figure in the London Lodge, a fact which assured Blavatsky of significant local support when she arrived in London in 1887. Kingsford's demise shortly afterwards no doubt also helped to clear London's esoteric stage for the veteran spiritualist. Blavatsky indeed flourished in this setting, and pretty soon launched into intense activity with the aim, it seems, of creating a new and powerful European base that would compete with the headquarters in Adyar for the leadership of the international Society. Towards the end of 1887 two of the central institutions created for the purpose were in place – Blavatsky had founded a new esoteric monthly by the name of *Lucifer*, which soon threatened to overshadow *The Theosophist*, and her disciples had formed a new organization, named the Blavatsky Lodge. The periodical and the new lodge worried Olcott, who has presumably imagined that his erstwhile friend had come to the end of her political road.[79]

The first issue of *Lucifer* appeared in September 1887.[80] The January 1888 issue might indicate Blavatsky's state of mind at that time. Her leading article was downhearted: 'It is not likely that much happiness or prosperity can come to those who are living for the truth under such a dark number as 1888; but still the year is heralded by the glorious star Venus-Lucifer, shining so resplendently that it has been mistaken for that still rarer visitor, the Star of Bethlehem. This too, is at hand; and surely something of the Christos spirit must be born upon earth under such conditions.'[81]

But 10 months later, the October 1888 issue reveals a sharp upturn in Blavatsky's state of mind. Her leading article attacked all the current spiritual movements, which she described as charlatan, and

---

79. Olcott, *Old Diary Leaves*, III, pp. 436–37.
80. *Lucifer* appeared continuously until August 1898. Its title was then changed to '*The Theosophical Review*'.
81. H.P. Blavatsky, '1888', *Lucifer* (January, 1888).

especially The Hermetic Brotherhood of Luxor.[82] She stressed that the monopoly on esoteric knowledge was held exclusively by the Theosophical Society, and that the real names of the Masters were known only to the founders of the Society – herself and Olcott.[83]

The changed mood was due to the relative success Blavatsky enjoyed at the end of 1888, chiefly thanks to her new book, *The Secret Doctrine*.[84] Written as a kind of sequel to *Isis Unveiled*, it contained answers to the great questions she had raised back in 1877. It claimed to be based on an ancient manuscript which had come into her possession, and was known to no other person in the West. She claimed that it contained the truth about the creation of the world and the lore that was transmitted to initiates through the ages.

The English press excoriated *The Secret Doctrine* – all but one paper, *The Pall Mall Gazette*, whose editor was the well-known journalist William Stead (1849–1912). Stead was then associated with a Russian lady journalist, Madame Olga Novikoff (1840–1925), who resided in London, where she behaved as an unofficial representative of the Czar's government in England. A friend of Gladstone, Novikoff devoted her efforts to promoting friendly relations between England and Russia. At this time, her salon attracted politicians, artists and diverse mystics, among them Blavatsky.[85]

Novikoff introduced Stead to Blavatsky, who asked him to review *The Secret Doctrine* in his magazine. Stead was daunted by the massive tome and asked Annie Besant, his friend and a well-known liberal journalist at the time, to undertake the task. As she recalled it,

---

82. The brotherhood gained success in England and the US, simultaneously with Theosophy. Blavatsky and Olcott themselves were listed as members in the brotherhood between 1875–1878, Joscelyn Godwin, Christian Chanel, John P. Deveney, *The Hermetic Brotherhood of Luxor: Initiatic and Historical Documents of an Order of Practical Occultism* (York Beach, 1995), pp. 341–48, 370–72, 432.

83. H.P. Blavatsky, 'Lodges of Magic', *Lucifer* (October, 1888).

84. The book was printed in October, having being edited by several English Theosophists, chiefly by Bertram Keightley, the London Lodge secretary, Countess Constance Wachtmeister, *Reminiscences of H.P. Blavatsky and The Secret Doctrine*, by the Countess Constance Wachtmeister, ed. A Fellow of the Theosophical Society (London, 1893), pp. 89–95.

85. For further details on Novikoff's relations with Stead and Blavatsky, see, Olga Novikoff, *The M.P. for Russia: Reminiscences and Correspondence of Madame Olga Novikoff*, ed. W.T. Stead, I (London, 1909), pp. 130–33; Ann Taylor, *Annie Besant: a Biography* (Oxford, 1992), p. 202; Nethercot, *The First Five Lives of Annie Besant*, p. 285; Bernard Shaw, *Collected Letters, 1874–1897*, ed. Dan H. Laurence (London, 1965), p. 172.

Annie Besant, President of the Theosophical Society 1907–1933, wearing Blavatsky's signet ring, reproduced by Yanai Zeltzer.

since 1886 there had been slowly growing up a conviction that my philosophy was not sufficient; that life and mind were other than, more than, I had dreamed... I studied the obscurer sides of consciousness, dreams, hallucinations, illusions, insanity. Into the darkness shot a ray of light – A. P. Sinnett's "Occult World"... and by the early spring of 1889 I had grown desperately determined to find at all hazards what I sought. At last... I heard a voice... bidding me take courage for the light was near. A fortnight passed, and then Mr. Stead gave into my hands two large volumes. "Can you review these? My young men all fight shy of them, but you are quite mad enough on these subjects to make something of them." I took the books; they were the two volumes of *"The Secret Doctrine"*, written by H.P. Blavatsky... As I turned over page after page the interest became absorbing... the light had been seen, and in that flash of illumination I knew that the weary search was over and the very Truth was found.[86]

Besant wrote a very favourable review of the work, and asked Stead to introduce her to the author. Their first meeting took place soon after at Blavatsky's place. Blavatsky charmed Besant, who arrived with her friend Herbert Burrows (1845-1921). Besant was surprised that the elderly spiritualist did not seem at all mysterious.

> She talked of travels, of various countries, easy brilliant talk, her eyes veiled, her exquisitely moulded fingers rolling cigarettes incessantly. Nothing special to record, no word of Occultism, nothing mysterious, a woman of the world chatting with her evening visitors. We rose to go, and for a moment the veil lifted, and two brilliant, piercing eyes met mine, and with a yearning throb in her voice: "Oh, my dear Mrs. Besant, if you would only come among us!"[87]

That one short phrase abruptly changed the life of Annie Besant and determined the future of the Theosophical Society. A few years later Besant succeeded Blavatsky and Olcott, raised the Society to a height beyond the dreams of its founders, and materially helped change the destiny of India, which became her second home.

---

86. Annie Besant, *An Autobiography* (Adyar, 1995), pp. 308-10, first published 1893.
87. Besant, *An Autobiography*, p. 311.

Chapter 4

The Theosophical Doctrine

This chapter presents the Theosophical doctrine as created and elaborated between 1877, when Blavatsky published *Isis Unveiled*, and the second decade of the twentieth century, in which Annie Besant developed her spiritual-national platform. Blavatsky was undoubtedly the main creative force responsible for the corpus of Theosophical theology, but her successor Besant contributed to it by honing her mentor's universal message into a doctrine which was primarily adapted to Theosophy's activity in India. Blavatsky and Besant were supported in this by an important Theosophical 'theologian', Charles Webster Leadbeater, who had trained as a clergyman and whose teaching stressed messianic-esoteric elements. He was among the first in the Western world to engage in the subjects of auras, chakras and channelling, which would later become central preoccupations of New Age movements.[1] The writings of these three Theosophists form the basis for this survey, both in the ideological sphere and in their chronological order, to show how the Theosophical doctrine developed in the first four decades of its existence.

Great caution must be exercised in examining the Theosophical writings in two main areas. The first and more problematic one is the irrational character of these writings, as well as their credibility. Anthony Grafton, who investigated forgeries of purported antique texts from ancient times to early modern times, could not have designed better guidelines for the investigator of the modern Theosophical writings. He stated that when certain texts are said to have reached the author by a miraculous route, or when the

---

1. For further discussion on the Theosophical Society's role in generating the New Age Movement, see, Wouter J. Hanegraaff, *New Age Religion and Western Culture: Esotericism in the Mirror of Secular Thought* (Albany, 1998), first published 1996; Olav Hammer, *Claiming Knowledge, Strategies of Epistemology from Theosophy to the New Age* (Leiden, 2001).

author claims to have made a fair copy of the original, the text is most probably a forgery. As he put it, the typical forgery is presented with the claim that an ancient document or text had been discovered by accident, or that it is based on a text located very far away, preferrably in an unknown language. Grafton states that the forger must carry out a number of moves – he must give his text a distinctive philological and physical appearance, demonstrably belonging to an earlier period than his own. The forger must imagine two things – first, how the text must have looked at the time of its presumed writing; second, how it must look now that it has been 'found'. Moreover, the forger must explain where the text originated and how it conforms to other, authoritative, texts. Another characteristic of such forgers is the invention of mysterious but impressive tales to account for how the previously-unknown treasures had come into their possession.[2] All these criteria seem to apply to Blavatsky's works, in particular her second great book, *The Secret Doctrine*.

The second area calling for great caution has to do with the broad historical setting of movements with similar theologies to that of Theosophy. To understand the religious cults of our era, we must examine the religious-historical contexts in which they arose, which may well stretch back centuries.[3] This is seen in the characteristic Theosophical kind of thought, whose roots go back to the Renaissance, if not earlier. Thus an analysis of the Theosophical writings must be accompanied by constant evaluation both of their inner logic and their claim to originality. This is why the analysis of Theosophical philosophy will be done in two stages. The present chapter deals with the Theosophical primary sources, and the following chapter investigates the sources predating Theosophy and their influence on the formulation of the Society's platform.

The first phase in the development of the Theosophical doctrine spread over the dozen or so years between the publication of *Isis Unveiled* and *The Secret Doctrine*. The Society's primary ideological and theological programme was formulated during this interval. It offered seekers of the occult a new way of searching for the unknown, beginning with a geographical reorientation of the object

---

2. Anthony Grafton, *Forgers and Critics, Creativity and Duplicity in Western Scholarship* (Princeton, 1990), pp. 8–9, 49–50, 58.

3. David S. Katz and Richard H. Popkin, *Messianic Revolution, Radical Religious Politics to the End of the Second Millennium* (New York, 1998), p. xi.

of the search. When Blavatsky first began, her ideas displayed the unmistakable influence of Hermetic and neo-Platonist philosophy. But gradually ancient Hindu philosophy came to occupy a greater place in her theory. Blavatsky already expressed high regard for ancient Indian culture in *Isis Unveiled*, but at that stage the genealogical hierarchy of ideas she ascribed to the sources of the esoteric lore had not yet crystallized. Reading *Isis Unveiled* one gains the impression that it was written in mid-transition in Blavatsky's thought, as if while writing it she was trying to blend the Hermetic beliefs she had held before with some new conclusions apparently drawn from current scientific study.

As stated before, this is especially noticeable with regard to Blavatsky's references to the geographic sources of magical lore. In the early stage, the founder of the Society referred mainly to ancient Egypt as the fount of ancient knowledge, but as time went on India increasingly became the destination for the search after the occult. The change inevitably affected the decision of Blavatsky and Olcott to move the centre of their project to India in 1879. The move to India led Blavatsky to pore over ancient Hindu literature, primarily *The Bhagavad Gītā*, which as we have seen, was translated into English by Charles Wilkins back in 1784. The Theosophical interest in *The Bhagavad Gītā* remained crucial even after the end of the Blavatsky period. As noted, it was the first book Besant translated into English.[4]

The Theosophical preoccupation with *The Bhagavad Gītā* and other sacred Hindu texts rested on their tendentious identification as ancient Gnostic texts, belonging in reality to the Western Hermetic tradition. In this way, the ancient Hindu literature influenced the Theosophical theology mainly by broadening the spectrum of its sources of reference, rather than on its contents. And since Blavatsky and her disciples were never content to read these texts as they had been written, but insisted on discovering in them secret meanings associated with Hermetic philosophy, the influence of the Hindu scriptures upon the substance of Theosophical theology was fairly limited, as it continued to revolve around the same Hermetic and

---

4. Unlike Max Müller, Blavatsky claimed that the *Bhagavad Gītā*'s importance exceeded the importance of the Vedas, H.P. Blavatsky, *Isis Unveiled: A Master-Key to the Mysteries of Ancient and Modern Science and Theology*, II (Pasadena, 1998), pp. 562-63, first published 1877; *The Bhagavad Gītā, or, the Lord's Song*, trans. Annie Besant (London, 1895).

somewhat fantastic thinking. I shall now analyse Blavatsky's two major works, examining the world view they reflect, the change that took place in the time between their respective writing, and the evident impact of the contemporary Orientalist and comparative religion research upon the author.

Isis Unveiled

This work, in two thick volumes, appeared in 1877, two years after the founding of the Theosophical Society in New York. The book was reprinted many times, translated into various languages, and became the Theosophists' 'Bible', being Blavatsky's first great oeuvre. It served as the guidebook in the quest for the truth the Theosophists seek to discover, mainly in formulating the questions that the student of the occult should ask, and defines the correct way to find the answers. Later Blavatsky herself sharply criticized her first book, arguing that *Isis Unveiled*, 'with its misprints and wrong quotation-marks, has given me more anxiety and trouble than anything else during a long lifetime which has ever been more full of thorns than of roses.' She claimed that her poor opinion of the book was always consistent and unequivocal, from her first reading of it after she finished writing it to the end of her life, and that she had never hidden her opinion of it all through the years, despite repeated warnings that this might harm its sales.[5] But her criticism focused on the book's external defects, not on its substance. It could hardly be otherwise – after all, as she always maintained, she had been only the mediator in its writing, as it had been dictated to her in a trance by the Mahatmas of the Great Brotherhood.

The introduction to the first volume of *Isis Unveiled* declares: 'Our work, then, is a plea for the recognition of the Hermetic philosophy, the ancient universal Wisdom-Religion, as the only possible key to the Absolute in science and theology.'[6] The assertion indicates Blavatsky's presumed motives – *Isis Unveiled* was meant to legitimize the search for answers to humanity's eternal existential questions through the Hermetic philosophy. The key Hermetic formula, 'As below, so it is above,' which proclaims the identity of the materials and laws in all the worlds and all the dimensions, appears also in *Isis Unveiled*, alongside the assertion that ancient Egypt is the source

5. H.P. Blavatsky, 'My Books', *Lucifer* (London, May, 1891).
6. Blavatsky, *Isis Unveiled*, I, p. vii.

of our world's esoteric knowledge. Egypt was where Moses learned the ancient magic lore, which he transmitted to the Jews. Egypt was also the place where Jesus passed his youth, and where, according to Blavatsky, he was trained in the occult and in working miracles.

Blavatsky argued that ancient Egypt attained the summit of human civilization, and everything that came after it was a decline. She declared that ancient Egyptians knew everything there was to know about electricity, that it was the centre of knowledge in its era for all who took an interest in the sciences, and the source of all the Greek philosophical doctrines, including those of Pythagoras and Plato. The Egyptians left evidence of their scientific skills, as for example in embalming, and also dominated the world geographically. This was deduced from Blavatsky's astounding conclusion, that the navy of the Pharaoh Necho II reached America, long before the infant Columbus dipped his toes in the ocean.[7]

All the above meant that Egypt was the cradle of global esoteric lore, but this applied only to the first phase of the history of magic, as outlined in the Theosophical doctrine of *Isis Unveiled*. The second historical phase showed that those who created the ancient magical lore were not the Egyptians, as they had actually received it from an even earlier source – namely, ancient India. According to Blavatsky, the source of Platonic philosophy was indeed in Egypt, but it was important to note that Plato had been influenced by the *Vedas*. Consequently, ancient Indian magic was not inferior to that of ancient Egypt, but actually greater. India, Blavatsky maintained, was the source of all human knowledge. Everything the Egyptians, Phoenicians, Jews, Greeks and Romans knew, they had learned from the Indians.

There is a visible connection between the altered perception of the history of ideas that the academic world experienced in the nineteenth century and Blavatsky's historical 'discoveries'. As we have seen, Max Müller, the leading figure in the academic study of India, himself developed a refurbished history, romantic and charged with moral-cultural messages, about the supposed links that had existed in the past between India and the rest of the world. Max Müller who, following Schopenhauer, asserted that Christianity was a synthesis created in Egypt between the Semitic and the Aryan

---

7. Blavatsky based these arguments chiefly on Bunsen's (Max Müller's patron) Egyptologist research, Blavatsky, *Isis Unveiled*, I, pp. 518, 528-31, 539-42, see also II, pp. 92-93, 366-68, 431-32.

thought, unwittingly influenced Blavatsky's elaboration of her own version of history. Following in his footsteps, she argued that the religion taught by Jesus was not Christianity but Buddhism. Moreover, it was a secret Gnostic doctrine he had learned in Egypt. She solved the problem of the assumed connection between the ancient Indians and Egyptians by declaring that the latter were actually descendants of the Aryan Indians, who reached Egypt as a colonial Aryan outpost. Not coincidentally, this assertion echoed William Jones' hypotheses. In this matter Blavatsky was clearly inspired by the spirit of the Orientalists. Thus, for example, in her attack on Darwin's theory of evolution she quoted Max Müller's statement in 'Comparative Mythology', that Man's condition had not necessarily been more backward in the past.[8]

Max Müller's objective in 'Comparative Mythology', as well as in other writings, was to demolish English prejudices regarding India. As we have seen, his argument was that the ancient Aryan Indians were not barbaric, and that the West would do well to learn from them in order to secure a better future for itself. Blavatsky turned to his writings to support the overarching worldview she had created, in which humanity, having a cyclic history, had once been more developed than at present, and nearer to understanding the cosmos and the deity. She contended that humanity was currently undergoing an historical cycle, but was not necessarily at its peak.

The doubtful evidence on which Blavatsky rested in this connection demonstrates the muddled nature of *Isis Unveiled*, which interwove precise statements and references by serious scientists and scholars with outright journalistic fabrications.[9] There are a good many of these in the book, which is packed with incoherent passages and reports about marvels and miracles based on pure hearsay, and sometimes not even that. Such trivial elements may not matter much, and might be regarded as harmless, but they are surprising in a book that is laden with quotes from the leading scholars of the age. Among these was John William Draper (1811–1882), a well-known historian of religion, whose controversial book, *History of the Conflict between Science and Religion*, had appeared some three years before *Isis Unveiled*. Blavatsky knew the book well – Draper's

---

8. Blavatsky, *Isis Unveiled*, I, pp. xi, 4, 90, 92, 583–88, see also II, pp. 123, 192, 435.
9. See, for example, her quotation of the *Kansas City Times*, that reported an archeological discovery of a giant human skeleton: Blavatsky, *Isis Unveiled*, I, p. 304.

argument that Christianity had been responsible for a fixed hostility to science over the previous centuries was music to her ears, as she was always a fierce opponent of the Christian establishment. She fully adopted this position, while tilting it somewhat to suit her tendency. For example, Giordano Bruno, whom Draper viewed as a victim of the anti-scientific Church, was turned by Blavatsky into a martyr who paid with his life for his Hermetic-esoteric beliefs. He is still depicted thus by the *Theosophists* to this day.[10]

Quotes and references from other leading contemporary Orientalists, scientists and scholars of religions, abound in *Isis Unveiled*, among them Champollion, Schliemann, Whitney, Darwin, Jones, and of course Max Müller, whom Blavatsky especially favoured. His name appears in the book as frequently as Moses or Hermes Trismegistus, the eponymous central figure of the Egyptian Hermetic corpus. The writings of these respected scholars were quoted alongside some highly dubious testimonies. This mixture characterized Blavatsky's work throughout her life, and reflected her inner world, in which the scientific pretension of an autodidact mingled with esoteric theories. This hodge-podge frequently provoked ridicule.

We have noted the two cultures, the Egyptian and Indian, to which *Isis Unveiled* attributed the origins of occult lore, but towards the end of the first volume it transpires that Theosophist history included a third, mind-boggling, stratum. The true source of human knowledge, it asserted, lay not in Egypt or in India, but in another place, mentioned by Plato – namely, the lost world of Atlantis, which perished because of its sovereign's penchant for black magic. According to Blavatsky, fugitives escaping from Atlantis as it sank beneath the waves – among them the biblical Noah – settled in various parts of the world, notably in a mysterious island in the prehistoric ocean, which became the refuge of the last Atlanteans. These islanders could live in water, on land or in fire. There was no marine communication with the island, but it was linked to other parts of the world by subterranean tunnels. The Atlantean survivors who lived in that island bequeathed the esoteric secrets to the present human race. According to Blavatsky, their story was the

---

10. John William Draper, *History of the Conflict Between Religion and Science* (New York, 1903), pp. 151–82, first published 1874; Blavatsky, *Isis Unveiled*, I, p. 95; Annie Besant, *Giordano Bruno: Theosophy's Apostle in the Sixteenth Century* (Adyar, 1913).

source from which arose the mythologies of many cultures which referred to defying the deity and the fall, or expulsion from the deity's domain – among them the story of Adam and Eve, Lucifer and Prometheus.[11]

The second volume of *Isis Unveiled* is somewhat less fantastic. It discusses the historical and philosophical bonds between Christianity, Judaism and the religions of India, opening with a bitter attack against Christianity, which Blavatsky accused of tyranny. Her principal argument was that the Church was not the true inheritor of Christ, since it does not practise compassion and peace. The Christian Church's inequity was demonstrated in its conduct in India, where the missions propagated slander about Hindu rites.

Blavatsky was no less critical of Judaism, Christianity's spiritual parent, arguing that the latter suffered from a congenital defect because it had chosen to ally itself with the Semites, which, she claimed, was the least spiritual race. The Semites had never succeeded in developing a language capable of holding moral or intellectual ideas, and was never able to convey anything higher than sensual idioms. That was why their literature never created anything original that had not been borrowed from Aryan thought. Their science and philosophy could at best hope to approximate the high metaphysical systems of the Indo-Europeans. To prove the inferiority of Judaism and the fact that it, and hence Christianity, derived its sources from older myths, Blavatsky again quoted Max Müller, who, as we have seen, showed that Sanskrit was much older than Hebrew. Clearly then, she argued, the source of the biblical narratives lay in the Vedic literature.[12]

Isis Unveiled concludes with the statement that most members of the white race simply lack magical abilities. If there was scarcely any magic in the West it was because only one European in a million might have the ability to become a practising magician.

---

11. Blavatsky, *Isis Unveiled*, I, pp. 298–99, 589–93.

12. Blavatsky, *Isis Unveiled*, II, pp. 411, 434–35. Despite her undermining description of the Hebrew language, Blavatsky did try to etymologically analyse many Hebrew words, thus following Max Müller's methods, not always very successfully. For example, she claimed that St. Peter's name, which phonetically derived from the Greek term for a rock, originally derived from the Hebrew root 'peter' (to decipher). 'Isis Unveiled' is abundant with many similar false interpretations: Blavatsky, *Isis Unveiled*, II, pp. xxviii, 29, see also I, p. 570.

This reflected the Orientalist view of the East as a place of mystery, where the native population is endowed with natural magical gifts, denied to the magicless West. This view must have strengthened Blavatsky's decision to move to the Orient a couple of years after the publication of *Isis Unveiled*, in which she declared at the end: 'Pre-Vedic Brahmanism and Buddhism are the double source from which all religions sprung; Nirvana is the ocean to which all tend.'[13]

Isis Unveiled is packed with information, imagination and connections (though also many errors), and seeks to tie together three 'historical' views about the source of human wisdom. The reader wandering through its various layers finds himself following Blavatsky's footsteps as she, influenced by a number of scholars, undergoes a change of mind and begins to see India replacing Egypt as the source of Aryan culture. The third and most fantastic layer, which casts human history back to the very distant past, to Atlantis and even earlier, is the most impressive in terms of the imagination invested in its creation. The same kind of imagination and thinking characterizes Blavatsky's other major work, *The Secret Doctrine*.

The Secret Doctrine

The Secret Doctrine, which also comprised two thick tomes, provided the followers of the Theosophical Society with fresh theological material and supplied answers to some of the questions first posed in *Isis Unveiled*. The purpose of this work was to reveal to the world an ancient secret doctrine, or a body of knowledge that contained the essence from which all religions, especially the ones based on Aryan thought, derived: '... to show that Nature is not "a fortuitous concurrence of atoms", and to assign to man his rightful place in the scheme of the universe.'[14]

The book included a translation with partial commentary of an ancient poem named 'The Book of Dzian', which had come into Blavatsky's possession by marvellous means. Her copy of it, she claimed, was the only one extant in the West. It was written in an ancient language called Senzar, known to practitioners of the occult in ancient times, and *The Secret Doctrine* offered its first translation

---

13. Blavatsky, *Isis Unveiled*, II, pp. 635-39.
14. H.P. Blavatsky, *The Secret Doctrine: The Synthesis of Science, Religion, and Philosophy*, I (Pasadena, 1999), pp. vii-viii, first published 1888.

into a Western language. According to Blavatsky, the translated stanzas of the poem contained an abstract algebraic formula whose decipherment helped to understand the cosmic evolution from the low to the high.[15] Blavatsky explained that the reason she had a unique copy of this ancient and unknown text was that it had been given to her in 1880 by the leader of Arya Samaj, Dayananda Saraswati: 'If Mr Moksh Mooler... were a Brahmin and came with me, I might take him to a gupta cave near Okhee Math, in the Himalayas, where he would soon find out that what crossed the Kalapani from India to Europe were only the bits of rejected copies of some passages from our sacred books.'[16] The conclusion to be drawn from this account was that if 'The Book of Dzian' was unknown in the West, this did not make it any less authentic.

This fantastic tale, in which Blavatsky made free with the reputations of both Dayananda Saraswati and Max Müller, tells us something about her. Long before 1888, when *The Secret Doctrine* appeared, it was already evident that both these men regarded Blavatsky as a crank, harmless at best, or – at worst, from her own viewpoint – as actually harmful. Apparently Blavatsky had grown a sufficiently thick skin to ignore such criticism. Despite Max Müller's known opinion of her, she continued to quote him and make use of his research. *The Secret Doctrine*, like *Isis Unveiled* before it, is full of references to him, giving the impression that she greatly admired him.

The first volume of *The Secret Doctrine* analyses the contents of 'The Book of Dzian', purporting to juxtapose it with current scientific information. This volume describes the creation of the universe and its diverse component parts, ranged in a hierarchy of seven divine forces which shape and create their surroundings. These forces are responsible for creating the cosmos, from the cosmic material to the galaxies, from a single planet to a planetary chain. This creative process continues in the various evolutionary stages of every world, until the appearance of life and of humanity. The seven divine forces, according to Blavatsky, correspond to the Hermetic philosophers' seven planets. As she describes it, there are in the universe

---

15. Blavatsky, *The Secret Doctrine*, I, pp. 1, 21-23. Gershom Scholem thought that the 'Book Dzian' was an adaptation of 'Sifra D'tzniuta', a Cabbalistic text, attributed to Rabbi Shimon Bar Yochay: Gershom Gerhard Scholem, *Major Trends in Jewish Mysticism* (Jerusalem, 1941), pp. 398-99.

16. Blavatsky, *The Secret Doctrine*, I, p. xxx.

planetary chains, each of which comprises seven worlds, but only one of these is physical and visible. The other worlds are made up of different energy materials and exist on parallel planes. There is an infinite number of planetary chains, and they exist only in the four lower planes of the seven planes of creation. The highest planes exist in an archetypical universe. Each planetary chain is the offspring of a chain which had completed its function, has died and remains on a lower plane, so that it may be regarded as a reincarnation of the defunct chain.[17]

The Secret Doctrine then proceeds to discuss symbols and their meanings. Blavatsky referred to Max Müller's theory of the Solar Myth, arguing that modern scholars did not have the wherewithal to comprehend the ancient myths and symbols. These had been originally created by the practitioners of esoteric religions, who understood the magic power of the words and used pictorial symbols to describe what they had learned. The Egyptian hieroglyphs were a typical example of such a mysterious symbolic language, which is made up of anagrams, each of which represents a whole world. Nowadays the key to such knowledge, she argued, existed only among initiates in India.[18]

Blavatsky then returned to the subject of the Jews. Quoting her own *Isis Unveiled*, she wrote: 'They became a hybrid people... not alone with the Canaanites, but with every other nation or race they came in contact with.' The implication was that a nation of hybrids could not produce an original culture. Its religion and heritage would likewise be hybrid, a mongrel mixture derived from diverse sources and therefore unworthy of respect or study.[19]

The first volume of *The Secret Doctrine* concluded with arguments against modern historians, who distance themselves from the truth of ancient times, diminish it and demolish every position based on

---

17. Blavatsky, *The Secret Doctrine*, I, pp. 21–34, 101, 152, 574–75. For further reading, see, Julie Hall, 'The *Saptaparña*: The Meaning and Origins of the Theosophical Septenary Constitution of Man', *Theosophical History*, ed. James Santucci, Vol XIII, no. 4 (October, 2007), 5–38.

18. Blavatsky, *The Secret Doctrine*, I, pp. 303–11.

19. Blavatsky's criticism was directed primarily at the Christian Church. Taunting Judaism served her claims against its offspring. Indeed, she was never a fanatical anti-Semitist. However, It is worth noting that one of her close disciples, the Russian Theosophist Juliana Glinka (1844–1918), was the one who transferred the Protocols of the Elders of Zion from Paris to Russia, Norman Cohn, *Warrant for Genocide, The Myth of the Jewish World-Conspiracy and the Protocols of the Elders of Zion* (London, 1967), pp. 15–24, 100–101; Blavatsky, *The Secret Doctrine*, I, pp. 313, 444–45.

recognizing the wisdom of the ancients. Blavatsky also criticized the Orientalists, comparing their work to the damage caused by termites to ancient buildings in India. In the twentieth century, she maintained (prophetically?), history as an academic discipline would become a ragbag of meaningless details and be buried under an avalanche of hypotheses.[20]

Most of the second volume of *The Secret Doctrine* is devoted to a further expansion on issues that were raised in *Isis Unveiled* – the true history of the world, the civilizations and races that preceded mankind, and the conclusions to be drawn from these matters regarding the future of humanity. According to the secret doctrine as deduced from 'The Book of Dzian', seven human races developed simultaneously in seven different regions of the globe. They had been created by the seven divine forces described earlier. Man was essentially Logos, a reflection containing everything that exists. Man's creation was dual, because it entailed the creation of both body and soul.[21]

Back in the distant past there were four ancient continents which sank under the sea, among them Atlantis and Lemuria.[22] They were inhabited by the four human races that preceded our own. The fifth continent in the scale of human evolution (our species being the fifth), is contemporary Europe, in which the civilization of the Aryan race matured. Humanity is far older than the scientists maintain. It first appeared on our planetary chain exactly 1,664,500,987 years ago. Present-day humanity appeared as far back as 18,618,728 years ago. These figures, Blavatsky stated, were based on the calculation methods of the Arya Samaj. This meant that the great pyramid of Egypt was built very much earlier than the archaeologists maintain – in fact, 78,000 years ago. The new reckoning of human history would

20. Blavatsky, *The Secret Doctrine*, I, p. 676.

21. Accordingly, Blavatsky maintained that the Hindu swastika was a mystical Aryan symbol, which reflected the human condition. Its right side symbolized the human arm, pointing at the sky, while its left part symbolized the human connectedness with the earth. Thus, unintentionally, Blavatsky contributed to the later adaptation of the swastika by the Nazis: Blavatsky, *The Secret Doctrine*, I, pp. 25, 82, 98–99.

22. The myth of Lemuria was born in the 1860s in the minds of several Darwinists, headed by the German Ernest Haeckel (1834–1919) and the English Philip Scalter (1829–1913). When trying to explain the similarity between Indian and South African fossils, they invented the theory of 'Lemuria' – a continent believed to have formerly connected Asia and Africa.

promote the understanding that our civilization was preceded by ancient civilizations which were higher than our own.

As we have seen, Blavatsky wrote in *Isis Unveiled* about a mysterious island, settled by fugitives from Atlantis, that was linked to the rest of the world by subterranean tunnels. She returned to it in *The Secret Doctrine*, described the life of the inhabitants in great detail, and stated that every Brahmin or Yogi knew that the ancient temples in his country stood above the subterranean labyrinth which spread in all directions. The giant statues in the Easter Islands provided further visual evidence for the existence of ancient human civilizations and races. These statues depicted the fourth human race, the one directly preceding our own, whose members had fought against the Atlanean magicians. Understanding the true history as shown in *The Secret Doctrine* inevitably leads to the conclusion that a new human race, the sixth in the series, would appear simultaneously with the rise of a new, sixth continent, to which all the lucky survivors of the concurrent catastrophe would escape. The growth of the new race, with its diverse nations, would parallel the slow demise of our race over the next several thousand years.[23]

In the final part of *The Secret Doctrine* Blavatsky referred to Darwin's theory of evolution, and declared it to be baseless. She maintained that the similarity between man and gorilla did not indicate a common origin, but an ancient merger between astral beings and ape-like mammals. In a related connection she argued that the human races had mixed with the earlier races in history, which accounted for the 'mental superiority' of the Aryan race. The ancient Aryans mated with the last sons and daughters of Atlantis, and inherited some of their evolved spiritual abilities. In other words – the Aryan race was the direct heir of the Atlantean civilization.[24]

23. Blavatsky, *The Secret Doctrine*, I, pp. 6–8, see also, II, pp. 66–69, 221–24, 432, 445–46.
24. Blavatsky, *The Secret Doctrine*, II, pp. 688–89, see also p. 743. It is worth noticing that the Theosophical Karma doctrine served as an alternative to Darwin's evolution theory. Blavatsky's unique blend of science and spiritualism might have unintentionally influenced several serious scientists, who involved non-materialistic elements in their work. A good example of that is 1977 Nobel Prize recipient for Chemistry, Ilya Prigogine's (1917–2003) work, which formulated the theory of self-organization, which involves factors that balance chaos and equilibrium in nature. His follower, Erich Jantsch, crystallized these ideas into an orderly evolutionary theory, Hanegraaff, *New Age Religion and Western Culture*, pp. 72–73; Ilya Prigogine and Isabelle Stengers, *Order Out of Chaos: Man's New Dialogue with Nature* (Toronto,

This brief survey of *Isis Unveiled* and *The Secret Doctrine* shows that they were similar in content, in fanciful thinking blending fantasy with reality, and in their method of presentation involving constant confrontation with prominent academic scholars. While *Isis Unveiled* was published in the early days of the Theosophical Society, *The Secret Doctrine* appeared when the Society was already fairly well established in India, England and the United States. Its role, therefore, was to reinforce ideas presented in the earlier book, and offer new material to clarify the Theosophical worldview and to define the Society's goals henceforward. Blavatsky composed for the Society's followers an alternative history of the universe as a whole and of humanity in particular. Furthermore, she defined the 'historical' route by which the secret lore was transmitted through the various human races, from the era of Atlantis to our day. Her attitude towards India, as the source of esoteric lore in our time, was reworked since *Isis Unveiled* and refined in *The Secret Doctrine* into a more comprehensive concept, describing in detail the way in which the occult lore was passed from Atlantis to the ancient Aryans of India.

Blavatsky's self-presentation as the person responsible for bequeathing the occult knowledge to the world deserves scrutiny. While the overall impression made by *Isis Unveiled* is of a highly developed imagination and a longing for the magic of a fabulous world, *The Secret Doctrine* presents Blavatsky as the indispensable interpreter of ancient Oriental scriptures, notably the probably fictitious 'Book of Dzian.' While *Isis Unveiled* raised questions and queries and picked ideas from any number of sources, *The Secret Doctrine* offered decisive and authoritative answers. The difference between them reflects the personal development that Blavatsky underwent in the intervening period. Whereas in 1877 she was an unknown spiritualist, by 1888 she had become the grand priestess of a fashionable movement, a position she was able to retain despite the Hodgson Report and the breakup with Olcott. The continued rise of the Theosophical Society in the following years was undoubtedly helped by the success of Blavatsky's theological doctrine. This doctrine continued to develop after her death, mainly by her two most able disciples, Besant and Leadbeater.

1984); Erich Jantsch, *The Self-Organizing Universe: Scientific and Human Implications of the Emerging Paradigm of Evolution* (Oxford, 1980).

Besant's Doctrine

It has been the accepted view of historians of the Theosophical Society that Blavatsky was the Society's sole theologian, probably because Besant saw herself exclusively as Blavatsky's faithful disciple, and her contribution has been seen as adding feminist and political, rather than theological, elements. This, in my opinion, overlooks an important point. Though Besant adopted Blavatsky's doctrine, the way she developed it contributed significantly to two crucial aspects. First, she popularized the Theosophical esoteria by presenting its principal ideas in an ordered and straightforward manner, in contrast to the disorder and excess which characterized Blavatsky's presentation. Secondly, she helped to further develop the idea of the World Teacher, which from the second decade of the twentieth century became a paramount one for the Theosophists.

Annie Besant succeeded Blavatsky as the leader of the esoteric current of the Theosophical Society following the founder's death in 1891. In 1907, after Olcott's death, Besant was elected president of the international Society. In the next decade the Theosophical message grew increasingly nationalistic, as the Theosophical Society became a decisive factor in the modern Indian national awakening. Having concluded her role in India's national leadership, Besant concentrated on the promotion of the World Teacher – Jiddu Krishnamurti. What follows is an analysis of selected articles and books by Besant, with the emphasis on the area in which she made the decisive contribution – the renewed appearance of a World Teacher.

Besant's first important book, *Esoteric Christianity*, was published in London in 1901. It contained the principal elements of her thought, some of which would later evolve further and distinguish her doctrine from that of her mentor. The most noteworthy were the Christian religion (or, at any rate, Besant's interpretation of it), Hermetic and neo-Platonic philosophy, early Theosophical philosophy (mainly that of Meister Eckhart (1260–1328) and Jacob Böhme (1575–1624), and a Blavatsky-like mixture of scientific influences based on the current scholarship of comparative religion and anthropology.

The underlying argument in *Esoteric Christianity* was that the Christian church distorted the original message of Christ, preferring to entrust to a few individuals the true esoteric lore that he taught, rather than broadcast it far and wide. Besant sought to correct this distortion and present to as many people as possible the instructions of Jesus, which she claimed constituted the real Theosophy. Yet, as people vary in their capabilities while being in a constant evolutionary process, they are offered religious teaching in different measures, according to their needs. That is why the high esoteric lore is possessed by a very few, those who are fit, in evolutionary terms, to receive it and employ it correctly. Accordingly, there are some rules of conduct that the students of esoteric studies must follow – principally purity, selflessness and self-control. The Masters, who laid down these rules, considered strong moral fibre to be more important than intellectual development.

Esoteric Christianity surveyed the history of the occult lore, with references to various neo-Platonist sources, such as Iamblicus (d. c. 330), Proclus (c. 410–85) and Porphyry (c. 232–c.304). Besant also drew on contemporary studies of comparative mythology, which claimed that religious teachers in ancient times had risen above their cohorts and taught Truth, which deteriorated into mythology over the centuries. She made no reference to Max Müller, whose scholarly career was based on developing this formula, but made use of the work of his rival, Andrew Lang, and his studies in the field of religious anthropology. According to Besant, the sources of secret knowledge were found in Central Asia, where the Grand Lodge of the Masters was located. This lodge – whose siting conformed with the Orientalist theses concerning the origin of the ancient Aryan race – helped to propagate the occult lore in various countries, including ancient Egypt and the land of Israel. Throughout Western history, the Masters made sure to introduce this knowledge to select individuals, among them Thomas Aquinas, Giordano Bruno, Meister Eckhart, Jacob Böhme, Paracelsus (1493–1541), Christian Rosenkreuz, St. Germain and others.

In *Esoteric Christianity* Besant defined the elements that made up the image of Jesus. These elements would later become essential parts of the Theosophical campaign to promote the World Teacher. The figure of Jesus, according to Besant, could be divided into three categories – the historical, the mythical and the mystical Jesus. The historical Jesus (i.e., the real person known by that name) was born, according to Besant, in 105 BCE, and studied the mystical tradition in a monastery in the Judaean desert, later in a monastery in the Sinai Peninsula, on Mount Serbal, which housed a library of secret wisdom that had originated in the Himalaya. Later Jesus went to

Egypt, where he was initiated by the Egyptian Lodge of the Masters. Western civilization had not yet been born, but the time had come for the appearance of the powers which arise at the start of a new era and attend the birth of the new civilization. The spiritual hierarchy which directs human evolution sent a guide to help the new Western civilization on its way, and this guide materialized in Jesus' physical body in his last three years.

The mythical Jesus was an image connected with the Solar Myth, itself an expression of belief in the Logos as the ancient truth. The life stories of sun deities in ancient cultures older than Christianity contained elements of death and resurrection similar to those of Jesus and Mary – for example, the story of Isis and Horus in Egypt and the Hindu Devaki and Krishna. The mystical Jesus is the embodiment of the Logos in human flesh. The story of his earthly crucifixion was the human interpretation of Man's cosmic crucifixion. The mystical image was linked to the human figure of Jesus and became part of his human biography, unconnected to reality – like the Holy Trinity, which in fact expressed the three divine aspects of the human spirit: intelligence, love and will.[25]

These ideas would remain the foundation of Besant's thought in the coming years. The emphasis given in this book to the supposed original nature of Christianity would remain one of the dominant issues that preoccupied her when she was building up the myth of the World Teacher around her protégé Krishnamurti during the first three decades of the twentieth century. The myth served to link Christian messianic beliefs to Theosophical theology. Although the subject was of Indian origin, his intended public was Western. In effect, the myth of the World Teacher was essentially a Christian one, as the Western followers of the Theosophical Society identified Krishnamurti not merely as a modern personification of Jesus Christ, but as his actual physical incarnation.[26]

This idea – the birth of the new human race and the appearance of a new World Teacher who would guide it –matured significantly in Besant's writings. In 1912, she declared that the current World Teacher, who arose in order to guide the fifth (Teutonic) Aryan sub-race, was the successor of the Buddha and Jesus. She also asserted

---

25. Annie Besant, *Esoteric Christianity, or the Lesser Mysteries* (London, 1901), pp. vii-x, 15-19, 33-35, 112-19, and 130-83.

26. Annie Besant, *The Coming Christ* (Chicago, 1927), p. 24.

that there were signs of a new continent rising in the Pacific Ocean. Every time a new continent rose, she stated, there were indications of the birth of a new human root-race destined to inhabit it. However, our fifth root-race had so far comprised only five sub-races, though six are needed before a new root-race can arise. The solution to this problem, Besant suggested, lay in America, where scientists report the rise of a new man, unlike his predecessors in physical measurements and facial features. She stated that English people who visit their American 'cousins' every few years are amazed by the spreading of this new sub-race, which looks intellectual and strong-willed, as indicated by the set of his jaws, different and distinct from his forerunners. History shows, she asserted, that each time a new sub-race appears, so does a new World Teacher. She contended that this development was now due.[27]

Besant listed other reasons for expecting the imminent appearance of a World Teacher. Aside from the social need for change, evidenced in the economic exploitation of certain classes, more and more people with supernatural abilities were making their appearance in the world, chiefly in the United States. This, she said, was due to changes in the global climate and the electric charge in the atmosphere, which affects the human nervous system and enhances its capacity to foresee the future. Such changes characterized the inter-era periods, which herald the birth of a new human race.[28]

In 1913 Besant published a collection of lectures, some of which she had given in London and some in Stockholm at the annual world conference of the Theosophical Society. In these lectures she discussed the divine plan for the development of human civilization. She maintained that all the great civilizations of antiquity appeared to spring, like the one in Egypt, from nothing. Nevertheless, it must be understood that human civilization grows incrementally, like the floors of a building, logically and at an orderly pace. There are, therefore, differences among the descendants of the Aryan sub-races which reflect the progress of human evolution. The descendants of the fourth Aryan sub-race, the Celts, reached Europe via Greece and spread through the Continent. Their characteristics, which we observe in their descendants, the French, are marked by their admiration for aesthetics per se. In this they differ from the

27. Annie Besant, *Initiation: the Perfecting of Man* (London, 1912), pp. 97, 117–23.
28. Annie Besant, *Theosophy and the New Psychology* (London, 1904), p. 73.

offspring of the fifth sub-race, the Teutons, in whose German and English descendants we find a greater tendency to science than to art. The sixth sub-race, which was just beginning to arise and take shape, is characterized by a strong development of the intuition. The future society, to which this sub-race would give rise, would need to use a political and social structure characterized by the strong commitment of all its children. Something of this nature, Besant argued, had existed in ancient India, where – as the caste system showed – all the inhabitants saw themselves as inseparable parts of the social organism.

In these lectures Besant connected the figure of the Western World Teacher, or Christos, with that of the Oriental World Teacher, the Bodhisattva. She argued that the history of the five Aryan sub-races corresponded to the history of the five Aryan religions – Hinduism, the religion of ancient Egypt, the Zoroastrian religion, the Greek school of philosophy, and Christianity. The World Teacher who came in the past to guide the first Aryan sub-races concluded his task after having materialized as Gautama the Buddha. The World Teacher now expected by the Theosophists, the one who was once incarnated as Jesus, had earlier been incarnated as Krishna.[29]

World Teachers belong to remote branches of humanity that we cannot conceive of. Their spiritual growth, from the human to the super-human, led their minds to merge with the divine Logos itself, like a prodigal son returning to his father. Thanks to the evolutionary process they undergo, they can become incorporated anew in any race and in any world they choose. For the ancient Egyptians the term that described it was the birth of Horus, for the Christians – incarnation, and for the Hindus – avatar. The Bodhisattva, or World Teacher, is the highest being there is, the supreme teacher not only of men but also of angels and archangels, who are called Devas in the Orient. The seat of the Bodhisattva is always occupied, because the world is never left without a Teacher to guide it.

The World Teachers who came to planet Earth in the past in order to guide the Aryan sub-races were known by various names, though in most cases they were the same entity. The first World Teacher of the first Aryan sub-race was the Buddha, who in his earlier life as a man belonged to the Aryan root-race. The World Teacher of

---

29. Annie Besant, *Superhuman Men in History and in Religion* (London, 1913), pp. 6–12, 37–51.

the second Aryan sub-race – which had spread westwards from East Asia and led to the Aryanisation of the Arab countries, North Africa and the Mediterranean littoral – was known as Hermes, and according to Besant, was known in the Hermetic literature by the name of Hermes Trismegistus. The World Teacher of the third Aryan sub-race, who brought about the Aryanisation of Persia, was known as Zoroaster (Zarathustra). The World Teacher of the fourth sub-race, the Celtic, was Orpheus, and the World Teacher of the fifth sub-race was known as Jesus. Besant stated that there was little likelihood that the Teacher whose arrival was imminent would be widely welcomed. Nonetheless, he would come and would walk among us, as he had done before in Palestine. It was possible, she noted hopefully, that the human race had reached a sufficiently high spiritual development so that the World Teacher would be able to stay among us longer than the three years he had spent on earth the last time.[30]

Another important sphere which always preoccupied Besant was psychology. In 1904 she published a book in which she tried to associate modern psychology with Theosophy. The timing reflected the rising importance of psychology in the contemporary scientific discourse.[31] Besant proposed a 'vital theory' for

---

30. Annie Besant, *The Coming Christ*, pp. 5-27.

31. Sigmund Freud (1856-1939) published 'The Interpretation of Dreams' in 1899, 'Psychopathology of Everyday Life' in 1901, and 'Three Essays on the Theory of Sexuality' in 1905. Besant's book was published, therefore, in the midst of a rising tide of interest in psychology. One should notice that Freud himself had researched for many years subjects that appear to belong to Besant's spheres rather than to the arena of rationalistic science, speaking mainly of his lifelong interest in telepathy, which he was researching together with his daughter, Anna (1895-1982) and colleague, Sandor Ferenczi (1873-1933), Sigmund Freud, 'The Uncanny', in *The Standard Edition of the Complete Psychological Works of Sigmund Freud*, ed. James Strachey, XVII (London, 1953), pp. 219-52, first published in German 1919; Sigmund Freud, *Psychopathology of Everyday Life*, trans. Anthea Bell (London, 2002), first published in German 1901; Sigmund Freud, *The Interpretation of Dreams*, trans. Joyce Crick (Oxford, 1999), first published in German 1899; Sigmund Freud, *Three Essays on the Theory of Sexuality*, trans. James Strachey (London, 1962), first published in German 1905; Sigmund Freud, *The Collected Papers of Sigmund Freud*, ed. Philip Rieff, x: Studies in Parapsychology (New York, 1963); Roger Luckhurst, *The Invention of Telepathy, 1870-1901* (Oxford, 2002), pp. 71-76.

Freud's esteemed colleague, and for sometime heir, Karl Gustav Jung (1885-1961), delved into the occult studies, in his search for archetypical elements in the religions of the East and of the West. Jung contributed greatly to the formation of New Age thought, and was one of the first to mix modern psychology and Eastern

what she dubbed 'the new psychology' – that which was ready to examine exceptional facts with an open mind. She maintained that in the course of evolution, Man had acquired several kinds of consciousness, which co-existed in his mind, layer upon layer. Our bodies still contain traces of animal consciousness, as well as the consciousness of a savage and of a partially-civilized man, capped by the 'larger consciousness', which is our true Self. Beyond all these there is another, higher consciousness, linked to the Higher Self, which is neither born nor dies. It is ancient, continuous and consistent, and can be identified with the divine element that is in us. The mechanism of this consciousness is made up of obsessions, dreams and telepathy.[32] Besant remained interested in the elements of human consciousness throughout her life. For example, in 1922 she argued that it is possible to change one's character by the daily use of the power of thought, imagining all that one wishes and thus turning the wishes into reality in one's lifetime. Character is not fixed, and may therefore be changed by the meditative practice of feeling and thought.[33]

The two principal subjects discussed above – the appearance of the World Teacher and the analysis of Man's higher consciousness – were the dominant issues that preoccupied Annie Besant. Her close friend Charles Webster Leadbeater developed these themes in his own way and helped to make them into integral elements of the Theosophical doctrine.

---

philosophy. His primal therapeutic interest in spiritualism is evidenced in several cases he reported, among them the case of a young patient (S.W.) who claimed to communicate with spirits. Jung participated in séances and tried to scientifically explain automatic writing, table turnings, and the like. In order to understand his patient's hallucinations, he spent many hours in reading occultist literature. His work was primarily rationalistic and scientific. Nevertheless, Jung's reports of his interest in the occult may indicate the field's relative legitimacy in the early twentieth century: C.G. Jung, 'On the Psychology and Pathology of So-Called Occult Phenomena', in *Psychology and the Occult* (Princeton, 1977), pp. 6–91: first published in German 1902; C.G. Jung, 'On Spiritualistic Phenomena', in *Psychology and the Occult*, pp. 92–107, first published in German 1905; C.G. Jung, *The Psychology of Kundalini Yoga*, notes of the Seminar Given in 1932, ed. Sonu Shamdasani (Princeton, 1996), p. 68; C.G. Jung, *Psychology and the East* (Princeton, 1978); Paul Heelas, *The New Age Movement: The Celebration of the Self and the Sacralization of Modernity* (Bodmin, 1996), p. 46; Hanegraaff, *New Age Religion and Western Culture*, pp. 496–501.

32. Besant, *Theosophy and the New Psychology*, pp. 23–29.
33. Besant, *Theosophical Christianity* (London, 1922), pp. 34–35, 50–55.

Leadbeater's Doctrine

Charles Webster Leadbeater joined the Theosophical Society in 1884, and quickly rose through its ranks, perhaps because he was a clergyman. The leaders of the Society probably regarded his conversion as a triumph over the Christian establishment they detested. Leadbeater was trained by Sinnett, the strong man in the London Lodge during the 1880s, and soon became a favourite with Blavatsky during her stay in England in 1884, shortly before the publication of the Hodgson Report. Leadbeater accompanied Blavatsky on her journey back to Adyar that year, and stayed on in India after his patroness returned to Europe. After her death, in 1891, he set out to succeed her in para-normal subjects, and indeed most of his writings dealt with similar matters to those that preoccupied Blavatsky, and he too claimed to examine occult lore with scientific tools. Leadbeater became Annie Besant's confidant and close friend and accompanied her for many years as her Number Two in the Society's hierarchy (although not formally), until 1914, when he decided to move to Australia. The two friends would spend together many hours, sometimes stretching into several days, during which they experienced supernatural visions. These visions, and the insights derived from them, were the raw material for books which covered diverse issues, from the qualities of Man's non-physical bodies to reconstructions of the 'true' history of the world. The following is a survey of a few of Leadbeater's principal writings, some of which he wrote in collaboration with Besant and some on his own. Their joint writings are markedly different in character and style from those written by Besant alone – so presumably the dominant contributor was Leadbeater.

Leadbeater's originality, as well as the impact of his ideas on the New Age movement, can already be found in his book *Thought Forms*, published in 1901. Written in collaboration with Besant, it described experiences of super-natural vision. The book discussed the auras which supposedly envelop all living creatures, claiming to analyse scientifically the aura's features and the way they are affected by thought. Wilhelm Röntgen's (1845–1923) discovery of the x-rays, six years prior to the publication of *Thought Forms*, might have influenced Leadbeater's pretension to scientifically analyse the rays produced by the astral body. Leadbeater and Besant believed that a human being has astral and mental bodies

Charles Webster Leadbeater, 1914 (reproduced by Yanai Zeltzer)

in addition to the physical one. The astral body, which is that of the passions, accounts for the aura of an undeveloped human being. It is limited to the astral plane, which is dominated by the animal nature of the human consciousness. By contrast, the mental body radiates brilliant colours that shine brightly the more developed the intellect and the more it engages in pure and sublime matters. Leadbeater claimed that the thought process produces vibrations associated with the mental body, visible to those who are capable of seeing them. The further it is from its source the weaker the vibration, but when it encounters another mental body it affects it and creates in the encountered mind similar thoughts to its own. *Thought Forms* offered a number of visual examples of various kinds of thoughts and auras. It interpreted the significance of the different colours the human auras supposedly radiate, and proposed a kind of guide to evaluating human beings according to the colours of their auras.[34]

Leadbeater and Besant went on with a series of supposedly scientific experiments of this sort. A book they published in 1908 described the most outstanding experiment, detailing 57 chemical elements, some of them unknown to science, such as Adyarium and Occultum.[35] A curious reference to this book was made in 1943 by the Ceylonese Jinarajadasa (1873–1953), a former disciple of Leadbeater's, who would later preside over the world Theosophical Society between 1945 and 1953. He wrote to Cambridge Professor Francis Aston (1877–1945), recipient of the Nobel Prize for Chemistry in 1922, to inform him that a considerable portion of his scientific discoveries had in fact been made long before by Leadbeater and Besant.[36]

The year 1913 was especially fruitful for Leadbeater. He published two thick volumes, one all his own and one written in collaboration with Besant. The first, *The Hidden Side of Things*, was a kind of summary of his long years of occult research. It surveyed,

---

34. For example, the presence of black colour in one's aura indicates hatred and evil, while red implies anger, and pale yellow indicates high intellect. Moreover, there are archetypical symbols that may appear in one's aura, which may be perceived by people who are capable of super-natural sight. Such is the golden star of David, surrounded by a pale yellow circle, which stands for the comprehension of the cosmic order, Annie Besant and C.W. Leadbeater, *Thought-Forms* (Wheaton, 1986), pp. 5–13, 21–25, 59–67, first published 1901.

35. These terms may indicate their graveness rather than their developed sense of humor, Annie Besant and C.W. Leadbeater, *The Book of Occult Chemistry* (Adyar, 1908).

36. Annie Besant and C.W. Leadbeater, *Occult Chemistry Investigations*, ed. C. Jinarajadasa (Adyar, 1946), pp. 1–4.

over two volumes, the influence of the external world upon Man, and Man's influence upon the external world, as interpreted by the principles of occult lore. The book purported to guide the person seeking the right way of life, from the food one consumes and the habits of drinking and smoking, to the right perception of the world and of one's place in the natural and human systems. The motive for writing this book was the recognition that an era was about to end and a new one begin, in which Man would need to attain perfection, to a far greater degree than at present.[37]

A similarly prophetic and portentous air hangs over the collaborative work produced by Leadbeater and Besant, *Man: Whence, How and Whither*, which appeared the same year. It purported to survey the 'true' history of the world and of humanity, in the spirit of Blavatsky's *The Secret Doctrine*, and offered a vision of the future with answers to questions about the future of the human species. This vision of the future was especially intriguing, because, as we shall see, it revealed the authors' political-racial philosophy. The book was based on research carried out at Adyar in the course of 1910, when Leadbeater and Besant would go into a trance, while two of their confidants recorded their words, which the authors predicted would be viewed in the future as 'pioneering work'.

In the historical narrative in *Man: Whence, How and Whither* certain figures appear and are reborn in various incarnations, and always influence the unfolding of history. The most prominent of these reincarnations were the one originally named Mars, now Master Morya; Mercury – now Master Koot-Hoomi; Vulcan – later Thomas More; and Mahaguru – the Bodhisattva who has previously been incorporated as Hermes-Toth, Zoroaster, and the Buddha. Significantly, among these entities who kept being reborn in order to play crucial roles in human history were many members of the Theosophical Society, such as Alcyone – now Krishnamurti, Herakles – now incorporated in Annie Besant's female body, Phocea – currently William Quan Judge, Sirius – now Leadbeater himself, and Ulysses, incorporated as Olcott.

The first five chapters of the book discuss the planetary chains, such as the chain of the moon (originally a separate planet), which was an evolutionary precursor of the chain of planet Earth. The chain of our sister-planets was also different in the past, when the surface

---

37. C.W. Leadbeater, *The Hidden Side of Things*, II (Adyar, 1913), pp. 347–48.

of Mars was inhabited by developed life forms and resembled Earth. At a certain point, determined by the programme of creation, various kinds of entities began to arrive on earth, coming mainly from other planets linked to our chain, namely Mercury and the Moon, the latter too having once been inhabited and about to end its evolutionary role. About 200,000 BCE the continent of Atlantis met a catastrophe, caused by the practice of black magic. Most of the continent disappeared under the waters, leaving only two large islands – Ruta and Daitya. In 75,025 BCE another catastrophe plunged these islands too under the ocean we call the Atlantic. While the Atlantean civilization flourished, its offspring built daughter-civilizations in Egypt, India, Mesopotamia and America. In that early era those civilizations reached technological and spiritual attainments that the present members of the Aryan race are still far from achieving. For example, the Atlantean conquerors of Egypt built the great pyramids, including the one that the Pharaoh Cheops would much later claim as his own achievement. Nevertheless, Leadbeater and Besant assumed that in another few centuries the heirs of the Atlanteans, namely the members of the Aryan race, would attain even greater achievements.

The plans that led eventually to the creation of the Aryan race had begun to take shape a million years ago, when the Lord of the Moon, named Manu in the ancient Hindu texts, decided to create his civilization on Earth. The career of the Aryan race began not long before the second catastrophe that befell Atlantis, when the Lord of the Moon initiated the enhancement of a group of human beings, who were five-sixths of Aryan origin and one sixth Atlantean. These people settled 60,000 years ago in the region of today's Gobi Desert, and after a long time, during which they were further shaped, began to settle the globe. The Aryan migration began about 40,000 BCE, when the first and second Aryan sub-races conquered China and Japan, Formosa and Siam, Sumatra and Java, as well as Australia, which was previously inhabited by the members of Lemuria, of the third root-race. The first effort to improve the members of the Aryan race involved a large group of people, who in their current incarnations held leading positions in the Theosophical Society. Leadbeater and Besant claimed that these individuals repeatedly opened the paths for humanity and served as its vanguard. This description reflects the self-image of the leaders of the Theosophical Society in the beginning of the twentieth century – or at any rate, the image they wished to convey to their followers.

Like Blavatsky's major writings, *Man: Whence, How and Whither* also discussed the Jews. According to the authors, the Jews had originally been a fanatical sect in Southern Arabia, who regarded themselves as pure by comparison with the corrupt culture surrounding them. At a certain stage they were induced by a prophet to leave their homeland and cross the Red Sea to the coast of Somalia. From there, after a few hundred years, they migrated to Egypt, where the Pharaohs welcomed them and even granted them privileges. But after a long stay in Egypt they fell out with a Pharaoh who wanted to cancel those privileges, and consequently moved to Palestine, where they became known as Jews. They still adhere to the theory that they are the Chosen People, without knowing its origin.

The people of the third Aryan sub-race, the Iranians, set out on their campaign of conquest in 30,000 BCE. The fourth Aryan sub-race, the Celts, were sent by the Lord of the Moon in 20,000 BCE to the Caucasus, from where they spread into Europe. Among their descendants were the ancient Greeks, who finally defeated the last Atlantean empire (an argument that was perhaps intended to show that Aryan superiority went that far back). The fifth Aryan sub-race, the Teutons, were developed in parallel with the fourth, and enhanced with various racial elements. The improvement produced tall, strong, good-looking people, fair-haired and blue-eyed.

Their migration took place in three settlement stages. The descendants of the first wave were today's Russians, Croats, Serbs and Bosnians; of the second wave – the Latvians, Lithuanians and Prussians; of the third – Germans, Scandinavians, Goths and Englishmen. These conquered central, western and southern Europe, and later (in our time) took possession of Australia, North America and India. With this 'historical' description Leadbeater and Besant explained the supposedly-natural and pre-planned developments, which had led up to the political world order at the start of the twentieth century. They stated that the fifth sub-race had not yet accomplished its historical role – in the course of the next few centuries this sub-race was destined to take over the entire world, aided by a union between Germany, England and the United States. In the resulting empire there would be a distinguished place for India, which was already beginning to rise again and occupy its proper position. The reason for India's high status was her unique historical role as the mother of Aryan wisdom. She first rose to that status in 18,875 BCE, when she began to be Aryanized. India was responsible for founding the Egyptian civilization, when a mission she sent over there in 13,500 BCE started a dynasty of Aryan kings, who ruled for thousands of years and made Egypt into a world centre of knowledge.

Man: Whence, How and Whither concludes with an interesting vision of the world in the distant future. Leadbeater and Besant proclaimed that the world would be ruled by a federation of nations centred in Europe, where there would be an institution similar to the German Reichstag, in which representatives of all the nations would serve in turn. The man who would create this new world order would be a reincarnation of Julius Caesar. The new order would make it possible for a reincarnation of Jesus to appear and bring back the one true religion. The future condition of the world would be positive, free from fear or wars. The people of the world would speak a new international language, a kind of shorthand version of English. Although all the world's nations would continue to exist, the world would in fact be ruled over by the British Empire, led by a king and a ministerial council, without a parliament, but guided by principles of justice. London, the world's capital, would be cleansed of its characteristic smog, and preserve many of its present buildings, such as St. Paul's Cathedral. The world's spiritual centre would naturally be in Adyar, where a university would be founded to investigate the Theosophical Society's second and third tenets – the first one having already been achieved. A palace resembling the Taj Mahal, only much bigger, would be built there. The role of the Theosophical Society in that world would be to assemble all the fields of science, literature and the ancient religions.[38]

This future vision, with its high position for Theosophy in a global political structure led by an Aryan empire, was the summit of the collaboration between Leadbeater and Besant. The work of Blavatsky's theologian-successors added new levels to the original Theosophical programme, and produced a prophetic foundation to provide the followers of the Society with a vision that would endow their activity with significance. This vision motivated

---

38. Annie Besant and C.W. Leadbeater, *Man: Whence, How and Whither* (Adyar, 1913), pp. 1-3, 7-8, 114-19, 133-40, 237-73, 275-76, 287-89, 293-322, 328-30, 454-66.

Besant's political aspirations in India in the second decade of the twentieth century. Understanding it helps to examine her work for India's national liberation, which she saw as an essential step towards constructing the future world that would live under Aryan hegemony.

Chapter 5

The Sources of the Theosophical Doctrine

The Theosophical doctrine had come a long way from the publication of *Isis Unveiled* in 1877 to the works of Besant and Leadbeater in the early twentieth century. By now there was a theological corpus designed to answer all the questions asked by the followers of the Society. Its authority rested on the implicit claim to a unique Theosophical 'revelation'. Though Theosophy never called itself an institutionalized religion, its leaders clearly sought to create the impression that they alone knew the road to the Truth.[1] Hence the present chapter will examine the degree of the Theosophical doctrine's uniqueness and originality. I seek to show that many of the Theosophical ideas were borrowed from diverse Western sources, and were worked by the theologians of the Society into a single doctrine. I try to answer the question under investigation by isolating and analysing these sources, while locating Theosophy on the map of the history of ideas, and show that it was part of an intellectual current that began long before Blavatsky.

The following is a review of pre-Theosophical persons and works that dealt with occult lore and obviously influenced Theosophical thought. The subject of occultism, with its multifarious sources, requires a very large study, both for the number of persons involved and the vast amount of material. I shall therefore concentrate on occult literature in the nineteenth century. Though this literature drew on earlier sources, it was this that influenced Blavatsky. Though the founder of Theosophy claimed to know Greek, Latin and even Sanskrit, in all probability her presumed familiarity with esoteric and religious writings, whether dating from antiquity or the renaissance, derived mainly from their descriptions in contemporary literature. This conclusion is based on the great similarity

---

1. See, for example, H.P. Blavatsky, 'Lodges of Magic', *Lucifer* (London, October, 1888).

between Blavatsky's writings and various accessible nineteenth century books. In fact, as we shall see, the synthesis she claimed to have created between the wisdom of the Orient and the wisdom of the West was largely a synthesis of the existing, diverse Western literature on occult lore.

I shall confine myself to a general survey of the various sources so as to shed light on their connection with Theosophy. Uncovering these connections may broaden the investigation of the Society's operations in India. In the first place, it sharpens the apparent discrepancy between the esoteric nature of the Society and its contribution to India's national liberation. The political-historical story of the early Indian national movement, with its links to the Theosophical Society, takes on a different hue in light of the esoteric elements of the Theosophical doctrine and its sources. On the other hand, isolating the sources of that doctrine helps to examine the real extent of the Theosophists' openness to the Indian culture. The political success of the Society in India, especially in the second decade of the twentieth century, was achieved on the basis of an intellectual equation that claimed to combine the wisdom of the Orient with that of the West. In this equation the Orient was assigned equal importance with the West, at least in terms of its philosophical-religious contribution. The equation was, at least formally, the main concern of the Theosophical Society during the many years when it laboured to revive the ancient Hindu philosophy. An examination of the theological sources of the Theosophical doctrine may challenge this perception, and if it is found that Theosophy drew its sources overwhelmingly from Western tradition, then this would diminish the true share of the Oriental tradition in Theosophical thought. Indeed, it would place some question marks over the Theosophical claim to promote a synthesis between East and West, and would make it possible to study the Society from a somewhat different viewpoint, as having been inspired by a typically Western approach to the ancient Hindu scriptures.

The implications are considerable, both with regard to the place of the Theosophical Society in the national Indian consciousness – as an ultimately Western institution – and to the motives of the Society itself, which might be seen to have acted from a patronizing spiritual-cultural position, rather than from a sincere appreciation of the real Hindu civilization. If Blavatsky, Besant and Leadbeater were indeed influenced by Hindu and Buddhist literature to the point when the Oriental thought became an integral part of their doctrine, then this could be taken as a genuine attempt at creating an East-West synthesis. But if the major part of their ideas was drawn from an essentially Western intellectual current, this would indicate a more patronizing stance, underpinned by an intellectual dogma that forced the wisdom of the Orient into a mental mould imported from the West.

Early Sources: Pre-Nineteenth Century

a. Hermeticism

Blavatsky's doctrine drew on a variety of sources, notably the Hermetic current in renaissance philosophy which was influenced by the neo-Platonic Gnostic school. In Blavatsky's day, Hermetic ideas were familiar to aficionados of esoteria, either from the original writings or via the esoteric renaissance of the nineteenth century, when numerous Hermetic works were published. Aside from the importance of this current in the history of occult lore, many of the esoteric writings of the nineteenth century (which in turn influenced Blavatsky) were its known and avowed inheritors. We may, therefore, locate Theosophy in that current, which is repeatedly mentioned in Blavatsky's writing. After all, she herself defined *Isis Unveiled* as 'a plea for the recognition of the Hermetic philosophy.'

The term 'Hermeticism' refers to a philosophy that is primarily identified with a set of ancient Egyptian texts known as the *Corpus Hermeticum*. It claimed to have been written by an early, semi-divine priest named Hermes Trismegistus in pharaonic times. This self-dating led to the Hermetic corpus being thought of as one of the oldest written texts, if not the oldest of all. In reality, it was compiled in Egypt circa the second century CE.[2] It concerns the ways in which Man may achieve enlightenment and advance towards the deity, and also offers an alternative story of the Creation. In it the deity, or Logos, is an androgynous being which exists in the form of light. The deity created two other major forces before it created

---

2. Isaac Casaubon, the Anglo-Swiss humanist (1559–1614), was the first to accurately date the *Corpus Hermeticum* to the second century: Frances A. Yates, *Giordano Bruno and the Hermetic Tradition* (Chicago, 1991), pp. 398–402, first published 1964; Anthony Grafton, *Forgers and Critics, Creativity and Duplicity in Western Scholarship* (Princeton, 1990), pp. 88–89.

Man in its own image, fell in love with him and taught him the secret of Creation. The first force was a generative god who created the physical universe we inhabit, and the second in the form of seven rulers, or 'deans' (identified with the seven planets in ancient astrology), who live in the sphere of Creation and are responsible for the world of the senses and for fate. Man, having once become aware of the acts of his 'brother', the creative god, wished likewise to possess the powers of creation. The Logos god agreed and brought Man into the sphere of creation, among the deans who endowed him with their powers. Man was thus originally an equal of the creative deity, and his high position in the hierarchy of creation was almost identical with that of the Logos god itself. According to the Hermetic view, Man's creative potential turned him from a helpless creature, bearing the consequences of the original sin (as held by the Christian dogma), into a divine being empowered to take part in ruling the world and directing its moves.

The Hermetic narrative, like the Bible, describes a fall from paradise, or a cosmic disruption which occurred when Man became enamored with nature, which is described as a feminine being. Their union resulted in Man having a dual nature, whose soul remained immortal but who became mortal when he acquired a physical body following his union with nature. Man is master of all ephemeral things, yet is still a subject of death, being bound by the forces of fate. Although Man's original nature was above the cosmic system, following his union with nature he became subjugated by it. Thus Man became subordinate to the laws of nature, fertility and death, whose nature derives from the world of the senses, the dark and watery element. The Hermetic conclusion is that it may be possible to set right the cosmic error which caused Man to fall from his primordial state. The way to achieve this begins with liberation from the world of the senses and concludes with the recovery of Man's original powers, the restoration of his divine image and the abolition of the curse of death.[3]

The magic means of attaining this goal arises from the central Hermetic view that the universe, at all levels, is made up of the same materials – i.e., that which is above, in the divine spheres, is the same as that which is below, in the earthly worlds. Therefore a magical

---

3. Brian P. Copenhaver, *Hermetica: The Greek Corpus Hermeticum and the Latin Asclepius* (Cambridge, 1992), pp. 1–7.

operation in our world would affect the other worlds, too, and vice versa. This conclusion was further refined during the renaissance by magicians, or magi, who rediscovered the Hermetic lore which had been forgotten in the West following its suppression by Catholic Christianity.[4] In effect, they reworked the theoretical basis for the modern practice of esoteria. The leading figure was Marsilio Ficino, the court translator of the Medici family in Florence. He was the first to translate the *Corpus Hermeticum* into Latin, when it was brought to Florence by Greek monks who fled from Constantinople after it fell to the Ottomans in 1453.

The influence of the Hermetic Corpus is plain to see in Ficino's writing. He wrote that Man was the deity's representative on earth. Man has a dual nature, because while dominating the material work, he also exists in the ethereal sphere. This duality is also found in the human soul, which has a divided nature, being in part on the divine plane and in part on the earthly one.[5] He was preoccupied with this duality his entire life. 'Were there not within us divine power, and were our minds not of heavenly origin, we could in no way acknowledge the insufficiency of mortal things and we should certainly never reason beyond, or pursue anything above, the physical level.'[6]

Ficino defined the soul as the centre of human existence, apart from the physical existence, because it belonged to another, astral body which was influenced by the planets and imprinted by their distinctive operations. He stated that each soul, as it falls into a physical body, bears a basic pattern corresponding to its dominant planet, and imprints it on its astral body.[7] His belief in the existence of the astral body matured in his book *De Vita* (Book of Life),

---

4. St. Augustine was one of the chief suppressors of the Hermetic doctrine and its 'prophet', Hermes Trismegistus, whom he widely objected in his *Civitas Dei*. It seems that of all the pagan rituals he had objected, the Hermetic ritual of Theurgy (the summoning of spirits into sculptures) attracted his harshest criticism, St. Augustine, *City of God* (New York, 1958), pp. 165–69.

5. Marsilio Ficino, 'The Soul of Man', excerpt from 'Theologia Platonica', *Journal of the History of Ideas* (April, 1944), pp. 28–30; Marsilio Ficino, *Meditations on the Soul: Selected Letters of Marsilio Ficino*, trans. Members of the Language Department of the School of Economic Science, London (Letter to Jacopo Bracciolini), (Rochester, 1996), p. 41, first published 1975.

6. Ficino, *Meditations on the Soul*, (Letter to Giovanni Nesi), pp. 53–56.

7. Marsilio Ficino, *Commentary on Plato's Symposium on Love*, trans. Sears Jayne (Dallas, 1964), p. 113.

published in 1489, which dealt with medicine based on Hermetic principles, and is regarded as one of the most comprehensive works on magic in the renaissance. This work made a major impact on the Hermetic movement as a whole, including Theosophy.

De Vita expressed the Hermetic view that 'as below, so it is above' – meaning, that the higher and nether worlds consist of the same elements. To Ficino, this meant that Man is made up of the same substances as the celestial worlds – soul, spirit and body – and was therefore a microcosm reflecting the divine macrocosm. Hence Man's soul works in the same way as the soul of the universe, and serves as the link through which life streams into the physical body, through the mediation of the spirit. The man who wishes to develop spiritually must strive to take in as much as possible of the higher elements of the universe, by drawing the world spirit into his own. This process is facilitated by cleansing his spirit as much as possible of material and mental pollution. It is likewise possible to draw astral influence from the world of stones and plants, which store planetary powers. For example, a man seeking a particular planetary influence may wear a ring set with the stone associated with the said planet, thus affecting his health or fate accordingly.[8]

This was the basis of Ficino's belief that, once having understood the connections and reciprocal influences of the world elements, Man can work a magic of creation, or natural magic. By way of illustration, Ficino described the resonance created by two facing lutes – the sound produced by plucking a string of one lute causes the same string to vibrate in the other, although it is untouched. In a similar way, a magus can use music to cure insanity, as Saul was healed by David.[9] Thus by means of natural magic the diverse elements of the universe are linked together until they become identical.[10]

---

8. Marsilio Ficino, *Book of Life*, trans. Charles Boer (Woodstock, 1994), pp. 96, 115, 123–24, first published 1980. These ideas remind, not surprisingly, of one of the more fashionable fields in New Age thought – the belief in the healing power of crystals: Wouter J. Hanegraaff, *New Age Religion and Western Culture, Esotericism in the Mirror of Secular Thought* (New York, 1998), p. 18, first published 1996.

9. Blavatsky used the same analogy, almost word by word: H.P. Blavatsky, *Isis Unveiled: A Master-Key to the Mysteries of Ancient and Modern Science and Theology*, I (Pasadena, 1998), p. 215, first published 1877.

10. Brian Vickers, 'Analogy Versus Identity: The Rejection of Occult Symbolism, 1580–1680', in *Occult and Scientific Mentalities in the Renaissance*, ed. Brian Vickers (New York, 1986), p. 123, first published 1984.

The Sources of the Theosophical Doctrine

Another interesting point in Ficino's thought is his seven-runged ladder of creation, or planetary chain, which must be climbed in order to join the deity. Each stage of that ladder is connected to one of the planets to certain physical or spiritual substances.[11] This could have inspired Blavatsky's planetary chains, but where Ficino contented himself with a description of the planets in keeping with current cosmology, Blavatsky developed the chain to include planets made of other, non-physical, matter.

Ficino was the first of a long line of European magi. Probably the most prominent of his successors was Giordano Bruno, whom Western historical perception, including that of the Theosophists, has depicted as a martyr of progress and the enlightenment, sacrificed by the ignorance and intolerance of the Church of Rome. This image rests mainly on Bruno's attempts to promote the Copernican theory, which conflicted with the Church dogma. The image was created in the nineteenth century by such scholars as Draper, who ignored Bruno's actual ideas, which were basically Hermetic, as his writings show. Indeed, to Bruno the appeal of the Copernican theory was that it was heliocentric, like the Hermetic doctrine.

Bruno's reputation rested on his 'art of memory', which he demonstrated and taught in a number of royal courts, including that of France's Henri III, who invited him to an audience in 1581. Bruno's description of the interview sheds light on his Hermetic thinking: 'I gained such a name, that King Henri III summoned me one day and asked me whether the memory which I had taught was a natural memory or obtained by magic art; I proved to him that it was not obtained by magic art but by science.'[12] This would seem to support the widespread notion that Bruno was an early scientist whose main interest was in knowledge per se, rather than in magic.[13] But that is because he regarded the fields of Hermetic magic as belonging to natural magic and as a natural science that could be investigated, taught and developed. His theory of memory was no exception, and he made it into a Hermetic art of memory,

---

11. Ficino, *Book of Life*, p. 159.
12. Frances A. Yates, *The Art of Memory* (Chicago, 1999), p. 200, first published 1966.
13. Some historians regard Bruno as an early philosopher of science. Such views are based on a shallow reading of Bruno, disregarding the true nature of his beliefs. See, for example, Hilary Gatti, *Giordano Bruno and Renaissance Science* (New York, 1999), pp. 2-9.

bound up with occult lore.¹⁴ There was no great distance from this idea to the Theosophical claim of including the study of the occult among the sciences.

Bruno's magical practice involved the art of bonding different elements, an idea which rested (like Ficino's) on the concept of a seven-runged ladder of creation along which all the movement in the cosmos flows. The deity is located above this ladder and acts upon all the different entities that exist on its rungs. The flow is two-directional and ceaseless, so that the deity, whose benevolence emanates from the top level down to the least life-form, in turn receives what flows up the ladder from the bottom. Bruno's theory also included an extensive hierarchy of demons, and was based on the magical levels of the ladder of creation.

Bruno maintained, furthermore, that there exists in the world an ancient symbolic language of divine origin, with which it is possible to communicate with the spirit world. He thought that the Egyptian hieroglyphs were originally such a language, whose knowledge was lost together with the Egyptian magical lore. This language was one of the objectives he pursued, because he saw it as the solution to the cognitive problem that preoccupied him, namely, the indirect connection with reality. Knowledge of this language would provide the means of creating a consciousness of uniform images and symbols, which would enable the soul to come into direct contact with reality.¹⁵ Bruno's thought was of a kind that influenced much later theories, including Blavatsky's. It rested on the idea that the magical world is inseparable from the one we know, and that the art of magic should be regarded as a science.

Ficino and Bruno represented a widespread phenomenon that would be further developed by a large number of magi in the sixteenth and seventeenth centuries, among them Pico della Mirandola (1470–1533), Paracelsus, John Dee (1527–1608), Tommaso Campanella (1568–1639) and others.¹⁶ Their ideas persisted into the

---

14. Yates, *The Art of Memory*, pp. 199–230.

15. Giordano Bruno, 'On Magic', in Giordano Bruno, *Cause, Principle and Unity, and Essays on Magic* (Cambridge, 1998), pp. 105–109, 113–15, 130–31.

16. For further reading on the renaissance magi, see, D.P. Walker, *Spiritual and Demonic Magic from Ficino to Campanella* (London, 1958); *Secrets of Nature, Astrology and Alchemy in Early Modern Europe*, ed. William R. Newman and Anthony Grafton (Cambridge, MA, 2001); *Art, Science, and History in the Renaissance*, ed. Charles S. Singleton (Baltimore, 1968); *Hermeticism and the Renaissance: Intellectual History and*

nineteenth century and flourished among students of the occult, including Blavatsky.

b. Orders, Fraternities, Magicians

The development of Theosophy found another source of inspiration in seventeenth century secret societies, notably the Free Masons and the Rosicrucian Fraternity. The Order of the Free Masons was founded in the belief that its rites and rituals dated from the temple of Solomon, and contained truths given by God directly to the builders of the temple. The exact date when this Order was founded is uncertain, though it probably took place in Scotland in the seventeenth century. After a period of secrecy, the political and religious circumstances in Europe changed, and the Order was able to emerge in the open. The Grand Lodge, founded in London in 1717, was the first to make its existence public, and thereafter the Order flourished throughout Europe. In every country it entered it established a Grand Lodge, headed by a Grand Master, responsible for an intricate hierarchy of functionaries. The Order underwent many splits, from the eighteenth century through the twentieth, arising chiefly from the tension between Christianity and atheism.[17]

There is no doubt that Blavatsky was influenced by the Free Masons, if only by their terminology – for example, the terms Masters and Lodge. Moreover, the Masons were the first to operate an international network of Lodges, all loyal to the mother movement – a model which the Theosophists emulated. Another interesting point in this connection is the exclusion of women (which still exists) by most of the Orders of the Free Masons. Blavatsky was displeased by this patriarchal attitude.[18] Besant fought against it when she joined

---

the Occult in Early Modern Europe, ed. Ingrid Merkel and Allen G. Debus (London, 1988); *Occult and Scientific Mentalities in the Renaissance*, ed. Brian Vickers (New York, 1986); David S. Katz, *The Occult Tradition, from the Renaissance to the Present Day* (London, 2005).

17. For further reading on Freemasonry, see, David Stevenson, *The Origins of Freemasonry: Scotland's Century, 1590–1710* (Cambridge, 1988); Margaret C. Jacob, *Living the Enlightenment: Freemasonry and Politics in Eighteenth-Century Europe* (New York, 1991); William R. Weisberger, *Speculative Freemasonry and the Enlightenment: A Study of the Craft in London, Paris, Prague, and Vienna* (New York, 1993); Marsha Keith Schuchard, *Restoring the Temple of Vision: Cabalistic Freemasonry and Stuart Culture* (Leiden, 2002).

18. Blavatsky, *Isis Unveiled*, II, pp. 349, 77.

in 1902 the Co-Masonry, an alternative Order of Free Masons, unrecognized by the official orders, which accepted women members.

The myth of the Rosicrucian Fraternity flourished in Europe throughout the seventeenth century. Its origins went back to the mediaeval myth of the Templars, revived by three pamphlets published in the German city of Kassel between 1614 and 1616, which became known as the Rosicrucian Manifestos. Their protagonist was the priest Christian Rosenkreutz, who announced the founding of an order, or fraternity, and invited new members to join. The first two pamphlets aroused interest, which intensified in 1616 with the publication of the third, entitled 'The Chemical Wedding of Christian Rosenkreutz'.[19] The tenets of the order, which described itself as a secret fraternity of enlightened scholars, influenced nineteenth century writers, among them Blavatsky. For example, the first pamphlet, entitled 'Fama Fraternitatis', contained biographical information about the founder C.R. (Christian Rosenkreutz). Born to a noble but poor family, he was educated in a monastery, where he learned Greek and Latin. Later he travelled in the Orient, spent two years in Fez in Morocco, where he was taught by local sages, and later founded the fraternity. The tenets of the fraternity were as follows:

* The members had to practise charity and heal the sick.
* The members had to keep secret their affiliation with the fraternity, and to observe the local customs where they lived.
* The fraternity would hold annual meetings in specified places.
* Each member would choose a successor to follow him after his death.
* The initials C.R. were the seal and symbol of the fraternity.
* The faternity would remain secret for 100 years.[20]

The main idea in this and the other pamphlets was that the mission of the fraternity was to do good by studying wisdom and keeping

19. It is quite obvious that at least the third pamphlet was, in fact, a part of a hoax, made by Johan Valentine Andrea (1586–1654). The pamphlets, which were distributed all over Europe, created a severe turmoil, when various people were suspected as members of the Rosicrucian Fraternity, which ironically probably never existed. For further discussion on this peculiar phenomenon, see, Frances A. Yates, *The Rosicrucian Enlightenment* (London, 1974), first published 1972; Antoine Faivre, *Theosophy, Imagination, Tradition: Studies in Western Esotericism* (Albany, 2000), pp. 171-90: first published in French, 1996; Susanna Akerman, *Rose Cross Over the Baltic: The Spread of Rosicrucianism in Northern Europe* (Leiden, 1998).

20. Yates, *The Rosicrucian Enlightenment*, pp. 238-51.

the secret. This idea, of a kind of shadow government operating in various countries and subject to a central body, is quite similar to Blavatsky's Great Brotherhood.

It seems that Blavatsky did not know the pamphlets at first-hand, otherwise she would probably have quoted them in her writings. But the impact of the pamphlets lingered in Europe long after their publication. As we shall see, the story of the Rosicrucian Fraternity inspired such writers as Hargrave Jennings (1817–1890) and Bulwer-Lytton, whose books on the occult Blavatsky knew well. Certainly, reading the 'Fama' recalls some marked similarities with Blavatsky's story, both the real and the imaginary elements. She, too, like Rosenkreutz, was of aristocratic background, claimed to know Latin and Greek, and studied occult lore in an exotic location. Whereas Rosenkreutz was content with Morocco (which was regarded by sixteenth century Europeans as sufficiently remote), Blavatsky had to go to the Far East and study in distant Tibet. Both created their fraternities after their studies, and dedicated themselves to good works. Moreover, one of the usages adopted by the Theosophists, the use of initials instead of whole names, was already found in the pamphlets of the Rosenkreutz Fraternity. Likewise, the use of the term fraternity stands out, both with regard to the Great Brotherhood and to the second aim of the Theosophical Society, which was, as we have seen, 'the formation of a nucleus of universal brotherhood.'

From the seventeenth century on, the myth of the Rosicrucian Fraternity inspired many esoteric movements which claimed to derive from the 'original' Rosenkreutz order. Among them was a Theosophical order, The Temple of the Rosy Cross, founded in London in 1912. Yet while the members of the Rosenkreutz Fraternity were committed to total secrecy, this was not necessarily part of the Theosophical agenda, except for the Esoteric Section, the ES, as we shall see further on.

Christian Rosenkreutz was a mythical person. Likewise, the Count of St. Germain, another protagonist of the modern esoteric tradition, was a semi-fictitious figure that excited the Theosophical imagination.[21] Unlike these two, there were some flesh-and-blood individuals

---

21. St. Germain, who probably died in 1784, was a French aristocrat, known for his alchemical pretensions. Rumors of his appearance in various locations in Europe had spread widely since his presumed death date, thus promoting his mythical

who engaged in magic, or in practices viewed as borderline in the tension between magic and science, and who prepared the scene for Blavatsky. Most prominent among them were Franz Anton Mesmer (1734–1815) and Alessandro Cagliostro (1743–1795). Mesmer, a Viennese physician, became famous after he settled in Paris in 1778 where he practised healing by magnetism. He became so renowned, that the Royal French Academy of Sciences formed a committee that included Benjamin Franklin (1706–1790) to examine his theories. Its conclusion, published in 1784, was that he was a charlatan.

In New Age terminology, Mesmer might be called an early healer. His technique involved the use of magnets, laying of hands and the manipulation of what he described as a fine invisible fluid that streams around the body and links it to the planets and the higher worlds. The healing process entailed a hypnotic state (the origin of the verb 'to mesmerise'), which supposedly activated the said forces. Despite its dismissal by the French Academy of Sciences, Mesmer's theory became widely popular, spreading beyond France.[22] The controversy around it continued through the nineteenth century and clearly revealed the blurred boundary, as it was then, between science and the occult. This was especially noticeable at the end of the century, when such invisible forces as electricity were given their scientific definitions. Nowadays mesmerism might be treated with greater tolerance, given that similar Oriental practices, such as shiatsu, reflexology, or acupuncture, have been introduced into the Western medical consensus. The connection between it and the Theosophical belief in such forces is plain to see, especially in regard to Olcott, who used to lecture on Mesmerism and often practiced healing.[23]

image as an immortal sage. Blavatsky referred to him as an Adept and counted him within the members of the Great Brotherhood. His name appeared in many Theosophical publications. For example, see Judge's claim, that St. Germain sailed to America during the war of independence, where he fought for freedom alongside the American revolutionary militias, William Q. Judge, 'Adepts and Politics', *The Theosophist* (Adyar, June, 1884).

22. For further discussion on Mesmer, see, Joscelyn Godwin, *The Theosophical Enlightenment* (Albany, 1994), pp. 151-67; Janet Oppenheim, *The Other World: Spiritualism and Psychical Research in England, 1850–1914* (Cambridge, 1985), pp. 110-12.

23. Blavatsky, *Isis Unveiled*, I, p. 72; Blavatsky, *The Secret Doctrine: The Synthesis of Science, Religion, and Philosophy*, II (Pasadena, 1999), p. 156, first published 1888; Henry Steel Olcott, *Old Diary Leaves, Fifth Series* (Adyar, 1932), pp. 18, 461, 464 (Hereafter *Old Diary Leaves*, V).

Mesmer's contemporary Cagliostro won a reputation as a healer and alchemist in the 1770s and 1780s, after his return to Europe from travelling in the Middle East. He too, like Christian Rosenkreutz, spent a long period in the Arab countries, where he claimed to have acquired his knowledge of the occult. He treated many people of all walks of life and gained a following that served as the basis for the formation of a new Free Mason movement, led by him, called The Egyptian Rite of Freemasonry. Unlike the original Free Masons, it accepted women and Jews. Cagliostro set up lodges of his order all over Europe, but while he was popular among seekers of the occult, political circles viewed him with suspicion.

In reality there was nothing Egyptian in the rites of his order, which mainly claimed to communicate with the seven angels of the Apocalypse, whom Cagliostro used to contact through a mediator, usually a boy or a girl who went into a trance and answered his questions on behalf of the angels. Towards the end of his life he attracted the attentions of the Catholic Church, was accused of heresy and won the dubious reputation as the last person to be burnt at the stake by the Roman Inquisition.[24] Cagliostro is remembered as a charlatan and mountebank, but his story is a good example of the mysterious magus, commanding occult powers, a cosmopolitan figure hobnobbing with the highest society in various countries. The charm of this image kindled the imagination of many nineteenth century Europeans, and inspired Blavatsky, whose own image contained similar elements.[25]

Early Theosophy

Another source of influence on Blavatsky was the early Theosophical philosophy of the Baroque period, beginning with Jacob Böhme and continuing with Emanuel Swedenborg (1688–1772). The thinking of both men included esoteric elements, characterized by

---

24. Godwin, *The Theosophical Enlightenment*, pp. 99–106.
25. Blavatsky described Cagliostro as one of the greatest initiates of his time, and included him within the Great Brotherhood, H.P. Blavatsky, 'Was Cagliostro a Charlatan?', *Lucifer* (January, 1890); Blavatsky, *Isis Unveiled*, I, p. 100; Blavatsky, *The Secret Doctrine*, II, p. 156. For further reading on the common attraction to the Orient, as manifested in the stories of Blavatsky, Rosenkreutz, and Cagliostro, see, Isaac Lubelsky, 'The Star in the East: the Theosophical Perception of the Mystical Orient', ed. Andreas Önnerfors and Dorothe Sommer, *Sheffield Lectures on the History of Freemasonry and Fraternalism, Vol. 1: Freemasonry and Fraternalism in the Middle East* (Sheffield: Sheffield University Press, 2009), 85–108.

the great importance they set on revelation (especially its mythical aspects), belief in direct contact with higher worlds and preoccupation with the relations between God, Man and Nature. Both thinkers influenced the Romantic Naturphilosophie current in early nineteenth century Germany, which sought to answer existential questions by considering the cosmos as a text to be deciphered, identifying spirit with Nature, and with an animistic view of the world as a living entity.

Böhme, a German cobbler from Görlitz, received no formal education, but studied the Scriptures by himself and familiarized himself with Hermetic literature, especially the writings of Paracelsus. His books laid the groundwork for the Western Theosophy of the Baroque period, and won him a following which continued long after his death, even outside Germany. In 1610 he experienced a mystical revelation which, he claimed, enabled him thereafter to understand simultaneously the reciprocal relations among the various planes of reality, by willing oneself to approach God. His mystical philosophy called for direct observation of the nature of Creation through first-hand experience, and sought to resolve the paradox of evil existing in the world side by side with the omnipotent good deity. Böhme was influenced by the Hermetic philosophy then widespread in Europe, but his mysticism was anchored primarily in Christianity.

Swedenborg, born in Sweden to an upper-class family, also developed a philosophy that began with Christian mysticism. He studied at the University of Uppsala, where his bishop father was a professor, travelled widely in Europe and spent two years in England, which later became his second home. After his return to Sweden in 1716 he worked as an engineer in the kingdom's mining management. Later he was ennobled and entered the Swedish chamber of peers. He spent many years doing scientific research, published papers on various subjects from mining engineering to anatomy, the latter being a subject he studied in the hope of finding the connection between the physical body and the soul. He spent long periods outside Sweden, mainly in Amsterdam and London, where he associated with Jewish Kabalistic circles.

In 1745, aged 57, Swedenborg experienced a revelation and began to communicate with the world of spirits and angels. These entities helped him to set up the basis for a new church, which he hoped to found in the belief that the Second Coming would take place in his lifetime. He published commentaries on the Scriptures, which he claimed had been given him at first-hand. He wrote books on metaphysics, the meaning of the relations between the sexes and ways of understanding the meaning of existence. His final years passed mainly in London, where he died in 1772.

Swedenborg sought to bring into his church believers of all the religious movements of his time, rather than launch a new religious sect. Nevertheless, in 1788 his followers in London founded the Church of the New Jerusalem, which before long crossed the Atlantic and founded branches in the United States, where it still flourishes. Although the mysticism of Böhme and Swedenborg was inspired by Christian devotion, which Blavatsky disliked, she did regard these two as part of the visionary trend which began in ancient times and ultimately reached her.[26]

Nineteenth Century Sources

In early nineteenth century Europe there was a revival of interest in the Hermetic and mystical tradition of previous centuries. The principal works written in this trend were composed by academics and clergymen, as well as by independent writers who took an interest in the study of the occult. A characteristic of this current was the persistent attempt by various writers to create a synthesis between diverse sources, including between East and West. As we shall see, these efforts were by no means confined to Blavatsky and the Theosophists, who were influenced by preceding writers and their ideas. What follows is a survey of the main works which gave rise to the comparative and critical current of thought which ultimately gave birth to Theosophy.

26. For further reading on Böhme and Swedenborg, see, Antoine Faivre, 'Questions of Terminology Proper to the Study of Esoteric Currents in Modern and Contemporary Europe', in *Western Esotericism and the Science of Religion*, ed. Antoine Faivre and Wouter J. Hanegraaff (Leuven, 1998), pp. 1–10; Antoine Faivre, *Theosophy, Imagination, Tradition*, pp. 7–26; Godwin, *The Theosophical Enlightenment*, pp. 93–98; Jacob Böhme, *Essential Readings*, ed. Robin Waterfield (Wellingborough, 1989); Jacob Böhme, *Six Theosophic Points, and Other Writings* (Ann Arbor, 1958); Andrew Weeks, *Böhme: An Intellectual Biography of the Seventeenth-Century Philosopher and Mystic* (Albany, 1991); Emanuel Swedenborg, *The Universal Human and Soul-Body Interaction*, ed. and trans. George F. Bole (New York, 1984). Blavatsky, who praised Böhme and claimed that his mysticism was very close to her modern Theosophy, treated Swedenborg somewhat differently, perhaps because of the competition between Theosophy and his church, Blavatsky, *The Secret Doctrine*, II, 634; Blavatsky, *Isis Unveiled*, I, p. 306.

The History of Gnosticism

The revived interest in esoteria was preceded by studies, which indirectly influenced Theosophical thought, about Church history, early heretical movements and Gnostic sects in early Christian times. These studies set the parameters for the discussion of the history of Christianity for a long time. One of the leading works was *An Ecclesiastical History* by Johann Lorenz von Mosheim (1693-1755), which appeared in Göttingen in 1755. This was an early attempt at the subject, with an emphasis on the Protestant Reformation to give it historical justification. Mosheim examined early heretical movements, such as the Arian and the Manichean, as well as pagan philosophers from the time of the Roman Empire. He included in the survey of Christian history the renaissance revival of neo-Platonist philosophy, describing some of its prominent figures, including Ficino, whom he described as a perfect example of the connection between mediaeval scholasticism and mysticism.[27]

Another influential early work, *A History of Early Opinions Concerning Jesus Christ*, by the Unitarian chemist Joseph Priestly (1733-1804), appeared in London in 1786. It aimed to convince the readers that the Christian church was originally Unitarian – namely, believing in a single God, rather than the Trinity. Priestly tried to substantiate his argument with critical readings of the Old and New Testaments, contrasting their statements on the singular God with the history of the Christian Church and the Arian heresy. His firm conclusion from this re-examination of the Christian scriptures was that their original thinking differed from the Church's doctrine.[28] Such writings opened the way to criticism of the doctrine of the Christian Church in all its diverse movements, and furthermore led to a scientific and almost secular history of Christianity. This critical spirit also affected Blavatsky, a century later, in connection with her sharp criticism of the Church and her claim that its original tenets were quite unlike the ones upheld at present.[29]

27. Johan Lorenz von Mosheim, *An Ecclesiastical History, Antient and Modern, from the Birth of Christ, to the Beginning of the Present Century* (2 vols., London, 1765), first published in German, 1755.

28. Joseph Priestley, *A History of Early Opinions Concerning Jesus Christ* (4 vols., London, 1786); *Asian Religions in America: a Documentary History*, ed. Thomas A. Tweed and Stephen Prothero (New York, 1999), pp. 44-48.

29. Blavatsky quoted Priestly's criticism in regard to the characteristics that were attributed to Jesus Christ long after his time and claimed that Priestly's courage was exceptional, Blavatsky, *Isis Unveiled*, II, p. 239.

The writings of Mosheim and Priestly influenced later writers. One of these was Charles William King (1818–1888), a respected academic, member of Trinity College, Cambridge, who specialized in gemology. His book, *The Gnostics and Their Remains*, published in 1864, sought to present a comprehensive synthesis of all the manifestations of Gnosticism through an analysis of amulets, jewels and polished gems. King argued that all the Gnostic sects originated in India, and that the Hellenistic mystical schools resulted from the establishment of the link between the Hellenistic and Indian cultures, under the Seleucian and Ptolemian dynasties. He also asserted that the Jewish Kabala – which he described as very ancient – alongside the religion of Zoroaster, had had a major influence over Western Gnosticism, in addition to the Indian mystical tradition. His book was written in a scientific spirit, free from esoteric claims. King did, however, make some curious assertions, such as that the Order of the Free Masons was the outstanding modern preserver of the Gnostic legacy and the direct heir of the Templars, whose traditions stemmed from India.[30] Blavatsky made many references to this book, which made a major contribution to the formation of her own doctrine, especially with regard to King's assertion that the source of the Gnostic philosophy was India.[31]

A book by Henry Longueville Mansel (1820–1871), *The Gnostic Heresies of the First and Second Centuries*, which appeared in 1875, reinforced the idea that India was the source of the Gnostic philosophies. The book, written by an Oxford professor of Church History, comprised a number of lectures he had given in 1868, which offered a coherent definition to the term Gnosticism and reviewed Gnostic sects from the beginning of the Christian era. Mansel, like Max Müller, bound together diverse religious systems from the Orient, and argued, inter alia, that there was a great similarity between the Zoroastrian and Mosaic religions, and that Hinduism had influenced ancient Egypt. Accordingly, he too maintained that many Greek Gnostics had been indirectly influenced by India.[32]

---

30. C.W. King, *The Gnostics and their Remains, Ancient and Mediaeval* (London, 1864), pp. 1, 10, 172–73.

31. Blavatsky, *Isis Unveiled*, II, pp. 149–50, 186–88, 254–56; Blavatsky, *The Secret Doctrine*, I, p. 410.

32. Henri Longueville Mansel, *The Gnostic Heresies of the First and Second Centuries*, ed. J.B. Lightfoot (London, 1875).

164   *Celestial India*

The History of Magic

The floodgate of books about the history of magic opened in 1801, with Francis Barrett's *The Magus*. The book clearly followed the tradition of Hermetic philosophy, and became the first guide of its kind to occult lore. Barrett described himself as a professor of chemistry, Kabala, natural philosophy and the occult, and promised his readers information about the sciences of natural magic, employing a terminology that would be adopted, consciously or not, by Blavatsky. For example, 76 years before Blavatsky he defined the term 'adept' as one who constantly seeks the true spiritual way.[33]

Barrett's book was a kind of summary of the extant magical lore and most probably inspired Blavatsky's *Isis Unveiled*.[34] The first part of *The Magus* dealt with alchemy and Hermetic philosophy, looking like a direct product of the school of Ficino and Bruno. It described Man's place on the ladder of creation, and discussed the powers of gemstones, rings and scents associated with certain planets. It described the spirit of the universe, the seven planets with their symbols and natures, as well as the magical powers of numbers from one to twelve. The second part of the book dealt with magnetism, the power of imagination, Kabalistic magic, good and evil spirits, the magical power of the days of the week and methods of summoning spirits. In addition, *The Magus* included a biographical-chronological index of various magicians, such as Hermes Trismegistus, Zoroaster, Raymond Luly (c. 1232–1315), Paracelsus, John Dee, Albertus Magnus (c. 1200–1280), and Roger Bacon (1214–1292) (the latter two were persistently comprehended by many as alchemists, despite the absence of any solid proof). The book concludes with a passage of astonishing resemblance to Theosophical terminology:

> Finally, to conclude, we are chiefly to consider one thing to be attained as the ground of perfection in the rest: i.e. The great First Cause, the Eternal Wisdom, to know the Creator by the contemplation

---

33. Francis Barrett, *The Magus, or Celestial Intelligencer: Being a Complete System of Occult Philosophy* (London, 1801), p. 57.

34. A large part of The Magus is probably a direct copy of Cornelius Agrippa's (1486–1535) De Occulta Philosophia, which was translated to English in the seventeenth century. It is most probable that Barrett obtained that book in an occult book store in Covent Garden, right after it had purchased the library of the famous astrologer Ebenezer Sibley (1751–1800), Godwin, *The Theosophical Enlightenment*, pp. 116–20.

of the creature. This is the grand secret of the philosophers, and the Master-key to all sciences both human and divine...[35]

The Magus was only reprinted in 1875, about two years before the appearance of *Isis Unveiled*. Possibly the interest it aroused influenced Blavatsky, even if she had not been familiar with it before. She herself did not refer to Barrett as a source of inspiration.[36]

In 1815 Barrett published another important book, *The Lives of Alchemystical Philosophers*, which served as a useful biographical source for any nineteenth century person interested in alchemy. It was in three parts – the first, 'The Lives of the Adepts', contained brief biographies of individuals whom the author classified as alchemists, among them the biblical Tubal Cain, Averroes (who translated Aristotle into Arabic, 1126-1198), Albertus Magnus, Thomas Aquinas (c. 1225-1274), Raymond Luly, Pico della Mirandola, Jacob Böhme (in the usual English mis-spelling, Behmen), John Dee and Cagliostro. Barrett reviewed their lives and described supposedly-documented cases of transmutation they performed. The second and more significant part of the book was a bibliography of 751 books on alchemy, and the third reviewed 34 short investigations carried out by the best alchemists through history. This part concludes with the passage from the famous emerald table, attributed to Hermes Trismegistus: 'This is true, and far distant from a lie; whatsoever is below, is like that which is above; and that which is above, is like that which is below: by this are acquired and perfected the miracles of the one thing.'[37]

Barrett might have been guilty of plagiarism, but he made a significant contribution to the foundation of a literary genre that dealt with magic, by treating it as comparative research – a genre that would grow and flourish right through the nineteenth century. Aside from laying the groundwork for this genre, he brought the Hermetic tradition into the nineteenth century and did so in readable English.

35. Barrett, *The Magus*, p. 198.
36. It was Olcott who mentioned Barrett alongside Blavatsky, in regard to astral magic literature, Olcott, *Old Diary Leaves*, V, p. 41.
37. Francis Barrett, *The Lives of Alchemystical Philosophers; With a Critical Catalogue of Books in Occult Chemistry, and a Selection of the Most Celebrated Treatises on the Theory and Practice of the Hermetic Art* (London, 1815). The Emerald Table, attributed to Hermes Trismegistus, was translated in late-mediaeval Europe from Arabic to Latin and later was adopted as a motto by the renaissance alchemists.

In the 1850s, two of Francis Barrett's successors, Mary Ann South-Atwood and General Ethan Allen Hitchcock (1798-1870), published influential books (in England and the United States respectively), on the history of Hermeticism and alchemy. Both individuals belonged to the circles which believed that the secrets of esoteria could be discovered by a systematic study of its history. South-Atwood's book, *A Suggestive Inquiry into the Hermetic Mystery*, was in four parts. The first reviewed the Hermetic alchemical tradition from an exoteric (open) viewpoint, the second reviewed it esoterically, the third dealt with the Hermetic laws, and the fourth with Hermetic practice. There were quotes from various Hermetic sources, as well as from the 'Book of Yetzirah' (a part of the Kabalistic Book of Zohar). South-Atwood ended her book with the following:

> They, we repeat, who can understand the language of the philosophers, will understand their Art; for this we have opened the way only, which if any one will consent to travel in, we assure him of success, but not otherwise...But he who desires to enter, let him search for the Root of Reason rationally...if he would have Truth at last...Let him search into the enigmas, pursue the fables, and consider the parables and maxims of the wise Adepts...[38]

Hitchcock's book, *Remarks upon Alchemy and the Alchemists*, asserted that alchemy was not properly understood in modern times, yet was closely related to the intellectual and moral spheres in the same way that studying dinosaur fossils teaches us about ancient geology. His main idea was that the alchemists' search for the philosopher's stone aimed at attaining wisdom, not material wealth. Therefore, seekers after wisdom might gain from the experiences of many alchemists whose work he reviewed in his book.[39]

38. Mary Ann South, née Atwood, *A Suggestive Inquiry into the Hermetic Mystery, with a Dissertation on the More Celebrated of the Alchemical Philosophers, Being an Attempt Towards the Recovery of the Ancient Experiment of Nature* (London, 1850), pp. 530-31. South-Atwood became interested in Mesmerism and the Hermetica in her youth. In the 1880s, she met Sinnett and bequeathed the London Lodge her father's reach occultist library. Later, she maintained close relations with Gerald Massey and George Mead, Blavatsky's secretary.

39. Ethan Allen Hitchcock, *Remarks upon Alchemy and the Alchemists, Indicating a Method of Discovering the True Nature of Hermetic Philosophy* (Boston, 1857), pp. iii, 17. Hitchcock, a retired general from the US army, wrote other books that dealt with Swedenborg and with the original symbolic nature of Christianity. He tried to prove that the image of Jesus Christ was a symbol used by the Essenes. Hitchcock's influence exceeded the occultist circles, and reached the early modern psychoanalytical arena, as evidenced by Herbert Silberer's (1881-1923) references to him in his

Edward Bulwer-Lytton and the Esoteric Novel

It is possible to draw a direct line from Francis Barrett to Edward Bulwer-Lytton. The latter's esoteric novels bear more than a hint at the esoteric insights described in Barrett's books. Bulwer-Lytton was a successful politician who entered the British Parliament in 1831, and was appointed Colonial Secretary in 1858.[40] He was rewarded for his successful service by being raised to the peerage. His descendants played important parts in the history of India and of the Theosophical Society. His son was Viceroy of India between 1876 and 1880; his granddaughter was a patron of Krishnamurti, the world-teacher cultivated by Annie Besant. In addition to his political career, he was a prolific writer who became known for historical novels, notably *The Last Days of Pompeii*, published in 1834. He also appears to have engaged in esoteric practice. His interest in the subject is evident in some of his fantastic novels, steeped in esoteric ideas, which clearly influenced Blavatsky, who made frequent references to him. I shall review his best-known esoteric writing – *Zanoni*, published in 1842, and his last esoteric novel, *The Coming Race*, which was published in 1871, two years before his death.

If Barrett helped launch a sort of comparative study of magical and Hermetic traditions, *Zanoni* marked the start of a literary genre focused on the occult. This novel, which influenced many seekers of the occult in the nineteenth century, was full of imagery taken from Hermetic myths and the traditions of the Rosenkreutz Fraternity. The book's preface introduces an old gentleman named Clarence Glyndon, whom the narrator meets in a Covent Garden bookshop specializing in occult subjects. The narrator, who was for some time interested in the Rosenkreutz Fraternity, suspects that the shop is associated with it and contains books written by its members. At his meeting with Glyndon, the old man says to him, 'Who but a Rosicrucian could explain the Rosicrucian mysteries! And can you imagine that any members of that sect, the most jealous of all secret societies, would themselves lift the veil that hides the Isis of their wisdom from the world?' Glyndon goes on to say that the

---

'Problems of Mysticism and its Symbols', which psychoanalysed various symbols that were common within secret Orders: Herbert Silberer, *Problems of Mysticism and its Symbols* (New York, 1917), first published in German, 1914.

40. L.S., 'Lytton, Edward George Earl Lytton Bulwer – first Baron Lytton (1803–1873)', *The Dictionary of National Biography*, XII (Oxford, 1921–1922), pp. 280–87.

Brotherhood of the Rosy Cross was but part of the great body of 'Platonists', students of the occult, who belonged to far nobler fraternities than that of Rosenkreutz. Glyndon dies some time later and bequeaths to the narrator all his fortune and some manuscripts in code, having obtained his promise to publish them after his death. The novel is presented as a translation of the said manuscripts.

The story takes place in the final years of the eighteenth century. It is divided into seven parts, comprising the stories of the young Glyndon, an opera singer and actress named Viola, and a nobleman by the name of Zanoni. Viola, the daughter of a Neapolitan musician and an English mother, meets on the opening night of an opera composed by her father and in which she performs the leading role, a mysterious young man who enchants her with his gaze and inspires her with power and courage when she is struck by stage-fright. She learns from porters in the street that the young man, Zanoni, is immensely wealthy and arrived in Naples in a splendid boat. Its sailors say that before coming to Naples, their master had lived for a long time in India. The porters hold opposing views about the young man – one says that he gave him a valuable diamond, while another argues that he is a sorcerer. The first man dismisses the latter's story, saying it was spread by an old man who claimed to have met Zanoni in Milan 70 years earlier, looking as young as he did at present. Moreover, the same old man claimed that already then, 70 years earlier, he had heard an old man state that he had met Zanoni 60 years previously in Sweden.

After her parents' death, Viola finds herself attached to Zanoni and to the Englishman Glyndon, a troubled young artist, for whom she feels a sisterly affection. Zanoni tells her that if he married her he would have to renounce his immortality, and urges her to forget him and marry Glyndon. Nevertheless, Viola falls in love with him, discovers that he has perfect command of many languages, and is a member of a mysterious order whose history has never been told. The two settle on a Greek island where they live from 1791 to 1793, a son is born to them and, impelled by Viola's illness, they move to Venice, where she recovers. Meanwhile, Glyndon engages in occult study and is initiated as a neophyte by Zanoni's friend Mejnour. He fears for Viola, because he suspects that Zanoni belongs to the dark forces. He comes to Venice and warns Viola against her husband. She decides to investigate and takes advantage of Zanoni's absence in Rome for a few days to search his private apartment, where she discovers medical herbs and a vessel containing a crystal. When she opens the vessel and breathes its scent she has a revelation – she soars to the celestial spheres, or the world of ideas, where her soul joins Zanoni's ideal image. At the same time she sees demonic forms that threaten to steal her son from her.

Persuaded that Zanoni indeed belongs to the forces of evil, and is part of a conspiracy to kill her baby by witchcraft, she flees to Paris in July 1794 – at the height of the Terror, which according to Bulwer-Lytton was the work of sorcerers, like the whole of the French Revolution. Zanoni follows her to Paris, where he meets Glyndon and tells him his true life story. He says that he was born in ancient times in a civilization of sages in whose lands the only desire was for knowledge, or magic, as it is called by the ignorant today. At that time a number of people, including Zanoni, discovered how to achieve immortality. Zanoni, who turn out to be a magus and theurgist and can summon spirits, insists to Glyndon that he belongs to the forces of good and that his soul always seeks the light. He says that he and his friend Mejnour are the only survivors of that ancient community of sages, the others having renounced immortality as they were unable to persist in the life of celibacy, which is the prerequisite of immortality. At the end of the novel Viola is imprisoned by the revolutionary government and sentenced to die, and so too is Zanoni, who could in theory use his magical abilities to escape the guillotine. Before his execution, he manages to reach Viola and give her an amulet, thus sacrificing his immortality for love. That day Robespierre (1758–1794) himself is guillotined, and the Terror ends. The prison guards find Viola's body, with an ecstatic expression on her face, having been united with her lover. Their son, however, survives.

Bulwer-Lytton appended to the novel clues to his protagonists. The two immortal men, Mejnour and Zanoni, personify the two idealistic aspects of the human spirit. Mejnour symbolizes the spirit of science, and Zanoni the moral idealist, who always seeks new knowledge and discovers that self-sacrifice is the perfect way to becoming a better man.[41]

For lovers of the occult, Zanoni's character represented the essence of certain core myths. While the author does not provide

---

41. Edward Bulwer Lytton, *Zanoni* (London, 1853), pp. 302–303, first published 1842.

precise details about his origins, he does hint that he was a Chaldean. Blavatsky was more influenced by *Zanoni* than by any other novel.[42] She adopted Bulwer-Lytton's view of the French Revolution as the work of the forces of evil, and was impressed by his central idea – the existence of a secret brotherhood far older than the Rosicrucian, which preserved ancient knowledge. It is probably that the reference to Zanoni's origin inspired her imagination when she composed her own ideas about Atlantis and its ancient sages, who supposedly passed their gifts to the early Aryans.

Bulwer-Lytton's last esoteric novel, *The Coming Race*, is regarded as one of the forerunners of the genre of science-fiction. An elderly American of English ancestry, from a prosperous upper middle-class family, describes what happened to him in America in his youth. He met a scientist who had found indications of human life in a deep mine. The two proceed to go down the mine to explore it, and there the scientist dies in an accident. The narrator goes on exploring and reaches an underground world, where he finds a big city with advanced structures and agriculture. The inhabitants are called 'Vril-Ya'. They are very tall, their complexion resembled that of the American Indians, and they emanate quiet power. Despite their resemblance to humans, their technological and spiritual abilities are far more developed. The narrator is invited home by one of the inhabitants, and associates with his son and daughter, who are endowed with impressive gifts. For example, the host's son has healing abilities, and by laying his hands on the narrator heals the injuries he had suffered on the journey.

The Vril-Ya rule by means of a magnetic force called Vril. It enables them to control the weather, apply mesmerism (sic!), and transfer an entire consciousness from one individual to another – by this means the narrator speedily learns his hosts' language and teaches them his own. He learns that this race moved underground in ancient times, after an internecine war following the discovery of the Vril between those who were pacific and those who wanted to use the force for evil purposes. Their system of government is simple, consisting of periodic elections of a leader, aided by a council of magician-sages. The institution of marriage among the Vril-Ya differs from the form on earth's surface – they marry for three years, at the end of which they are free to change spouses. In addition

---

42. Blavatsky, *Isis Unveiled*, I, pp. 1, 17, 64, 285–86.

to their command of the Vril force, they have a highly developed mechanical ability. For example, they have a pair of wings each, with which they can fly. They also possess robots which perform the simple tasks. Their mythology describes an ancient Buddha or Prometheus, who is also the ancestor of all the Vril-Ya. They believe in the reincarnation of the soul, and therefore do not fear death.

The narrator grows alarmed the more he learns about the beliefs of the Vril-Ya, and realizes that they are waiting for the right moment to return to the surface of the earth and dispossess the human race. Aware that the 'coming race' is more highly developed than his own species, he concludes that the human era is about to end. The plot includes a story about the unrequited love that Zee, the host's daughter, feels for the narrator, whom she instructs about her civilization. In the end she saves him and shows him the way back to the upper world, where he returns to his previous life, though tormented by his acquired knowledge. He tells his story when he is an old man, retired from his work, in order to warn humanity about the imminent danger.[43]

An interesting element in *The Coming Race* is Bulwer-Lytton's description of the grammar of the Vril-Ya language – clearly a product of the philological research of his time. He quoted extensively from Max Müller's writing, especially from his article 'On the Stratification of Language', and devised a comparative-philological study, in Max Müller's style, purporting to isolate the roots of the Vril-Ya language and analyse its grammatical logic.[44]

Both *The Coming Race* and *Zanoni* contain elements that influenced Blavatsky, who treated some of the novels' ideas as though they were actual discoveries. For example, in *Isis Unveiled* she discussed the Vril-Ya and the power of Vril, which she said represented the primordial force of creation. Similarly, in a letter she wrote Sinnett three years later she quite seriously discussed the Vril force, arguing that knowledge of it had been common among the ancient races that had perished.[45] The discussion of the origin of the Vril-Ya also points

---

43. Edward Bulwer Lyton, *The Coming Race* (London, 1886), first published 1871.
44. 'The Coming Race' was published anonymously in 1871. Its first edition was dedicated to Max Müller, who in 1873, following Bulwer-Lytton's death, was happy to find who the author of the book really was. However, Max Müller did not think highly of the novel, F. Max Müller, *Auld Lang Syne* (New York, 1898), pp. 189–90.
45. Blavatsky, *Isis Unveiled*, I, pp. 64, 125, 296; *The Mahatma Letters to A.P. Sinnett from the Mahatmas M. & K.H.*, transcribed and compiled by A.T. Barker, letter no. 1 (Koot-Hoomi to Sinnett), 15 October 1880 (Adyar, 1972), p. 2, first published 1923.

to Bulwer-Lytton's influence on Blavatsky on the subject of the myth of Atlantis and on her belief in the existence of advanced technological civilizations in pre-history. Likewise, the imminent threat to humanity, described in *The Coming Race*, resembles the theory of Blavatsky and Besant about the changeover of races and sub-races in the course of world history. As we have seen, they argued that the last Aryan sub-race was taking shape in their lifetime in America. According to their theory, the final days of this new sub-race would also be the final days of the present human race. In this way, the substance of some of Bulwer-Lytton's ideas found its way into the Theosophical doctrine.

A Religious History of India

A characteristic of Blavatsky's thinking was her effort to create a synthesis between the religions of East and West, which she believed had stemmed from a single ancient source she named 'the secret doctrine'. As we have seen, this approach was influenced principally by the comparative method that dominated the new discipline of comparative religion. As noted, the predominant influence on Blavatsky in this matter was Max Müller, but several other influential writings on the subject of India and her religious movements were available during the time when Blavatsky was constructing her doctrine. Four of these are described below. Aside from their contents, they generally familiarized the public with Indian concepts and thus prepared the ground for the acceptance of the Theosophical doctrine.

Edward Moor's (1771–1848) *The Hindu Pantheon* (published 1810) was regarded through the nineteenth century as the basic textbook on Hinduism, mainly thanks to its vivid depictions of the Hindu gods. Moor was a member of the Asiatic Society and the Literary Society of Bombay. His book was based on a scientific approach and he stated that he had followed Wilkins' working method. The lavish illustrations by an artist named Haughton enriched the colourful text. Moor apologized for having written the survey of the Hindu gods without knowing Sanskrit, but maintained that his book drew on the information available in the writings of Jones, Wilkins and Colebrooke, as well as his own research among the Hindus.

Blavatsky was quite familiar with the *The Hindu Pantheon* and undoubtedly impressed by the splendid illustrations, as her frequent references to the book indicate.[46] However, some of the specific insights offered by this book, and their possible impact on the Western understanding of the religious aspect of India, are worth a closer look. One of these is Moor's basic assumption that the Hindu religion is monotheistic, since all the Hindus believe in a single eternal entity, which manifests itself allegorically in various deities. Moor emphasized, in this connection, the supposed similarity between the stories of Jesus and Krishna. He also devoted much space to a discussion of the numerous divine avatars, describing both Krishna and Jesus as avatars of Vishnu. Significantly, he maintained that Krishna's character resembled that of Hermes-Mercury, the messenger of the Graeco-Roman gods. Moor discussed extensively Hindu concepts and symbols – for example, he devoted five pages to the concept of Om – described the Vedic literature and reviewed archaeological findings made in India, including coins, medals and commemorative tablets. The book ends with the Hindu god of love, Kama, discussed in such a way as to hark back to the supposed monotheism of the Hindus and its common roots with the West. According to Moor, in this sense the Hindu concept of love did not differ greatly from the Christian one.[47]

Another book, the four-volume *Account of the Writings, Religions and Manners of the Hindoos*, which appeared about a year after *The Hindu Pantheon*, provided much valuable information about the Indian culture. Published in Shrirampur in West Bengal, it was the work of the missionary William Ward (1769–1823), who had come to India in 1799 and collected data about the local culture. A very comprehensive survey of the Hindus, it drew on such academic sources as Jones and Colebrooke.[48] It seems that Blavatsky was not familiar with this old book, but its relevance to the present discussion lies in its influence over later writings which she did know well. The most important of these was Hargrave Jennings' 1858 book, *The Indian Religions*, which mentions Ward's book as one of its principal bibliographical sources.

As well as the missionary from Shrirampur, Jennings listed '*Asiatick Researches*' (the organ of the Asiatick Society), and Cornelius

---

46. Blavatsky, *Isis Unveiled*, II, pp. 95, 465, 539, see also, 557–58.
47. Edward Moor, *The Hindu Pantheon* (London, 1810), pp. ix–xi, 1, 180–89, 205, 410–14, see also, 447–51.
48. W. Ward, *Account of the Writings, Religions, and Manners, of the Hindoos: Including Translations from their Principal Works* (4 vols., Serampore, 1811).

Agrippa, Albertus Magnus, Plato and Swedenborg – unlikely combinations that place him neatly in Blavatsky's circles. Jennings lived all his life in London, eking out a living by his pen. Inevitably, the publication of *The Indian Religions* was associated with the great Indian revolt that had broken out the previous year. Jennings expressed a decidedly anti-imperial opinion in his book, arguing that the rebellion was a result of poor governance by the English administration. His book reads like a defence of Buddhism, opening with the claim that in all of England there were not five people who understood it, and by way of background, he reviewed Brahmanism and the caste system. This is not the place to point out his factual errors, such as dating Buddhism before Brahmanism. Nevertheless, there are two prominent elements in Jennings' *Indian Religions* that deserve attention. One is the claim that the Buddha appeared in India 1,000 years before Christ, that he had been preceded by three Buddhas, and Gautama – known as the famous Buddha – was the fourth. Jennings stated that another Buddha (Maitari) would appear before the end of the world. The other important element is Jennings' attempt to compare the principles of Buddhism (the existence of Nothingness, the non-existence of God, etc.) with Judaism and Christianity.[49] The contribution of these elements to Theosophy is clear, especially in reference to the theme of a World Teacher and the idea of hidden kernels of truth in all religions. Jennings' later book, *The Rosicrucians*, had even a greater effect on Blavatsky, thanks to its survey of all the various orders and beliefs that attributed themselves to the Rosicrucian fraternity. Blavatsky referred to Jennings as an unquestionable authority.[50]

It is not possible to conclude this survey without mentioning *The Light of Asia* by Edwin Arnold (1832–1904).[51] Though published after *Isis Unveiled*, its importance in shaping English public opinion on the subject of Buddhism is directly connected to the subject of the present chapter. Arnold was a poet, journalist and educator who ran the Sanskrit college in Pune for several years, before returning

---

49. Hargrave Jennings, *The Indian Religions: or Results of the Mysterious Buddhism* (London, 1858), pp. 1-2, 16, 19, 138-67.

50. Hargrave Jennings, *The Rosicrucians, their Rites and Mysteries* (London, 1870), pp. 338-39; Blavatsky, *Isis Unveiled*, II, p. 444.

51. Edwin Arnold, *The Light of Asia, or the Great Renunciation (Mahabhinishkramana), Being the Life and Teaching of Gautama, Prince of India and Founder of Buddhism* (London, 1879).

to England in 1861. He then worked as a journalist at the Daily Telegraph, and among other things, organized the journey of Henry Morton Stanley (1841–1904) to Africa. *The Light of Asia* was published in 1879 and was immediately acclaimed. It is a long poem about the story of the Buddha, supposedly communicated to Arnold by an Indian Buddhist. The poem enchanted many readers and is held to be one of the leading works that gave the Western public a direct access to non-Christian protagonists. In this sense it may be linked to the Theosophical efforts to introduce such ideas to the Western public mind, and in fact *The Light of Asia* became one of the popular books among Theosophical circles.[52]

American Transcendentalism

Another source of influence on the Theosophical doctrine was the American Transcendentalism movement, which though it was not directly associated with Theosophy, certainly helped pave the way for it.[53] The moving spirits of this movement, which included some of the leading American intellectuals of the nineteenth century, were Ralph Waldo Emerson (1803–1882) and Henry David Thoreau (1817–1862).[54] Emerson was a minister of the Unitarian church, but left it and formed his own romantic theory, which entailed an attempt to achieve direct experience of the deity as existing in all parts of nature and in all human beings. Emerson was interested in Platonic philosophy, metaphysics and mysticism, as can be deduced from his descriptions of Plato and Swedenborg. Like the European mystics, he discovered the spiritual Oriental world through reading Hindu scriptures, including the *Bhagavad-Gītā*, which he mistook for a Buddhist text. His writing was filled with concepts that appear to have been drawn from those scriptures, such as 'Over-Soul', 'Higher-Self' and 'Illusion', which resemble the Hindu concepts Brahman, Atman and Maya. So did his poem 'Brahma', published

---

52. Many Theosophists mark Blavatsky's passing day – 8 May – or 'White Lotus Day' – by reading from the *Light of Asia*, alongside the *Bhagavad Gītā*, Emily Lutyens, *Candles in the Sun* (London, 1957), p. 16.

53. Robert S. Elwood, Jr., 'The American Theosophical Synthesis', in *The Occult in America: New Historical Perspectives*, ed. Howard Kerr and Charles L. Crow (Urbana, 1983), pp. 111–34.

54. Hanegraaff, *New Age Religion and Western Culture*, pp. 457–61; Carl T. Jackson, *The Oriental Religions and American Thought: Nineteenth-Century Explorations* (Westport, CT, 1981), Chapter 3, pp. 45–62.

in 1857.[55] His view of India was not especially profound, but he was the first American thinker to study Oriental philosophy seriously and try to incorporate it in the Western cultural tradition.

Thoreau, Emerson's renowned Transcendentalist associate, went further in adopting Hindu philosophy. Thoreau's famous book *Walden*, the product of two years' sojourn in nature, is replete with thoughts about human existence that seem to have been inspired by his reading of Hindu texts.[56] Even stronger evidence of Thoreau's interest in India crops up repeatedly in his journals of the 1840s and 1850s.[57] Emerson and Thoreau brought into their circle other writers, such as Margaret Fuller (1810-1850) and Bronson Alcott (1799-1888), and influenced many American artists and thinkers, including the poet Walt Whitman (1819-1892). The work of three other late Transcendentalist writers is relevant to the present discussion. The first, James Freeman Clarke (1818-1888), was a minister of the Unitarian church in Boston and a Harvard lecturer. His book, *Ten Great Religions*, published in 1871, was the most widespread work on Oriental religions in America in the late nineteenth century. Clarke's comparative study of Hinduism, Buddhism and Confucianism, was written with an open mind and emphasized the beautiful aspects of these religions, even in comparison with Judaism and Christianity. Like Priestly a century earlier, he was guided by the idea that a single great truth underlies all the world's great religions.[58]

A similar thought characterized the first volume of *Oriental Religions* by Samuel Johnson (1822-1882), published in 1872, which was devoted to India. Johnson, also a Harvard graduate and Unitarian minister (he founded his own independent church in 1853), surveyed Brahmanism and Buddhism from the premise that religion is universal. Johnson quoted the leading scholars of the age, such as Schlegel, Colebrooke, Wilson, Bernouf and Max Müller, and adopted the principles of the Aryan Myth. His book opens with the

55. Ralph Waldo Emerson, 'Plato; or, the Philosopher', in 'Representative Men', *The Complete Works of Ralph Waldo Emerson*, Vol. 4 (New York, 1903), pp. 37-79; Ralph Waldo Emerson, 'Swedenborg; or, the Mystic', *The Complete Works of Ralph Waldo Emerson*, Vol. 4. pp. 91-146; Ralph Waldo Emerson, 'Brahma', *The Complete Works of Ralph Waldo Emerson*, Vol. 9, p. 195.

56. Henry David Thoreau, *Walden* (Köln, 1996), first published 1854.

57. *The Journal of Henry D. Thoreau*, ed. Bradford Torrey and Francis H. Allen, I (New York, 1962), pp. 266-67 (August 4, 1841); pp. 275-76 (28 August 1841); see also, II, pp. 4-5 (1842).

58. James Freeman Clarke, *Ten Great Religions: An Essay in Comparative Theology* (Boston, 1871).

The Sources of the Theosophical Doctrine

statement that the human race arose in the highlands of Iran (or at any rate, the races responsible for civilization). However, unlike many serious scholars, he maintained that Hebrew culture also arose in that region.[59]

Another American Transcendentalist was Moncure Daniel Conway, like the other two a Harvard graduate and Unitarian minister. The son of a prosperous Virginian family, he was an opponent of slavery and in 1863, during the American Civil War, he moved to London, where he engaged in the study of religions. Conway, who made friends with Max Müller and kept up the association for many years, is seen as one of the leading figures who brought Oriental Studies from England to the United States. In addition, he and his wife befriended Annie Besant in 1873, after her separation from her husband, helped her financially and maintained a warm friendship with her for a long time.

With reference to the present discussion, in 1879 Conway met Blavatsky in London, when she and Olcott were travelling to India. Later, in the early 1880s, he witnessed the success of the Theosophical Society in England. In 1884 he was invited to give a series of lectures in Australia, then went on an extensive tour of Ceylon and India, and even reached Adyar, where he again met Blavatsky. He described this journey in his book, *My Pilgrimage to the Wise Men of the East* – despite its title, a very clear-headed book, in which he noted that the Westerners' concept of the Orient differed substantially from the daily reality of India. In this he discerned the problematics which also affected the leaders of the Transcendentalist Movement, whose imaginary India was not necessarily related to reality.[60]

---

59. Samuel Johnson, *Oriental Religions, and their Relation to Universal Religion: India* (Boston, 1872), pp. 1, 39–40.

60. Conway, who first met Blavatsky on her first trip to London, described her as an amusing and unsophisticated lady who based most of her conversation on gossip. Therefore, he found it hard to believe that she was the author of *Isis Unveiled*. Despite his negative tendency towards Theosophy, Conway's interest in the movement was growing side by side with the growth of the Society's influence within London's elite circles. This was the reason for his short visit to Adyar, where he spent a few hours with Blavatsky. His impressions from that meeting were again negative. He asked Blavatsky to show him some of the spiritualistic phenomena associated with her, but was informed that just a short while before his arrival, the Mahatmas decided to postpone their miraculous correspondence with their disciples. Conway's reaction was: 'That was just my luck in such matters. Wherever a miracle occurs I was always too soon or too late to see it.' Accordingly, when discussing miracles, Blavatsky's comment was: 'It is all glamour – people think they see what they do not see, that is the

Early Attempts at a Synthesis of an Occult Doctrine

Long before Blavatsky, there were attempts to synthesize various religions and magical theories and locate their common origin. The following are some of the works which paved the way for the Theosophical synthesis.

One of the first books to provide a stylistic inspiration for *Isis Unveiled* was *Anacalypsis* (from the Greek 'to unveil'), by Godfrey Higgins (1772–1833). The first volume of this book was issued in 1833, but the second appeared in 1836, after the author's death. Higgins, a Yorkshire gentleman, declared that his aim was to isolate the common sources of human civilization. He conducted this search through obsessive attempts to discover similarities among the diverse alphabets, numbers, myths and religions around the world. He argued, for example, that 'the letters of the old Synagogue Hebrew are nearly the same as the English, only in a different form.' Likewise, he said that the different numbering systems in the world sprang from a single source. The world's religions also sprang from a single source, far older than any known religion. He maintained that there were ancient philosophical doctrines that culminated in various religions, including Christianity. Thus, he stated, there was a single source behind the myth of the Crucifixion and the myth of Krishna, whose name he spelled Cristna.

Higgins was undoubtedly influenced by Jones, and quoted him extensively on the origin of the Hindus. Like him, he stated that the Hindus and Ethiopians were genetically connected, as demonstrated by the Buddha's 'negroid' features. Higgins, however, differed from those who cultivated the Aryan Myth. He expressed great appreciation for the Jewish race, and even asserted that the Jews and Brahmins had a common origin – namely, from Ur of the Chaldeans, the native land of Abraham, and that Sanskrit and Hebrew grew from the same source. To prove it, he compared several languages, including Arabic and Ethiopian (which he probably did

whole of it.' While in Adyar, Conway saw Koot-Hoomi's portrait, and was convinced that it was really an old portrait of the Hindu reformer Rammohan Roy. Moreover, Conway claimed that the Master's name was just a combination of Blavatsky's two most sincere followers, Olcott, and Hume (*Olcott+Hume* = Koothume = Koothoomi), Moncure Daniel Conway, *My Pilgrimage to the Wise Men of the East* (London, 1906), pp. 195–213; Moncure Daniel Conway, *Autobiography, Memories and Experiences*, II (Boston, 1905), pp. 286–90, 309–14; *The Life and Letters of the Right Honourable Friedrich Max Müller*, ed. Georgina Max Müller, I (New York, 1902), pp. 70, 405–407, also 475, see also, II, pp. 21, 53, 213; Jackson, *The Oriental Religions*, pp. 134–37.

not know), and concluded that they had the same origin, common to Hebrew, Sanskrit and Greek. *Anacalypsis* puts forward quite unfounded examples to support its author's basic hypothesis, and their presentation recalls Blavatsky's style. To illustrate his point that the inhabitants of pre-Columbian America descended from the same primordial nation as all mankind, Higgins made a 'philological' analysis leading to the conclusion that the Hebrew word 'messiah' was the origin of the Aztec word 'Mexico' – or, as he chose to spell it, 'Mesi-co'. Similarly, he claimed that myths from various parts of the world grew from identical sources. He too, like Blavatsky, described the history of the earth as made up of cycles. He stated that the era of mankind might be about to end, like other eras when the earth was populated by unknown races, which perished following a comet strike.[61]

The resemblance between *Anacalypsis* and *Isis Unveiled* is plain to see, in substance and in style. Blavatsky was greatly influenced by *Anacalypsis*, and viewed Higgins as an authority.[62] But Higgins was not interested in the occult, and was one of several independent scholars who were searching for the sources of human civilization, while various spiritualists engaged in similar attempts at a synthesis though from an esoteric position. One of the most prominent was the American medium Andrew Jackson Davies (1826–1910), who published his influential book, *The Principles of Nature*, in 1847. Davies – who was a cobbler like Böhme before he discovered his powers – claimed to communicate with famous spirits, such as Galen and Emanuel Swedenborg. *The Principles of Nature* was made up of three parts. The first, or 'The Key', reviewed existing theories; the second part sought to explain the structure of the world, and the third purported to analyse human society, with the aim of creating a 'Brotherhood' of all mankind.[63] Most of the book was devoted to the

---

61. Godfrey Higgins, *Anacalypsis, an Attempt to Draw Aside the Veil of the Saitic Isis; or, an Inquiry into the Origin of Languages, Nations, and Religions*, I (London, 1833), pp. xi, 57, 144–45, 448–49, 452, see also, II, pp. 23, 445 (London, 1836). The book's title was probably the first to use the 'unveiling of Isis' motif. The first writer that had used that motif was the Parisian professor Charles François Dupouis (1742–1809), who researched ancient fables and symbols: Godwin, *The Theosophical Enlightenment*, pp. 32, 76–90.

62. Blavatsky, *Isis Unveiled*, I, pp. 13, 32–34, 242, 284, 347, see also II, pp. 43–44, 120–21, 490–91; Blavatsky, *The Secret Doctrine*, II, p. 105.

63. Andrew Jackson Davies, *The Principles of Nature, Her Divine Revelations, and A Voice to Mankind*, in Three Parts (London, 1847), pp. 1–2.

history of humanity from antiquity to the present, with descriptions of the various societies that had existed in Asia, Europe, Africa and America, stressing the significance of the biblical flood and its effect on humanity.

The contribution of this book to the formation of Blavatsky's doctrine lay not so much in its contents as in its framework, which sought to create a synthesis of all the existing knowledge and to describe pre-historic events. Unlike Blavatsky's later effort, Davies surveyed human society in terms of class, rather than from an esoteric viewpoint. His approach therefore tended to analyse the past on the basis of the present, and was more practical than Blavatsky's. He frequently used illustrations from the Bible in support of his arguments. His aim, ultimately, was to help bring about a better future for humanity, and in that sense his work was definitely related to the Theosophical message. Davies argued that by understanding the truth, ' ... mankind will discover that the mind must be refined and perfected, and that when this is properly accomplished, the social world will be correspondently elevated, and thus be advanced to honor, goodness and UNIVERSAL PEACE' (original emphasis).[64]

However, Davies' influence on Blavatsky was minor compared with the inspiration she drew from one of the leading teachers of the occult in the nineteenth century, Alphonse-Louis Constant, who became known as Eliphas Lévi (1810-1875). Lévi, a gentile, chose a Jewish name because of his interest in the Kabala, and as such was one of main authors of the revived European interest on Jewish mysticism and magic. His father having been a cobbler, he shared this association with Böhme and Davies. He was an ordained Roman Catholic priest, but left the Church after a crisis of faith which made him turn to the occult. He went on to write a number of esoteric books which made an impact, notably *Transcendental Magic* (1856)[65] and *The History of Magic* (1860). The latter has several features in common with *Isis Unveiled*. Lévi seemed to examine the history of magic from a supposedly scientific viewpoint, arguing that it was

64. Jackson Davies, *The Principles of Nature*, p. 677.
65. Eliphas Lévi, *Transcendental Magic, its Doctrine and Ritual*, trans. Arthur Edward Waite (London, 1995), first published in French 1856. The book surveyed various historical magical traditions and symbols. It defined an ancient occultist doctrine, which reappears in history under different names. Obviously, this idea more than reminds of Blavatsky's Secret Doctrine.

an ancient science which was persistently and erroneously confused with deception. To dispel this prejudice, he described forms of occult lore through history and in various parts of the world.

The book consisted of seven parts which examined occult lore from various angles. The first part highlighted the Book of Enoch as an ancient source, and reviewed the practice of magic in the ancient cultures of India, Egypt and Greece. To the present discussion, it is significant that Lévi dated ancient India and its magical practitioners earlier than those of Egypt and Europe. He argued that India was in the distant past populated by the descendants of Cain, and later by the offspring of Abraham and Keturah. He described the Upanishads (spelling it Oupnek'hat – following the translation by Anquetil Duperron) as being full of black magic, on the one hand, and expressions of morality and liberty, on the other. Having reviewed the practice of magic in ancient Egypt and Pythagoras' Greece, he described the Jewish Kabala as the original expression of the ancient doctrine of the occult. He maintained that the Kabala originated from the land of the Chaldeans, whence it was brought by Abraham to the Holy Land. The Egyptians learned it from Joseph, and in turn taught it to Moses. Moses passed its secrets back to the Jews, who incorporated it in the Bible by means of a symbolic language.

The second part dealt with the history of magic and described initiation into the occult. The third focused on the Christian revelation as a synthesis between magical doctrines, and on Jesus – who, Lévi asserted, practised magic, as did all the early Christian priests. The fourth concerned the historical role of magic as a shaping force of culture, focusing on the history of magic among pagan people and mediaeval magicians, such as Albertus Magnus and Thomas Aquinas. The fifth part discussed the adepts of the early Modern Age, such as Raymond Luly, Paracelsus, the Order of Rosenkreutz and the Free Masons. The sixth concerned magic during the French Revolution, focusing on Swedenborg, Mesmer, the Count of St Germain and Cagliostro. Lévi argued that the Jacobin revolutionaries practised magic,[66] and mentioned the Bavarian Illuminati in

---

66. This certainly is reminiscent of Bulwer Lytton's claim in 'Zanoni'. Lévi and Bulwer Lytton were indeed colleagues, and have probably practiced occultism together. For example, it was reported that in 1861 they summoned the spirit of Apollonius of Tyana. The location they chose for the ceremony was the roof of the 'Pantheon', in Regent Street, Godwin, *The Theosophical Enlightenment*, p. 215.

this connection.⁶⁷ The final part of *The History of Magic* dealt with occult lore in the nineteenth century.⁶⁸

Lévi's other books are also similar to Blavatsky's writings. She often quoted him, and regarded him as one of the leading Kabalists and authorities on the occult in Europe. She stated that the Theosophists set great value on Lévi's writings, because they promoted the comparison between the Oriental and Western traditions.⁶⁹

The same could be said for the Countess of Caithness, another expert on occult lore who associated with Blavatsky and Olcott in the 1880s. Her book, *Old Truths in a New Light*, appeared about a year before *Isis Unveiled*, and looks like an early edition of it. There is a marked resemblance between the two books, in content and in style. The chapter division, the numerous quotes from scientists and the academic pretension to juxtapose what Caithness calls 'practical' and 'spiritual' sciences, are unmistakably similar to *Isis Unveiled*. The statement, 'Science is most important, but it cannot stand alone, it must go hand in hand with Spiritism, or it will inevitably stumble every third step,' as well as her motto of testing old 'truth' in the light of new science, reinforces the resemblance between the two books.

Caithness, like her predecessors, surveyed the history of occult lore and various heretical movements, including the Manichean. She asserted that the present was a special era in which spirituality advanced faster than ever before, and spoke of an ancient esoteric doctrine common to all religions. She illustrated her arguments by analysing identical symbols in diverse cultures, and made references to many scientists, such as Kepler, Newton and Darwin. As for the last-named, her answer to the problem of the 'missing link', was

---

67. The sect of the Illuminati was founded in Bavaria in 1776 by Adam Weishaupt (1748-1830). In 1784 it was banned by law and thus attracted ongoing accusations regarding its subversive activities, in a manner reminiscent of the Rosicrucian hysteria that swamped Europe earlier.

68. Eliphas Lévi, *The History of Magic*, trans. Edward Waite (London, 1982), pp. 29, 55, 72, 77, 98, 147-56, 203-205, 242-49, 256-59, 283-87, 292, 295-304, 299-311, 317-21, first published in French, 1860.

69. *The Theosophist* (Bombay, October, 1881); Blavatsky, *Isis Unveiled*, I, pp. 280-81, 480-81, 484-85, see also, II, pp. 201-202, 250, 467-68; Blavatsky, *The Secret Doctrine*, I, pp. 196, 243, 253, see also, II, pp. 268, 409, 511, 589; Eliphas Lévi, *The Book of Splendours* (Wellingborough, 1973), pp. 42, 69-70, 83-94, first published in French 1894; Eliphas Lévi, *The Mysteries of the Qabalah, or the Occult Agreement of the Two Testaments* (Wellingborough, 1974), first published in French, 1920.

The Sources of the Theosophical Doctrine

belief in the existence of spirits at various levels, and the assertion that Man is of divine origin. Like Lévi, Caithness drew comparisons between various Eastern and Western scriptures, including the *Zohar*, and declared that the *Bhagavad-Gītā* greatly resembled the New Testament. She concluded her book with the statement, 'These three great doctrines (the unity of God, the plurality of inhabited worlds, the succession of existences)... were inculcated in the sacred mysteries of all the ancient religions of this earth...'[70]

An equally influential book appeared in New York in the same year as *Old Truths in a New Light* – it was *Art Magic*, by Emma Hardinge Britten (nee Floyd, 1823–1899).[71] Hardinge Britten was a founding member of the Theosophical Society in New York. Born in England, she emigrated with her mother to the United States in the 1850s. She became interested in spiritualism at an early age, and took part in séances with Robert Dale Owen (1801–1877; the son of Scottish utopian industrialist Robert Owen, 1771–1858) and the Fox sisters.[72] Hardinge Britten was personally familiar with the spiritualist circle in London, including Gerald Massey. In the early 1870s she and her wealthy husband (who printed some of her books) moved to Boston, where she gave lectures on spiritualism every Sunday.[73]

There is a marked resemblance between *Art Magic* of 1876 and *Isis Unveiled* of 1877. Like Blavatsky, who claimed that she wrote her books in a trance, Hardinge Britten stated that she was only the editor of her book, and that the real author was a European who did not wish to reveal his identity. Her book claimed to present a synthesis between all the ancient magical practices and modern spiritualism. She devoted entire chapters to India and her magical practices, and linked them to the magical systems of ancient Egypt

70. Countess of Caithness, *Old Truths in a New Light, or, an Earnest Endeavour to Reconcile Material Science with Spiritual Science, and with Scripture* (London, 1876), pp. 4, 12, 27, 152-58, 252-72, 361-63, 443.

71. Emma Hardinge Britten, *Art Magic; or, Mundane, Sub-Mundane and Super-Mundane Spiritism* (New York, 1876).

72. The case of the American Fox sisters (who on 31 March 1848 began their communication with spirits in their house in Hydesville), is considered as the first ever reported case of modern spiritualism: Emma Hardinge Britten, *Nineteenth Century Miracles; or, Spirits and their Work in Every Country of the Earth: A Complete Historical Compendium of the Great Movement Known as 'Modern Spiritualism'* (Manchester, 1883), pp. 27-42.

73. Emma Hardinge Britten, *Autobiography*, edited and published by Margaret Wilkinson (her Sister and sole Relative) (London, 1900), pp. 106, 107-108, 214, 224.

and the Jewish Kabala, arguing that they all stemmed from a single ancient source. *Art Magic*, like *Isis Unveiled*, was also designed rather like an encyclopedia of the occult, with surveys of the history of magic among various nations, mesmerism, the proportions of the Egyptian pyramids, and a long list of occult teachers in the renaissance, including Cornelius Agrippa, Paracelsus, John Dee and Christian Rosenkreutz.

No doubt when the Theosophical Society was founded, Blavatsky and Olcott were delighted by the participation of Hardinge Britten, who was a respected member of spiritualist circles on the East Coast of the United States. Some of the Society's early gatherings in fact took place in Hardinge Britten's residence in New York. Nevertheless, Blavatsky made no mention of *Art Magic* in *Isis Unveiled*, just as she ignored Caithness' book – possibly because both books appeared so close to her own. Or perhaps the reason was not literary. A personal rivalry developed between the two women spiritualists not long after they met. Their relations were still satisfactory in 1881, by which time Blavatsky and Olcott were already living in India, as shown by a notice published by Hardinge Britten in '*The Theosophist*', asking members of the Society to contribute their experiences to a new book on the history of the spiritualist movement. Two years later, when the book appeared, Hardinge Britten was already at odds with Blavatsky and Olcott, argued that the Theosophical Society had lost its way, and stated that she no longer regarded herself as a Theosophist.[74]

Let me conclude this survey with one other writer – Edward Schuré (1841–1929), whose influential book *The Great Initiates* appeared in 1889 (the same year as *The Secret Doctrine*).[75] Schuré clearly did not influence Blavatsky, but the timing of his book shows that the information she claimed to reveal in her books was hardly unique to her. Schuré, like Lady Caithness, Hardinge Britten and Blavatsky herself, sought to produce a synthesis of all the known esoteric lore. He stated that every religion has two histories – one open and one hidden, secret and esoteric. His premise was that the rivalry between the Church and science was the source of all the greatest troubles of mankind. His central idea was that all the

---

74. *The Theosophist* (October, 1881); Emma Hardinge Britten, *Nineteenth Century Miracles*, pp. 295–305.

75. Edouard Schuré, *The Great Initiates, Sketch of the Secret History of Religions* (2 vols., London, 1912), first published in French 1889.

great civilizations and religions were linked, so that their diverse prophets belonged, in effect, to a single tradition and adhered to the same secret doctrine.

He maintained that the Indian civilization was the oldest one, and from it issued the wisdom that the Egyptians, Jews and Greeks subsequently learned. Schuré, too, like Blavatsky, held that Jesus had practised an esoteric creed and linked him to ancient teachers, such as Krishna, Rama, Hermes, Moses, Orpheus and Plato. Like many of his predecessors, Schuré engaged in the obsessive attempt to re-create history according to the familiar narrative that all the civilizations prized by the Europeans stemmed from India and Egypt, and to tie them directly to Jesus. Thus the thought that characterized *Anacalypsis* continued with Eliphas Lévi, reached its peak with Blavatsky, and continued after her.[76]

The Myth of Atlantis

Both *Isis Unveiled* and *The Secret Doctrine* were largely impressive attempts at a synthesis of the various magical systems in the world, together with a review of the occult doctrine through history. As we have seen, both books were based on extensive previous literature which dealt with similar ideas. However, Blavatsky could claim the copyright for introducing what we might call 'the myth of Atlantis' into the heart of New Age thinking. Although popular interest in Atlantis began in the West in 1882, with the publication of Ignatius Donnelly's *Atlantis: The Antediluvian World*, Blavatsky's *Isis Unveiled* had dealt with Atlantis already in 1877, as did *The Secret Doctrine* in 1888. I shall now describe the sources of this myth, which became one of the leading themes among followers of the occult in our time.

The myth of Atlantis is mentioned in two famous Dialogues of Plato, the 'Timaeus' and 'Critias'. The story in both – slightly longer in the former than in the latter – describes an advanced civilization that

---

76. There are indeed plenty of other later examples, such as William Stainton Moses' (1839-1892) *Spirit Teaching*. Moses, a well-known medium and one of the SPR founders, described India as the source for all of the world's religions, William Stainton Moses, *Spirit Teaching* (London, 1894); Arthur Conan Doyle (1859-1930) published his *History of Spiritualism* in 1926, pretending to become the first ever historian of the Spiritualist movement. Conan Doyle was a great sympathizer of Blavatsky, and accordingly ruled against Hodgson's report: Arthur Conan Doyle, *The History of Spiritualism*, II (London, 1926), pp. 64, 71.

existed 9,000 years before Plato on a large island west of Gibraltar, which was linked by a chain of islands to a vast continent beyond the ocean. The civilization was founded by the god Poseidon, who placed his first son Atlas on its throne – that is why the island itself and the surrounding ocean bear his name. The Atlanteans ruled over the Mediterranean world, including Egypt and Greece. Their civilization was destroyed by an earthquake, followed by a flood that submerged the island. In the 'Timaeus' it is also said that the Athenian people sprang from a handful of Atlantean survivors.[77]

The rediscovery of Plato's writings in the renaissance revived interest in the myth of Atlantis, notably demonstrated by Francis Bacon's 1627 work, *The New Atlantis*. This utopian work describes how a group of mariners, tossed by a severe storm at sea, are washed up on an island called Benshalem by its inhabitants. These long-lived, highly advanced people produce artificial metals, various minerals, poisons and medicines. They have tools that enable them to observe things invisible to the naked eye (telescope and microscope), and 'also engine-houses, where are prepared engines and instruments for all sorts of motion'. The source of their knowledge is the civilization of Atlantis, which according to Bacon, existed in America until 3,000 years ago and dominated the sea lanes. The islanders tell the mariners that 1,900 years earlier they were ruled by a king named Solamona, who founded a society or order which they call Salomon's House. Every 12 years the order sends out two ships bearing three members of that order, to gather information about events in the outer world. The information is added to the store of knowledge preserved by the islanders, whose goal is to gather knowledge about 'God's first creature, which was Light'. The head of the order blesses the narrator and permits him to return to England and publish what he has seen, for the good of the nations of the world.[78]

Ignatius Donnelly's *Atlantis* appeared in 1882 and became a best-seller, sparking a widespread interest in lost continents. Its success undoubtedly gave a measure of legitimacy to the earlier *Isis Unveiled* and to *The Secret Doctrine*, which appeared six years after it, at any rate in connection with the subject of Atlantis and

---

77. Plato, *The Timaeus and the Critias or Atlanticus*, trans. Thomas Taylor (New York, 1944).

78. Francis Bacon, 'New Atlantis', in *The Advancement of Learning and New Atlantis* (Oxford, 1974), pp. 215–47, first published 1627.

the legendary pre-historic continent in the Pacific Ocean – Lemuria. Donnelly, an attorney and a US Congressman from Minnesota in 1863–1869, attempted a kind of scientific investigation based mainly on circumstantial evidence to verify the pre-historic existence of the continent of Atlantis, following its description by Plato. His book included seismological observations and surveys of fossils found in various continents, side by side with such absurdities as the discovery of smoking pipes in various parts of the world long before the discovery of America and the tobacco plant, or reports of pre-Columbian American paintings depicting bearded men, although the Amerindians were famously beardless. Donnelly quoted many different authorities, including Jones, Wilhelm von Humboldt and Max Müller, and argued that the ancient Atlanteans must have been descendants of Japhet, the son of Noah. He concluded that the Aryan race had originated in Atlantis, and the Indian Aryans in particular had reached India from Europe and Atlantis.[79]

Donnelly continued his would-be scientific attempts to reconstruct the civilization of Atlantis in his next book, *Ragnarök*, published in 1883, which theorized that the destruction of Atlantis was due to a huge meteor that struck the earth thousands of years ago.[80] His two books probably enhanced the public acceptance of Blavatsky's further development of the Atlantis myth in *The Secret Doctrine* in 1888.[81] The myth went on growing in the twentieth century, taking root in the Western subconscious, spawning dramatic versions in the cinema and television. It also became one of the leading subjects for discussion in modern esoteric societies, which include individuals who claim to communicate with the spirits of the Atlanteans and receive their spiritual guidance.[82]

******

79. Ignatius Donelly, *Atlantis: The Antediluvian World* (New York, 1973), first published 1882.

80. Ignatius Donelly, *Ragnarök: The Age of Fire and Gravel* (New York, 1883).

81. G.W. Trompf, 'Macrohistory in Blavatsky, Steiner and Guénon', in *Western Esotericism and the Science of Religion*, pp. 269–96.

82. This tendency was greatly enhanced by the work of the twentieth century's medium, Edgar Cayce, who, from 1924 until 1944 claimed to have had many trances in which he communicated with incarnations of Atlanteans. Cayce predicted that the continent of Atlantis will rise again in a slow process that was supposed to begin in 1968: Edgar Evans Cayce, *Edgar Cayce on Atlantis* (New York, 1968); Another

The above review may shed light on the degree of originality and uniqueness of the Theosophical doctrine, as well as on its Western orientation. As I have shown, the bulk of the material used by Blavatsky in her books was drawn from preceding work. Even if she did not access all the sources listed above, particularly the early ones, there is no mistaking their influence upon the sources she did know. This seems especially significant, given that Blavatsky described herself as an agent of information, rather than its fount. Yet the information in her books was supposed to have been passed to her by the Masters of the Theosophical Society, superhuman beings claiming to possess a broad historical perspective. It would seem that isolating the literary sources which influenced Blavatsky, and especially pinpointing the ones which contained the exact same information, might dent the prestige of those Tibetan Masters.

In the same way, it is evident that Blavatsky's information about the Hindu civilization was drawn from Western sources which contained many errors and largely supported the same premise – namely, that the wisdom of the East and the wisdom of the West stemmed from a common origin. This viewpoint was wholly adopted by Blavatsky and her successors, and it led them to perceive India and her culture through an essentially Western prism. Accordingly, we may conclude that the Theosophical interpretation of the Hindu scriptures was cast in a Western light and in fact forced those texts to conform to an esoteric Western doctrine.

Blavatsky, in fact, produced a synthesis of all the available Western sources of her time, rather than between East and West. Thus the place of the Oriental tradition in the corpus of Theosophical theology was far smaller than the Society claimed. In the final analysis, the

---

contribution to the myth of lost continents was made in 1931, when Harvey Spencer Louis (1883–1939), published (under the pseudonym 'Cervé') his book on Lemuria, in which he determined that the modern Indians possess the purest Lemurian blood: W.S. Cervé, *Lemuria: The Lost Continent of the Pacific* (San Jose, 1931). Louis was the Imperator of the American Rosicrucian Order – Antiquus Mysticus Ordo Rosae Crucis (AMORC) – which was established as the branch of the European Ordo Templ Orientis (OTO), a Rosicrucian Order that was founded in the early twentieth century by the German Theosophist Theodore Reuss (1855-1923). *Lemuria* was the 12th volume in The Rosicrucian Library Series, which Louis wrote and edited. The myth of Lemuria gained popularity in America, perhaps not less than that of Atlantis. Several Lemurian communes exist in the US to this day, preparing the ground for the future reappearance of the lost continent, Timothy Miller, *The Quest for Utopia, Vol. 1: 1900–1960* (Syracuse, 1998), pp. 189–90.

The Sources of the Theosophical Doctrine

thinking that animated the Society was largely Western, and so it remained for many years, at least until Besant's death in 1933.

These conclusions may help clarify the true place of the Theosophical Society in the Indian society in the time of Blavatsky and Olcott, with their claim to reveal to the Hindus the secrets of their own religion. These conclusions may also help to put in perspective the political-Theosophical period under the leadership of Annie Besant, who tried, as we shall see, to deepen her mentor's pretentious synthesis and to link the Theosophical-theological programme with the Indian national one. These insights will shed light on Besant's motives, and provide an added explanation for her problematic Indian image. It was this image which ultimately led to her failure in India's political arena, and to the loss of much of the influence of the Theosophical Society.

Chapter 6

Annie Besant – Her Pre-Theosophical Career

An analysis of Annie Besant's personality, activities and complicated life-story is somewhat problematic, as it involves a number of historical issues that seem tenuously related. Besant was a prominent woman in her time even before she discovered Theosophy, and especially afterwards. Her personal story involved various gender and feminist issues, as she was a strong woman whose achievements stood out in the conservative landscape of Victorian society. In addition to the feminine aspect of her story there was the religious one in a life marked by crises of faith. These crises led her through various ideological and theological stations, from devout Christianity via militant atheism and uncompromising socialism to the wholehearted adoption of the Theosophical doctrine. And each of these stations represents some aspect of English society of its time.

Another historical issue raised by a study of Besant's personality has to do with her 26-year presidency of the Theosophical Society. The Theosophical doctrine, reviewed in the previous chapters, raises many question marks in rationalist minds. With Blavatsky known as the Society's main representative, the organization evoked a very particular reaction from the British Establishment and public opinion, ranging from (at best) raised eyebrows to outright mockery. From the moment Besant succeeded Blavatsky, this attitude began to change. Though the Theosophical Society never became widely popular in England, Besant's standing, fame, background, connections and rhetorical gifts made the Society seem less absurd and more appealing. This was especially noticeable in India, the Empire's Oriental flank – there Besant effected a marvellous transformation of the Theosophical Society into a respected and influential organization that rivalled other Western institutions, such as the Christian Mission, and local Indian movements, both religious and national. This was clearly corroborated by Besant's political success.

Another historical issue arising from Besant's work in India concerns the colonial angle. In Blavatsky's time, the Theosophical claim to a cultural synthesis between East and West was expressed in the idealization of the sacred Hindu texts; it reached its zenith in Besant's time in the veneration of Jiddu Krishnamurti as a World Teacher, or the new messiah. This chapter in the history of the Theosophical Society – analysed in detail in the last chapter of this book – seems to me to encapsulate the problem inherent in the Western composition of the Society's leadership in its early days in India. The cultural imperialism which the Society claimed to oppose became one of its own characteristics, when its essentially Western Theosophical and messianic ideas were adapted to the personality of an Indian lad, who was in effect abducted from his father, removed from his culture and educated in accordance with Western ideas. The case of Krishnamurti is a representative test-case, which clearly reflects the equivocal attitude towards the Orient and its inhabitants on the part of Besant and her Society associates. It was this attitude which culminated in the Society's lapse from the influential political position it had achieved up to 1919 under Besant.

Annie Besant's biography is rich in diverse motifs, each of which calls for an historical study in its own right. Indeed, the historiography of the Theosophical Society as a whole – and of Besant in particular – is affected by this diversity, not always favourably. Many of the studies tend to focus on one or the other aspect of her personality and her work – as embodying the Victorian crisis of faith, as a militant feminist, as a socialist activist associated with the Fabians, or a Theosophical leader. Some of the studies are overly sympathetic to their subject and fall into the well-known trap of losing the necessary objectivity. It seems to me to be due to empathy and the appreciation for Besant's pioneering role as a feminist, as well as in the Victorian crisis of faith. My own conclusion is that the various phases of Besant's life, her diverse activities and contributions, should be viewed together. In the final analysis, they all led up to her eventual 'incarnation' as the President of the Theosophical Society, and they should therefore be integrally comprised in her life-story and personality.

It must be said that, as a subject, Besant is much easier to like and to describe sympathetically, than Blavatsky. Ostensibly, they were totally different women. The first, Blavatsky, was a rootless wanderer, physically unattractive, even intimidating, overweight, a compulsive smoker, a spouter of endless verbiage, who claimed to possess tremendous spiritual powers, and who was ultimately ridiculed by a representative of the English Establishment, the SPR. The other, Besant, was an Englishwoman (for all her insistence on her Irish origin), a good-looking woman who was liked by many influential men in England's cultural elite. Moreover, the usual image of Blavatsky was fairly clearcut and based mainly on her spiritualist pretension. Besant, by contrast, was a more complex case, as her various 'incarnations' projected different images, most of them positive. Yet Besant remained devoted to Blavatsky throughout her life, regarding the older woman as her leading mentor. Blavatsky's theological legacy was the foundation of Besant's Theosophical thought and the background of her practical political activity in India.

In the final analysis, though, the proper way to evaluate these two women cannot be based on the social impression they made, or their public image, but only on their ideas, as reflected in their writings. And since Besant remained constant in her Theosophical faith from 1889 to the end of her life, we may assume that her Theosophical writings represent her most unequivocally – this, despite the fact that a rationalist historian finds it easier to empathize with her pre-Theosophical self. However, an attempt to evaluate her general life's work must also take into account her early writings. Not wishing to judge Besant, I will present the tools which may help to evaluate her work and her complex personality.

Besant was 42 years old at her first encounter with Theosophy. The powerful impression made on her by Blavatsky's piercing gaze, as she described so dramatically in her memoirs, led to a spiritual turning-point.[1] The abrupt change in her life appears all the more drastic given the ideological features of her journalistic and public career prior to her conversion. The following is a review of her life before Theosophy, which is significant for several reasons. Besant's public activity during the 1870s and 1880s made her into one of England's most famous (or notorious) women.[2] Her being so

1. Carol MacKay observes the important symbolic role that the image of vision had played in Besant's writing. It seems that this image is especially prominent in the description of her first meeting with Blavatsky, Carol Hanbery MacKay, *Creative Negativity: Four Victorian Exemplars of the Female Quest* (Stanford, 2001), p. 107.

2. Mark Bevir, 'Annie Besant's Quest for Truth: Christianity, Secularism and New Age Thought', *Journal of Ecclesiastical History* 50 (1) (January, 1999), p. 62.

well-known at this early state no doubt enhanced the public impact of her Theosophical work later on.

Furthermore, during those years Besant formed contacts with leading figures in the secular, liberal, socialist and anti-monarchist circles in which she acted. As we shall see, these would be useful to her after her election as president of the Theosophical Society, giving her access to the English elite, in both the cultural and political spheres. What is more, Besant's pre-Theosophical life had been full of struggles, both personal and public. Those years may therefore be regarded as a formative period which prepared her for her role as president of the Theosophical Society from 1907 to her death.

The Formative Years

Annie Besant was born at 5.39 pm on 1 October 1847. Her father, Henry Wood, was a London businessman, of Irish origin on his mother's side. Her mother was Irish on both sides. Besant valued her origins very highly,stating, 'three-quarters of my blood and all my heart are Irish.' Though brought up as an Englishwoman, as an adult she sought to trace her Irish roots, probably from a romantic urge to sustain her anti-Establishment role.[3]

She was five when her father died of influenza, leaving his family badly off, so that her childhood was marked by continuous hardship. Three years after Wood's death, in 1855, eight-year-old Annie was given into the care of a friend of the family, a well-off widow named Charlotte Marryat, a respectable society lady and a devout Christian. Besant spent most of her childhood and adolescence in Mrs. Marryat's home, where she was taught French and German, which she perfected in European travels with her patroness.[4] Mrs. Marryat stressed religious study and reading the Scriptures, and the

---

3. H.V. Lovett and Patrick Cadell, 'Besant, Annie (1847–1933)', *The Dictionary of National Biography, 1931–1940* (Oxford, 1961), pp. 72–74, first published 1949; Annie Besant, *An Autobiography* (Adyar, 1995), pp. 1, 3, first published 1893; Ann Taylor, *Annie Besant: a Biography* (Oxford, 1992), pp. 1–3.

4. Valuable autobiographical information in regard to Besant's early years was published in a series of articles, entitled 'Autobiographical Sketches', which Besant published in her magazine, *Our Corner*, from January 1884 until June 1885. For her reflections on her language lessons and European travels, see, Annie Besant, 'Autobiographical Sketches', *Our Corner* (March, 1884); For further biographical information, although somewhat shallow, see, Rosemary Dinnage, *Annie Besant* (Middlesex, 1986).

endless poring over the Gospels led Besant to take a great interest in Christianity. This may have led her decision to marry the deacon Frank Besant (1840–1917), whom she met in the spring of 1866, when she was just 19 years-old.[5] Their marriage lasted only six years, producing, after a short honeymoon in Paris, a son and a daughter – Arthur Digby, born in 1869, and Mabel Emily, born in 1870.[6]

The marriage was an unhappy one, though probably through neither partner's fault. Frank Besant was a conservative clergyman, whose expectations from his young wife were quickly disappointed. Annie Besant herself described thus the difficulties of their relationship:

> All my eager, passionate enthusiasm, so attractive to men in a young girl, was doubtless incompatible with the "solid comfort of a wife", and I must have been inexpressibly tiring to the Rev. Frank Besant. And in truth, I ought never to have married, for under the soft, loving, pliable girl there lay hidden... a woman of strong dominant will, strength that panted for expression and rebelled against restraint...[7]

Besant's early attempts at writing illustrate the poor communication between the couple. Her first pamphlet, 'On the Duty of Fasting', written in 1866, was published in 1870. But she wrote another pamphlet on the same theme, 'Fasting Communion', which was never published due to her husband's objection. Her son found that his father had written on the manuscript, 'I would not publish this, thinking that she ought to be satisfied with the publication of preceding pamphlet.'[8]

In 1871 the family moved to the village of Sibsey in Lincolnshire, where Frank was appointed vicar. Rural life left Annie Besant with ample leisure to read religious and philosophical literature, which helped her to develop a new secular and skeptical world-view. That year she also experienced a crisis of faith when her daughter

---

5. Besant declared that in her youth she was obsessed with religious dreams. Therefore, marrying a clergyman was a logical consequence, since 'To me a priest was a half-angelic creature, whose whole life was consecrated to heaven': Besant, 'Autobiographical Sketches', *Our Corner* (April, 1884).

6. For further information on Besant's marital life, see, Arthur Digby Besant, *The Besant Pedigree* (London, 1930), p. 198.

7. Besant, *An Autobiography*, p. 65. It seems that this analysis is far more objective than those given by Besant's biographers, who usually describe Frank Besant as a violent and obsessive man, Taylor, *Annie Besant*, pp. 33-34; Arthur H. Nethercot, *The First Five Lives of Annie Besant* (Chicago, 1960), p. 43.

8. Arthur Digby Besant, *The Besant Pedigree*, pp. 200-201.

fell gravely ill. As she described it, the ideas that simmered in her mind at this time kept seeking expression. Before long this would be found in journalistic writing.[9]

Her marriage came to an end in the summer of 1873, when her husband despaired of her unbelief. They agreed on a legal separation, which remained in force for many years. Reverend Frank Besant refused to give his wife a divorce, and she remained legally married to him until his death in 1917. The separation agreement left their son in the father's custody, while the daughter, Mabel, stayed with her mother. Reverend Besant gave his wife a small allowance, which, she said, sufficed for 'respectable starvation'.[10] For some time she stayed with her mother, but when Mrs. Wood died on 10 May 1874, it seemed to Annie Besant that her life was going downhill fast. It is not difficult to imagine how the atheistic separated wife of a clergyman felt in the last quarter of the nineteenth century. The hope of employment, adequate income and respectable social life must have seemed unattainable. At this time Besant was helped by friends, among them the American Transcendentalist Moncure Daniel Conway, who was staying in London.[11] The solution to her problems came in the form of a new friend, Charles Bradlaugh (1833-1891), whom she met on 2 August 1874.

Secularism and Neo-Malthusianism

Charles Bradlaugh was a prominent liberal in England in the last third of the nineteenth century.[12] Throughout his long career, which reached its height in the 1880s with his repeated election to Parliament, he preached atheism, free thought, improved worker rights, and against the monarchy.[13] Born into the lower middle class,

---

9. Besant, *An Autobiography*, pp. 71, 97-98.

10. In 1878 the Reverend Besant succeeded in getting his daughter in his custody. Nevertheless, the anger he felt towards his wife would make his children miserable for many years to come. For example, when the 20 year-old Arthur Digby decided to renew his relations with his mother, his father refused to stay in contact with him: Besant, *An Autobiography*, p. 101; Arthur Digby Besant, *The Besant Pedigree*, p. 221.

11. Moncure Daniel Conway, *Autobiography, Memories and Experiences*, II (Boston, 1905), pp. 286-87.

12. J.R.M., 'Charles Bradlaugh (1833-1891)', *The Dictionary of National Biography*, XXII (Oxford, 1965), pp. 248-50, first published 1922.

13. Bradlaugh wrote an enormous number of articles that dealt with these issues. For some fine exemplars, see, *A Selection of the Political Pamphlets of Charles Bradlaugh,*

Bradlaugh was widely-read though self-taught, having left school at the age of 11. He served in the army for several years, and once discharged settled in London, where he mingled in liberal circles.[14] He quickly rose to prominence thanks to his rhetorical and writing abilities. In 1859 he was elected president of the London Secular Society and was greatly in demand as a speaker in the capital and elsewhere.

Bradlaugh's provocative lectures dealt with atheism, attacked Christianity from a rationalist viewpoint, included debates with churchmen, and in the course of the 1860s made him famous throughout the country. He was also involved with events on the Continent – for example, in the 1850s he helped raise funds for Garibaldi in Italy.[15] In 1860 he founded the weekly '*The National Reformer*', an organ for radical writers, and in 1866 he launched the National Secular Society, which called for secular education, the separation of Church and State and the abolition of restrictions on religious minorities. The National Secular Society spread rapidly through the kingdom, integrating numerous free-thinking societies. By 1880 the Society numbered 6,000 registered members, active in 60 branches. This membership comprised the hardcore of Bradlaugh's support, while a far greater number of people were interested in his ideas.[16] The Society's central venue was London's Hall of Science, where Bradlaugh spoke every Sunday evening in the 1870s to an audience consisting mostly of artisans and small traders. That Sunday, 2 August 1874, did not differ from Bradlaugh's other public appearances, except for one detail – that evening Annie Besant came to hear him speak.

Besant had first read an issue of *The National Reformer* a fortnight earlier, on 17 July 1874, from which she learned of the existence of the National Secular Society. She decided to join it and came to the Hall of Science in order to receive her membership card from Bradlaugh himself. After the lecture – which dealt with Christian superstitions and the similarity between the myth of Krishna and

ed. John Saville (New York, 1970); Hypatia Bradlaugh Bonner, *Humanity's Gain from Unbelief, and Other Selections from the Works of Charles Bradlaugh* (London, 1932), first published 1929.

14. Hypatia Bradlaugh Bonner, *Charles Bradlaugh, A Record of His Life and Work*, I (London, 1902), pp. 1–41.

15. Bradlaugh Bonner, *Charles Bradlaugh*, p. 152.

16. Walter L. Arnstein, *The Bradlaugh Case, A Study in Late Victorian Opinion and Politics* (Oxford, 1965), pp. 8–15.

Jesus – the two talked briefly.[17] This was the start of a long and productive association, with Bradlaugh being Besant's patron and spiritual mentor until she spread her wings and became known in her own right, at first on the basis of the articles she published in *The National Reformer*. A few days after their first meeting, Bradlaugh offered her a position on the paper. Her first article appeared on 30 August 1874, and before long she became a regular columnist in the liberal weekly.[18] In 1877 she became the paper's deputy editor, and part of the time its acting editor. The experience she gained in that period, as a journalist and an editor, would serve her well years later in India, where she founded Theosophical publications that spread the Theosophical ideas and her political-national ideology.

At this time Besant also discovered and began to develop her rhetorical ability. Her first lecture on behalf of the National Secular Society, given in London on 25 August 1874, three weeks after her first meeting with Bradlaugh, was devoted to the rights of women.[19] She gave her successful first speech in London's Hall of Science on 28 February 1874, after which she became a regular speaker alongside Bradlaugh in meetings of the National Secular Society all over Britain. She set out on her first lecture tour on 12 February 1875, going to Scotland, where she addressed small audiences in Glasgow and Aberdeen. That year she was chosen to be vice president of the Society, and held the position until 1890. At the gatherings of the Society Bradlaugh and Besant preached atheism, the advancement of the working class and a rational, neo-Malthusian economy. These were provocative ideas for much of English society at that time. Besant's early days as speaker and public figure were often marked by resistance that occasionally erupted into violence.[20] No doubt the hardships she had personally experienced gave her the strength to withstand these stresses. In this sense, her work alongside Bradlaugh was a practical political apprenticeship that would serve her well in her later, Theosophical, life.

17. Besant, *An Autobiography*, pp. 115–16.
18. During this early period, Besant used the pseudonym Ajax.
19. This lecture was printed on September 1874 as Besant's first political pamphlet, Annie Besant, 'The Political Status of Women', in *A Selection of the Social and Political Pamphlets of Annie Besant*, ed. John Saville (New York, 1970), section 2, pamphlet no. 8 (1877 edition), 14 pages: first published 1874.
20. Besant, *An Autobiography*, pp. 176–78.

Public opposition to Bradlaugh and Besant reached a climax in 1877, when the two produced a new edition of *The Fruits of Philosophy* [written in 1832 by the American doctor Charles Knowlton (1800–1850)], a book about family-planning and birth-control. The first British edition of the book was printed in 1876 by Bradlaugh's colleague, Charles Watts (1835–1906). This could have been done in relative peace, if not for the over motivation expressed by Watts' Bristol agent, who decided on his own initiative to add two provocative illustrations to the Bristol edition. The law authorities reacted immediately, sentenced the agent for two years in prison and eventually made Watts renounce the book and halt its distribution. Besant and Bradlaugh used the opportunity, and on 20 January 1877 established a new publishing house, 'Freethought Publishing Company', in which they produced their edition of the book.[21] The publication led to Bradlaugh and Besant being arrested on 7 April 1877. They were released without bail after a few hours and their trial was set for 18 June 1877. During this interval the book sold very well and made a good deal of money for the two, as well as producing tremendous press coverage. The Knowlton Trial, as it became known, provided Besant with a public platform, from which she argued for the right of public debate and freedom of expression on the subject of family-planning. This was an extremely difficult issue, despite its obvious urgency, because open discussion about sex in general, and birth control in particular, was considered immoral in the Victorian age.[22]

---

21. The new publishing house was dedicated to the printing of pamphlets which were written by its owners. One of the more provocative of those was Bradlaugh's 'The Impeachment of the House of Brunswick', which fiercely attacked the royal family. It seems that such provocations went hand in hand with the publication of *The Fruits of Philosophy*: Charles Bradlaugh, 'The Impeachment of the House of Brunswick', in *A Selection of the Political Pamphlets of Charles Bradlaugh*, section 2, pamphlet no. 15 (1877 edition), 103 pages, first published 1871; Charles Knowlton, 'The Fruits of Philosophy: An Essay on the Population Question', in S. Chandrasekhar, *'A Dirty Filthy Book': The Writings of Charles Knowlton and Annie Besant on Reproductive Physiology and Birth Control, and an Account of the Bradlaugh-Besant Trial* (Berkeley, 1981), pp. 87–147, first published 1832.

22. The question of birth-control was first raised in England in 1789 by Thomas Malthus (1766–1834). Malthus maintained that as long as the world's population growth would not be limited, it was bound to rise in geometric series, while its food supply would grow only in arithmetic series. He predicted bitter consequences, especially to the population of England. During the 1870s, the subject was still considered very sensitive, so that when Annie Besant became its spokeswoman at

The court's decision was that, although the book contained material that offended public morality, the defendants who published it had not intended to corrupt. Nevertheless, they were sentenced to six months imprisonment and a fine of 200 pounds. But before the sentence could be carried out, the Court of Appeal dismissed the penalty, on the grounds that the conviction was technically flawed. Thus, despite being convicted, Besant and Bradlaugh emerged from the trial strengthened, and enjoyed increased support from liberal circles.[23]

The Knowlton Trial also gave Annie Besant's name some celebrity outside of the British Isles. In all probability, Blavatsky and Olcott, who were still in the United States, were also aware of the affair.[24] A later confirmation (from the India period) that the affair interested Blavatsky appeared in a letter sent by the Master Koot-Hoomi to Sinnett (who had already returned to England) in January 1884:

> I'm sorry you took the trouble of posting me about Bradlaugh. I know him and his partner well. There is more than one trait in his character I esteem and respect. He is *not* immoral... Yet the book published by them – '*The Fruits of Philosophy*' is infamous and *highly pernicious* in its effects whatever and however beneficent and philanthropic the objects that led to the publication of the work... I *have not* read the work – nor ever will; but I have its unclean spirit, its brutal aura before me... They are the fruits of Sodom and Gommorah rather than of philosophy...[25]

Blavatsky's early interest in Besant may suggest that there was a long-term plot and an intricate web spun to capture Annie

---

the courthouse, she immediately gained considerable attention, T.R. Malthus, *An Essay on the Principle of Population, and, a Summary View of the Principle of Population*, ed. Anthony Flew (Harmondsworth, 1970), first published 1798.

23. By 1879, Freethought Publishing Company printed 185,000 copies of *The Fruits of Philosophy*, alongside another bestselling publication, Besant's *The Law of Population*, which dealt with similar issues and sold 40,000 copies. Since 1877, statistics show a dramatic decrease in birth rates in England. This decrease might have been directly influenced by the Knowlton Trial: Annie Besant, 'The Law of Population: Its Consequences and Its Bearing upon Human Conduct and Morals', in *A Selection of the Social and Political Pamphlets of Annie Besant*, section 2, pamphlet no. 10 (1891 edition), 46 pages, first published 1877; Besant, *An Autobiography*, pp. 204, 211-12; Arnstein, *The Bradlaugh Case*, p. 22; Taylor, *Annie Besant*, pp. 121, 342 f4.

24. Henry Steel Olcott, *Old Diary Leaves, Fifth Series, 1893-96* (Adyar, 1932), p. 301; Taylor, *Annie Besant*, p. 236.

25. A.T. Barker, *The Mahatma Letters to A.P. Sinnett from the Mahatmas M. & K.H.* (Adyar, 1972), p. 399, Letter No. 86 (January, 1884), first published 1923, p. 241, Letter No. 33 (undated).

Besant for the Theosophical cause.[26] But whether or not Blavatsky nurtured a long-term plan to initiate Besant into Theosophy, it was understandable that she took an interest in one of the most prominent women in contemporary England. As for Besant's own interest in Theosophy before her 'conversion', it is certain that before 1889 she showed no interest whatever in spiritualism. On the contrary – during those years she became the outstanding representative of the secular-rationalist movement, and clearly objected to spiritualism.[27]

The Knowlton Trial and the press hullabaloo around her cost Besant dearly. Her estranged husband, Frank Besant, used the scandal to start legal proceedings to obtain custody over their daughter Mabel, as well as their son. His petition of January 1878 stated that Mrs. Besant was morally unfit to be a mother, on account of her atheistic activity and her connection with Bradlaugh – 'an infidel lecturer and author'.[28] The case went very badly for her. She felt that the judge, Sir George Jessel (1824–1883), favoured her husband's side, and that she was being judged on her political opinions rather than her fitness as a mother. Jessel decided for the father, and even denied her the right to visit her daughter. Since in the late 1870s Jessel regularly presided over the Court of Appeal, it was he who heard Besant's appeal against his own decision. Nevertheless, he ended by permitting her to visit her children, but she herself soon realized that her presence was causing them great distress and confusion. She therefore decided to give up even her authorized visits.[29]

There is no doubt that having to give up her children was one of the main experiences that shaped Besant's personality. Aside from the tragic personal situation, the sense of helplessness in the face of the conservative masculine Establishment must have heightened her rebellion and militancy, which intensified through the years.

26. Taylor, *Annie Besant*, pp. 236-37.
27. Besant, *An Autobiography*, p. 252.
28. The case gained a severe public interest, and once again Besant had to protect herself publicly. She was criticized particularly by the *London Times*, which from then on became hostile towards Besant's activities, and later against the Theosophical Society in general. For Besant's reply to *The Times*' allegations, see, *The Times* (London, 17 April 1878).
29. Besant, *An Autobiography*, pp. 191-92, 195; Besant, 'Autobiographical Sketches', *Our Corner* (June, 1885).

Bradlaugh was first elected to Parliament in 1880, as the Liberal candidate for Northampton. This was a real triumph for the members of the National Secular Society and all supporters of Freethought, to whom it was a vindication of their long struggle for secularism.[30] Besant continued to work as Bradlaugh's associate until 1885. During this period, as well as writing articles for *The National Reformer*, she published a number of pamphlets on the same issues as those that Bradlaugh sought to promote in Parliament. They mainly concerned the promotion of atheism, the struggle against social injustice in the operations of the Christian Establishment, and arguments about the Church's distortion of the Gospels.[31] Yet as Bradlaugh's parliamentary efforts began to bear fruit, Besant began to distance herself from him. The harmony of their collaboration, consistent since 1874, was disrupted in June 1885, when Besant defected from the secular-liberal camp and joined the Fabian Society, which Bradlaugh viewed as an ideological rival.[32] Nevertheless, the two remained on good terms until Bradlaugh's death in 1891.

Socialism

At the end of September 1882, Bradlaugh and Besant moved their publishing offices to 63 Fleet Street, and there Besant worked until December 1890, (when the business association between the two was dissolved). In January 1883, not long after the move, Besant launched a new monthly, '*Our Corner*', to provide an alternative platform for writings on culture, art and politics. Judging by its price (6 pence) and contents, the magazine aimed at a fairly popular readership.

Among the persons who were close to Besant in the years up to 1889 were Charles Bradlaugh's eldest daughter Alice,[33] Edward

---

30. For further discussion on Bradlaugh's provocations at the Parliament, see, John M. Robertson, 'An Account of his Parliamentary Struggle, Politics and Teachings', in Hypatia Bradlaugh Bonner, *Charles Bradlaugh*, II, pp. 211-367.

31. See, for example, several two pence pamphlets: Annie Besant, *Giordano Bruno* (London, 1883); Annie Besant, *The Gospel of Atheism* (London, 1882); Annie Besant, *True Basis of Morality* (London, 1882); Annie Besant, *God's Views on Marriage, as revealed in the Old Testament* (London, 1883).

32. Charles Bradlaugh, 'Some Objections to Socialism', *Our Corner* (March, 1884); Charles Bradlaugh, 'Socialism: Its Fallacies and Dangers', in *A Selection of the Political Pamphlets of Charles Bradlaugh*, section 1, pamphlet no. 14 (1887), 16 pages.

33. Her premature death, in 1888, marked Besant's early interest in spiritualism, Taylor, *Annie Besant*, pp. 220-21.

Bibbins Aveling (1849-1898) and John Mackinnon Robertson (1856-1933). She was also close to George Bernard Shaw, who was beginning to make a name for himself as a journalist and writer. The two were on intimate terms from 1885 until Besant's conversion to Theosophy. Two other notable friends at this time, notably in the late 1880s, were William Stead, the editor of the *Pall Mall Gazette*, and Herbert Burrows, the person with whom Besant first called on Blavatsky. Besant's relations with each of these individuals illustrate the stations of the last secular decade of her life, and shed light on the strong social connections which would serve her later in her Theosophical life.

Aveling was one of the most inconstant men in the liberal (and later socialist) circles in London in the 1880s. He and Besant had met in 1879, when she had decided to study Law. The five compulsory preparatory courses included science – Aveling's speciality as university lecturer. Besant attended his lectures in company with Bradlaugh's younger daughter Hypatia, and was greatly impressed.[34] Although she never did complete her studies, their meeting led Aveling to make an abrupt change in his professional life. He had always longed to be a playwright and journalist, and shortly after meeting Besant he began to publish articles in *The National Reformer*. At first he published them anonymously (for fear the association with the radical movement would harm his professional position), and later under his real name, having asserted his loyalty to the secular movement. In time, Aveling became a regular contributor to *Our Corner*, and later published a number of plays under the pseudonym Alec Nelson. Besant brought him into the National Secular Society, and soon after, in 1880, he became its vice-president, side by side with her.

Aveling quit the National Secular Society in 1884 and joined its chief political rival, the SDF – Social Democratic Federation, which was founded by Henry Hyndman (1842-1922) in 1881. Shortly afterwards he quit the SDF, too, and helped found the Socialist League, which competed successfully against its mother-movement, and went on growing until the end of the nineteenth century. Between 1886 and 1895, the Socialist League published an

---

34. Conway reports that most of the students at University College London did not favour Besant's presence, due to her negative reputation, Conway, *Autobiography, Memories and Experiences*, II, pp. 287-90.

influential weekly named 'The Commonweal', to which Aveling was a regular contributor. It competed with the SDF's weekly, 'Justice', and gave favourable coverage to Besant's public activity in the latter half of the 1880s.[35]

Aveling's circle of associates included some of the most prominent socialists in England, among them Friedrich Engels (1820–1895), George Bernard Shaw, and Eleanor Marx (1855–1898), Karl Marx's youngest daughter. Aveling had married a woman named Isabel Frank in 1872 but separated from her when he became a secular socialist. He and Eleanor Marx began to live together in June 1884 (about a year after her father's death), and collaborated in promoting socialism in England and abroad.[36] It was understood that they would marry when his legitimate spouse died. When she finally passed away in 1897, Aveling broke his promise and secretly married a young actress named Eva Frye, with whom he had had an affair. Eleanor Marx took it very badly and on 31 March 1898 committed suicide by poison. Aveling was so affected by her suicide that he died on 2 August that year.[37]

John Robertson was a regular contributor to *Our Corner* from May 1883, writing about socialism. However, he only met Besant for the first time in October 1884, at a farewell party thrown in his honour by the Edinburgh Secular Society. The occasion was his departure for London, where he would join *The National Reformer*, replacing Aveling who had withdrawn from the National Secular Society shortly before. There was immediate chemistry between him and Besant. As soon as he arrived in London he became a lodger at her house, where he lived until 1887. It was during 1884, the year Robertson came to London, that Besant became interested in the socialist ideas which were beginning to spread at that time. According to Besant, Robertson played a crucial role in attracting her to socialism.[38]

35. Years after, when Besant began her political activity in India, she published a weekly, which bore the title *The Commonweal: A journal of National Reform*, thus combining the names of Aveling and Bradlaugh's two influential weeklies.
36. Eleanor Marx-Aveling and Edward Aveling, 'The Woman Question', in *Thoughts on Women and Society*, ed. Joachim Müller and Edith Schotte (New York, 1987), pp. 10–29, first published 1886.
37. Yvonne Kapp, *Eleanor Marx, I: Family Life (1855–1883)* (London, 1972), pp. 253–86; Chushichi Tsuzuki, *The Life of Eleanor Marx, 1855–1898: a Socialist Tragedy* (Oxford, 1967), pp. 316–19.
38. Besant, *An Autobiography*, p. 274.

Robertson also gained Bradlaugh's sympathy, despite his being a socialist, and later became his first biographer. Beside his position at *The National Reformer*, he regularly contributed to Besant's *Our Corner*, and was her right hand in editing the monthly. After Bradlaugh's death in 1891, he became the chief editor of *The National Reformer*. He began his long political career, and in the years 1909-1918 was a Liberal Member of Parliament for Tyneside. At the same time he also cultivated an extensive literary career, not only writing on political issues, history and the science of religions, but making a serious contribution to modern literary research and publishing books on the authenticity of Shakespeare's writings.[39]

Robertson's literary talents manifested themselves only after his working relations with Besant had ended. However, it appears that already in the mid-1880s, when he was working at *Our Corner*, he regarded himself as an authority in literary matters. This is attested in an angry letter to him, sent on 19 January 1885, from a young writer who had submitted an early work of his for publication in the magazine. '... refrain from telling Mrs. Besant,' it said, 'that my books are immoral and dull. I have no doubt that you have gone that length, though she is too kind to say so.'[40]

The angry writer was George Bernard Shaw, who was then 29 years old, and the novel in question was *The Irrational Knot*, which Robertson considered unworthy of publication. Eventually *Our Corner* published it by instalments. At this time Shaw became a regular contributor to Besant's magazine.[41] Their friendship developed in parallel with her passage from the National Secular Society to the Fabian Society, which she joined in June 1885, of which Shaw was already one of the leading spokesmen.[42] Her addition to its ranks was a major catch. Compared to the current Fabian activists, Besant was quite well-known, being a member of an older generation than

---

39. Harold J. Laski, 'Robertson, John Mackinnon (1856-1933)', *The Dictionary of National Biography, 1931-1940* (Oxford, 1961), pp. 736-37, first published 1949; Taylor, *Annie Besant*, pp. 170-71; J.M. Robertson, *Did Shakespeare Write Titus Andronicus?* (London, 1905); J.M. Robertson, *Pagan Christs: Studies in Comparative Hierology* (London, 1903); J.M. Robertson, *A History of Freethought: Ancient and Modern, to the Period of the French Revolution* (London, 1936), first published 1899.

40. Shaw, *Collected Letters, 1874-1897*, ed. Dan H. Laurence (London, 1965), pp. 112-13.

41. Besant, *An Autobiography*, p. 274; Shaw, *An Autobiography, Vol. 1, 1856-1898*, Selected from his Writings by Stanley Weintraub (New York, 1969), pp. 101-102.

42. Edward R. Pease, *The History of the Fabian Society* (London, 1916), pp. 40, 44.

that of the Society's founders, who were mostly in their twenties (in 1885 she was 38). Quite soon, Besant became a central figure in the Fabian circle. During her years of membership she contributed to the Society's fame and success by putting to use the dynamic public experience she had gained in her work with Bradlaugh.

The Fabian Society was probably the world's first socialist organization and one of the progenitors of the British Labour Party. It was founded in January 1884 by Frank Podmore (1856-1910) and Edward Pease (1857-1955), who were also founding members of the SPR.[43] Podmore's house, 14 Dean's Yard, Westminster, was the Society's headquarters in its early days, and it was also the venue of many of SPR's early meetings. Shaw humorously described how he and other members of the Fabian Society would attend a Fabian meeting in those early days, and immediately afterwards join a SPR meeting, both in the same rooms.[44]

The two societies remained linked for several years, although they appeared to be concerned with unrelated issues. The fact that key members of the Fabian Society and the SPR (such as Podmore and Pease) were active in both indicates a common intellectual basis, probably arising from a similar intellectual position. Podmore probably regarded the SPR as the proper venue for discussing universal spiritual issues, while the Fabian Society was his setting for considering intellectual questions in their social context. Possibly it was this atmosphere which originally attracted Besant to the

---

43. Podmore and Pease founded the Fabian Society to promote social equality in England. The name of the new society was inspired by the tactics that the Roman Consul, Fabius Maximus Cunctator, used against Hannibal. Later, Podmore was losing his position in the Fabian Society in favour of other members, particularly Shaw and Sydney Webb (Baron Passfield, 1859-1947). Eventually, he retired and was made honorary secretary of the SPR. Later, he wrote the biography of Robert Owen, and dedicated himself to the research of telepathy. Pease, his co-founder, maintained his Fabian activity and served as the Fabian honorary secretary until 1939: Pease, *The History of the Fabian Society*, pp. 28-40; Frank Podmore, *Robert Owen: a Biography* (2 vols., London, 1906); Frank Podmore, *Modern Spiritualism: a History and Criticism*, ed. R.A. Gilbert (2 vols., London, 2000), first published 1902; A.M. McBriar, *Fabian Socialism and English Politics, 1884-1918* (London, 1962), p. 3; Margaret Cole, *The Story of Fabian Socialism* (London, 1961), pp. 1-6; Margaret Cole, 'Pease, Edward Reynolds (1857-1955)', *The Dictionary of National Biography*, 1951-1960 (Oxford, 1971), pp. 799-800; Mary Agnes Hamilton, 'Webb, Sidney James, Baron Passfield (1859-1947)', *The Dictionary of National Biography*, 1941-1950 (Oxford, 1959), pp. 935-40; Roger Luckhurst, *The Invention of Telepathy, 1870-1901* (Oxford, 2002), p. 55.

44. Shaw, *Collected Letters, 1898-1910*, ed. Dan H. Laurence (London, 1972), p. 497.

Fabians. Thus, at any rate, did Shaw analyse the reasons that led her eventually to quit the Fabians in favour of Theosophy.[45]

Shaw and Besant first met at a gathering of the Dialectical Society, founded to promote a free discussion of the ideas of John Stuart Mill. Shaw went there to speak on the subject of socialism, but on arrival was surprised to meet Annie Besant, who asked him to introduce her to his fellow Fabians.[46] This was the beginning of a long and close relationship. Like the friendships between Besant and several other men during this time, it is hard to assess to what extent the one with Shaw went beyond the Platonic. Besant wrote very matter-of-factly but discreetly about her relations with such close associates as Aveling and Robertson, and so she did about Shaw. He, on the other hand, wrote a good deal about her. Thus any conclusions about the nature of their relationship must be based on the way he presented it. Shaw was well-known for his passionate affairs and intimate descriptions of his relations with women, yet where Besant was concerned he asserted that their relationship was characterized by 'intimacy [of]... a very close and personal sort, without however going further than friendship.' Yet a biography of Shaw written (in 1942) with his collaboration paints a different picture. From a distance of 55 years, Shaw recalled that in 1887 Besant presented him with a detailed cohabitation agreement, which he declined, supposedly because she was married. She was distressed, he recalled, demanded that he return her letters and tearfully returned his letters to her. The biography goes further, suggesting that Besant had a nervous breakdown after the end of her relations with Shaw: 'Her hair turned grey; she even thought of suicide.'[47]

The two undoubtedly had an unusual friendship based on a common goal, mutual admiration and perhaps even Shaw's Irish background (given Besant's deep attachment to her own Irish origins).[48] But we must remember that Besant was nine years older than Shaw, had greater experience and fame, and therefore a stronger

45. Shaw, *An Autobiography*, I, p. 140.
46. Shaw, *Everybody's Political What's What?* (London, 1944), pp. 74, 152; Shaw, *An Autobiography*, I, pp. 111, 141.
47. Shaw, *An Autobiography*, pp. 302–303 f11; Hesketh Pearson, *Bernard Shaw, His Life and Personality* (London, 1943), p. 114, first published 1942.
48. The Irish question did indeed bother Besant at the time. This is evidenced in her articles in *Our Corner*, as in the *National Reformer*. See, for example, Annie Besant, 'England's Jubilee Gift to Ireland', in *A Selection of the Social and Political Pamphlets of Annie Besant*, section 3, pamphlet no. 20 (1887), 8 pages.

position than his in their relationship. Hasty assumptions have been made about her supposed affairs with several male friends, but in fact there is no solid foundation for any of them – not with reference to Bradlaugh, Aveling, Robertson, Burrows and Stead, and not with regard to Shaw. Yet, aside from the speculations and gossip, there can be no doubt that Besant was one of the most important women in Shaw's life. His frequent references to her in his writings testify to this, as well as the fact that she inspired several characters in his plays.[49]

The Fabians' new acquisition, Annie Besant, rapidly joined the Society's leadership and was elected to its executive committee in 1886. Her rhetoric skills made Besant a breath of fresh air for the Fabians, who had so far engaged mainly in theoretical discussions, as described by Shaw: 'Now at this time Annie Besant was the greatest orator in England, perhaps the greatest in Europe...'[50] Her extensive political and organizational experience – the fruit of her decade of collaboration with Bradlaugh – led her to suggest reorganizing the Fabian Society as a political party, in order to get into Parliament. She promoted the opening of branches all over England, the formation of a league (with elected officers), and starting a publishing house to be funded by contributions.[51] In 1886 she produced for the Fabians her first socialist pamphlet, '*Modern Socialism*', which appeared by instalments in *Our Corner*, then published in full in June 1886, by Freethought Publishing House.[52] At the same time she was the moving spirit in organizing the great Fabian conference that was held in London, with the participation of all the socialist movements in England, except the SDF.[53] She devoted space in *Our Corner* to articles about Fabian socialism. This pro-Fabian activity became so crucial, that in October 1887 she was obliged to give up her position

---

49. Shaw based the character of Mrs. Clandon in his 1896 *You Never can Tell* on Besant, Shaw, *An Autobiography, Vol. 2, 1898-1950: The Playwright Years*, Selected from his Writings by Stanley Weintraub (New York, 1970), p. 284 f4. In an undated letter (probably 21 April 1898), Shaw mentioned that the character of Raina in his *Candida*, was also based on Annie Besant: Shaw, *Collected Letters, 1898–1910*, p. 34.

50. Shaw, *An Autobiography*, I, p. 138.

51. Patricia Pugh, *Educate, Agitate, Organize: 100 Years of Fabian Socialism* (London, 1984), p. 11.

52. Annie Besant, 'Modern socialism', in *A Selection of the Social and Political Pamphlets of Annie Besant*, section 4, pamphlet no. 26 (1890 edition), 51 pages: first published 1886.

53. McBriar, *Fabian Socialism and English Politics, 1884–1918*. p. 23.

as deputy editor of *The National Reformer*, after ten years of unbroken work beside Bradlaugh. 'I therefore resume,' she wrote, 'my former position as contributor only, thus clearing *The National Reformer* of all responsibility for the views I hold.'[54]

Besant's work for the Fabians was most intensive in 1887-1888, notably in connection with two major events in which she took an active part – 'Bloody Sunday' and the strike by the women workers at the Bryant & May match factory. On Sunday, 13 November 1887, the SDF, the Fabian Society and the Socialist League held a mass meeting in London's Trafalgar Square to protest against the attack on the right of assembly. The meeting turned riotous and on the orders of the commander of the Metropolitan Police, Sir Charles Warren (1840-1927), was dispersed with great violence by the police, who caused the death of several persons, and the wounding and arresting of many others. Besant witnessed 'Bloody Sunday' in company with other Fabians, including Shaw, who noted: 'The heroine was Mrs. Besant, who may be said without the slightest exaggeration to have all but killed herself with overwork in looking after the prisoners.'[55]

The police arrested many socialist activists, and Besant helped some of them (with the help of Eleanor Marx) by paying their bail and fines and obtaining legal representation for them. The cost was covered by a fund created by William Stead, the editor of *Pall Mall Gazette*. One interesting outcome of this affair was Besant's meeting with Richard Burdon Haldane (1856-1928), then a young barrister who helped defend the accused. Like several other young people Besant met at this time, Haldane was at the start of a grand career, and their acquaintance would serve Besant well many years later.[56]

Following the events of 'Bloody Sunday', the relationship between Besant and Stead quickly grew stronger. During the 1880s Stead was one of the most influential journalists in England, if not the most influential. He became the chief editor of the *Pall Mall Gazette* in 1883. Under his management, the daily newspaper, which cost a halfpenny, enjoyed wide distribution and a strong presence

---

54. Besant, *An Autobiography*, p. 291.
55. Bernard Shaw, 'The Fabian Society, What It has Done and How It has Done It' (1892), in *Essays in Fabian Socialism* (London, 1949), p. 134: first published 1932.
56. E.S. Haldane, 'Haldane, Richard Burdon, Viscount Haldane, of Cloan (1856-1928)', *The Dictionary of National Biography*, 1922-1930 (Oxford, 1961), pp. 380-86, first published 1937; Pugh, *Educate, Agitate, Organize*, p. 17.

that helped promote public discussion on various political and social issues. Stead's journalistic style came to be known as 'the new journalism' (an expression coined by Mathew Arnold in 1887). His editorial articles were regarded as highly significant, whether about major political questions or social issues.[57]

Stead was a devout Christian and was regarded as an unbiased investigating journalist. At this time he was interested in spiritualism, an interest which began when he first took part in a séance and grew over the years. In 1890 he left daily journalism and founded the spiritualist publication '*Borderland*'. In 1897 he published a collection of communications with the spirit of an American journalist named Julia Ames, whom he had met in London in 1890, shortly before her death. The communications were made by means of automatic writing, a skill Stead discovered in himself in 1892. Not content with communing with the spirit of Julia Ames, he later reported constant communication with the spirit of his son Willy, who died in the age of 33.[58] But Stead's spiritualist skills did not help him to foresee his own end – he went down with the Titanic in 1912.[59]

Stead's popularity gradually declined, due both to his interest in spiritualism and to his opposition to the Boer War in South Africa (1899–1902), but when he met Besant he was at the zenith of his career. In 1887 they founded together the Law and Liberty League, in defence of victims of police violence. The League published a halfpenny weekly magazine entitled '*Link*', which Besant and Stead produced together. It dealt with social issues, such as fair wages for the working-class, women's employment and protection against exploitation by employers. In June 1888 the *Link* began to promote

57. Stead was said to have influenced the decision to send General Gordon (1833–1885) to Khartoum in 1884. In 1885 the *Pall Mall Gazette* published a series of reports (The Maiden Tribute of Modern Babylon), in which it revealed the problem of under-age prostitution in England: Frederic Whyte, *The Life of W.T. Stead*, I (London, 1925), Chapters 6 and 8, pp. 117–44, see also 159–86.

58. Whyte, *The Life of W.T. Stead*, I, pp. 327–34.

59. Stead's daughter, Estelle, claimed to have communicated with her deceased father for many years. In 1937 she published a detailed description of the communications, which were transferred by a French medium, Madame Hyver. In one of these messages from the other world Stead complained about the communication difficulties he encountered, due to the substantial number of radio communications which have polluted the atmosphere in the beginning of World War I, Estelle W. Stead, *Communication with the Next World, the Right and Wrong Methods: A Text-Book Given by William T. Stead from 'Beyond the Veil' through Madame Hyver* (London, 1937), p. 68.

a public debate about the miserable working conditions of the women employees at the Bryant & May match factory, and called for a boycott of the company's products. At that time the 1,400 women working in that factory, most of them very young, were paid a pittance, while, according to Besant, the shareholders of the company received huge dividends.

The affair aroused the interest of Herbert Burrows, who rallied to the aid of the match workers.[60] He and Besant resolved to devote themselves to the fight against the management of the match factory. Besant wrote: 'If we ever worked in our lives Herbert Burrows and I worked for the next fortnight. And a pretty hubbub we created.'[61] Shaw noted:

> Her powers of continuous work were prodigious. Her display of personal courage and resolution... were trifles compared to the way in which she worked day and night to pull through the strike of the over-exploited match-girls... An attempt to keep pace with her on the part of a mere man generally wrecked the man.[62]

Burrows, though, was not wrecked. He and Besant interviewed workers and managers at the match factory and published their impressions in the press.[63] These reports created a public outcry, which flared up when Besant personally went to the workers' aid and led a strike at the factory. After the successful strike Besant and Burrows organized the match workers into a union. Besant personally headed it for many years, and Burrows was its treasurer. A couple of years after the strike Besant opened a club for the union members. It was to provide 'the atmosphere so familiar to all who have grown up in the blessed shelter of a happy home, so strange, alas! to too many of our East London girls.'[64]

60. Burrows met Besant in 1879, when he was an activist in the National Secular Society. In 1884 he joined the SDF, but still kept close relations with Besant during the 1880s, during which he introduced her to the Marxist theories and the terminology of revolutionary socialism. In 1885 he was elected to the London School board, having enjoyed Besant's enthusiastic support in *The National Reformer*. Later, he led her to join the SDF, which became the last stop in her pre-Theosophical journey. Following Besant, Burrows joined the Theosophical Society, but quit his membership in 1908, just after his old friend became its president, Taylor, *Annie Besant*, p. 213; Besant, *An Autobiography*, p. 283.

61. Besant, *An Autobiography*, p. 305.

62. Shaw, *An Autobiography*, I, p. 140.

63. See, for example: Annie Besant and Herbert Burrows, 'The Strike of the East End Matchmaker', *The Pall Mall Gazette* (9 July 1888).

64. Besant, *An Autobiography*, pp. 304-307.

Shortly after this affair, Besant was elected to the London School Board as the Fabians' representative, replacing Burrows who had held the position since 1885. At this time the Board was quite conservative, despite having been one of the first institutions in England to allow women on its board from its foundation in 1870. Besant devoted much of her time to the Board's work, bringing up matters of vital concern to the schoolchildren, such as free meals and the abolition of fees for primary schools.[65] She continued to lecture, but there was less demand for her as a speaker after she joined the SDF. Despite that move, she remained a member of the Fabian Society, and took part in a course of lectures given in the autumn of 1889. The lectures were subsequently issued as a book, *Fabian Essays in Socialism* – including her own contribution, entitled 'Industry under Socialism' – by Besant's publishing house.[66]

After publishing favourable reviews of *The Secret Doctrine* in the *Pall Mall Gazette* and *The National Reformer*, and causing quite an uproar, Besant announced that she was joining the Theosophical Society. The atheistic readers of *The National Reformer* were astounded by her new views. She stated, *inter alia*, that '... the wisdom of those "masters", in whose name Madame Blavatsky speaks... has given only into the hands of the selfless the control of those natural forces which, misused, could wreck society.'[67]

A little after the appearance of her reviews of *The Secret Doctrine*, Besant published a pamphlet entitled, 'Why I Became a Theosophist'. It discussed non-corporeal phenomena such as Mesmerism and hypnosis. She explained that these led her to understand that the materialistic worldview she had always upheld no longer satisfied her, and addressed the members of the

---

65. Taylor, *Annie Besant*, pp. 214-20.
66. The book sales went well, but shortly after Besant's conversion to Theosophy, the Fabian Society decided to hand the printing rights to another publishing house. Besant was mad and delivered the unsold copies, with her resignation letter, to the offices of the Fabian Society. The Fabian executive committee discussed the Besant affair in its meeting on 21 November 1890. The protocol reads: 'Gone to Theosophy'. Four days later, Shaw wrote that Besant did not explain her resignation, and blamed Theosophy for the change in her manners, Annie Besant, 'Industry under Socialism', in *Fabian Essays in Socialism*, ed. George Bernard Shaw (London, 1889), pp. 150-69; Pugh, *Educate, Agitate, Organize*, pp. 21-23; Shaw, *Collected Letters, 1874-1897*, pp. 270, 273.
67. Annie Besant, 'Review of the Secret Doctrine', *The National Reformer* (23 June 1889), 390-91.

National Secular Society with a dramatic statement, asserting her new quest for the truth.[68]

Besant indicated that her interest in spiritualism and the occult had begun in the first half of 1889, before she met Blavatsky, and that she read *The Secret Doctrine* when she was already mentally prepared to take the Theosophical ideas on board.[69] Nevertheless, her conversion to Theosophy must have stunned most of her associates. Shaw offered several explanations for this transition, and mentioned that according to the Shakespearean view, Besant was a tragedian, while the Fabians were comedians. This, according to Shaw, made Besant realize that she had spent her time as fifth wheel in the Fabian carriage.[70]

Shaw made a similar comment in a letter to his friend H.G. Wells (1866–1946), dated 22 November 1906. He said that the Fabian Society found it difficult to keep competent women, such as Besant, because they discovered pretty soon that they had no actual function that could not be fulfilled without them.[71]

Shaw's interpretation of Besant's transition to Theosophy clearly differed from hers. He maintained that he had been personally responsible for the sequence of events that led to her meeting with Blavatsky, and reacted to her conversion to Theosophy cynically.[72] Bradlaugh's reaction was much more critical:

> Modern Theosophy, according to Madame Blavatsky... asserts much that I do not believe, and alleges some things that, to me, are certainly not true. I have not had the opportunity of reading Madame Blavatsky's two volumes, but I have read during the past ten years many publications from the pen of herself, Colonel Olcott, and of other Theosophists. They appear to have sought to rehabilitate a

---

68. Annie Besant, 'Why I Became a Theosophist', in *A Selection of the Social and Political Pamphlets of Annie Besant*, section 4, pamphlet no. 27 (1889), 31 pages; Blavatsky published the complete pamphlet in *Lucifer, a Theosophical Magazine* (London, August, 1889); Shaw said that he learnt of Besant's conversion by accident, having laid his eyes on the pamphlet while attending the offices of *The Star*, Shaw, *An Autobiography*, I, p. 141.

69. Besant, *An Autobiography*, p. 309.

70. Shaw, *An Autobiography*, I, pp. 138–39.

71. This strange comment indicates its speaker' chauvinism rather than the real reason for Besant's resignation from the Fabian Society: Shaw, *Collected Letters. 1898–1910*, pp. 653–54, 716.

72. Shaw, *An Autobiography*, I, pp. 141–42; Shaw, *Collected Letters, 1874–1897*, p. 505.

kind of Spiritualism in Eastern phraseology. I think many of their allegations utterly erroneous, and their reasonings wholly unsound. I very deeply regret indeed that my colleague and co-worker has, with somewhat of suddenness, and without any interchange of ideas with myself, adopted as facts matters which seem to me to be as unreal as it is possible for any fiction to be. My regret is greater as I know Mrs Besant's devotion to any course she believes to be true.[73]

Thus did one of the great women rebels against the Victorian Establishment turn into a devout Theosophist. Annie Besant's life-story, which until then had swung through rationalist ideologies – from a militant atheism to Marxist socialism – underwent a profound change when she began to believe in Theosophy. Nevertheless, the political experience she acquired in her pre-Theosophical career would serve well the interests of the Theosophical Society. The widespread connections acquired in her secular incarnation would also serve to consolidate the Society as a more respected body, and empower her in her relations with the Establishment in England and in India. Her experience as a journalist and publisher enabled her to construct the efficient propaganda machinery she founded in India. All these experiences formed the foundation on which Besant built the Theosophical structure in the following years, from 1889 to her election as president of the Indian National Congress in 1917. In this sense, Blavatsky had shown foresight in choosing her successor. The next chapter discusses Besant's career in fulfilling her mentor's expectations.

---

73. Charles Bradlaugh, 'Some Words of Explanation', *The National Reformer* (30 June 1889), 409; Blavatsky published the complete article in *Lucifer*: Blavatsky, 'Force of Prejudice', *Lucifer* (July, 1889).

Chapter 7

The Struggle Over the Leadership of the Theosophical Society, 1889-1907

Besant's Initiation by Blavatsky, 1889-1891

The last two years of Blavatsky's life were filled with intense activity – writing books, editing the magazine *Lucifer* and promoting the Theosophical activity in London. Soon after meeting Besant, Blavatsky turned her into her confidante and marked her as her chosen successor. Blavatsky's Indian summer seems to have been vitalized by the presence of Besant, Theosophy's latest acquisition. It probably gave her hope that her doctrine would survive after her.

Shortly after joining the Theosophical Society, Besant went to Paris with Burrows, to participate as SDF delegates in the international Socialist congress that was held in Paris between the 15th and 20th of July 1889, one of the events marking a century since the French Revolution. At this time Blavatsky was in Fontainbleau, near Paris, where she took a vacation for several weeks. Having finished their duties at the congress, Besant and Burrows visited their new mentor, and stayed with her for 'a day or two'.[1] This was when Besant first experienced an encounter with one of the Masters. The vision of Master Morya was the first of many she would describe in the coming years.[2] It was a clear indication that Besant was wholly inducted into Blavatsky's imaginary world at the very start of her Theosophical life.[3]

Blavatsky had chosen to stay in Fontainbleau because at this time the foreign relations of the London Lodge were concentrated in

---

1. Annie Besant, *An Autobiography* (Adyar, 1995), p. 321, first published 1893.
2. According to Besant, she woke up from a deep sleep, and saw the Master's glowing image in front of her: *Lucifer, A Theosophical Magazine* (London, June, 1891).
3. For further discussion on Annie Besant's new spiritualism, see, Mark Bevir, 'Annie Besant's Quest for Truth: Christianity, Secularism and New Age Thought', *Journal of Ecclesiastical History* 50 (1999), 83-85.

The Struggle Over the Leadership of the Theosophical Society 215

France. The Society's first French Lodge had been launched a few months earlier, in March 1889, and its founding was seen as the most significant event in the occult sphere in France of the 1880s.[4] While resting in Fontainbleau, Blavatsky wrote *The Voice of the Silence*, which became one of the most popular Theosophical texts. Besant and Burrows read this short book while staying with their mentor in France, and admired its polished English style. Their admiration rested on the claim that it was a translation from Senzar, the lost ancient language in which the original texts of *The Secret Doctrine* had also been composed. Blavatsky claimed that *The Voice of the Silence* was part of a more comprehensive composition entitled 'The Book of Golden Precepts', used by the Tibetan mystical sect with which it was identified. She claimed that Senzar, the book's mysterious original language (known in the West only to Blavatsky herself), was the oldest Aryan language. *The Voice of the Silence* was, thus, part of India's original Aryan, Buddhist civilization.[5]

At about the same time Blavatsky published another popular book, entitled *The Key to Theosophy*. While it did not add anything new to the material in the massive volumes of *Isis Unveiled* and *The Secret Doctrine*, it did compress Blavatsky's central ideas into a more readable form than the earlier, less organized books. Besides reviewing the main Theosophical principles, Blavatsky listed the dangers faced by the Theosophical Society, and promised its members a brilliant future:

> Then the Society will live on into and through the twentieth century. It will gradually leaven and permeate the great mass of thinking and intelligent people with its large-minded and noble ideas of Religion, Duty, and Philanthropy... Through its teaching... the West will learn to understand and appreciate the East at its true value... Mankind will be saved from the terrible dangers, both mental and bodily, which are inevitable when that unfolding takes place, as it threatens to do, in a hot-bed of selfishness and all evil passions.[6]

As we shall see, that 'hotbed of selfishness' would characterize the wars of succession among the leadership of the Theosophical Society.

---

4. Joscelyn Godwin, *Music and the Occult, French Musical Philosophies, 1750–1950* (Rochester, 1995), p. 151.

5. H.P. Blavatsky, *The Voice of the Silence, Being chosen Fragments from the 'Book of the Golden Precepts'* (Wheaton, 1992), pp. v–vii, first published 1889.

6. H.P. Blavatsky, *The Key to Theosophy* (London, 1938), pp. 152–53, first published 1889.

These began immediately after Blavatsky's death in 1891, and in a matter of a few years culminated in the Society's irreparable split.

In the summer of 1890, Blavatsky moved to Besant's house at 19 Avenue Road, St John's Wood, London. In an announcement she made in *Lucifer*, Blavatsky nominated herself the president of the Theosophical Society in Europe. Thus, her new premises were turned into the European headquarters of the Theosophical Society. Olcott, reluctantly, authorized that self-nomination in September.[7] Besant made some major changes in the house, gave Blavatsky rooms on the ground floor, and set aside a conference room for meetings of the Blavatsky Lodge, (established, over Olcott's objections, shortly after Blavatsky's arrival in London). The new headquarters soon became the residence of certain privileged associates, such as the editor of *The Secret Doctrine*, Bertram Keightley, and his brother Archibald, the Countess Wachtmeister, and George Robert Stow Mead (1863–1933), who was becoming one of the leading figures in the Theosophical Society in England.[8] This privileged circle observed a strict daily regime, at their mentor's demand, with a pedantic daily schedule that set the times for all activities, from mealtimes to lights-out.[9]

This colourful group was conspicuous not only for its upscale residence, but also for representing the core of the elite circle of Theosophy in London, namely, the ES – Esoteric Section – founded by Blavatsky shortly after settling in England. This faction was designed to support her in the dispute with Olcott and the Adyar centre. Membership in it was viewed by the Theosophical Society rank and file as a real privilege, mainly because it involved direct instruction by the Society's founder. The precise activities of the ES membership are not easy to determine, there being no regular record of their meetings or of the experiments they conducted. Both were hidden under a thick shroud of secrecy rigidly maintained

---

7. *Lucifer* (July and September, 1890).

8. Mead joined the Society in 1884 and became Blavatsky's secretary in 1889. He served as deputy editor of *Lucifer* for several years and was appointed chief editor of *The Theosophical Review* in 1897. Mead gained scholarly reputation, due to his translations and his own writings. See, for example, George Robert Stow Mead, *Orpheus* (London, 1965), first published 1896; G.R.S. Mead, *Pistis Sophia: A Gnostic Miscellany: Being for the Most Part Extracts from the Books of the Savior, to Which are Added Excerpts from Cognate Literature* (London, 1921); G.R.S. Mead, *Thrice-Greatest Hermes: Being a Translation of the Extant Sermons and Fragments of the Trismegistic Literature with Prolegomena and Notes* (3 vols., London, 1964), first published 1906.

9. Besant, *An Autobiography*, pp. 329–31.

by Blavatsky. New members who joined the ES had to sign an application form that included a commitment to complete confidentiality. This form, composed by Blavatsky, also listed numerous rules and restrictions phrased in supposedly legal language. This meant that their signatures were indeed legally binding, as was demonstrated in some cases when members of the faction withdrew from it and believed themselves free to reveal its inner workings.

One of the most prominent members of the ES at this time was the Irish poet and playwright, the future Nobel winner (1923), William Butler Yeats. He had been greatly interested in mysticism and the occult from an early age, and first encountered Blavatsky's teaching when he presided over a small esoteric group, the Dublin Hermetic Society, founded in 1885. He was drawn to Theosophy from reading Sinnett's *Esoteric Buddhism* and meeting Blavatsky and Olcott's associate Mohini Chatterji, who had been sent to Ireland to promote Theosophy. Following their meeting, Chatterji brought Yeats into the Theosophical Society, and caused him to change the name of his society. In April 1886 it became known as the Dublin Theosophical Society.[10] Yeats moved to London in 1887 and met Blavatsky a few months later. He joined the ES in December 1888, but was expelled from it at the end of 1890. His descriptions of Blavatsky and the ES (mostly written during those two years) provide an interesting insight about her and events inside the ES.

Yeats described his first meeting with Blavatsky in a letter he wrote in December 1887 to his friend, the Irish nationalist John O'Leary (1830–1907). 'I was at Madame Blavatsky's. She abused me over the spiritualist affair... They all look to Ireland to produce some great spiritual teaching.'

Another letter to O'Leary, from September 1888, mentions that he visited Blavatsky every six weeks or so. It appears that associating with her was good for Yeats' literary career, which was then in its early stages. In 1888 he co-edited an anthology of Irish folklore together with the editor and journalist (and friend of Shaw's) Ernest Rhys. In September that year he wrote Rhys to ask him to send a copy to Blavatsky, promising that she would review it in *Lucifer*.[11]

---

10. Terence Brown, *The Life of W.B. Yeats: A Critical Biography* (Oxford, 1999), pp. 32-33; R.F. Forster, *W.B. Yeats: A Life, Vol. 1: The Apprentice Mage, 1865–1914* (Oxford, 1997), p. 47.

11. *The Letters of W.B. Yeats*, ed. Allan Wade (London, 1954), pp. 56-57, 86, 90-91. See also, W.B. Yeats, 'Irish Fairies, Ghosts, Witches etc.', *Lucifer* (January, 1889).

A little after this, around Christmas time in 1888, Yeats joined the ES. His memoirs of that period reveal that the powerful attraction he felt for Blavatsky was somewhat weakened by his mental resistance to the obedience she demanded of the members, and his uncertainty about the existence of the Masters.[12] In his journal he noted on 20 December 1889 that a few days earlier, on the first anniversary of his joining the ES, he had renewed his loyalty oath to the group. The ceremony, conducted by Blavatsky, was attended by several new members of ES, among them Annie Besant and Herbert Burrows.[13] Yeats used the occasion to propose a working programme for the members to carry out research and experiments in the sphere of the occult. He worried that Blavatsky might reject it, for fear of applying black magic, but to his surprise (as he noted in his journal), his proposal was adopted on 30 December. On 19 January 1889 it was decided to form a 'Recording Committee', headed by Yeats, to research occult lore. The committee carried out experiments in clairvoyance, and Yeats noted that Blavatsky kept the report of these experiments.

During his two years of membership in the ES, Yeats wrote extensively about his experiences in it to his friend, the Irish poet Katharine Tynan (1861–1931). On 21 December 1888, a few days before he joined the group and some time after the death of Anna Kingsford, Yeats wrote Tynan about Blavatsky's claim that, 'There were two Mrs Kingsfords, "a good woman and a woman of the world who dyed her hair... She was good, but her progress came from intelligence."'

His unreserved faith in his mentor was gradually diluted by doubt. On 26 December 1889, after having his beard shaved, Yeats wrote Tynan, a touch humorously, that 'Madame Blavatsky promised me a bad illness in three months, through the loss of all the mesmeric force that collects in a beard one has gone by.' On 4 December 1890, he reported to his friend: 'I too had a quarrel with the followers and withdrawn from all active work in the society. I wrote some articles they objected to about *Lucifer*.'[14]

---

12. W.B. Yeats, *Memoirs*, ed. Denis Donoghue (London, 1972), pp. 281–82; *The Letters of W.B. Yeats*, p. 125.

13. Yates and Besant became close for a while, probably because of the latter's Irish sentiment, Elisabeth Butler Cullingford, *Gender and History in Yeats's Love Poetry* (Cambridge, 1993), p. 40.

14. *The Letters of W.B. Yeats*, pp. 97, 145, 162.

Yeats' criticism of *Lucifer* marked his decision to transfer his allegiance to another esoteric society, the Hermetic Order of the Golden Dawn, which he joined on 7 March 1890, a few months before he was ejected from the ES by Blavatsky. The Golden Dawn, which counted among its members the famous occultist Aleister Crowley (1875-1947), had become the Theosophical Society's most serious rival in England. Yeats' decision to switch to the Golden Dawn resulted from his dislike for the Theosophical claim to reconcile the occult with science, and his interest in the more mystical aspects of the occult, which Blavatsky repudiated.[15]

Yeats acknowledged a debt to Blavatsky even after she ejected him from the ES. Aside from the literary analyses of his work which describe its characteristic magical symbolism as drawing deeply on Blavatsky's teaching, it appears that Yeats held her in high esteem to the end of his life. In 1920 he described appreciatively how Blavatsky was the first to introduce him to Oriental philosophy and the world of the spirits. His *Autobiographies* quotes her sympathetically in connection with the very issue which led him to turn away from her: 'Beware of mediumship; it is a kind of madness; I know, for I have been through it.'[16]

Yeats' reports reveal that members of the ES experimented with phenomena associated with the occult – precisely the sort of activity from which Olcott sought to distance the Theosophical Society after the scandal of the Hodgson Report. It was therefore to be expected that Olcott would regard the ES as undesirable and a threat to the Society. Nevertheless, during the next two decades, under Besant's leadership following Blavatsky's death, the ES became the Society's elitist body, despite Olcott's strenuous objections. As we shall see, Besant's power-base on her way to the presidency of the international Theosophical Society was the ES, and this was the main source of the friction between her and Olcott. One of Besant's notable qualities as the Society's leader – in contrast to Olcott and Blavatsky – was the skilful way she amalgamated the two approaches, the political and

---

15. On Blavatsky's objection to black and practical magic, see, H.P. Blavatsky, 'The Blessing of Publicity', *Lucifer* (August, 1891); Blavatsky, 'Ormuzd and Ahriman', *Lucifer* (March, 1891); Richard Ellmann, *Yeats: The Man and the Masks* (New York, 1948), p. 86.

16. Frank Kinahan, *Yeats, Folklore, and Occultism* (London, 1988), pp. 218-19; W.B. Yeats, *Later Essays*, ed. William H. O'donnell (New York, 1994), pp. 270-72; W.B. Yeats, *Autobiographies* (London, 1973), p. 177, first published 1955.

the esoteric, which had characterized her two predecessors respectively. Her dizzying rise in India's political sphere was largely due to this combination. Her fall, too, which was no less dramatic, was also largely due to it.

Relations between Blavatsky and Besant grew closer during the time of the Yeats affair. Though unusually creative at this time, Blavatsky became increasingly weak and ailing in the last two years of her life. She was aware that her approaching demise would hand the final victory to her former associate Olcott in the contest for the leadership of the Theosophical Society. This awareness reinforced her relationships with Besant, whom she indicated as her chosen successor. This was demonstrated not only in their joint residence, but also in their work on *Lucifer*. Besant's first article in the magazine appeared in the June 1889 issue.[17] Thereafter she became a regular contributor to the Theosophical monthly, and after Blavatsky's death its chief editor.

Nevertheless, Blavatsky was careful not to rely exclusively on her new friend. At this time she also took pains to renew her ties with William Judge, the president of the American Section, whom she named in her will as head of the ES (alongside Besant). She saw proofs of leadership abilities in both Besant and Judge, who had been her partner in the founding of the Theosophical Society. Her main concern was to leave a successor who would be able to stand up to Olcott about the Society's future way. In all probability, she envisaged cooperation between the two heads of the ES, Besant and Judge, who were both eager to expand the esoteric aspect of the Theosophical doctrine. In this scenario she foresaw them resisting Olcott, who was trying to cast the Theosophical Society in a more rationalist, respectable and established light, with a strong tendency towards Buddhism.

Blavatsky's pugnacious approach to Olcott and his supporters was expressed in a series of articles she published in *Lucifer* between 1889 and 1891. In August 1889, for example, her column, entitled 'A Puzzle from Adyar', attacked the editorial article of the previous month's *The Theosophist*, which claimed that it was her intention to take over and 'to boss Adyar' through her ES. In response, Blavatsky wrote: 'Owing to such undignified quibbles, Adyar and especially

---

17. Annie Besant, 'Practical Work for Theosophists', *Lucifer* (June, 1889).

The Theosophist are fast becoming the laughing stock of Theosophists themselves, as well as of their enemies.'[18]

Another article she wrote in April 1890, entitled 'Why I do not return to India', which would be published in *The Theosophist* only in 1922, many years after both she and Olcott were dead, stated:

> In India... ever since my departure, the true spirit of devotion to the Masters and the courage to avow it has steadily dwindled away. At Adyar itself, increasing strife and conflict has raged between personalities... There seems to have been something strange and uncanny going on at Adyar... so long as I remained at Adyar, things went on smoothly enough, because one or other of the Masters was almost constantly present among us...

Blavatsky declared that she could not return to India, and 'live at the Headquarters from which the Masters and their spirit are virtually banished.'[19]

Further evidence of Blavatsky's efforts against Adyar is found in her 'Letters to the American Conventions', sent between 1888 and 1891. The letters were read aloud at the annual conferences of the American Section, which Judge organized from 1887 on. They shed light on the rivalry between Blavatsky and Olcott and the balance of power in the Society's leadership. When Blavatsky sent her first letter, early in 1888, she was at a low ebb. She had recently arrived in London and the positive reaction to the publication of *The Secret Doctrine* had yet to appear. Judge was probably aware of her vulnerable position at this time, but he treated her with utmost respect and read out her letter to the delegates of the American Section on the second and final day of the second American conference. No doubt he regarded her public support as crucial. It accorded nicely with his plans against Olcott and his ambition of becoming the leader of the international Theosophical Society.

Blavatsky used Judge as a pawn. In all probability, her original estimate of him was much the same as Olcott's – namely, that he was of lesser degree than either of them. But Blavatsky could not ignore Judge's substantial success in the United States.[20] Compared

---

18. *The Theosophist* (July, 1889); H.P. Blavatsky, 'A Puzzle from Adyar', *Lucifer* (August, 1889).

19. Blavatsky, 'Why I do not return to India', *The Theosophist* (January, 1922), originally written in April 1890.

20. Judge's charisma and skills helped the American Section become the world's largest Theosophical section. In 1896, there were already 108 Theosophical lodges

to any other prominent Theosophist outside Adyar, Judge was the likeliest candidate to lead the opposition to Olcott. Accordingly, her first letter contained fulsome praise for Judge, whom she dubbed 'My dearest brother and co-founder of the Theosophical Society,' adding that the Society's very existence was due to him. Her second letter, sent to the third annual conference of the American Section, which took place in April 1889, resembled the first, and warned against allowing the Society to grow too fast, for fear of a premature fall. The third letter, addressed to the fourth American conference in April 1890, was read out by her special representative Bertram Keightley.

When the fifth American conference was held in April 1891, Blavatsky was already on her deathbed. Perhaps that was what prompted her to send Annie Besant as her personal representative to the conference. She probably used this last opportunity to unite the powers of Judge and Besant as her joint successors. Besant sailed to the United States on 1 April 1891 on board the ship 'The City of New York', arrived in New York on the 9th, and gave a series of lectures there and in Washington DC, before joining the American Section for its conference in the middle of the month in Boston. There she read out two letters from her mentor, who again flatteringly praised Judge.[21]

Madame Blavatsky died from complications of influenza on 8 May 1891, a few days before Besant's return from the United States. One of her last instructions was to appoint Besant as general secretary of the inner circle of the ES. As things stood at the time of her death, it looked as though the union of Besant and Judge's forces was in fact materializing. As it happened, the old spiritualist's prophetic vision was impaired, at least in this matter.

Blavatsky's death was the second tragedy to hit Besant in a short space of time. Bradlaugh, her patron during her atheistic phase, had died three months earlier. Thus ended another chapter in Besant's life, with the demise of the two people who had made the greatest

across the USA: E.T. Hargrove, 'Progress of Theosophy in the United States', in *The North American Review* 162 (June, 1896), 698–704.

21. H.P. Blavatsky, *Letters to the American Conventions*, Letter 1 (3 April 1888), Letter 2 (7 April 1889), Letter 3 (26 April 1890), Letter 4 and 5 (15 April 1891). (Republished Online by The Theosophical University Press, available at: http://www.theosociety.org/pasadena/hpb-am/hpb-am1.htm); *Lucifer* (May, 1890, April and May, 1891).

impact on the course of her life. From now on she would have to fight for her convictions without any patrons to assist her – except, of course, the Masters, with whom she would be in close contact through the coming years. In September 1889, some 18 months before she died, Blavatsky wrote that,

> ...our Society has done more within its fourteen years of life to familiarize Western thinkers with great Aryan thought and discovery than any other agency within the past nineteen centuries. What it is likely to do in the future cannot be forecast; but experience warrants the hope that it may be very much, and that it will enlarge its already wide field of useful activity.[22]

In this her foresight was correct. Besant would expand the sphere of influence of the Theosophical Society far beyond what her mentor had achieved, bringing Indian thought closer to the West, but primarily bringing Western thought to India.

At a Crossroads

Blavatsky's death left an obvious vacuum in the worldwide Theosophical milieu, and marked the start of a series of struggles over the Society's leadership and character. The wars of succession lasted into the first decade of the twentieth century, and featured two climatic moments – the American Section's split from the international Society in 1895, and Besant's election as the Society's president in 1907. Another dramatic crisis, though unconnected to Blavatsky's legacy, occurred in 1912, when the German Section quit the Theosophical Society. As we shall see, this section, led by Rudolf Steiner (1861–1925), would be reborn as the Anthroposophical Society.

A study of Besant's conduct, her uncompromising character and utter confidence in the rightness of her way, can lead one to conclude that she herself largely contributed to those crises. Her decision to turn her back on Judge and cooperate with Olcott (apparently in opposition to Blavatsky's directives), was a leading cause of Judge's isolation and the American Section's secession. Yet even after this dramatic development, Besant continued resolutely to advance her own position and convictions, causing great uneasiness to many members of the Society and a growing fear that it was going astray.

22. H.P. Blavatsky, 'Our Three Objects', *Lucifer* (September, 1889).

These apprehensions came to the fore when Besant was elected president of the Society – some long-standing members, among them Sinnett, Burrows and Keightley, quit the movement. Besant's equally unbending manner during the sharp ideological rift with Steiner led to the loss of the German Section in 1912. Perhaps if Besant had been more pluralistic, more diplomatic and less militant, these crises might have ended differently. In other words, but for Besant's trenchant personality, it is possible that the Theosophical Society would today be a unified and much larger body.

Yet Besant's character was not the only cause of the various schisms that broke up the movement. There were ideological conflicts as well as personal rivalries. From the moment Besant decided to cooperate with Olcott her doctrine grew increasingly pro-Indian, clashing with the mindset of the American and German sections. The American Theosophists did not see India as the exclusive source of occult lore, and their position was reinforced by Judge's successor, Katherine Tingley. She preferred the Egyptian Hermetic tradition over the Hindu esoteria, and maintained that the significant spiritual centre in the modern world was America, rather than Asia. The ideological dispute between Besant and Steiner also revolved around the former's insistence on the centrality of India. As we shall see, Steiner was animated by Christian ideas, and resisted the World Teacher concept which became the heart of Besant's doctrine from the moment she was elected the Society's president. To him, her belief in the Hindu Krishnamurti as the avatar of both Krishna and Jesus was an absurdity.

Before she could become the president of the Theosophical Society, Besant had to overcome several adversaries within the Society, notably William Judge and later his successor Katherine Tingley, who headed the American Section from 1896. The alliance forged between Besant and Judge a little before Blavatsky's death lasted only two years. It was ended by Besant's calculated decision to switch her support to Olcott. This decision matured in the course of 1893, a year of major developments for Besant and the Theosophical Society. The Society appeared to be recovering from the Hodgson Report and regaining international recognition. The event which best symbolized this was the World's Parliament of Religions, which met in Chicago in September 1893. Two months later Besant went on her first journey to India, which would become her second home.

The World's Parliament of Religions

The July 1893 issue of *The Theosophist* carried a letter from William Judge, the president of the American Section, giving a detailed description of the World's Parliament of Religions, scheduled to be held in Chicago for 17 days, from the 11th to the 27th of September that year. Judge noted proudly that the Theosophical Society would be represented in the unique gathering, alongside representatives of the world's other religions.[23] He was entitled to feel proud – the occasion was one of the most talked-about events of the time, despite the fact that it had originally been planned as a sideshow to that year's Chicago World's Columbian Exposition.

The relative representations in the World's Parliament of Religions reflected the priorities and areas of interest for the contemporary research of Comparative Religion. Besides the various Christian denominations and Judaism, it was mainly the religions of the Far East which were represented, while Islam was allocated a minor representation which did not reflect its global dimension.[24] In other ways, however, the very existence of this conference marked a turning-point in the relations between East and West. Spokesmen for Oriental religions were for the first time at the forefront, winning public sympathy and press coverage. This event may be seen as the starting point of one of the most interesting phenomena in the intellectual history of the modern United States, where there is still today widespread interest in the religions of the East.[25]

The moving spirit behind this extraordinary project was an American cleric called John Henry Barrows (1847–1902). Having graduated in Theology at Yale University, he was ordained minister of the Congregational Church in 1875. His interest in a dialogue between the religions of the East and Christianity arose mainly from his ambition to unify the world's religions by a gentle propagation of Christianity in the East, as the faith that contained the main tenets of both Eastern and Western beliefs. In this, his ideas closely resembled those of Max Müller who also hoped to Christianize India, not by the methods of the old missionary societies, but through openness, acceptance and understanding of the ancient Aryan religions.

23. *The Theosophist* (July, 1893).
24. Richard Hughes Seager, *The World's Parliament of Religions: The East/West Encounter, Chicago, 1893* (Bloomington, 1995), pp. 101–102.
25. Carl T. Jackson, *The Oriental Religions and American Thought* (Westport, 1981), pp. 257–58.

Essentially, this approach meant building a religious bridge between East and West, and for Barrows, as for Max Müller, the bridge was to be constructed of Christian planks. Barrows, acting as the chairman of the World's Parliament of Religions, was in touch with Max Müller and met him in Oxford in 1895, on his way to India, where he spent two years lecturing all over the country.[26]

Prominent among the participants invited to the Parliament were Vivekananda, representing Hinduism, and Anagarika Dharmapala, representing Buddhism. As noted before, Vivekananda had been a disciple of Ramakrishna. He had received a Western education, had a very good command of English, and would later become one of the leading neo-Hindu reformers, in part thanks to his participation in the World's Parliament of Religions. When he arrived in Chicago he was relatively unknown, but in the course of the 17-day Parliament he became the most popular of the delegates. He presented the principles of Hinduism, especially the philosophy of the Vedânta – the theological foundation of the Vedânta Society he later launched in the United States. In the twentieth century this society would do more than any other Indian-originated body to disseminate Hindu philosophy in the United States.[27] After the conference Vivekananda went on an extensive lecture tour through the United States, receiving enthusiastic press coverage. After his return to India a core of faithful supporters continued to disseminate his ideas in the US through the Vedânta Society. On his way back to India, in 1896, he met Max Müller in Oxford. Later, between August 1899 and July 1900, he again went on a tour of the US, lecturing widely, especially on the West Coast.

Although he died fairly young, in 1902, Vivekananda established the image of a Hindu preacher of a new kind, and it became the model for the religious Hindu nationalists who followed him. His books on yoga were published in the United States and England, and apparently pioneered this subject in the West.[28] Thus his participation in the World's Parliament of Religions was a major event and a landmark in the history of the export of ideas from India

26. *The Life and Letters of the Right Honourable Friedrich Max Müller*, ed. Georgina Max Müller, II (New York, 1902), p. 351.
27. Carl T. Jackson, *Vedânta for the West: The Ramakrishna Movement in the United States* (Bloomington, 1994).
28. For further reading, see, Swami Vivekananda, *The Yogas and Other Works, Including the Chicago Addresses, Jnana-yoga, Bhakti-yoga, Karma-yoga, Raja-yoga, Inspired Talks, and Lectures, Poems and Letters* (New York, 1953).

to the West. But Vivekananda was still a relatively anonymous figure when the Parliament met, and the Theosophists had a clear advantage over him in public relations and publicity for the defence of Hinduism, as they had over all the Hindu reform movements of the time.[29] His relations with the Theosophical Society were in the nature of rivalry, and he eventually launched a sharp attack on Theosophy. Curiously, much of his popularity stemmed from the interest he aroused in occultist circles in America, including some members of the Theosophical Society. This ran counter to his own critical attitude towards occult lore.[30] According to Vivekananda,

> It goes without saying that a certain amount of good work has been done to India by the Society; as such every Hindu is grateful to it, and especially to Mrs Besant... she is doing the best in her power to raise our country... But that is one thing – and joining the Society of the Theosophists is another. Regard and estimation and love are one thing, and swallowing everything any one has to say, without reasoning, without criticising, without analysing, is quite another.

He resented the Theosophists in the context of the Parliament of Religions:

> There is a report going round that the Theosophists helped the little achievements of mine in America and England. I have to tell you plainly that every word of it is wrong... I saw some Theosophists in the Parliament of Religions, and I wanted to talk and mix with them. I remember the looks of scorn which were on their faces, as much as to say, "What business has the warm to be here in the midst of the gods?"... Thus they prepared the way for me all over America![31]

Olcott responded condescendingly to Vivekananda's criticism, arguing that the Hindu reformer was in error when he denigrated the Theosophical Society, this being due to his youth and inexperience. The crass conclusion of his attack was that Vivekananda's early death was a punishment for his conduct: 'Karma can take care of itself.'[32]

29. Jackson, *Vedânta for the West*, pp. 5–6.
30. Steven F. Walker, 'Vivekananda and American Occultism', in *The Occult in America: New Historical Perspectives*, ed. Howard Kerr and Charles L. Crow (Urbana, 1983), pp. 162–76.
31. Swami Vivekananda, 'My Plan of Campaign', in *The Complete Works of Swami Vivekananda*, Vol. 3 (Mayavati, Almora, Himalayas, 1945–1948), pp. 254–57, first published 1908.
32. Olcott, *Old Diary Leaves*, Sixth Series (April 1896 – September 1898) (Adyar, 1935), pp. 128–29 (Hereafter Old Diary Leaves, VI).

However, he conceded magnanimously that Vivekananda had 'a precious gift which it is a pity is not more generally shared by modern Hindus, viz., earnestness.'[33]

The other prominent Oriental participant in the Parliament of Religions was the Sinhalese Buddhist reformer Dharmapala from Ceylon, who became by far the most popular Buddhist representative at the conference. His lectures, rich in Western philosophy and the contemporary science of religions, presented the principles of his organization, Maha Bodhi, and called for a revival of Buddhism and the restoration of sacred Buddhist sites to their believers. After the conference he went on a lecture tour around the United States, and conducted well-publicized conversions to Buddhism. In the summer of 1896 he again visited the United States, stopping on the way to meet Max Müller in Oxford. Georgina Max Müller was impressed by him, noting that he was 'a strikingly handsome man'. Max Müller had earlier, in July 1895, written to Dharmapala to persuade him to take part in an international congress of religions in England. He urged him to keep up his efforts to revitalize his original pure religion, noting that his Theosophical friends were charlatans: 'Nothing has injured Buddhism so much in the eyes of scholars and philosophers in Europe, as what goes by the name of Esoteric Buddhism. Madame Blavatsky may have been a dear friend to you, but Truth is a dearer friend.'

After Max Müller's death, Dharmapala wrote to his wife, Georgina, and told her that he had been a devoted reader of her husband's writings since 1883. 'In obedience to nature's law,' he wrote, 'the physical body of the illustrious individual known as Professor Max Müller has ceased to exist, but his name will continue to exist in influencing future generations.'[34]

Possibly Max Müller's strictures affected Olcott's close ally. Dharmapala's relations with the Theosophical Society cooled in the late 1890s, and in the end he broke off with Olcott. But in 1893, during the World's Parliament of Religions, his relations with the

---

33. Olcott, *Old Diary Leaves*, Fifth Series, 1893–1896 (Adyar, 1932), p. 412 (Hereafter *Old Diary Leaves*, V).

34. Seager, *The World's Parliament of Religions*, pp. 110–11; Thomas A. Tweed, *The American Encounter with Buddhism, 1844–1912: Victorian Culture & the Limits of Dissent* (Chapel Hill, 2000), p. 54, first published 1992; *The Life and Letters of the Right Honourable Friedrich Max Müller*, II, pp. 350–51, 369, 448.

Society's leadership were good, and his success in Chicago probably struck them as favourable to their cause.

The Theosophical Society sent several delegates to the World's Parliament of Religions, led by Judge, as Olcott's official representative, and Besant, as the Society's official spokeswoman.[35] Another delegate, Gyanandra Nath Chakravarti, a Brahmin professor of mathematics from Allahabad, a long-standing member of the Theosophical Society, accompanied Besant from London to America and stayed with her in Chicago. Judge gave a lecture about the principles of Theosophy, explained that it did not claim to be a new religion but proposed a new method of looking at the world's religions. Besant spoke about Theosophy's higher aim – the recognition of Man's true evolution, whose goal was a higher spiritual state. She told the audience about Blavatsky's mission and the Masters who were behind the Society and provided its spiritual vitality.[36]

In their reports to *The Theosophist* in India and *Lucifer* in England, the representatives of the Theosophical Society at the conference described a huge success, halls packed with large masses of avid listeners. The obvious euphoria in these reports reveals the state of mind of the Theosophical Society at that time. It seemed that the long crisis caused by the Hodgson Report was finally over, and the Society was at last winning the sort of worldwide establishment recognition it had longed for.

The project of rehabilitating the reputation of the Theosophical Society had begun in India in 1885, from the moment Blavatsky left Adyar. Remaining as the sole leader in the Orient, Olcott did a great deal to win respect for the Society, emphasizing its national-spiritual nature and playing down its esoteric aspect. In England, however, the situation was quite different. Blavatsky nurtured the esoteric element in the London Lodge and the ES as the spearhead of the Theosophical efforts in Europe. Her death in 1891 saved the Society from the constant criticism she attracted, and opened new possibilities for the Society's relations with the press and the academic world. From the political point of view, Blavatsky's choice of Besant as her successor was clearly the right one. Besant,

---

35. Olcott, *Old Diary Leaves*, V, pp. 36–38.
36. William Q. Judge, 'Theosophy Generally Stated', *Lucifer* (December, 1893); Annie Besant, 'The Evolution of Man' (An Address at the Parliament of Religions, Chicago, 1893), in Annie Besant, *Evolution and Occultism* (Adyar, 1913).

one of the best-known women in England before her conversion to Theosophy, was viewed more favourably than her foreign mentor. For some time, at least, her connections in the higher circles made for a more tolerant reaction.[37] In this way the year 1893 seemed to augur a more promising future. The World's Parliament of Religions, from which Besant emerged in the highest spirits, was seen as the start of such a future. Yet it was just then that Max Müller chose to launch a strong attack against the Theosophical Society. It began before the Parliament in Chicago, but was most probably connected with it.

Max Müller versus the Theosophical Society

Max Müller was involved in the moves that led up to the World's Parliament of Religions, as well as the debates held in the course of it. His interest in the conference stemmed from his desire to advance the discipline he had founded – Comparative Religion – which was still in its infancy. As we have seen, he knew Barrows, the man who organized the conference, and in 1894 he noted that there were few things in his life he regretted missing so much as the World's Parliament of Religions.[38] Very likely he disliked the fact that the Theosophical Society had been invited to take part in the conference. In the two months leading up to the event he attacked the Society with unprecedented ferocity.

The attack signalled a sharp change in his attitude towards the Society and its leaders, as his previous expressions had been much more tolerant. Indeed, he had corresponded with Olcott for several years and regarded him as a contributor to the study of India's religions. Their communication began with the founding of the library at Adyar in 1886. The library increased rapidly and accumulated a considerable number of valuable manuscripts.[39] Max

37. Similarly, the Russian Theosophical Society began to flourish only years after Blavatsky's death, when her scandalous reputation was somewhat forgotten. The Russians accepted Besant's Theosophy more favourably, since her preaching involved some fundamental Christian ideas, unlike her predecessor, Maria Carlson, 'No Religion Higher than Truth', A History of the Theosophical Movement in Russia, 1875–1922 (Princeton, 1993), pp. 43–53.

38. Eric J. Sharpe, *Comparative Religion, A History* (La Salle, 1987), p. 252, first published 1975; Seager, *The World's Parliament of Religions*, pp. 126–27.

39. The library is still highly regarded by scholars worldwide. See, for example: Daniel H.H. Ingalls, 'The Heritage of a Fallible Saint: Annie Besant's Gifts to India', *Proceedings of the American Philosophical Society* 109 (1965), 86. However, visiting the library nowadays might cause disappointment due to its non-Western standards, and the overall atmosphere of neglect.

Müller viewed this work favourably and agreed to advise Olcott. His supportive attitude is shown in a letter he wrote to Olcott on 24 July 1888, praising the Theosophical effort in translating Sanskrit texts, and urging him to devote his best efforts to translating the Upanishads.[40] Olcott naturally valued the connection with Max Müller, whose authoritative standing was precisely what he needed after the Hodgson Report fiasco.

In their early association Max Müller's attitude to Olcott was friendly and good-humoured, as may be deduced from the description of their single meeting, at Max Müller's home in 1888. As a convert to Buddhism, Olcott was uncomfortable about the placing of three Buddha images on the hearthstone in Max Müller's library. He advised his host to display them in a more respectful way, to avoid hurting the feelings of devout Buddhists. Max Müller replied that the images had been placed on the hearth because the ancient Greeks regarded it as the most sacred place in the house.[41]

Max Müller's tolerance turned to rigid dislike which became most intense in 1893. The opening salvo of his campaign against the Theosophical Society was the publication of *Theosophy or Psychological Religion*, with an introduction in which he claimed that 'It should be known once for all that one may call himself a theosophist, without being suspected of believing in spirit-rappings, table-turnings, or any other occult sciences and black arts.'[42] His decision to describe the collection of his lectures as a campaign against Theosophical activities was clearly due to the Society's relative success at this time and the anger it aroused in him.[43] On 22 March 1893 he wrote Olcott,

> ... that is what you and your friends have been looking for, that is what you will find... in my last volume of Gifford Lectures, entitled *Theosophy or Psychological Religion*. You should now try to persuade your friends in India to make a new start, *i.e.* to return to their ancient

---

40. Blavatsky published the letter in *Lucifer* (November, 1888).
41. *The Life and Letters of the Right Honourable Friedrich Max Müller*, II, pp. 245–46.
42. F. Max Müller, *Theosophy or Psychological Religion* (London, 1893), p. xvi.
43. Bosch, Max Müller's finest biographer, claims, perhaps somewhat naively, that the book's title was chosen in order to prevent possible confusion with Blavatsky's ideas. It seems to me that that choice was made carefully, as an aimed attack against the Theosophical Society, Lourens Peter van den Bosch, 'Theosophy or Pantheism?: Friedrich Max Müller's Gifford Lectures on Natural Religion'; published Online by *Here-Now4U* Online Magazine: http://www.here-now4u.de/eng/theosophy_or_pantheism__friedr.htm

philosophy in all its purity... If I have spoken and written against you, I should have done just the same against myself and my best friends, when I saw that they were seeking for the truth but were going on a wrong road to find it. You can do much good in India if you will treat the Hindus, not as children, but as men.[44]

Olcott evidently was unimpressed by these suggestions. The June issue of *The Theosophist* carried a harsh criticism of *Theosophy or Psychological Religion*.[45]

Max Müller's attack came to a head in May 1893, in an article entitled 'Esoteric Buddhism' – the title borrowed, consciously or not, from Sinnett's book – harshly denouncing the late Blavatsky and the Theosophical Society:

> It is sometimes represented as the height of professorial conceit that scholars like myself, who have never been in India, should venture to doubt statements made by persons who have spent many years in that country. This has always been a very favourite argument. If Sanskrit scholars differ from writers who have been twenty years in India, they are told that they have no right to speak; that there are MSS. in India which no one has ever seen, and that there are native scholars in possession of mysteries of which we poor professors have no conception. When asked for the production of those MSS., or for an introduction to these learned Mahatmas – for India is not so difficult to reach in these days as it was in the days of Marco Polo – they are never forthcoming... The fact is, that there is no longer any secret about Sanskrit literature, and I believe that we in England know as much about it as most native scholars.

Max Müller argued that the confusion in these matters had to be laid at the door of,

> .... the late Madame Blavatsky, the founder of Esoteric Buddhism. I have never met her, though she often promised, or rather threatened, she would meet me face to face at Oxford... At first she treated me almost like a Mahatma, but when there was no response I became, like all Sanskrit scholars, a very untrustworthy authority. I have watched her career for many years from her earliest appearance in America to her death in London last year... Like many people in our time, she was, I believe, in search of a religion which she could honestly embrace. She was a clever, wild, and excitable girl... Like Schopenhauer, she seems to have discovered through the dark mists of imperfect translations

---

44. *The Life and Letters of the Right Honourable Friedrich Max Müller*, II, p. 309.
45. *The Theosophist* (June, 1893).

some of the brilliant rays of truth which issue from the Upanishads and the ancient Vedânta philosophy of India... Unfortunately, she took it into her head that it was incumbent on every founder of a religion to perform miracles... We see that Madame Blavatsky might have achieved some success if she had been satisfied to follow in the footsteps of Rider Haggard... but her ambition was to found a religion, not to make money by writing new *Arabian Nights.*

The conclusion of 'Esoteric Buddhism' was that Blavatsky was ignorant and egocentric in her pretension to found a religion of her own, while Max Müller himself – her polar opposite – aimed to provide scientific knowledge to the whole human race and to all who were interested in religion as such.[46]

On 10 June 1893, soon after the publication of 'Esoteric Buddhism', Max Müller wrote Olcott:

> I can quite understand your feelings for Madame Blavatsky... particularly after her death... but I felt it my duty to protest against what seemed to me a lowering of a beautiful religion. Her name and prestige were doing real mischief among people who were honestly striving for higher religious views... Madame Blavatsky seems to me to have had that temperament, but she was either deceived by others or carried away by her own imaginations. There is nothing esoteric in Buddhism... Buddha protests against the very idea of keeping anything secret... You can help to forward or retard the good work that has to be done in India. If I can be of any use, I am always willing to help.[47]

The July issue of *The Theosophist* reported Max Müller's article ironically and complacently: 'We cannot, at any rate, complain of want of attention just now: we are receiving it on every hand.' The August issue carried an article by Olcott reviewing Stead's spiritualist magazine *Borderland,* and quoted the following: 'A truth for Prof. Max Müller to ponder before again prodding Mme. Blavatsky, through the sod of her grave, so to say.' The September 1893 issue carried an extensive review of Max Müller's article by the Hindu Purnedu Narayan Sinha, expressing great disappointment with the Professor's ideas.[48]

---

46. F. Max Müller, 'Esoteric Buddhism', *The Nineteenth Century* (London, May, 1893), 767–88.
47. *The Life and Letters of the Right Honourable Friedrich Max Müller,* II, pp. 312–14. Olcott later quoted the letter in his diaries, Olcott, *Old Diary Leaves,* V, pp. 42–45.
48. *The Theosophist* (July, August, September, 1893).

Another indication of Max Müller's attitude at this time was brought up later by George Mead in the March 1904 issue of *The Theosophical Review*. Mead described his correspondence with Max Müller some ten years earlier, soon after the publication of *Theosophy or Psychological Religion*. He wrote that Max Müller had asked him why he was wasting time on Theosophy, when the entire sphere of Oriental research was open to him. 'Above all, he was puzzled to understand why I treated seriously that charlatan, Mme. Blavatsky, who had done so much harm to Oriental studies by her parodies of Buddhism and Vedânta, which she had mixed up with Western ideas.'[49]

Max Müller summed up his opinion of Blavatsky and Theosophy in the second volume of *Auld Lang Syne*, published a little before his death:

> Madame Blavatsky might certainly have done a good work if she had joined some really learned Pandits... nor would it have been too much for a person endowed with such extraordinary, if not miraculous, powers as she was said to have possessed, to have mastered the grammar of Sanskrit. But what has been the result of all her labours?... the true teaching... has been obscured rather than illuminated by being mixed up with poor and contemptible conjuring tricks... There is no mystery about that philosophy... there is nothing esoteric in their teaching... It is difficult, therefore, not to get angry if one sees the elevated views of these ancient philosophers being dragged down to the level of cloudy hallucinations, and rendered absurd by being mixed up with vulgar trickeries.[50]

The leaders of the Theosophical Society were not particularly concerned about Max Müller's harsh criticism. Olcott expressed regret that Max Müller had never been to India, where he might have understood '... that man's consciousness is able to grasp the ultimate truth by functioning on a plane higher than that on which dictionary, grammar and encyclopaedia are milestones by which a man's progress towards the attainment of knowledge is marked.'[51]

Annie Besant responded to Max Müller's 'Esoteric Buddhism' by saying that he was merely a petty, narrow-minded scholar, whose

---

49. *The Theosophical Review* (London, April, 1904).
50. F. Max Müller, *Old Lang Syne, Second Series, My Indian Friends* (New York, 1899), pp. 164-69.
51. Olcott, *Old Diary Leaves*, V, p. 45.

criticism was irrelevant to the students of esoteria.[52] It is interesting to follow Besant in India in the coming years gradually adopting a preaching method that seems taken directly from Max Müller's thinking, so that she appeared to be unconsciously recycling his established ideas. It is ironic that Besant, who regarded esoteric studies to be the heart of Theosophy and objected to the 'narrow-minded' academic approach to Oriental philosophy, would become the leading practitioner of Max Müller's approach, as we shall see.

Besant's Journey to India

Besant travelled to India for the first time after the World's Parliament of Religions. The geographic trajectory she followed in late 1893 – from America to Asia – symbolized the political turn she made then, when she distanced herself from Judge in favour of Olcott. It seems that her moves were dictated by political expediencies, led by her ambition to lead the Society. The same ambitions animated both Olcott and Judge, the other two sides of this political triangle. Unlike them, Besant did not at this time head a particular Section and her status rested on her position in the ES. Perhaps this was the reason she was the least contented and the most avidly ambitious of the three. Her standing as Blavatsky's disciple and successor gave her the swing vote between Olcott and Judge, and made her choice a fateful one for the Society's future. Had she supported Judge, it would have meant an open revolt against Olcott in the effort to dominate the international Theosophical Society. On the other hand, her support for Olcott would certainly damage the Society, though at this time no one foresaw an actual breakup.

Another problem affecting these considerations was the strength of the American Section, which was the biggest in the world and no less influential than the movement in India. The appeal of leading a large movement in the United States, where, according to Besant, the new Aryan race was evolving, was doubtless as powerful as the appeal of the Aryan homeland in the East. But the most she could hope for if she joined Judge was to be number two in the Society's hierarchy. It is also possible that she took into consideration Olcott's advanced age – he was 19 years older than Judge. She certainly could not foresee that the older man would outlive the younger.

---

52. *Lucifer* (June, 1893).

Besant arrived in Colombo, the Ceylonese capital, on 9 November 1893, accompanied by Countess Wachtmeister, Blavatsky's faithful companion. Olcott received her and arranged an extensive lecture tour for her, which began on her first day in the Orient. According to him, her first lecture was attended by many important personages, including the British governor of Ceylon and the commander of the British forces on the island. After three days in Colombo, Besant set out with Olcott on a brief tour through Ceylon, visiting sacred Buddhist sites and addressing Theosophical schools. The two sailed to India on 16 November, and spent several months crisscrossing the Subcontinent, with Besant addressing mixed audiences of Indians and Europeans. The lecture tour began in south India and reached its first high point in Adyar, where the annual conference of the Theosophical Society opened on 21 December 1893. There Besant addressed representatives of the various lodges, which by then numbered 352. On 1 January 1894, Olcott and Besant left Adyar and travelled to Bengal, where Besant gave a series of lectures, then proceeded to Benares and other major cities, including Agra and Delhi. Then they travelled to the Punjab, where Besant lectured in Lahore, and later in Lucknow. According to Olcott, his new ally's lecture tour was a huge success. He stated that she had addressed a total of some 100,000 people in 121 lectures. A simple calculation indicates that she lectured every day in the course of a tour that lasted four and a half months.[53]

The British Establishment did not take kindly to Besant's tour, as *The Times* of London confirmed in an editorial article in February 1894. It referred to Besant as a dubious spiritualist sermonizing the Indian subjects on political matters that might provoke unrest and sedition. *The Times'* main argument was that Besant's call to the Indians to return to their ancient heritage meant to help them break free of the alien British rule over their country. Besant responded to this article in a letter she sent the *Times* in March, strongly denying having any political intentions or connections with political elements. She asserted that her aim was to bring about a spiritual revival in India, to counteract the corrupting materialistic influences reaching it from the West. Her ideas sprang from ancient Aryan sources and were opposed to the Western idea of progress. Her goal was to promote the unification of all the Aryans

---

53. Olcott, *Old Diary Leaves*, V, pp. 52-162; *The Theosophist* (January-April, 1894).

under a single spiritual ideal and a single religion, without having any dealings with political elements whatsoever.[54] Her assertions, which seemed to be direct quotes from Max Müller, would later be severely tested as she grew more deeply involved in India and became an actual political leader.

Besant's long tour, like a preliminary royal progress undertaken by an heir to the throne, was her first introduction to India's principal cultural centres and its diverse inhabitants, both local and European. Her impressions of the landscapes, the unfamiliar customs and the local audiences who cheered her and Olcott, led her to the decisive resolution of her political quandary. After travelling for four and a half months, Besant knew she had found the field of action she had been looking for since her youth. She found India to be her second homeland, if not the first. As we shall see, the Oriental fantasy syndrome, which had affected numerous Westerners in the nineteenth century, affected her too. Influenced by Leadbeater, she would discover that she had lived in India in one of her former lives, and the discovery prompted her to settle there permanently, and dedicate the rest of her life to her old/new homeland's future.

Besant sailed from India on her way back to England on 20 March 1894. The conclusion of her tour was summed up dramatically by Olcott: 'Thus ends one chapter of the world's history.'[55] The hyperbole notwithstanding, it may be said that her journey did conclude a chapter in the history of the Theosophical Society. The political dilemma which marked the year 1893 and underlay Besant's voyages to America and India was resolved, and from now on she would collaborate with Olcott and turn her back on Judge. The decision would lead to the greatest upheaval experienced by the Theosophical Society in its entire history.

The Breakaway of the American Section and the Tingley Affair

The Theosophical war between the Indian and American sections flared up in 1894 and culminated in 1895. The signs had already been evident in 1893, but the signal for the start of open hostilities was given only when Olcott was assured of Besant's support and after she herself moved against Judge. Olcott thought he could

---

54. *The Times* (London, 5 February 1894, 30 March 1894).
55. Olcott, *Old Diary Leaves*, V, p. 162.

disparage Judge, and convince him of his subordinate position by relatively moderate means, and by using his authority as president of the international Theosophical Society. Accordingly, he laboured throughout 1893 to collect proofs that Judge had deceived the members of the Theosophical Society. He maintained that Judge had forged letters supposedly written by the Mahatmas, and hoped thereby to embarrass him publicly and eject him, or drive him to resign to avoid the shame of exposure. Judge's purpose in publishing messages from the Masters at that time was clearly to demonstrate that the Mahatmas of the Theosophical Society had chosen him to succeed their deceased emissary, rather than Olcott, whose growing interest in Buddhism he saw as a deviation from Blavatsky's legacy.

On 6 February 1894, towards the end of her first tour of India, Besant opened the campaign by presenting Olcott with an official demand to submit the issue of the forgeries to an internal commission of inquiry. Olcott accepted the demand, and sent a copy of it to Judge, offering him a choice of two courses of action – resignation, or a summons to appear before a commission of inquiry. Judge was not alarmed by this opening salvo – he may well have expected some such move. He telegraphed back to say that he was not guilty and was willing to be questioned about the matter. This left Olcott no choice, as he put it, but to announce on 27 April the formation of a commission of inquiry against the president of the American Section. The commission included some of the Society's leading figures, such as the brothers Keightley, Sinnett, Burrows, Mead and Olcott himself. It was supposed to hold its first sitting on 27 June, but was postponed to the first week in July 1894.

The commission interviewed the accused, Judge, who arrived from America, and the claimant, Besant. The decision was published on 10 July, and though original and creative, it was not exactly what Olcott had aimed for. It stated that although Judge might have committed the deception he had been accused of, it had to be examined as if it were committed by a private person – which the commission was not legally empowered to do.[56]

The members of the commission probably wanted to preserve the unity of the Society and merely issue a strong warning to Judge, in the hope that he would mend his ways and accept Olcott's

---

56. Olcott, *Old Diary Leaves*, V, pp. 79–82, 163–65, 170–74, 178–209.

authority. But the outcome was very different from Olcott's expectations. Judge realized that the leaders of the Theosophical Society in Europe were loyal to Olcott and that Besant, who had so recently been his confederate, had turned her back on him. His reaction to this humiliation at the hands of his associates was sharp and quick. On 4 November 1894 he sent a letter to the members of the ES announcing that, in accordance with the directives of the Masters, it was he who had been chosen as Blavatsky's sole successor as leader of the Esoteric Section. Judge argued that Besant was influenced by black magic exerted upon her by her Brahmin friend, Chakravarty, and that her actions and decisions violated the rules of the ES. He further maintained that she had attempted to manipulate him by supernatural means, but failed. He stated that according to the Masters, the Theosophical Society had been founded in the West by Western individuals, and it must not be made exclusively Oriental. He concluded as follows: 'Hence, under the authority given me by the Master and HPB., and under Master's direction, I declare Mrs. Annie Besant's leadership in the EST at an end.'[57]

At the time Judge launched his counter-attack Besant was on a lengthy tour of the East. As soon as the commission of inquiry finished its work, she set out with Bertram Keightley on a lecture tour lasting several months in Australia and New Zealand, in the course of which she founded the Australasian Section, which would grow in the coming years into one of the world's biggest Theosophical Society sections. Towards the end of the year she reached Ceylon once more, and there on the 19 December she responded to Judge's attack. She circulated a letter among the members of the ES in England and the United States, stating that Judge's accusations were delusional, and that Blavatsky's legacy was inherently tied to India, the birthplace of the Masters. She announced that she rejected her 'dismissal' by Judge and intended to continue working: 'We have come to the parting of the ways. I recognise no authority in Mr. Judge. Not from his hands did I receive my work; not into his hands may I surrender it.'[58]

Judge responded in an article that appeared in the April 1895 issue of *The Path*, the Theosophical Society monthly in America. He argued that Besant's interpretation of the term 'East' was erroneous:

57. Olcott, *Old Diary Leaves*, V, p. 258.
58. Annie Besant, *Eastern School of Philosophy*. Republished Online by Blavatsky Study Center, available at: http://www.blavatskyarchives.com/besantes1894.htm

> Let us once for all give up the notion that the East is India. India is but a small part of it... India has been regarded carelessly as "the East" among Theosophists, because it is under English rule and hence more heard of than other parts. Were Tibet open and under English or French rule, we would speak of it as the East quite as much as, if not more than, we have done of India.

He reiterated that the Theosophical Society was Western in spirit, and had been founded by the Masters not in India but in America, because that was where the next evolutionary development would take place.[59]

This article appeared at the height of the battle between Judge and Olcott and Besant. Shortly after, in the last week of April 1895, at the annual conference of the American Section in Boston, Judge succeeded in passing a formal decision to sever the connection with Adyar. Some of the members who remained loyal to Olcott started a new section which still exists, subordinate to Adyar.[60] The split between the two major parts of the Theosophical Society never healed. Reunification might have been possible after Judge's death on 21 March 1896, had not his successor Tingley followed in his footsteps and waged unrelenting war against Adyar.

Katherine Tingley, who was known as the Purple Mother, was born in 1847 (the same year as her rival Besant) and died in 1929, following a fatal road accident in the Netherlands. She was married three times and after a short acting career engaged in charitable work in prisons and hospitals. She was running a kitchen for striking workers in New York in 1894 when she met Judge and became his closest associate. After his death she succeeded him as head of the breakaway American Section. Throughout her long leadership, until her death, she guided the American Theosophical Society in her own way, seeking to achieve a utopian society with the emphasis on education, community and an alternative

---

59. William Q. Judge, 'The Truth about East and West, in *The Path* (New York, April, 1895).

60. The Theosophical Society in America founded its present centre in 1927 in Wheaton, Illinois. Its main competition was the American Theosophical Society, which sprang from Judge's American Section, whose centre is located in Pasadena, California. The Pasadena International Headquarters operates a publishing house, a library and a university. It seems that the rivalry between these movements is presently at ease. Nonetheless, the impressive on-line database of the Pasadena Headquarters tends to ignore Besant's contribution to Theosophy. Accordingly, Adyar's database treats Judge and Tingley just the same.

philosophy of life. Tingley transferred the centre of Theosophical movement in America from the East to the West Coast. In 1897 she purchased a piece of land in Point Loma, near San Diego, California. The centre directed the Theosophical activities in America, and housed educational institutes for children and a school of yoga. Tingley expanded the Theosophical educational work in America beyond Point Loma, and established a Theosophical school system, culminating in the founding of the Theosophical University in 1919. The University functions to this day in Pasadena. The Point Loma centre declined after Tingley's death and in 1942 financial difficulties forced the Society to sell it, and the Theosophical centre moved to Los Angeles.[61]

Tingley continued Judge's anti-Indian policy. Like him, she believed that America, particularly California, was the place where human evolution would leap to its next stage. This American orientation led her to support the study of the Maya civilization – probably inspired by Blavatsky's argument that it was a remnant of the Atlantean civilization. Aside from her wish to interpret Blavatsky's ideas, she probably favoured these ideas as a way of challenging the pro-Indian headquarters in Adyar. But Besant also upheld ideas of this kind, and argued that the new Aryan race was taking shape in America. Nevertheless, despite the resemblance between their ideas in this and other matters, Besant and Tingley were bitter enemies and fought for years over the leadership of the Theosophical Society. At times their battles became absurd. For example, in 1899, having decided to spend more time in India, Besant chose not to renew the lease on her old residence in St John's Wood, which, as we have seen, had housed the Blavatsky Lodge, the European Headquarters and the London ES. The lease was then purchased by Tingley, presumably on the assumption that possessing Blavatsky's old residence would add to her prestige.[62] As for Besant, during the early twentieth century she spent a good deal of money in California, her adversary's home ground. The most prominent of her investments there was the Theosophical centre at

---

61. Timothy Miller, *The Quest for Utopia, Vol. 1: 1900–1960* (Syracuse, 1998), pp. 21–22.

62. For further discussion of the Besant-Tingley affair, see, Arthur H. Nethercot, *The Last Four Lives of Annie Besant* (London, 1963), pp. 67, 158, 186; Peter Washington, *Madame Blavatsky's Baboon: A History of the Mystics, Mediums, and Misfits Who Brought Spiritualism to America* (New York, 1995), pp. 112–14, first published 1993.

Krotona, which ran into financial difficulties and sold most of its land in 1924. Later in the 1920s Besant purchased a new plot in Ojai, California, for a centre that would serve as Krishnamurti's home, as we shall see.

As soon as she succeeded Judge, Tingley began a major assault on Olcott and Besant. Her worldwide campaign was launched under the heading, 'Crusade of American Theosophists around the World'. The crusade opened in Boston on 7 June 1896, with a speech in which Tingley compared the contemporary American Theosophists to the founding fathers of the United States.[63] Then she set out with some of her followers on a journey to Europe and India, seeking to undermine the dominance of the world movement's headquarters and create an alternative by bringing new recruits into the American Section.[64] The attempt ultimately failed, but Tingley's efforts did present a challenge to Besant for many years. The two contended for the same potential public, especially in Europe, and at times actually in parallel. For example, in June 1913 Tingley organized an international Theosophical peace congress in Stockholm, concurrently with the annual world conference of the Theosophical Society. In her opening speech at the conference Besant referred at length to Tingley and her movement, concluding with a call to the members of the world movement not to attack the dissident American Section, but respond passively and pacifically to its attacks.[65]

The history of the rivalry between Besant and Tingley would fill a book. In retrospect, the two heroines seem to reflect one another. Each regarded herself as Blavatsky's successor, each achieved a position of leadership at a time of unquestioned masculine dominance. Tingley published a good deal, though not as much as her adversary, who was a highly experienced writer. Her books and articles contain a good deal of material very similar to Besant's writings, except for the Indian theme, which grew increasingly paramount for the latter.[66]

---

63. Katherine Tingley, *A New Light Among All*; republished Online by Theosophy Northwest, available at: http://www.theosophy-nw.org/theosnw/theos/th-ktkt.htm

64. Olcott criticized Tingley, as 'She who must be obeyed', who 'rules her millionaire and pauper followers as autocrat at Point Loma', Olcott, *Old Diary Leaves*, VI, pp. 84–85, 331.

65. Annie Besant, 'The Policy of the Theosophical Society', in *Superhuman Men in History and in Religion* (London, 1913), pp. 129–30.

66. See, for example, Katherine Tingley, *Theosophy: The Path of the Mystic*, first published 1922: http://www.theosociety.org.pasadena/pathmyst/path-hp.htm;

Since the present book concerns the attempted synthesis between Theosophy and the Indian civilization, I cannot take the subject of the two women's rivalry any further. It is, however, fascinating to observe how this personal contest produced such a bitter split in a movement that claimed to uphold universal fraternity.

The Elections to the Presidency of the Society, 1907

In 1896, three years after her first journey to India, Besant decided to open a new Theosophical centre in Benares (now Varanasi), in northern India. This centre would grow in the coming years and become Besant's political power-base in India. The choice of Benares appeared to stem from ideological reasons – Benares is on the River Ganges, in the heart of northern India's ancient Aryan homeland, unlike southern Adyar, which lies far from the old Aryan kingdoms. In reality, it was due to Besant's desire to separate herself from Olcott. Despite her decision to collaborate with him against the American contingent there were major differences between their viewpoints. Olcott tended to Buddhism, while Besant increasingly adopted Hinduism. Olcott sought to win the Society respectable acceptability in the eyes of the Establishment, while Besant emulated Blavatsky in her provocative early ES phase, and regarded the study of the occult as one of her principal objectives. Her leadership of the Society entailed active political action, in opposition to the views of its ageing president, who wished to avoid clashes with the British Raj. Above all, Olcott saw himself as the Society's sole leader, while Besant had her own aspirations.

She had to keep these aspiration muted and control her impatience for a long time, before Olcott finally died in 1907. During the intervening years Besant established an impressive school system and formed connections with various local key figures, as we shall see in the next chapter. When the time came for the contest for the succession, Besant's position in India was strong enough to ensure her an easy win of the presidency of the international Theosophical Society. Surprisingly, some of her oldest allies opposed her election and made quite a scandal about it.

Katherine Tingley, *The Wine of Life*, first published 1925, available at: http://www.theosociety.org/pasadena/wine/wlchp1.htm; Katherine Tingley, *The Gods Await*, first published 1926, available at: http://www.theosociety.org/pasadena/kt-gods/tga-hp.htm

The struggle began a little before Olcott's death in February 1907. That month's issue of *The Theosophist* was the first to be edited by Besant, since Olcott was too ill to do it. The issue carried a statement made by Olcott on his deathbed:

> ...Last evening, in the presence of witnesses, Mahatma M. and Mahatma K.H. appeared behind my sick-bed, visible to our physical eyes and speaking in voices audible to our physical ears. They told me to appoint Annie Besant as my successor. They said, no matter whom I should appoint there should be some discontented ones, but that taking everything into consideration, They most decidedly considered her the best fitted for the office.
>
> I therefore appoint Annie Besant to take the office of President of the Theosophical Society at my death...[67]

Olcott died on 17 February 1907, a few days after the publication of this testament. *The Times* carried a report about his funeral, held the following day. Besant read out his final letter and conducted the rites, at the end of which the corpse of the defunct president of the Society (himself an early proponent of cremation in the West) was cremated and his ashes scattered both in the sea near Adyar and on the River Ganges.[68] His demise was followed by one of the more painful conflicts of Besant's life. Although her position as his successor was secure, she must have been dismayed by the membership of the opposition.

The campaign against her was led by George Mead, Blavatsky's former secretary, who proposed himself for the presidency, together with Bertram Keightley and Sinnett (who became in 1895 vice-president of the international Society, following Judge's retirement). They were joined by Herbert Burrows, who had once been Besant's close friend. In other words, the London leadership of the Theosophical Society, formerly Besant's own base, was rebelling against her. The reasons for this British mutiny were complex – to some extent they were prompted by anxiety about Besant's uncompromising character, which seemed to foreshadow tyranny. In addition, Besant's close friend, Charles Webster Leadbeater, was at this time being accused of the sexual exploitation of children in his care.[69] Besant supported Leadbeater in his hour of trial, provoking intense anger against her, especially in the London Lodge.

67. *The Theosophist* (February, 1907).
68. *The Times* (12 March 1907).
69. For a thorough description of the Leadbeater scandal, see chapter 9.

A supplement added to the April 1907 issue of *The Theosophist* carries detailed information about the climax of the struggle. It includes an article by Bertram Keightley expressing doubts about the propriety of Besant's election. Keightley argued that the constitution of the Theosophical Society permitted the outgoing president to recommend a suitable successor, not to appoint one. Keightley also attacked Olcott's testament, doubting the credibility of the appearance of the Masters, as reported in *The Theosophist*. Besant replied to Keightley in the same supplement, responding to his doubts as to her abilities by saying he was young enough to be her son. The attack against her continued in an article by George Mead, her rival contestant for the post, who also argued that her appointment was improper. Olcott, he stated, was 'not according to his normal best judgement.' Mead's arguments against Besant focused on her personality: 'Mrs. Besant is the absolute autocrat of the E.S., and it is highly inadvisable that this autocracy and the constitutional office of President of the T.S. should be in the hands of one and the same person.'[70]

The battle was not confined to the pages of *The Theosophist*. Sinnett, who as vice-president served as the acting president during the interregnum, expelled Besant from Adyar, declaring that she was under the influence of the dark forces. Nevertheless, the British opposition failed to defeat Besant – the general elections for the presidency, held on 28 June 1907, gave her an overwhelming victory. Her triumph was immediately followed by a crisis as momentous as the great split of 1895 – Sinnett, Keightley and Burrows quit the Theosophical Society in protest against Besant's election. They were followed by a large number of other Theosophists, among them the entire membership of the big Sydney Lodge, which Besant herself had founded in the previous decade.[71]

Besant survived this crisis. Here, too, she was served by her uncompromising character and utter belief in her own way. Perhaps if she had distanced herself from Leadbeater, or proposed someone

70. *The Theosophist* (Supplement April, 1907).
71. Shortly after his resignation in 1908, Sinnett founded The Eleusinian Society, but renewed his membership with the Theosophical Society in 1911. George Mead (who resigned the Society in 1908) founded The Quest Society, which functioned until the 1930s. For further discussion on the 1907 election crisis, see, Gregory Tillett, *The Elder Brother: A Biography of Charles Webster Leadbeater* (London, 1982), pp. 93, 298 f10; Washington, *Madame Blavatsky's Baboon*, pp. 124-25; Ann Taylor, *Annie Besant: A Biography* (Oxford, 1992), pp. 285, 290.

else to head the ES (defusing fears of autocracy), things might have taken a different course. Her obduracy, combined with the desire to control the Society, had characterized her conduct during the crisis with the American Section, and these features would reappear in the 1912 crisis with Rudolf Steiner. As we shall see, it ended with most members of the German Section quitting the Society. Whether or not things could have gone otherwise, the fact is that in the latter half of 1907 the Theosophical Society came under the leadership of a new person, whose agenda was essentially different from that of her predecessor.

The issue of Indian nationalism, which occupied a minor place in Olcott's reign, became under Besant the central issue in the Theosophical project in India. Henceforth, the Theosophical Society would join the local national forces and play a significant part in the growth of Indian nationalism, which would peak in the coming years. It was also in those years that Besant's career reached its summit. She was both the high priestess of Theosophy and one of India's prominent national leaders. This dual role was crowned with her election to the presidency of the Indian National Congress in 1917. The next chapter covers those years.

Chapter 8

The Struggle for the Leadership of the Indian National Movement – 1907–1919

The involvement of the Theosophical Society in the internal Indian politics intensified when Besant assumed the Society's presidency in Adyar in 1907. It became even stronger in the second decade of the new century, especially during the First World War, and culminated with Besant's election to the presidency of the Indian National Congress in 1917. In the course of this decade Besant developed and promoted her prescription for India's national liberation. It won the support of a good part of the Indian political elite, who regarded Besant as a colleague and as a legitimate local leader – at any rate until 1919. The present chapter examines some significant issues involved in the relations between Besant, the Theosophical Society and the Indian national movement. I shall try to shed light on the historical process which culminated in a white woman, a member of the colonial nation and president of an esoteric society, becoming one of India's central national leaders.

Theosophy and Early Indian Nationalism: Allan Octavian Hume and the Founding of the Indian National Congress

The Indian National Congress was the principal political body in India up to independence in 1947. The Congress (hereafter the INC) was founded in 1885 and functioned for a long time as a kind of state-in-waiting. Later, the INC became the political party which governed for many decades. Jawaharlal Nehru, independent India's first Prime Minister and Foreign Minister, was the leader of the INC in its early years. Later it was headed by his daughter Indira Gandhi (1917–1984), and his grandson Rajiv Gandhi (1944–1991). His widow, Sonia, restored the INC to government in 2004. Thus the roots of the present ruling party in India lie in the political organization of 1885, which marked the start of the organized national struggle in India.

The person behind the rise of the INC in 1885 was a Briton by name of Allan Octavian Hume, a senior officer in the Indian Civil Service who retired from it in 1882.[1] Hume was born in London, studied at University College London for two years, then at Haileybury, the academy of the East India Company. Then he joined the Indian Civil Service and sailed to India in 1849. Once there, he served in a number of posts, moving up the hierarchy of the Raj. In 1870 he was appointed by the Viceroy Lord Mayo as head of the Home Department, a post he held for three months.[2] Mayo created especially for him a commission in charge of agriculture, revenues and commerce. Hume, a proponent of the economic development of the Indian population, chaired this commission between 1871 and 1879. But his patron Mayo was assassinated in 1872, weakening Hume's position in the upper echelons of the government. In 1879 Viceroy Lytton (1876-1880) disbanded Hume's commission, and appointed him to a minor post in the administration of the North-West Provinces.[3] Hume apparently felt that after 30 years of service this post, which obliged him to move to Simla, was a humiliation, and two years later applied for and obtained early retirement.[4]

But though retired, Hume kept up his contacts in the upper circles of government, including with Lytton's successor Lord Rippon (1880-1884), who regularly consulted him.[5] Hume stayed on in

1. Hume's most comprehensive biography was written in 1913 by his close friend, Sir William Wedderburn (1838-1918), himself a senior officer in the Indian Civil Service, and later MP (1893-1900) and twice the president of the Indian National Congress (1889, 1910), Sir William Wedderburn, *Allan Octavian Hume, 'Father of the Indian National Congress', 1829-1912, A Biography*, ed. Edward C. Moulton (New Delhi, 2002), p. x, first published 1913.
2. A.J.A., 'Bourke, Richard Southwell, sixth Earl of Mayo (1822-1872)', *The Dictionary of National Biography*, II (Oxford, 1921-1922), pp. 929-32.
3. Lytton was Lord Edward Bulwer-Lytton's son, R.G., 'Lytton, Edward Robert Bulwer, First Earl of Lytton (1831-1891)', *The Dictionary of National Biography*, XII (Oxford, 1921-1922), pp. 387-92.
4. Hume's request was replied to favourably, due to his unpopular negative view of the British regime in India. The *Dictionary of National Biography* claims that he had retired 'under a cloud': H.V.L., 'Hume, Allan Octavian (1829-1912)', *The Dictionary of National Biography*, 1912-1921 (Oxford, 1961), pp. 277-78, first published 1927; For further information on Hume's career, see, Wedderburn, *Allan Octavian Hume*, pp. xiii-xvi, 12-32; Briton Martin, *New India, 1885: British Official Policy and the Emergence of the Indian National Congress* (Berkeley, 1969), pp. 53-56.
5. W.L-W., 'Robinson, George Frederick Samuel, first Marquis of Ripon (1827-1909)', *The Dictionary of National Biography*, Supplement, I (Oxford, 1963), pp. 216-21, first published 1920.

India until 1894, devoting himself to three major subjects. The first was ornithology, in which he went further than any amateur.[6] The second, and his main interest after his retirement, was the organization of the Indian national movement. The third, in which he was involved at least between 1879 and 1883, was the Theosophical doctrine.

The connection between Hume and the Theosophical Society began in December 1879, when Blavatsky and Olcott visited his friend Sinnett in Simla. Sinnett introduced Blavatsky and Olcott to a number of local pundits, as well as to Hume. Olcott was favourably impressed by Hume, 'who made an eloquent and altogether excellent address; far better than my own.' Hume, for his part, was captivated by Blavatsky's supernatural powers, which he witnessed. For example, in 1880, when she stayed at his house, she located his wife's lost brooch, which was found buried in the garden.[7] About that time he joined the Theosophical Society, and in 1881 he founded a Theosophical lodge in Simla – the Simla Eclectic Branch – which he headed until 1883.

But unlike Sinnett, who remained Blavatsky's devoted disciple to the end of his life, Hume's critical sense did not leave him even in their early acquaintance. When he was invited to join the Society at the end of 1880, he struggled with himself. 'I am no military machine – I am an avowed enemy of the military organization – a friend and advocate of the industrial or co-operative system, and I will join no Society or Body which purports to limit or control my right of private judgement.'

He wondered about the capability of the Society's president to guide its followers. '... I should not object in any way to dear old Olcott's supervision, because I know it would be nominal, as even if he tried to make it otherwise, Sinnett and I are both quite capable of shutting him up if he interfered needlessly. But neither of us could accept him as our real guide, because we know that we are intellectually his superiors.'[8]

6. For further information, see, Allan Octavian Hume, *The Game Birds of India, Burmah and Ceylon* (3 vols., Calcutta, 1879–1891); Wedderburn, *Allan Octavian Hume*, pp. lxxix–lxxx, 35–40.

7. Henry Steel Olcott, *Old Diary Leaves, Second Series, 1879–1882* (Adyar, 1900), pp. 118–19, 237–42.

8. *The Mahatma Letters to A.P. Sinnett*, from the Mahatmas M. & K.H., transcribed and compiled by A.T. Barker, Letter no. 99 (Hume to K.H.), 20 November 1880 (Adyar, 1972), pp. 430–31, first published 1923.

Despite these doubts, Hume joined the Society, adopted its customs (for example, he called himself H-X, in keeping with the Theosophists' penchant for initials), and at least for a while believed in Blavatsky's powers, her links with the Masters and the Theosophical aim of maintaining a close association with the local Hindus.[9] His opinion of Olcott, however, did not change after he joined the Society. In 1882 he wrote: 'But though Col. Olcott is a scholar, he can perform no phenomenon – except very rapidly developing clairaudient and clairvoyant powers – and is yet, as far as I can see, as far from the great secret as any of us.'[10]

Hume's belief in Blavatsky grew, until he became a regular correspondent of her Mahatmas, who began to manifest themselves from 1880. The more he corresponded with them, the more his skepticism gave way to belief, at least until the end of 1882. Whereas in 1880 he wanted to go to Tibet in person, to witness the Masters in person (an idea firmly rejected by Koot-Hoomi), by 1881–1882 he already regarded them unreservedly as real entities, and addressed them as a disciple addresses his mentors.[11] What is more, he continued to believe in their existence and mission even after he quit the Theosophical Society.

Hume's interest in the occult and his ready, if not unreserved, trust in Blavatsky's stories, could be attributed to several reasons in combination.[12] Among these might be the rebuff he experienced

9. For further discussion on Hume's conversion to Theosophy, see, Edward C. Moulton, 'The Beginnings of the Theosophical Movement in India, 1879–1885: Conversion and Non-Conversion Experiences', in *Religious Conversion Movements in South Asia: Continuities and Change, 1800–1900*, ed. Geoffrey A. Oddie (Richmond, 1997), pp. 109–72; A first-hand evidence in regard to Hume's Theosophical devotion may be traced in his letters compilation from 1882, entitled *Hints on Esoteric Theosophy*. See, for example, Allan Octavian Hume, *Hints on Esoteric Theosophy*, No. 1 (Benares, 1909), (A Letter Written by H-X), p. 23, first published 1882.

10. Hume, *Hints on Esoteric Theosophy*, p. 41.

11. *The Mahatma Letters*, Letter No. 100 (K.H. to Sinnett), p. 431 (undated), probably from 1880); Letter No. 20A (Hume to K.H.), August 1882, pp. 120–21. See, as well, the esoteric guidance letters from the Master Koot-Hoomi to his disciple Hume: Letter No. 28 (K.H. to Hume), possibly 1881, pp. 205–15; Letter No. 11 (K.H. to Hume), 30 June 1882, pp. 59–66; Letter No. 14 (K.H. to Hume), 9 July 1882, pp. 77–83; Letter No. 15 (K.H. to Hume), 10 July 1882, pp. 87–97; Letter No. 22 (K.H. to Hume), Late 1882, pp. 133–41.

12. Wedderburn, Hume's biographer, chose to ignore the subject. Mehrotra, on the other hand, claims that Hume's attraction to Theosophy was the result of his advanced age (50 years-old when he met Blavatsky), Wedderburn, *Allan Octavian Hume*, pp. 65–68; S.R. Mehrotra, *The Emergence of the Indian National Congress* (Delhi, 1971), p. 312.

towards the end of his service in the Raj, together with his profound interest in the local culture, especially its esoteric aspect. Possibly his interest in esoteria also derived from the kind of disposition that characterizes seekers of the occult in general. These are often people who seem to have an almost desperate need for a vocation. Nevertheless, unlike Sinnett, who accepted Blavatsky quite unreservedly, Hume retained his critical faculty. Towards the end of 1882 he began to doubt the authenticity of the Mahatma Letters. When he became convinced that Blavatsky had written at least some of the mysterious letters, he turned away from her and even assisted Hodgson, the emissary of the SPR, when he visited Adyar. Hume stayed in Madras in February and March 1885, a few months before the first INC conference, and witnessed the discovery of the hoax of the double doors in the Koot-Hoomi altar cabinet. A short time afterwards he also joined the SPR.[13]

Inexplicably, he continued to believe in the Masters even after he witnessed Blavatsky's fraud with his own eyes. This is evident in the Hodgson Report, which quotes Hume in regard to his firm belief that Blavatsky's Mahatmas are real, and that some of the Mahatma Letters were in fact genuine.[14]

Such an assertion made in 1885, a few months before the first conference of the INC, indicates that the man behind the Indian national organization believed in the occult, in Blavatsky's Tibetan Mahatmas and the Theosophical vision of India's future. It is therefore true to say that the Indian National Congress was founded on an ideological basis influenced by Theosophical ideas.[15] Although Hume himself quit the Theosophical Society, as we shall see, the link between the Society and the INC was not severed. Indeed, the connection between the two organizations grew closer under Besant's leadership. If Hume defined the initial goals of the INC, Besant contributed to its agenda at least until 1919.

---

13. The May issue of the SPR's Journal listed Allan Octavian Hume, Simla, India, in its 'New Members' section: 'New Members', *Journal of the Society for Psychical Research*, No. 16 (London, May, 1885).

14. 'Report of the Committee Appointed to Investigate Phenomena Connected with the Theosophical Society', *Proceedings of the Society for Psychical Research*, 3 (December, 1885), pp. 224, 275.

15. Martin, *New India, 1885*, p. 65; Mark Bevir, 'Theosophy as a Political Movement', in *Gurus and their Followers: New Religious Reform Movements in Colonial India*, ed. Antony Copley (Delhi, 2000), pp. 159–79.

Hume's efforts to establish an Indian national body were undoubtedly motivated by his profound interest in Theosophy. Although he had tried to promote reforms to improve the living conditions of the Indians even before he met Blavatsky, his attempts to push for a local political organization were clearly fortified by his growing interest in Theosophy. His biographer Wedderburn inadvertently provided clear evidence of this effect. He noted that among Hume's papers he found a strange memorandum concerning seven volumes of secret reports which had been entrusted to him. The people behind these reports, Wedderburn stated, were Gurus, leaders of religious sects who 'have purged themselves from earthly desires... These religious leaders, through their Chelas or disciples, are fully informed of all that goes on under the surface, and their influence is great in forming public opinion.'

The date of this memorandum is problematic, as those secret reports were delivered to Hume before he met Blavatsky.[16] However, it is clear that Hume deduced from the reports that British rule in India was under serious threat, due to a widespread organization of an insurgent Indian movement. He noted that the reports contained quotes from hundreds of thousands of diverse local sources, and believed that the danger to the British Raj was greater than that posed by the Indian Mutiny of 1857.

The subject came up again in 1886, after Hume had broken off relations with Blavatsky. He wrote a letter to the Viceroy, Lord Dufferin (1884–1888), warning him against this danger, stating that his information came from a confidential source that might not be revealed. He told Dufferin that he was being instructed and guided by 'initiates', whose standing was only slightly below that of Mahatmas.[17] We do not know precisely what he meant, what those volumes entrusted to him contained, or who had given them to him to peruse. Nonetheless, it is likely that Blavatsky was involved in the matter, just as she was probably involved in the Mahatma Letters. It is certainly possible to conclude from this story that Hume believed that higher spiritual entities were using him to prevent a major uprising. This may have been what drove him to organize a

16. Wedderburn, *Allan Octavian Hume*, pp. 65–66.
17. W.L-W., 'Blackwood, Frederick Temple Hamilton-Temple, first Marquis of Dufferin and Ava (1826–1902)', *The Dictionary of National Biography*, Supplement, I (Oxford, 1963), pp. 171–76: first published 1920; Wedderburn, *Allan Octavian Hume*, pp. lxxxi–lxxxiii.

national Indian body that would cooperate with the British Raj and avert an imminent disaster.

His efforts to bring this about came to a head during 1885, at the end of which the INC held its historic first meeting. Early that year Hume had founded an organization named the Indian National Union. Towards the end of the year the word Union was replaced by Congress, by which name it became known from then on. Preparations for its first conference continued through the year. Hume left Madras on 19 March and travelled all over India, meeting numerous local leaders and establishing committees of the new body in the main cities.[18] Having organized the infrastructure, he sailed to England, where he remained between August and November. His purpose was to persuade a number of influential persons, including the former Viceroy Lord Rippon and some Members of Parliament, to support his idea of creating an organization that would improve education, agriculture and India's general situation, out of abiding loyalty to the British crown. He urged the formation of a parliamentary commission dedicated exclusively to Indian issues, thus making the subject an integral part of parliamentary debate.[19] His ideas became popular among the British Establishment as well as in the Indian elite.

The Provincial Congress Committees Hume had set up acted as expected and sent delegates to the first INC conference that opened in Bombay on 28 December 1885. Altogether seventy-two

18. During 1885, Hume founded the Provincial Congress Committees in Madras, Pune, Bombay, Surat, Lucknow, Ahmedabad, Karachi, Calcutta, Benares, Allahabad, Agra and Lahore, thus efficiently covering the sub-continent: Wedderburn, *Allan Octavian Hume*, p. 46; Mehrotra, *The Emergence of the Indian National Congress*, pp. 392–402.

19. Hume's efforts contributed to the change in the English public opinion in regard to India. The impact of Hume's activity was first evidenced in 1888, as The British Committee of the INC was founded, headed by Dadabhai Naoroji (1825–1917), a wealthy Parsi who had resided in England since 1865. The Committee recruited influential politicians, among them Charles Bradlaugh, who became deeply involved in Indian affairs until his death, in 1891. In 1890 the committee began to publish the periodical 'India' (a monthly in 1892 and a weekly in 1898), which spread pro-Indian propaganda in England. A major advancement was made in 1892, when Naoroji became the first ever Asian MP, and in 1893, when Wedderburn was elected to the parliament. Both fresh MPs founded a parliamentary committee which dealt exclusively with Indian matters, and propagated pro-Indian ideas: Wedderburn, *Allan Octavian Hume*, pp. 71–78; B.R. Nanda, *Gokhale: The Indian Moderates and the British Raj* (New Delhi, 1977), p. 88; David Lewis Jones, 'Naoroji, Dadabhai (1825–1917)', *The Dictionary of National Biography*, Missing Persons (Oxford, 1993), p. 490.

delegates arrived from all parts of India, among them lawyers, journalists, university lecturers, leading figures in the economy, doctors and merchants. Most were Hindus, a minority Muslims. Among the prominent individuals at the conference were the lawyers Pherozeshah Mehta (1845–1915), Kashinath Trimbak Telang (1850–1899), and Womesh Chandra Bonnerjee (1844–1906), alongside the wealthy merchant Dadabhai Naoroji. The delegates elected Bonnerjee as president and chose Hume as the secretary-general of the organization, a post he held until 1894 (Hume was made honorary secretary after his return to England, a post he filled until 1904). The conference was also attended by senior representatives of the Raj – Lord Reay, the recently appointed governor of Bombay, was the honorary president of the Bombay Congress, and Viceroy Dufferin came and bestowed his patronage on the new organization.[20]

Thus was launched the body that would ultimately free India from British rule. Yet in its early days the INC closely cooperated with the British Establishment, which gave it its blessings and support. After a time, the relationship cooled considerably, when the reforms eagerly awaited by the Indian leaders failed to materialize. Nevertheless, Hume's main idea – cooperation between Indians and the British rulers – remained for a long time the motto of the organization he founded. It also characterized Besant's relations with the INC. In the final analysis, despite Besant's desire to be seen as a local leader, the way she was perceived by the INC's Indian leaders in her time resembled the perception of Hume by the early leaders of the INC. In this sense, the historical process in which Besant's political career evolved – from active participation through her election to the INC presidency to her fall from grace – reflected the progressive disillusion with the British sympathizers. It epitomized the transition from the childish stage of political dependence on England and the English to the maturity which produced the demand for national independence.

---

20. Wedderburn, *Allan Octavian Hume*, pp. lxxxiii–xcvii, 49–51; Mehrotra, *The Emergence of the Indian National Congress*, pp. 378–420; Gordon Johnson, *Provincial Politics and Indian Nationalism: Bombay and the Indian National Congress, 1880 to 1915* (Cambridge, 1973), pp. 5–43.

2. Annie Besant: Preparing the Ground for a Political Career in India

The Theosophical Society viewed the INC favourably from its inception, and even tried to take credit for its success.[21] Curiously, although Hume had assisted Hodgson and formally quit the Society, it seems that the Society did not hold a grudge against him, and after his death commemorated him as one of its prominent members.[22] Besant maintained this favourable attitude, and as president of the Society went beyond mere support for Indian nationalism in an effort to seek a synthesis between the Theosophical Society and the INC. Before the Besant era the relations between the Theosophical Society and the national movements in India and Ceylon rested on shared aspirations for India's spiritual liberation. The Society's work consisted of quiet, apparently non-political, efforts to achieve intellectual freedom, focusing on education and the revival of ancient Hindu cultural values. Annie Besant, with her militant personality and rhetorical gifts, changed the Theosophical rules of the game. Under her direction, the Theosophical Society became a lively nucleus of nationalist activism, winning growing support among the Indian public, which regarded it and its president as potential liberators from imperial rule.

Indications of Besant's future intentions were already evident in 1893, when she first sailed to India. She made a speech on board the Kaisar-I-Hind on its way to Ceylon, in which she described India as the homeland of the Aryans. They had created an advanced civilization, she said, with a highly developed religion and society. She emphasized that this was the civilization Max Müller spoke of,

---

21. In 1887 Olcott wrote that the Theosophical Society was no less but the sole parent of the INC: *The Theosophist* (Adyar, supplement, January, 1887); Besant too claimed that the INC's birth resulted from a Theosophical enterprise and specified its foundation moment during the annual Theosophical convention of 1884: Annie Besant, *How India Wrought for Freedom: The Story of the National Congress Told from Official Records* (Adyar, 1915), p. 1; Surprisingly, an official INC report from 1935 gives a similar impression. Its author, Sitaramayya (who was considered the INC official historian, and later, in 1948, became the INC president), claimed that the idea that gave birth to the INC was first raised in Adyar, in 1884, B. Pattabhi Sitaramayya, *The History of the Indian National Congress (1885–1935)*, published by the Working Committee of the Congress on the Occasion of the 50th Anniversary (Madras, 1935), pp. 16, 21.

22. See, for example, the references made in regard to Hume in Besant's weekly: *The Commonweal, A Journal of National Reform* (Adyar, 9 January 1914, 21 August 1914).

which had been preserved by the Brahmins of north-western India, the unquestioned inheritors of the ancient Aryans. She argued that these people represented the finest physical, mental and spiritual human type of all time. Moreover, their ancient social system, based on castes, was also perfect. The system should be revived, she argued, as it assured long-term stability and prevented internecine conflicts. The system had declined and deteriorated over the years, but would be recovered when the Brahmins were once more the servants of the people, rather than its oppressors.

Here the ideas of the nineteenth century Orientalists, from Schlegel to Max Müller, are plainly in evidence, but only up to a point. Besant justified the superior status of the Brahmins over the other castes in keeping with her Theosophical belief in reincarnation and the principle of karma. She maintained that the pure-blooded Brahmin caste was made up of the purest souls. Her lecture called for India's awakening, so that she would lead the human race to spiritual victory.[23]

Besant made these statements before she set foot in India. She had formed her idea of India before experiencing the reality that she proposed to influence. In this, she was following the example of William Jones – who, as we have seen, conceived of his mission while still at sea – and of Max Müller, whose Indian vision crystallized without his ever visiting the land of his dreams. Besant's vision of India's glorious future would become the heart of her doctrine and characterize the work of the Theosophical Society from 1907 on. George Bernard Shaw was perhaps most apt when he quipped that she aspired to become the 'queen of the Theosophists' and India's modernizer.[24] The remark, though cynical, was a good description of Besant's Indian life, her unassailed presidency (at least in India) of the Theosophical Society, and her own perception of her role in awakening Indian nationalism and promoting her political organization.

Upon arrival in India Besant promised not to dabble in politics, but her endeavours to promote Hinduism and condemn Christianity could not but be viewed as political. Thus her activity was seen from the start as opposing the British Raj and threatening to deny its legitimacy. Christianity underlay the legitimacy of the British

23. *Lucifer, A Theosophical Magazine* (London, January 1894).
24. Shaw, *An Autobiography*, Vol. 2: 1898–1950, The Playwright Years, Selected from his Writings by Stanley Weintraub (New York, 1970), p. 174.

rule over India, being the reverse of the fatalistic Hindu thought. The idea of 'Maya' meant that Hindu believers regarded reality as artificial and meaningless, and the earthly existence as undesirable. By contrast, Christianity was described as a modern, realistic alternative, being the religion of the practical-minded rulers.

It was this idea which led to the accepted English view of India as the perfect field for the Christian mission. It was upheld by the utilitarian administrators who believed that the degenerate Hindu civilization should give way to the religion of the modern rulers. It was also accepted by academics like Max Müller who maintained that the apparent similarity between the ancient Vedic religion and Christianity might be the basis for a dialogue between the two. For all their differences, they shared the assumption that the best outcome of such contacts would be the triumph of Christianity. In this sense, the efforts of the Theosophical Society to promote Hinduism had a distinct anti-Christian agenda which was deemed subversive. Besant adopted Jones' revolutionary idea, which was further developed by Max Müller – namely, that the ancient Aryan order had been perfect but degenerated in the course of the millennia; only she concluded that it should be revived, not integrated with Christianity. Needless to say, this outlook was at odds with the British aim of modernizing and 'Westernising' India.[25]

Besant's plans to advance these views turned from the theoretical to the operative in 1896, with the decision to start a new centre in Benares. With money donated by her friend Ursula Bright (the wife of MP and Privy Chancellour Jacob Bright) she bought a property in the Kammacha quarter, near the city centre. There she stayed every year between November and April, running her independent Indian Theosophical Section which existed in parallel with the international headquarters in Adyar. Offices, a conference hall and a printery were built on the property, which soon became the Theosophical centre of northern India and the administrative headquarters of the educational institutions Besant established in Benares.

Besant became attracted to Hinduism after her arrival in India. She devoted a great deal of time to the study of Sanskrit, and claimed to have acquired much better knowledge of it than had Blavatsky and Olcott. As early as 1895, two years after her first arrival in India,

---

25. Mark Bevir, 'In Opposition to the Raj: Annie Besant and the Dialectic of Empire', in *History of Political Thought*, Vol. xix, 1 (1998), pp. 61-77.

helped by local scholars, she published a new translation of the *Bhagavad Gītā*.[26] Although by this time there were many translations of this work in various European languages (as mentioned before, Wilkins' translation had given English readers access to the dialogue of Krishna and Arjuna as far back as 1784), Besant presented the world with a new one, complete with Theosophical commentary. This was in a way of asserting the superiority of the Theosophical approach over the academic in interpreting the ancient Hindu civilization. The same assertion was made in later writings of hers, such as *The Wisdom of the Upanishads*, published in 1907, which she defined as 'an attempt to draw a few drops from the ancient well of Indian wisdom.'[27]

The attempt to fuse Theosophy with the ancient Hindu civilization also inspired the foundation of the Central Hindu College in 1898. The boys' college was established in Benares with money that Besant raised from various sources, including the Maharajahs of Kashmir and Benares. The latter donated one of his palaces to the college. Western teachers taught side by side with local pundits. The most prominent of the latter was the honorary secretary of the college, Bhagavan Das (1869–1958). The curriculum of the college included Western as well as classical Hindu subjects. The aim was to bring up a new local leadership, heirs to the ancient Aryan ones. These young leaders would be nurtured on the best of the cultures of East and West, with a Theosophical orientation.[28]

In 1901 the University of Allahabad permitted the college to grant a B.A., thus making it officially an academic institution. In 1905 the college was permitted to grant an M.A. in Sanskrit and English. The college would later grow to become the Benares Hindu University, which is still active. In 1904 Besant founded the Central Hindu Girls School, affiliated with the central college and based on the same principles. On the basis of these two schools,

---

26. *The Bhagavad Gītā, or, The Lord's Song*, trans. Annie Besant (London, 1895); Another edition to that translation was published in 1905, in cooperation with Bhagavan Das. It included a free word-to-word translation to English, and an introduction to Sanskrit grammar: *The Bhagavad Gītā*, trans. Annie Besant and Bhagavan Das (Adyar, 1950), first published 1905.

27. Annie Besant, *The Wisdom of the Upanishats* (Adyar, 1907), p. i.

28. See, for example, Besant's lectures on the '*Mahābhārata*', which were saturated with Theosophical interpretation in regard to the invisible world: Annie Besant, *The Story of the Great War: Some Lessons from the Mahābhārata for the Use of Hindu Students in the Schools of India* (Adyar, 1927), pp. 2, 218.

Besant founded in 1908 two nationwide educational systems, Sons of India and Daughters of India. She had earlier, in 1901, launched a periodical, 'The Central Hindu College Magazine', which was distributed all over the Subcontinent, to publish her educational work together with Theosophical messages. It was the creation of these institutions which won her the trust of the local elites. Their trust, in turn, gave Besant the influence she needed on her way to the political leadership. Moreover, her educational activities won her a reputation among the English Establishment. Thus, for example, when the Prince of Wales (the future George V) and his wife Mary came to Benares, they visited the college and were received by Besant and her students.[29]

During those years, before she became the president of the Theosophical Society, Besant travelled extensively all over India, forming connections with influential Indians. At first these connections rested on the Theosophical substrate that already existed throughout India, but in time Besant expanded it and used it to strengthen her own position. A good example of the kind of contacts she was forming with the Brahmin elite was her friendship with Motilal Nehru (1861-1931), the father of Jawaharlal.[30] They were introduced by their joint friend Chakravarty, and before long Besant became a regular visitor to the Nehru residence in Allahabad. Motilal Nehru had joined the Theosophical Society back in Blavatsky's time, and he readily adopted Besant's recommendation to hire a Theosophical admirer of hers, an Englishman named Ferdinand Brooks, as a tutor for his son Jawaharlal. Brooks tutored the young Nehru between 1900 and 1903, educating him in the tenets of Theosophy. During this period Jawaharlal himself joined the Theosophical Society, and was initiated by Besant

---

29. For further discussion of Besant's educational activities in Benares, see, Arthur H. Nethercot, *The Last Four Lives of Annie Besant* (London, 1963), pp. 68-88; Ann Taylor, *Annie Besant: A Biography* (Oxford, 1992), pp. 277-80; Peter Washington, *Madame Blavatsky's Baboon: A History of the Mystics, Mediums, and Misfits Who Brought Spiritualism to America* (New York, 1995), pp. 106-108, first published 1993.

30. Nehru senior was a successful Allahabad lawyer. His family (originally from Kashmir) kept close relations with the English authorities for several generations. His grandfather was the East India Company delegate to the Mughal court in Delhi, while his father served as a police officer in Delhi. He was elected to the INC in 1888, and later became one of the leaders of its dominant moderate faction. Nehru senior was elected to the presidency of the INC in 1919 and 1928, B.R. Nanda, *Gokhale, Gandhi and the Nehrus: Studies in Indian Nationalism* (London, 1974), pp. 50-59.

herself.³¹ Besant's relations with father and son flourished for many years. As we shall see, they were among her leading backers for the presidency of the INC in 1917.

Another important link formed after Besant's election as president of the Theosophical Society was with Gopal Krishna Gokhale (1866–1915), the main figure in the leadership of the INC between 1905 and 1915. Gokhale had been a member of the Theosophical Society before taking up politics. He was a proponent of gradualism in the Indian national struggle, believing that national education and training must be advanced before Indians could govern themselves. He therefore favoured cooperating with the British with the aim of achieving self-government under the Empire's sheltering wing.³² These ideas closely resembled Besant's, and they became good friends and worked in tandem until Gokhale's death. Their first collaboration was in 1909, when they jointly supported Gandhi in his campaign for the rights of the Indian community in Transvaal in South Africa. Gokhale organized a conference in Benares in support of Gandhi, and invited Besant to chair it. The following year Besant called on Gokhale to support her, when she was accused of sedition against the British Raj.

That year the official attitude towards Besant hardened, following an open letter she published in February in the Central Hindu College Magazine. It was prompted by a complaint made by a graduate of the college who had come to its anniversary celebrations (on 19 and 20 January 1910), and was subjected to racist treatment from a British person at the event. Besant complained about the administration's racist policy towards its Indian subjects, and called on it to re-evaluate its attitude:

---

31. Jawaharlal Nehru, *An Autobiography, with Musings on Recent Events in India* (London, 1949), pp. 14–16: first published 1936.

32. Gokhale, who was of a poor Brahmin origin, began his political career in 1889, when he was elected as the Pune delegate to the INC. The INC president that year was Wedderburn, who recognized young Gokhale's potential and kept close relations with him for many years. Gokhale met Hume in 1893 and became his friend until the latter's death, in 1913. In 1910 he replaced Mehta as the Indian member of the Imperial Legislative Council, perhaps the most powerful post open for Indians in that time. In 1905 he founded the Servants of India, a society that dedicated itself to the advancement of India. That same year he was elected to the presidency of the INC. Being the leader of the moderate faction, he remained the central leader of the INC until his death, in 1915, Nethercot, *The Last Four Lives of Annie Besant*, p. 219; Nanda, *Gokhale*, pp. 56–172.

'We who have charge of nearly one thousand lads in the Central Hindu College, and who influence tens and thousands all over India, we... who love India, and hope to see her a self-governing part of this mighty Empire, we appeal to the Government of India not to allow this work of love and service to be wrecked by brutality and folly.'[33]

The British rulers in Benares responded furiously to this public letter. Bhagavan Das, the secretary of the College, was warned that he would be subject to legal measures against him. Members of the College's managing board were advised to distance themselves from Besant. The furore calmed down after Besant asked for Gokhale's help – he used his contacts, intervened on her behalf and soothed the ruffled spirits.[34] Their alliance grew even stronger when Besant became active in the INC in 1914. The patronage of the most highly respected Indian leader of the day reflected on Besant and helped to strengthen her complicated political image. Henceforth she would be seen not only as a British personage willing to act against her government, but also as a champion of the national honour of Indians.

3. *Annie Besant and the INC: 1914–1916*

Besant's plans for reshaping the Theosophical Society after being elected as its president combined the esoteric element, which was Blavatsky's legacy, with the national element, broadly identified with Olcott. Besant fused the two components into a single doctrine which aimed at advancing Indian nationalism from an esoteric historical perspective. The fusion was especially activated in the second decade of the twentieth century, especially during World War I, when Besant became a prominent member of the INC leadership. It seemed as if all her previous experiences, in journalism as in politics, bore fruit at this time. In the years 1914–1916 Besant became an established publisher as well as a senior political figure. As she approached her 70th birthday, Besant had finally reached the destiny she had always sought.

Besant's official entry into India's political arena began in the run-up to the 1914 Congress, which was held in Madras, when she became a regular part of the INC leadership. At this time her

33. Raj Kumar, *Annie Besant's Rise to Power in Indian Politics, 1914–1917* (New Delhi, 1981), p. 43.
34. Kumar, *Annie Besant's Rise to Power*, p. 44; Nanda, *Gokhale*, p. 359; Taylor, *Annie Besant*, pp. 287–90.

popularity among Indians reached an unprecedented level compared with other Westerners involved in Indian politics. Although the INC had had two Western presidents before Besant was elected in 1917, their positions had been mainly honorary.[35] As we shall see, Annie Besant was the first president of the INC who extended the authority of the post and turned it into a truly operative role.

In the course of 1914, a little before her official entrance into India's political scene, Besant founded two newspapers within a few months of each other. The first issue of '*The Commonweal*', a 16-page weekly, that was printed in Adyar, appeared on 2 January 1914. Its editorial, penned by Besant, stated the weekly's aims: 'To hold a free platform for the expression of varied opinions on religious, educational, social and political problems, so that burning questions in all parts of the world may be threshed out, and truth elicited by a thoughtful discussion.' Moreover, she declared, 'One thing that lies very near to our heart is to draw Great Britain and India nearer to each other,' and she promised that 'We would fain be the voice of the dumb, and defender of the oppressed, the reformer of evil, the upholder of righteousness.'[36]

The writers in the magazine were English and Indian, more of the latter than the former. Among the regular contributors was Besant's old friend George Bernard Shaw, who published in the 26 June 1914 issue a two-page article calling for the liberation of India. He argued that only the Indians can set themselves free, by educating their children to liberty.[37] But the heart of the magazine was Besant's editorial articles, in which she always called for social reforms in India and a change in its national status. Beginning in 1915, her call for Indian Home Rule became the magazine's principal subject.

Besant's daily newspaper, '*New India*', began to appear on 1 August 1914. It covered the course of the World War, its orientation strongly pro-British and anti-German.[38] Yet as the war wore on, the

35. As mentioned before, Wedderburn was elected twice to the INC presidency (1889 and 1910). His friend, Alfred Webb, was elected to the INC presidency in 1894: D.J.O'D., 'Webb, Alfred John (1834–1908)', *The Dictionary of National Biography*, Supplement, I (Oxford, 1963), p. 622, first published 1920.

36. Annie Besant, 'Our Policy', *The Commonweal* (2 January 1914).

37. Bernard Shaw, 'Indian Cowardice and English Pluck', *The Commonweal* (26 June 1914).

38. See, for example, the following articles, which referred to the Germans as the new barbarians, accused them of committing war crimes and called for the arrest of all German missionaries in India, *New India* (Madras, 20 October 1914, 5 February 1915, 10 February 1915 and 7 July 1915).

The Struggle for the Leadership

paper became increasingly combative towards the British.[39] *New India*'s main argument was that Britain was using the Indian troops without giving their country anything in return. As we shall see, the increasingly bitter line prompted the administration to impose restrictions on the paper.

Preparations for the INC conference of 1914 were preoccupied with attempts to reconcile the moderate faction of the INC, under Gokhale's leadership, and the radical opposition, led by the nationalist Bal Gangadhar Tilak (1856–1920), dubbed by his followers Lokamanya (the people's saviour).[40] The rift between the two factions appeared in the first decade of the century, when Gokhale's moderate and pro-British position overcame Tilak's militant anti-British one. Though the two prominent leaders came from a similar background, their conflicting views reflected the opposing approaches that for a long time characterized the Indian struggle against British rule. In this sense, Besant's national doctrine was a blend of both views. She too, like Tilak, called for a revival of the ancient Hindu heritage, while maintaining, like Gokhale, that the revival ought to take place under the protective guidance of the British administration. This may have been the reason she was asked to mediate between the opponents in early December 1914, a few days before the start of the INC conference in Madras. Besant held intensive discussions with Gokhale and Tilak, in search of a formula that would enable the latter to return to the INC. But in the end Gokhale withdrew his consent and the attempted reconciliation failed.[41]

---

39. For some of the daily's anti-British articles, see, *New India* (4 August 1914); Annie Besant, 'Behind War?', *New India* (29 August 1914); *New India* (1 October 1914). As the war advanced towards its end, Besant's articles became more aggressive. See, for example, her 'Message to British Democrats': 'Our people have died in your war for freedom. Will you consent that the children of our dead shall remain a subject race?', Annie Besant, 'A Message to British Democrats', *New India* (3 December 1917).

40. Tilak, a wealthy and upper-class Brahmin, called for a violent revolution against the English regime. Influenced by Vivekananda and Dayananda Sarawati, he too called for the revival of the ancient Hindu heritage. His views led to a harsh dispute with Gokhale, who in the 1907 Surat Congress made Tilak and his followers quit the INC. Tilak was arrested many times by the Raj authorities, and spent many years in jail. In 1914, after having spent, again, some time in prison, he was released, and immediately became an immensely important political factor, Stanley A. Wolpert, *Tilak and Gokhale: Revolution and Reform in the Making of Modern India* (Berkeley, 1962), pp. 13–26, 157–212.

41. Annie Besant, 'Interview with Mr. Montague', republished in Kumar, *Annie Besant's Rise to Power in Indian Politics*, Appendix iv, p. 160; Nanda, *Gokhale*,

Besant addressed the Madras Congress twice to expound her political philosophy to the INC delegates. It remained essentially unchanged until her election to the presidency in 1917. In her first speech she stressed the need for reciprocity between the British administration and the Indians, and called for autonomous self-government. She attacked the racial discrimination against Indians and argued that if Oxford graduates come to India to serve in its British administration, the Empire should enable public servants of Indian origin to serve in all its colonies. She called for a campaign against discrimination and suggested a number of possible lines of action, such as boycotting goods imported from other colonies where Indian workers were discriminated against. She described India as having matured and no longer willing to remain in the Empire's 'nursery'. If Indian soldiers could fight as men in Europe, she said, they were entitled to be free men in their own country.[42]

Besant's second address to the 1914 Congress was devoted to her main political motto – the need for home rule. She called on the INC delegates to prepare for self-government, starting from the most basic functions of urban administration, such as responsibility for sewage and water supply, in order to be ready to run their country as soon as possible. She claimed that the legitimacy of self-government was inherent in Indian history and rested on the ancient Hindu civilization. Indeed, she asserted, no other civilization in the world was so fit for self-government as the Indian one, which was more highly spiritual than any other nation on earth.

Besant urged the INC delegates to work out a programme of action for the achievement of self-rule, and present it to the pragmatic Englishmen. The programme had to be constructed in an orderly manner, on the basis of the English idea of law and order. That was how Indians were trained by the English, and that was how they would achieve their independence. She argued that Indian self-government should be based on the system of rural administration as practised in ancient India. It rested on the authority of the village council, or panchayat, which in ancient times had made for

pp. 453–54; Wolpert, *Tilak and Gokhale*, pp. 264–70; Johnson, *Provincial Politics and India Nationalism*, pp. 185–90.

42. Annie Besant, 'Reciprocity', *Congress Speeches* (Adyar, 1917), pp. 1–6.

autarchy and an almost wholly independent way of life, ensuring justice for all the inhabitants.[43] With the panchayat as the basis, there should be a wider administrative level upon which would rise the government of the district, the province, and ultimately all India. She stated that this national vision resembled the dreams that had animated the successful struggles for independence in Italy and Germany. As in those cases, India's national independence was within reach. India, or 'the Queen mother', as she phrased it, had already crowned herself with the crown of self-government. Now it only needed to wait for other nations to acknowledge it.[44]

The 1914 Congress marked Besant's successful entry as an active member of the Indian national leadership. She continued to build up her power-base in the following year, promoting the call for self-government in her newspapers.[45] A series of articles she published in the course of 1915 in *The Commonweal*, appeared as a book at the end of the year, under the title *How India Wrought for Freedom*. It appeared in time for the 1915 Congress, which was held in December in Bombay. Besant proposed her candidacy for the presidency of the INC ahead of the Congress, but the delegates elected Sinha, one of the veteran leaders of the moderate faction.[46]

The book *How India Wrought for Freedom* included the minutes of 29 conferences of the INC, from 1885 to 1914. As Besant proposed her candidacy for the presidency of the movement at that year's conference, the book may be regarded as her political visiting-card, designed to prepare the ground and legitimize her election. The

---

43. Besant was not the first person to suggest the revival of the panchayat. Max Müller hailed the Indian rural ruling system, already in 1882. Even before him, in 1878, Wedderburn called for the revival of the panchayat. The governments of British India discussed the idea long before Besant's call. For example, in 1903 the Viceroy, Curzon, ruled out the idea by saying that there was no point in reviving something that was already dead. However, there is no doubt that Besant deserves to be credited for the adoption of her idea (to a certain point) by the government of independent India, F. Max Müller, *India: What Can It Teach Us?* (Escondido, 1999), pp. 60, 71, first published 1882; Wedderburn, *Allan Octavian Hume*, pp. xvi–xvii; Dietmar Rothermund, *Government, Landlord, and Peasant in India: Agrarian Relations Under British Rule* (Wiesbaden, 1978), p. 53.

44. Annie Besant, 'Self-Government', *Congress Speeches*, pp. 6–12.

45. See, for example, Politicus, 'Home Rule in India', *The Commonweal* (17 December 1915).

46. S.V. Fitzgerald, 'Sinha, Satiendra Prasanno, first Baron Sinha, of Raipur (1864–1928)', *The Dictionary of National Biography, 1922–1930* (Oxford, 1961), pp. 776–78: first published 1937.

book depicted the ever closer connection that had grown since 1885 between the INC and the Theosophical Society. It revealed Besant's vision for India, blending an esoteric worldview with a passionate national appeal for her adopted home. Quoting Max Müller's patron Bunsen, she argued that the case of India differed from those of Egypt, Assyria and Persia. Those ancient civilizations were dead, whereas that of India was alive and showing signs of returning to the forefront of world history. The construction of India's nationhood must be founded on her antiquity, which embodied the eternal Aryan civilization. Though India had experienced conquests, invasions, periods of might and of weakness, she remained eternal, or in Besant's words, 'MOTHER imperishable'.

This book recapitulated the Aryan myth at its best and reviewed its principal elements concerning the migration of the Aryans to India and their kinship with the Europeans. Besant compared the ethnic and religious composition of India's population to that of England. Just as the latter was made up of Saxons, Normans and Danes, so India's population was composed of Hindus, Persians and Muslims, and she asserted that the mixture was at that very moment becoming a consolidated nation.

The existing connection between England and India, Besant explained, was due to the spiritual guidance of a higher power, and she concluded that the British Raj was the product of secret forces, intended to prepare and guide the Indians on their way to a national revival. However, she stated, the British had failed in their mission and it was time for India to enjoy self-government.[47]

Besant's speech at the 1915 Bombay Congress contained similar elements. She noted the three main reasons for India being entitled to self-government: one, the urgent need for legislation on vital issues and the abolition of restrictive and anachronistic laws; two, India's economic straits, aggravated by its exploitation by the English tax collectors; three, the historical justification for granting India self-government, namely, that it had been self-governing for 5000 years before its conquest by the British. Besant recapitulated for the INC delegates the idea expressed in *How India Wrought for Freedom* – that it was divine Providence which had brought about the English conquest. It was this historical situation that caused the only free state in contemporary Europe to be entrusted with

---

47. Besant, *How India Wrought for Freedom*, pp. i–lix.

event must have been a dream come true. Three months earlier she had celebrated her 69th birthday, and a year later she would realize her Oriental fantasy.

Besant's speech at the Lucknow Congress, like her speech at the Bombay Congress, was about home rule. She focused on the plans to change the character of the Empire after the World War, and declared that the British attitude to India was tainted with racism. She argued that any future British federation would have to include India as an equal partner, and that British plans negate this possibility because of the Indians' dark skin. She justified her call for equality by pointing out that the founders of all the great religions were coloured, including Jesus and Mohammed, beside Buddha.[56]

The Lucknow Congress not only raised Besant's profile, but also marked Tilak's return to the leadership of the INC, after many years in which he and his associates were boycotted by the moderate camp. The year 1916, in which these two founded their respective Home Rule leagues, had clearly been the preamble for the Lucknow Congress. By the end of it, the two were clearly the outstanding contenders to head India's political leadership. As we shall see, in the following year Besant realized her aspirations and became the most popular leader in India, retaining this position until 1919.

4. Annie Besant and Mahatma Gandhi[57]

The person principally responsible for Besant's political fall in 1919 was Mohandas Gandhi, who in 1920 became the unquestioned leader of the INC. To understand Besant's rapid fall, so soon after her rise to the most senior position in Indian politics, it is necessary to examine the special relations between her and Gandhi. I shall therefore briefly review their long acquaintance before continuing the story of Besant. The relations between the two deserve reassessment, in order to evaluate the influence of the Theosophical leader upon the man who more than anyone has been credited with freeing India from British rule.

---

56. Annie Besant, 'Self-Government', *Congress Speeches*, pp. 21–22.
57. It is most probable that Besant was the first to address Gandhi as 'Mahatma' (Sanskrit for 'great soul'). Naturally, there is a considerable mental gap between the Theosophical connotation associated with that title, and the average Hindu comprehension of it, Nethercot, *The Last Four Lives of Annie Besant*, p. 288.

The Struggle for the Leadership

League's organizational secretary in early 1917.[53] In addition, Besant persuaded Dadabhai Naoroji to accept the League's honorary presidency. Naoroji, who as noted was one of the founders of the INC and the first British MP of Indian origin, was already 91 years old. His acceptance of the position doubtless won the League great prestige. It also testified to Besant's genuinely high status in the eyes of nationalist Indians.

Based on the established Theosophical network, Besant's League spread throughout India quickly and efficiently. A few months after its founding, the League changed its name to the All-India Home Rule League, in order to distinguish it from the Indian Home Rule League founded at the same time by Tilak.[54] It seems that Besant's mediatory efforts between Gokhale and Tilak two years earlier strengthened her association with the latter. Tilak joined Besant's league soon after its founding, as a gesture of respect, and Besant returned the gesture and joined his organization. Her own league soon became the platform from which she launched her quest for the presidency of the INC.

The 1916 conference of the INC took place in Lucknow.[55] Besant arranged for the annual conference of the Theosophical Society and the first gathering of the all-India Home Rule League to coincide with it, also in Lucknow. It is probable that the psychological and propagandistic impact of these simultaneous events was considerable, and led to the identification of the two great organizations she headed with the INC. Moreover, Besant's dominant presence in all three organizations, vividly demonstrated in the three conferences, enhanced her popularity and fame. To her, the triple

---

53. Arundale, who received his MA from Cambridge University, arrived in Benares in 1903, and began teaching English at the Central Hindu College. His Aunt, Francesca Arundale, was a prominent Theosophist who in 1902 initiated Besant to the Co-Masonry Order. Later, in 1920, Arundale married a Hindu, Rukmini Arundale (1904–1986), and succeeded Besant as president of the Theosophical Society.

54. For further discussion on that subject, see, Sitaramayya, *The History of Indian National Congress (1885–1935)*, pp. 214–18; Wolpert, *Tilak and Gokhale*, pp. 276–77; Nethercot, *The Last Four Lives of Annie Besant*, pp. 250–51; Nanda, *The Nehrus: Motilal and Jawaharlal* (London, 1962), p. 132.

55. The Lucknow Congress marked a turning point in the history of the Indian national movement, as it involved the first major effort to unite the Hindu leadership with the Muslim leadership, headed by Muhammad Ali Jinnah (1876–1948). The failure of that unification was the starting point of the process that eventually led to the partition of India in 1947, and to the foundation of independent Pakistan.

there is no doubt that Besant and the Theosophists saw the war between Britain and the Axis nations as a battle between the forces of good and evil. In their view, the Great War was one more demonstration of the eternal struggle between the Great Brotherhood and the forces of darkness. Besant naturally identified Britain with the forces of good, and saw Germany and its allies as embodying the sort of evil which throughout history set the human race back and impeded its plan of evolutionary progress.[51]

This dichotomy was also influenced by Besant's quarrel with Rudolf Steiner, who in 1913 founded the Anthroposophical Society, following a bitter dispute with the international centre in Adyar. The Austrian Steiner had been president of the German Section until his break with the Theosophical Society, and when he quit, the majority of the German members quit with him. The ensuing crisis overlapped with the First World War. As the next chapter will show, the discord between Besant and the former Theosophical German Section was marked by elements that stemmed directly from the war between Britain and Germany.

The hardening of the administration's attitude towards Besant was first indicated by a conditional injunction to close down her newspaper, *New India*, on 22 May 1916. The injunction, which reached Besant on the 26th, was issued in accordance with the Press Act, which allowed the authorities to take steps against newspapers which endangered the public peace. The injunction stated that *New India* harmed state security, and ordered Besant to deposit 2000 rupees as pledge of good conduct.[52] It succeeded in igniting Besant's rebellion, and from that moment on her national fervour grew more radical. Three months later, in Madras, she announced the establishment of a new political organization named the Home Rule for India League. It's goal was to advance the idea of self-government in India, while educating Indians to believe in their right to independence.

Beside Besant (who was Acting President), the leading team of the League included Wadia, deputy-editor of *The Commonweal*, as treasurer, and George Arundale (1878–1945), who became the

---

51. Annie Besant, 'Presidential Address', *Congress Speeches*, p. 32.
52. Besant cleverly published the injunction in both her newspapers, thus using them as counter-propaganda: *New India* (27 May 1916) and *The Commonweal* (2 June 1916).

introducing Indians to Western ideas of liberty and state institutions. She called on the INC delegates to recognize their own value and discard their sense of inferiority. She asserted that the answer to this inferiority complex was faith in the power and knowledge of the Hindu civilization.[48]

Although Besant made sure to link the demand for Indian self-government with loyalty to the British crown, the British administration became increasingly hostile to her. Major elements in the British Establishment had for many years been antagonistic towards Besant and the Theosophical Society in general. This was clearly evident in the way the *London Times* wrote about Besant. The paper was seen as hostile to the INC from its inception.[49] In reality, it had detested Besant even before she joined the INC, as shown in its critical description of her first visit to India, and it remained overtly hostile to her. For example, in 1913, during the Krishnamurty custody hearings, the *Times* published an editorial that was highly critical of Besant, denouncing her harmful influence over Indian youth and the Indian educational system in general. It argued that requiring tender young minds to engage in esoteric and mystical studies could be damaging to them, especially in India, where East and West met and diverse religions coexisted. The newspaper declared that while so far Theosophy had been treated with tolerance, it was time to examine the Society with greater care. It concluding by stating that the Theosophical Society should be permitted to exist, but receive no support whatever from the administration. This hostile attitude persisted until the end of the war.[50]

It grew worse in 1916, which saw a turning-point in Besant's political activity. It was the height of the World War, and the administration was especially alert to any sign of rebellion in the empire. Besant's activities, both in the INC and in her newspapers, which kept calling for Indian home-rule, were increasingly perceived as a threat. It is necessary to keep in mind that despite the fears of the government in India, the Theosophical Society was utterly loyal to Britain and had no intention of jeopardizing her chances of winning the war. While the English rulers of India regarded the Theosophical agitation for Indian home-rule as less than patriotic,

48. Besant, 'Self-Government', *Congress Speeches*, pp. 14–20.
49. See Wedderburn's remark about *The Times'* anti-INC tendency, Wedderburn, *Allan Octavian Hume*, p. 79.
50. *The Times* (London, 8 May 1913, 1 July 1918).

Mohandas Gandhi, who was born in the state of Gujarat, was 22 years younger than Besant. His father was a known politician who served as chief minister of the government of Porbandar and Rajkot. In 1888, aged 19, Gandhi went to England to study law, and lived in London until called to the bar in 1891. As he himself described it in his Autobiography, this was an important time in his life, and not only in the professional sense. He was introduced to the Theosophical Society which, as we have seen, was then flourishing in England under the leadership of Blavatsky and Besant. He became especially attached to two unnamed members of the Society (he referred to them as 'two brother Theosophists'), probably fellow students. It was they who introduced him to the principles of Theosophy, and invited him to read the *Bhagavad-Gītā* in Sanskrit with them. He wrote that he felt ashamed about not having read the Gita before, much less in Sanskrit. Reading it with them made a great impression on him, and led him to think of it as the most important Hindu scripture, just as it was perceived by Blavatsky.

One day Gandhi's two Theosophical friends took him to Besant's residence in St John's wood to a meeting of the Blavatsky Lodge. He was introduced to Blavatsky and Besant and chatted with them. He said that he was invited to join the Theosophical Society but courteously declined, saying he was insufficiently familiar with his own religion, hence could hardly join any other religious organization. He did, however, read Blavatsky's *The Key to Theosophy* from 1889, and said that it prompted him to read books on Hinduism, and dispelled the disdain for it that had been inculcated in him, as though it were a mass of superstitions.

In 1891 Gandhi returned to India and began to practise law. In 1893 he was invited to South Africa to defend an Indian merchant in a civil suit. While there he became aware of the hardships of the Indian community, which was discriminated against by the whites. He decided to devote himself to the community, and remained in South Africa, with short intervals, until the end of 1914. It was a little after coming to South Africa that he read the *Upanishads*, in an English translation published by the Theosophical Society. He also read with interest Max Müller's *India – What Can It Teach Us?* As he described it, these two books made an impression on him and heightened his regard for Hinduism. He also continued to cultivate close relations with members of the Theosophical Society in South Africa. In 1903 some of these friends urged him to join the

Society, and though he still refused to do so, he did read various sacred Hindu texts with them. During the Boer War he sheltered two Theosophical friends at his house. He also kept in touch with Besant. On a visit to India in 1901, when he first took part in the INC Congress in Calcutta, he visited Besant at her house in Benares. At about that time he also spent a month in Pune, staying at the house of Gokhale, who became his patron.[58]

Gandhi maintained that Theosophy had introduced him to his own culture, and he acknowledged the contribution made by the Theosophical Society to the revival and fostering of India's ancient civilization. Nehru, too, thought much the same, and their statements on the subject cannot be ignored. They testified to the high regard for Theosophy among the leaders of the young Hindu elite in the early twentieth century, which helps to explain the key position Besant occupied in the national leadership at that time. For her part, Besant was aware of Gandhi's attitude and consistently supported him. As noted before, as early as 1909 she took part in a pro-Gandhi conference. Later she expressed her support in her newspapers, which regularly reported his actions and campaign, and gave the young leader the vital exposure that brought his name to the attention of the reading public in India.

An illustration of Gandhi's appreciation for the Theosophical Society is found in the second issue of *The Commonweal*, which reported a speech he made in South Africa. The quote below, taken from the news story, corresponds with the statements in his autobiography, and sheds further light on his relations with the Society:

'Mr. Gandhi, in a public lecture given some time back to a Theosophical meeting in S. Africa, declared in moving terms that he owed a debt to the Theosophical Society which he could never repay. He told his audience on that occasion that, after leaving college, he was practically a materialist, as indifferent to the religion of his forefathers as to that of his Christian associates; but that by coming into touch with some Theosophists, he had his attention turned to things spiritual, and that, through the influence of the writings of Mrs. Besant and other Theosophical authors, his whole life had been affected, and he had been led to realize that the spiritual side of man's nature was of paramount importance. The beauties of the Bhagavad-Gītā and other sacred Hindu Scriptures were revealed to

---

58. M.K. Gandhi, *An Autobiography, or the Story of My Experiments with Truth* (Ahmedabad, 1998), pp. 57–58, 123, 203, 220–21, 235, first published 1927.

him, and, while naturally preferring his own religion, he was able to see that other religions were but different facets of one diamond.'[59]

The Theosophists' espousal of Gandhi was thus a natural echo of his attitude towards the Society, even though he declined to join it. It was also sustained by his association with Gokhale, who was also Besant's good friend. This favourable relationship persisted while Gokhale lived and while Gandhi was in South Africa, far from the centre of political action in India. His return to India in 1915 marked the start of a certain cooling in his friendship with Besant and the Theosophical Society. Gokhale died in Pune in February, shortly after Gandhi's return, and for a little while the good relations between the latter and Besant continued. Yet it appears that the passing of their mutual friend dampened their relations.

Upon returning to India, Gandhi found himself in the decision-making nucleus of national Indian politics. He was probably disappointed not to be chosen to succeed Gokhale as the head of the Servants of India society. He therefore chose to settle in the city of Ahmedabad in his native state of Gujarat, where he began to plan his moves in the local political scene and to form a political philosophy that differed from that of his Theosophical friend. Gandhi understood that for the INC to become a real mass movement, it had to change its image so that it would not be associated only with the elite but also with the lower strata. In this sense, his ideology was the opposite of Besant's, who regarded the Brahmin elite as the heirs of India's ancient Aryan rulers. She also, as we have seen, supported cooperation between this class and the British elite, along the lines envisaged by Max Müller. The governing model she believed in, based on a revival of the panchayat system, was elitist rather than democratic. Inevitably, Gandhi's vision led him to view Besant as an obstacle on his path, and it was only a question of choosing the right moment to oppose her patronship and to take his place as a popular leader in his own right.

The answer came soon enough. The 7 February 1916 ended a four-day celebration in Benares to mark the laying of the cornerstone of the Benares Hindu University, one of Besant's central projects

---

59. 'Mr. Gandhi on Theosophy', *The Commonweal* (9 January 1914). For further reading on the influence of Western and Theosophical writings on Gandhi, see, Allon Gal and Isaac Lubelsky, 'The Disintegration of the British Empire and the Nationalist Cases of India and Israel: a Comparative Analysis', *Israel Affairs*, ed. Efraim Karsh, Vol. 14, No. 2 (London, April 2008), 166–67.

in the previous years. Besant had prepared an impressive climax for the final ceremonies. She invited great personages, both British and Hindu, including the departing Viceroy Lord Hardinge (1910–1916).[60] Beside him sat the Maharaja of Darbhanga, as president of the University board, and a number of Hindu princes. The solemn atmosphere, however, was marred by the prominent presence of C.I.D. officers assigned to protect the Viceroy, which annoyed the Indian dignitaries. Besant had invited Gandhi to take part, regarding him still as her protégé. He was to speak before her, leaving her, as the honorary president of the ceremonies, to give the closing address. Exactly what it was that caused the rift between them that evening is not clear. Their respective versions of the event are markedly different. It is certain that, intentionally or not, Gandhi arrived late and Besant had to make her speech before him. Gandhi's speech, which followed hers and had thus become the closing address of the ceremonies, was felt by the important guests as highly provocative, so much so that the most senior Hindu personage present, the Maharaja of Darbhanga, left the podium while Gandhi was still speaking.

It is the sequel that remains controversial. Besant claimed that Gandhi had acted disrespectfully, deliberately insulted the maharajas, and thus offended her personally. Gandhi claimed that Besant caused him to interrupt his address by quitting the platform together with the Maharaja. He said he did not know why his speech was seen as so extreme, and that he had suggested to her, from the podium, not to interrupt him but comment on his speech when he finished. He was annoyed with Besant and argued that if she had not interrupted him, he would have finished speaking in a few moments and his statements would not have been misunderstood. Gandhi's close friend Nehru had still another version of events. In his own Autobiography he stated that Gandhi had spoken on behalf of India's poor, and called on the maharajas to go and sell their jewels. He added ironically that the princes followed Gandhi's advice only in part – they did not sell their jewels but they certainly did go, leaving Gandhi alone on the platform, hurting Besant to the core. This description seems credible. While Besant described the incident as a deliberate provocation by Gandhi, and he wondered

---

60. Cromer, 'Hardinge, Charles, Baron Hardinge of Penshurst (1858–1944)', *The Dictionary of National Biography*, 1941–1950 (Oxford, 1959), pp. 356–58.

disingenuously what the fuss was about, Nehru's version seems more objective, depicting the two as caught up in tussle for primacy. Be that as it may, the consequences of the scandal in Benares were a serious cooling between Besant and Gandhi, and it was obvious that there could be no ideological collaboration between them. Gandhi identified with the poorest of the land, and dubbed Besant, rightly or wrongly, as an ally of the immensely rich.[61]

The rivalry between them intensified as 1916 wore on. Besant, as we have seen, founded her Home Rule League in early September. The League spread all over the country, flourishing also in Gandhi's stronghold, the state of Gujarat. Gandhi launched a counter-project, arguing that Besant's League represented only the elites. Towards the end of the year and in the course of 1917 he organized a counter-movement, and in November 1917 launched the Gujarat Political Conference, designed to be a rejoinder to the Home Rule League and to provide the rural sharecroppers with suitable representation in the INC.[62] Gandhi's endeavours on behalf of the lower strata spread and won fame and support. These classes became his political power-base and made him the most influential leader in India from 1919 on.[63]

Despite the obvious rivalry that burgeoned between Besant and Gandhi from 1916 on, the two continued to display mutual respect, at least until 1919. Their reciprocal attitude mingled suspicion and admiration, with each side careful not to go too far in criticizing the other. Besant was aware of Gandhi's rising power, while he acquiesced in her swelling popularity. The drama reached a second climax in December 1917, when Gandhi had to accept Besant's election to the presidency of the INC. In the event, he did not have to wait long for her fall. As we shall see, soon after her election to the presidency Besant herself provided him with the propaganda material to use against her. By the December 1919 Congress it was

---

61. *The Commonweal* (11 February 1916); M.K. Gandhi, *Speeches and Writings* (Madras, 1922), pp. 260; Jawaharlal Nehru, *An Autobiography*, p. 533; Nethercot, *The Last Four Lives of Annie Besant*, pp. 242–43.

62. David Hardiman, 'The Crisis of the Lesser Patidars: Peasant Agitations in Khed District, Gujarat, 1917–34', in *Congress and the Raj: Facets of the Indian Struggle, 1917–1947*, ed. D.A. Low (London, 1977), p. 57.

63. Nehru claimed that Gandhi allowed delegates from various classes into the INC, thus making it far more democratic, while Beasat's platform of political power was based solely on the Indian middle-class, Jawaharlal Nehru, *The Discovery of India* (New York, 1946), pp. 343, 363.

clear that Gandhi had taken over the leadership of the INC, and that his erstwhile friend and rival had fallen from her high position.

5. *The Theosophical Dream Fulfilled, 1917*

The year 1917 saw the pinnacle of Besant's efforts against the British Raj. The restraining measures adopted by the administration against her, notably the conditional closing order against the magazine *New India*, did not produce the hoped-for results. Indeed, Besant's demands for Indian self-rule grew all the more extreme. Furthermore, her joining forces with Tilak, leader of the radical faction of the INC, and an avowed enemy of the British, was viewed as seditious. She was becoming worryingly influential as her Home Rule League spread rapidly all over the country. The rulers decided to take more drastic measures. Lord Pentland, the governor of Madras (1912-1919), declared that Besant was inciting against the British government in India, and that her activities went beyond theoretical propaganda to actual support for local terrorism. He based his claim on the contacts Besant had made with terrorists in Calcutta – according to her, to persuade them to act within the law.[64] Things went so far that Lord Chelmsford, Hardinge's successor as Viceroy (1916-1921),[65] signed a detention and expulsion order from Madras against three of the League's leaders – Besant, Wadia and Arundale.

The order went into effect on 20 June 1917, as the three were exiled to Ootacamund (nowadays Udhagamandalam), south-east of Madras. Shortly afterwards they were moved a little further south, to Coimbatore, a place of milder climate, in consideration of Besant's poor health. The penalty was especially harsh in view of the fact that she was nearly 70 years old when she was detained, then removed from her residence for an indefinite period, which would have been punishment enough for a young person. A few days before the order went into effect, she published a dramatic editorial article in *New India*, sharply criticizing the government. 'What is my crime,' she wrote, 'that after a long life of work for others, publicly

64. M.F. Headlam, 'Sinclair, John, First Baron Pentland (1860-1925)', *The Dictionary of National Biography*, 1922-1930 (Oxford, 1961), pp. 775-76, first published 1937; Besant, 'Interview with Mr. Montague', republished in Kumar, *Annie Besant's Rise to Power in Indian Politics*, p. 161.

65. R. Coupland, 'Thesiger, Frederic John Napier, Third Baron and First Viscount Chelmsford (1868-1933), *The Dictionary of National Biography*, 1931-1940 (Oxford, 1961), pp. 854-55, first published 1949.

and privately, I am to be dropped into the modern equivalent of the Middle Age oubliette – internment? My real crime is that I have awakened in India the National self-respect, which was asleep, and have made thousands of educated men feel that to be content with being 'a subject race' is a dishonour... I go into enforced silence and imprisonment, because I love India and striven to arouse her before it was too late. It is better to suffer than to consent to wrong. It is better to lose liberty than to lose honour.'[66]

Included in the detention order was a sweeping ban on the distribution of any writings by Besant, Wadia and Arundale.[67] The prohibition threatened to prevent the publication of Besant's newspapers. She tried to prevent this by selling them fictitiously for a symbolic amount to two friends, T.K. Telang and B.R. Reddy, and announced that she had no further connection with the publications. This enabled the papers to continue to appear during her exile from Adyar, although at first there were editorial difficulties which resulted in reduced editions. After a few days the ban was limited to Besant's political writings, which made it possible to continue publishing the papers.[68]

Besant's detention provoked angry reactions throughout India and before long produced the opposite results from those the administration had hoped to achieve. The popularity of the Home Rule League soared, with large numbers of influential people swelling its membership. The most prominent of these new members were the Nehru father and son, who protested against Besant's detention by not only joining the League but creating a new branch of it in their city of Allahabad. On 23 June 1917, Motilal Nehru was chosen as its president and Jawaharlal as one of its secretaries. They became ardent supporters of Besant, and remained so until her release. Jawaharlal Nehru would retrospectively analyse the tremendous impetus that Besant's arrest gave to the Home Rule movement in India, stating that it caused intense agitation among the Indian intelligentsia and even upset the old guard which had been loyal to England. He also revealed that in protest against it, he and a long list of other young Indians renounced their intention of joining the Imperial army.[69]

66. Annie Besant, 'To my Brothers and Sisters in India', *New India* (15 June 1917).
67. The ban was published on *The Commonweal*'s front page, *The Commonweal* (29 June 1917).
68. *The Commonweal* (6 July 1917); Nethercot, *The Last Four Lives of Annie Besant*, p. 259.
69. Nehru, *An Autobiography*, pp. 31-32.

Besant's detention also set off a wave of public protests. By the end of June, a mere ten days after her arrest, there were 28 demonstrations in Madras and 12 in Bombay. Even Gandhi, who had by this time openly disassociated himself from Besant, protested against her detention. He did so in a private letter sent to the Viceroy's secretary, but made his position clear: 'In my humble opinion, the internments are a big blunder,' he stated. 'I myself do not like much in Mrs. Besant's method. I have not liked the idea of political propaganda being carried on during the war.'

Nevertheless, he concluded firmly that if Besant were not freed, there would be violent disturbances, which was precisely what he sought to prevent. Furthermore, on 30 July 1917, the INC called on the Viceroy to free Besant, threatening that if she were not freed by the end of September, passive protests would take place.[70]

These reactions had an effect. Besant and her associates were set free on 17 September 1917, three months after her detention and removal from Madras. The ban on the distribution of their writings was also lifted. The change in policy was due not only to the protests, but also to a political reshuffle in the British government in London. The Secretary of State for India, Austin Chamberlain (1863–1937), was replaced by Edwin Samuel Montagu (1879–1924), who was known to be sympathetic to India, and who was anxious to end the controversial detention.[71]

Montagu knew Besant, having met her on his first visit to India in 1913.[72] He thought that her idea of self-rule was not bad in itself, and even announced in August 1917 that he planned to make an extensive tour of India in the autumn, in order to look into the discord and seek ways to resolve it. On 20 August he made a dramatic speech in Parliament, in which he announced the government's new policy for India. From now on, he declared, it would foster institutions of self-rule in India, looking forward 'to the progressive realization of responsible government in India as an integral part of the British Empire.' Besant could not have phrased

70. Taylor, *Annie Besant*, p. 306-307; Nanda, *The Nehrus*, pp. 132-41; Nethercot, *The Last Four Lives of Annie Besant*, pp. 259-64.

71. C. Roberts, 'Montagu, Edwin Samuel (1879-1924)', *The Dictionary of National Biography*, 1922-1930 (Oxford, 1961), pp. 607-10, first published 1937.

72. Montagu's first impression of Besant was a bit odd: 'Poor old Lady! It is difficult to believe her sexual. I find her very attractive, but her legal difficulties are very great', S.D. Waley, *Edwin Montagu: A Memoir and an Account of his Visits to India* (London, 1964), p. 327.

it any better.⁷³ Shortly before leaving for India, Montagu wrote Viceroy Chelmsford to tell him about his meeting with King George V and Queen Mary. He was lunching alone with their Majesties at the palace, when the Queen asked him how he proposed to end the business of Besant's detention. He replied that the only question was when to release her, and that Lord Chelmsford already had the opportunity to do so, having obtained assurances of Besant's good conduct.⁷⁴ He was aware of possible British criticism when Besant was freed: 'There will of course be an outburst of anger at her release, and jeers that my visit has not produced a calm atmosphere, and that she has violated her pledges.'⁷⁵

Montagu stayed in India from November 1917 until May 1918. At the end of November he met Besant in Delhi and was favourably impressed. 'Mrs. Besant,' he wrote, 'in her white and gold embroidered Indian clothes, with her short white hair, and the most beautiful voice I have ever heard, was very impressive and read magnificently.'⁷⁶

He arrived in Bombay on Christmas Eve 1917, two days before the opening of the annual INC Congress, which was scheduled to take place in Calcutta. *The London Times* reported that the first interviews he granted after arriving in Bombay were to representatives of the Home Rule movement.⁷⁷ They were led by Annie Besant, who met him and Viceroy Chelmsford and presented them with her political ideology and her vision of India being a member of the British Empire as a community of equals. At the end of their meeting Montagu asked her: 'You said just now that India did not trust us, and I think you are right. Does it trust you?'

'To a certain extent, yes,' she replied. Montagu went on: 'Supposing we were to bring a scheme forward, will you take up that scheme and recommend it? They might take on your recommendation what they would not take on ours.'⁷⁸

The exchange sheds light on Montagu's plans, and his correct assumption that Besant's position was not far from his. His decision

73. Taylor, *Annie Besant*, p. 308.
74. Waley, *Edwin Montagu*, p. 138.
75. For Montagu's quote, see, Sitaramayya, *The History of the Indian National Congress (1885–1935)*, p. 232.
76. Waley, *Edwin Montagu*, p. 145.
77. *The Times* (31 December 1917).
78. Besant, 'Interview with Mr. Montague', republished in Kumar, *Annie Besant's Rise to Power in Indian Politics*, p. 166.

to involve her in promoting his reform plan paid off. The Montagu-Chelmsford Reforms, launched in 1919, and fully implemented in 1922, ultimately won Besant's support.[79] This militated against her, and would later be one of the main causes of the loss of her popularity to Gandhi, who strongly opposed the reforms.[80]

One of Besant's first acts after her release from detention was to go to Allahabad, home of the Nehru family. Arriving there on 5 October 1917, she was met at the railway station by Motilal and Jawaharlal Nehru, accompanied by Tilak, and driven in a carriage to the Nehru residence. The crowds shouted, 'Besant mata ki jai!' (Victory to Mother Besant!), and flowers were thrown at the carriage from rooftops. Motilal Nehru made a speech in her honour at the Home-Rule League offices in Allahahbad. He said, 'Two years ago you saw with the clear intuition of genius what the motherland needed... You saw the inner hopes and aspirations in the hearts of the dumb, inarticulate millions of people of this country.'[81]

The admiration of Motilal Nehru, one of the leaders of the INC, for Besant reflected the public wave of adoration for her after her release. It reached its summit when she was proposed as president for that year's INC Congress. The proposal was officially made by one of the oldest leaders of the moderate camp, Babu Surendranath Bannerji (1848-1915).[82] A professor of English, Bannerji had twice served as president of INC Congresses – in Pune in 1895 and in Ahmedabad in 1902. His proposal carried much weight and won the backing of most of the provincial committees of the Congress. Thus at the opening of the Congress in Calcutta Besant was swept by a majority of votes to the presidency of the Indian National Congress, borne on a wave of popularity due to her detention.

At that moment it looked as if Besant had succeeded in fulfilling all her aspirations. Her dual titles as president of both the Theosophical Society and of the INC looked like a realization of the dream nurtured by the Theosophists for the past four decades. The dream of a synthesis between East and West, conceived by Blavatsky in

---

79. The reforms offered some measures of power to Indians, chiefly in the fields of education, health, and agriculture. The reforms were far from satisfying the call for Home Rule. Nonetheless, they were an important step forward in that direction.

80. B.R. Nanda, *Gandhi: Pan-Islamism, Imperialism and Nationalism in India* (New Delhi, 1989), p. 240.

81. B.R. Nanda, *The Nehrus*, p. 140.

82. *The Commonweal* (28 December 1917).

New York, appeared to have materialized under her successor in India. This sense of a dream fulfilled was clearly voiced in Besant's inaugural speech. Yet that speech, the climax of Besant's political career in India, contained the seeds of her downfall. She began by noting that there was an advantage in the Congress having elected as president someone who was not a native of India but of England, the land where the free institutions grew. Nonetheless, she went on, it was not as though they had elected a stranger, given the historical relationship between the Aryans of Europe and Asia. Historians believed, she said, that the Saxon self-rule system had sprung from an Asian source, and that the freedom which developed in England was an offspring of the traditional freedom of Oriental villages. She described herself as Western by origin but Oriental in spirit, and as one who might symbolize the union between Great Britain and India.

Besant's long speech (104 pages!) covered numerous subjects, including the World War, the economic relations between England and India, and the causes of India's new national awakening – specifically the loss of faith in the superiority of the white race. She maintained that this was due to the efforts of the Arya Samaj and the Theosophical Society, the work of Western Sanskrit scholars, who had learned to admire Indian civilization, and the stirring of Hindu women, whose position in the ancient Aryan civilization had been especially noble. The style of her address to the INC delegates resembled an investiture speech of an actual state president. She declared that the duty of a leader is to lead, and since the responsibility ultimately falls upon the leader, his decision must be final. This statement set a historical precedent for the presidency of the INC. Until then it had been a purely ceremonial post, lacking operative authority and lasting only the few days of the Congress. Besant proposed and obtained for the first time operative authority as president, extending the post for a whole year. In addition, she proposed the foundation of several committees who functioned throughout the year. Another proposition made by Besant led to the INC's adoption of the Home Rule League tricolour (red, white, green) flag (in 1931 the INC changed the red in the flag to saffron), thus making Besant's League flag the national flag of independent India.[83]

83. Sitaramayya, *The History of the Indian National Congress*, pp. 248-52; Eugène F. Irschick, *Politics and Social Conflict in South India: The Non-Brahman Movement and Tamil Separatism, 1916-1929* (Berkeley, 1969), pp. 82-83.

The speech closed with characteristic pathos, with Besant proclaiming her goal – a free India, honoured for her past and engaged in building a still more glorious future. It concluded with a typical Christian-Theosophical image – India as a nation crucified and about to be resurrected.[84] During the Calcutta Congress Besant also delivered an official report to the INC delegates, describing her meeting with Montagu, and expressing the hope that India's liberation was imminent, thanks to the spiritual bond between India and England.[85]

Thus the zenith of Annie Besant's political career was marked by her effort to convince the Indians to believe in her Theosophical vision and its realization under her leadership. This vision, as I have sought to show, which began with Blavatsky and culminated with Besant, was clearly influenced by the Orientalist ideas of the nineteenth century, notably those of Max Müller. It comprised belief in the greatness of the ancient Indo-Aryan civilization, its perception as the mother of the Aryan civilization of the West, and the goal of fusing the two great Aryan currents, the Indian and the Anglo-Teutonic. According to Besant, this synthesis would be the climax of a predestined historical process, determined by higher powers. Perhaps such a vision would have been warmly received some 20 years earlier, when most of the Indian leadership was favourably-disposed to Britain and accepted the assumption that the British presence was needed in India. Unfortunately for Besant, by the time she was elected president of the INC things had changed drastically, so that her vision soon became irrelevant. The political scene had changed after the war, in part thanks to Besant, who during the war called for an end to the discrimination against Indians. If between 1917 and 1919 she was the most popular leader in India, by the latter half of 1919 the public mood had darkened and grown much more anti-British than before.[86] Besant's political downfall resulted both from this change, and from her own ill-judged positions.

Her errors were mainly connected to two issues. The first, as we have seen, was her support for the Montagu-Chelmsford Reforms. The second was her controversial reaction to the massacre in Amritsar on 13 April 1919. The outcome in both cases was that

---

84. Annie Besant, 'Presidential Address', *Congress Speeches*, pp. 30-133.
85. Annie Besant, 'A Message from the President of the Indian National Congress to the Indian People', *Congress Speeches*, pp. 135-38.
86. Nanda, *Gandhi: Pan-Islamism, Imperialism and Nationalism in India*, pp. 188-94.

she was increasingly perceived by the Indians as identifying with British interests.

With regard to the first issue, it is important to note that at first she opposed the reforms.[87] Then she decided to support them, because she feared that India would degenerate into anarchy with the rise of the revolutionary movement. She regarded the reforms as an important stage on the road to self-rule, even if they held things up for a few years longer. A personal aspect came into this matter, too. Besant was convinced that Montagu was sincerely interested in advancing Indian self-rule. In a letter she wrote him on 15 November 1919 she urged him to propose himself for the exalted post of Viceroy.[88] But the reforms were ultimately rejected by the Indians. Gandhi, who in the 1919 Congress expressed sympathy with them and even offered to cooperate with the British, changed his mind later and from 1920 on became their leading opponent. Besant had to pay the price for supporting the reforms as Gandhi rapidly advanced to the forefront of the Indian leadership.

The second issue that damaged Besant's popularity was the massacre in Amritsar. The root-causes of the event went back to the recommendations of the Rowlatt commission, appointed by Viceroy Chelmsford on 10 December 1917 to look into the revolutionary currents in India and propose a policy to counter them. The commission's recommendations were turned into two proposed decrees, known as Rowlatt Bills. These expanded the powers of the administration to prevent sedition, provoking an angry response from Gandhi, who on 28 February 1919 announced the formation of his movement, Satyagraha Sabha, based on the principle of non-violent protest. Gandhi also called for a general strike throughout India in protest against the Rowlatt Bills. The strike took place successfully on 6 April 1919, among other places in Amritsar in the Punjab, the holy city of the Sikhs. Four days later at least four Europeans were killed by a rioting mob in the city. The authorities banned all demonstrations, but masses kept pouring into the streets to protest against the prohibition. On 13 April the army fired on a protest gathering of 10,000, wounding some 1,200 and killing close to 400, according to official counts (some estimated the numbers as much higher). Besant reacted hastily, justified the army and argued that the duty

87. *The Times* (15 August 1918, 22 July 1919, 30 July 1919).
88. Waley, *Edwin Montagu*, p. 221.

of preserving law and order was paramount. A few days later she claimed that she had spoken before becoming aware of the full horror of the event.[89] The humiliation felt by the Indians following the massacre, which demonstrated that while Indians may not kill Europeans but the reverse was allowed, no doubt reverberated on Besant. She was seen as defending the Raj, and was increasingly opposed in the INC leadership.

Her relations with Gandhi deteriorated. Whereas in early April, when he had been arrested by the British, she praised him and wished success to the Satyagraha movement, in November she criticized him sharply and rejected the principle of non-cooperation that had become a central plank in his campaign.[90] The opposition to Besant grew so intense, that in May 1919 she was obliged to resign from the presidency of the Home-Rule League. Her successor in the presidency of the League she herself had founded three years earlier was Mohandas Gandhi, who was becoming the strong man in the INC. A year later his policy of non-cooperation was widely endorsed by the Congress in Nagpur. Gandhi instigated a series of anti-British decisions, calling for a boycott on the systems of government and education, including those of the Theosophists. The Indian revolt became less tolerant and much more nationalistic.

Although Besant continued to hold various positions in the INC through the 1920s, the rift between her and the Congress leadership which opened in 1919 was never mended.[91] And so, after many years of trying to achieve a synthesis between East and West, the Theosophical Society became identified, willy-nilly, as a Western movement, when the leadership of India's national movement could no longer contain people like Annie Besant.

89. *New India* (17 April 1919).
90. *The Commonweal* (11 April 1919, 14 November 1919).
91. Right after her resignation from the Home Rule League, Besant founded a new political organization, which she stubbornly named 'National Home Rule League'. Her political activity in the subsequent years was focused on England's public opinion. She never forgave Gandhi, and although her stand as a popular leader was no longer valid, she continued to criticize his policy. See, for example, her article from 1921: 'Many have been blaming the Government of India for a policy of drastic repression which has not only been unduly severe, but leads nowhere. Such censure ignores the fact that the policy of Mr. Gandhi has been deliberately and intentionally provocative and that defiance encourages a spirit of lawlessness among the ignorant and the criminal classes, which strikes at the very foundations of society', *New India* (22 December 1921); For further discussion of Besant's political career after her fall in 1919, see, Nethercot, *The Last Four Lives of Annie Besant,* pp. 290–304.

Chapter 9

Theosophy and the World Teacher – The Esoteric Alternative

The final chapter of this book deals with the World Teacher, who became the focus of the Theosophical activity after the First World War. It will also suggest that there was another important, non-political, reason for the waning of the Theosophical Society's influence. The perception of India as the cradle of esoteric lore underlay the Theosophical interest in India's political sphere, as well as its promotion of the World Teacher, but whereas the political endeavours were concentrated in India, the cult of the World Teacher was global. As Besant's political career declined, this cult grew predominant until it became the principal alternative.

The alternative appeared in the shape of a young Hindu named Jiddu Krishnamurti, who became in 1909 the hub around which the esoteric Theosophical project revolved, in the expectation that when he grew up he would be the new World Teacher. The idea of a World Teacher, based on the ancient Buddhist idea of a Bodhisattva – an ever-present incarnation of the Buddha – was the most crucial element in Besant's theology. As described earlier, Besant believed that the Masters of the Great Brotherhood saw to it that every time a new human sub-race arose, a spiritual teacher would appear to guide it. Such teachers had appeared in the past, notably the Buddha, Krishna and Jesus. And since Besant believed that a new Aryan sub-race, the last in the series of Aryan sub-races, was just then emerging, she naturally expected the appearance of a World Teacher who would guide the new people in their early steps in the world.

Discovering this figure and recognizing his qualities while the body, or 'vehicle', it occupied was yet young, would help to make the best use of his powers and avoid a needless waste of time. Moreover, for the Theosophical Society to identify this young World Teacher and nurture him would ensure that he would have the ideal conditions when he 'awakened' and began to fulfil his destiny.

Nevertheless, his discovery in 1909 in the form of a young Hindu boy was probably not entirely accidental, as this was the time when Besant started her intensive political activity in India. Depicting a young Hindu as the awaited World Teacher was also a demonstration that the Theosophical Society was free from racial prejudice or condescension, while personifying the synthesis between East and West, which had preoccupied the Theosophical Society for a long time.[1]

I shall now relate the discovery of Krishnamurti, the central position that he came to occupy in the Theosophical mind, the crisis that shook the Theosophical Society as a result of Besant's decision to pin everything on him, and his story up to 1929, when he disavowed his so-called destiny. The description may lead to some interesting conclusions about the real meaning of the longed-for synthesis between the two currents of the Aryan nation, and suggest another explanation for Besant's dramatic fall from the heights of India's national leadership.

Charles Webster Leadbeater

Charles Webster Leadbeater was one of the most controversial figures in the history of the Theosophical Society. From 1909 on he became one of the Society's foremost leaders, played a crucial role in the Krishnamurti affair and a greater role than anyone in choosing the esoteric alternative. His name was linked both to sex scandals and to claims of supernatural abilities. The duality characterizes his personal history, too, which remains somewhat obscure and made up of bits of information that are not always reliable. The following is his history up to the discovery of the World Teacher.

Leadbeater stated that he was born on 17 February 1847, eight months before Besant. His soul had undergone some important incarnations. In one of them, he asserted, he was born to a well-off family in Athens' golden age. In that life he sailed to Samos, where he met Pythagoras, and at the end of their encounter Pythagoras promised him that they would meet again. Leadbeater in his Greek persona did not understand what the philosopher meant, but in his modern life he discovered that Pythagoras had been one of the

---

1. For further reading, see, James Santucci, 'The Conception of Christ in the Theosophical Tradition', in *Alternative Christs*, ed. Olav Hammer (Cambridge, 2009), pp. 190–211.

early incarnations of the Master Koot-Hoomi, which explained his promise.

Leaderbeater also claimed that at the age of 12 he and his brother Gerald travelled to Brazil with their father, who had been appointed to a managerial position at a railway company there. During this period the young Leadbeater underwent some hair-raising experiences. On one occasion he himself drove a locomotive and captured a cashier who had absconded from his father's company. The South American phase ended badly, as once on a tour in the Brazilian backwoods he and his father and brother squabbled with some Indians, escaped from them and fell into the clutches of rebel soldiers. The rebels killed his young brother and tortured him, but his father got away and then freed him. After returning to England, the young Leadbeater began to study at Oxford (or Cambridge in other versions), but had to give up his studies when his family went bankrupt. His interest in the occult began when he met Bulwer-Lytton, the famous writer and politician, who was visiting his father and demonstrated supernatural experiments. The first time Leadbeater discovered his spiritual powers was when he was still a boy, when in the course of a séance with his mother the table at which they sat rose, and a hat that rested on it danced by itself.[2]

A probe at the general register office in London revealed that Leadbeater was in fact born on 16 February 1854 – seven years later than the date he claimed. His father was an impecunious accountant employed by a railway company. Leadbeater's name never appeared as a student at either Oxford or Cambridge, and there is no indication that he ever had a brother.[3] His recollections of his father's relations with Bulwer-Lytton were probably likewise imaginary – it is most unlikely that the lower middle-class clerk associated with the well-known politician. All in all, Leadbeater's colourful autobiographical details were typical of his general tendency to fantasize. Moreover, their exposure provided easy ammunition to anyone who wished to mock the Theosophical pretensions to occult powers. This had begun with Blavatsky, but

---

2. C.W. Leadbeater, *How Theosophy Came to Me* (Adyar, 1986), pp. 1–9, first published 1930; C.W. Leadbeater, 'Saved by a Ghost', *The Theosophist* (Adyar, January, 1911).

3. Gregory Tillett, *The Elder Brother: A Biography of Charles Webster Leadbeater* (London, 1982), pp. 16–17.

peaked with Leadbeater, with his magical claims and fantastical writings.

Leadbeater was ordained in the Anglo-Catholic Church in 1878. Like many Victorians, he was interested in spiritualism and the occult, and read the extensive literature about these subjects. As a result, he became preoccupied with questions which undermined his religious faith, as the church was unable to answer them. In 1883, having read Sinnett's book, *The Occult World*, he felt he had found the answers. He was so impressed by the book that he wrote to the author, who responded willingly and persuaded him to join the Theosophical Society. Leadbeater's initiation into the Society, conducted by Sinnett, took place in December 1883. Alongside Leadbeater was another initiate, a serious catch for the Society – the well-known scientist William Crookes, who joined with his wife.[4] Though not a well-known person, Leadbeater was probably also viewed as a worthy catch – a priest becoming a Theosophist was a rarity even during the good years before the Hodgson Report crisis.

In his early days as a Theosophist Leadbeater maintained a close association with a medium named William Eglinton (1857–1933), who claimed to channel a number of disembodied souls, including one which called itself Ernest. Ernest talked to Leadbeater about the Masters of the Orient, and promised to transmit to him a message from them. Leadbeater was intrigued and consulted Sinnett, who as we have seen had conducted an extensive correpondence with the Masters. With Sinnett's permission, Leadbeater sent a letter to Master Koot-Hoomi, by means of Ernest, in which he asked if it was necessary to spend the seven years of apprenticeship in the occult in India.[5]

Ernest conveyed the letter but did not keep his promise to obtain an answer. In the end the answer came from a quite different source – Madame Blavatsky, whom Leadbeater met in London in 1884, a few months after his initiation into the Society. On the eve of her own journey to India, she received a letter from Master Koot-Hoomi with an answer for Leadbeater. The Master stated that it was not imperative to remain in India throughout the seven

---

4. Gregory Tillett, *The Elder Brother*, p. 30; Leadbeater, *How Theosophy Came to Me*, pp. 15–21.

5. Leadbeater, *How Theosophy Came to Me*, pp. 25–29.

years of apprenticeship, and that a person can be a faithful 'chela' anywhere. Moreover, Koot-Hoomi took an interest in Leadbeater, and suggested that he go to Adyar for a few months. The enthusiastic Leadbeater quit his post in the church and joined Blavatsky on the lengthy journey to India. In the course of the journey, while the two stopped in Egypt, Koot-Hoomi sent Blavatsky another letter, personally praising the former priest who had become a Theosophist: 'Tell Leadbeater that I am satisfied with his zeal and devotion.'

Nor was Koot-Hoomi the only Master who was interested in Leadbeater. According to him, while in Egypt he met another member of the Great Brotherhood, Master Djwal Kul.[6]

Leadbeater and Blavatsky arrived in Colombo, the capital of Ceylon, on 17 December 1884, where they met Olcott. The president of the Theosophical Society arranged for Leadbeater to meet some Buddhist priests, who convinced him that there was no real difference between Buddhism and what he regarded as the true Christianity. Having reached this conclusion, the English priest resolved to follow Olcott and Blavatsky and convert to Buddhism. He was confident that his connection with the church had ended. Henceforth he devoted himself exclusively to Theosophy, though as we shall see, he returned to the fold of the Christian church some 30 years later.[7]

After two days in Colombo, Leadbeater, Blavatsky and Olcott sailed to Adyar, where the annual conference of the Theosophical

6. The name of the Master Djwal Kul was quite anonymous when Leadbeater first travelled to India. Many years later, his name would become famous among occultists, thanks to Alice Bailey, who 'channeled' his messages on a regular basis. See, for example, her book, *The Destiny of Nations*, which described a lengthy channeling with the Master, and dealt with the myths of Lemuria and Atlantis, Alice A. Bailey, *The Destiny of Nations* (Albany, 1968), first published 1949. Bailey became Besant's adversary in the 1920s. She claimed to have met Koot-Hoomi before in 1895, but had only realized who he really was in 1915, when she joined the Theosophical Society. She was initiated to the ES, but decided to resign from the Society after having heard 'the astounding statement that no one in the world could be a disciple of the Masters of the Wisdom unless they had been so notified by Mrs. Besant.' Later, Bailey founded her own society, The Arcane School, which is still active: Alice A. Bailey, *The Unfinished Autobiography* (London, 1951), pp. 34-37, 156-58.

7. In his first published book, Leadbeater explained the attraction of Theosophy as based on a successful substitute to Christianity, 'It is one of the most beautiful characteristics of Theosophy that it gives back to people in a more rational form everything which was useful and helpful to them in the religions which they have outgrown', W. Leadbeater, *Invisible Helpers* (Adyar, 1952), p. 1, first published 1896.

Society was about to take place. Leadbeater remained in Adyar, and a few months later was appointed director of *The Theosophist*, and when Blavatsky was obliged to leave India for good, he took over her position as the director of correspondence for the Theosophical Society.[8] But this was not the only thing Blavatsky bequeathed to him. Though she herself never mentioned it, Leadbeater presented himself as her unquestioned successor in all things occult. According to him, his abilities began to manifest themselves a little before Blavatsky's departure, when he began to see plainly the physical embodiments of the Masters, among them Koot-Hoomi and Morya, and his connections with them grew stronger after Blavatsky left. Koot-Hoomi taught him the practice of Kundalini meditation, which helps to open the energy channels needed to achieve clairvoyance. The climax of his initiation with the Masters was a 40 day period of seclusion, during which he practised this kind of meditation, and was repeatedly visited by the Masters who advised him and supported him in the difficult hours.[9]

Leadbeater wrote his memoirs about this period decades later, and they are full of dramatic effects meant to substantiate his claim that the Masters had chosen him to be Blavatsky's successor. Few people professed to have seen the Masters with their own eyes, and Leadbeater's claim to have maintained a constant, tangible association with them placed him in an enviable position. Equally, his assertion that Blavatsky had exempted him from the usual seven years of apprenticeship was supported by his description of the 40 days' seclusion in Adyar. The description had a mystic quality, probably inspired by Christ's 40 days in the desert.

Reality, however, was somewhat duller, and remained so for many years. Leadbeater's modest way of life in Adyar became even more austere after Olcott sent him to Ceylon, where he remained between 1886 and 1889. During this period he became embroiled in the attempted abduction of a local boy named Jinarajadasa, whom he claimed to have recognized as a reincarnation of his late (possibly fictitious) brother Gerald. The boy had been influenced by the tales of his English friend, who converted him to Theosophy and convinced him that if he wanted to advance in the occult lore he would have to go to England. In 1889 Leadbeater actually tried to

---

8. *The Theosophist* (June, 1885).
9. Leadbeater, *How Theosophy Came to Me*, pp. 36–133.

send Jinarajadasa secretly to England, but the boy's parents found out in time and fought to prevent his departure. In the end they gave in to Leadbeater's arguments that it was in the boy's interests, and allowed him to travel to England. Jinarajadasa remained in England for many years, studied Sanskrit and philology at Cambridge, married an Englishwoman named Dorothy Graham, and came to be a prominent Theosophical leader, and president of the Society, from 1945 until 1953.[10]

Leadbeater and his Ceylonese protégé left for England on 28 November 1889. They lived for two years at Sinnett's house, 7 Ladbroke Grove, Notting Hill, London. Sinnett was subsidizing Leadbeater, whom he had inducted into Theosophy six years earlier, and even entrusted him with the education of his son Denny. At this time Leadbeater acquired a reputation among members of the Theosophical Society as an expert in esoteric education for children. This speciality, as we shall see, would later lead to one of the worst scandals experienced by the Society, when Leadbeater was accused of sexually exploiting his pupils. But in the 1890s Leadbeater's name was unimpeachable, and he became known in Theosophical circles as a charismatic speaker and helpful counsellor to parents who wished to educate their children in the occult.

Leadbeater and Besant first met at Sinnett's house in 1890, a short time after Besant had been initiated into the Society by Blavatsky. He stated that he had long been aware of her public activities. Before discovering Theosophy, when he was still troubled by religious doubts, he had attended some of the lectures she gave while working beside Bradlaugh in the Freethought Movement. Her lectures roused him and intensified his inner conflict, as they 'raised other difficulties for which I saw no solution.'[11]

In the early stage of their association Besant was obviously in the superior position, being a well-known, respected and public figure. Perhaps this was the reason Leadbeater chose to embellish his biographical data, adding seven years to his age, bringing it close to Besant's, hoping to appear in a more impressive light.

---

10. Tillett, *The Elder Brother*, pp. 51-53; Peter Washington, *Madame Blavatsky's Baboon: A History of the Mystics, Mediums, and Misfits who Brought Spiritualism to America* (New York, 1995), pp. 115-18, first published 1993.

11. C.W. Leadbeater, *The Other Side of Death, Scientifically Examined and Carefully Described* (Adyar, 1954), p. 78, first published 1903.

Their relations grew closer in August 1895, when Besant invited Leadbeater to stay at her house at 19 Avenue Road, St. John's Wood, London. She also subsidized him and made him the junior secretary of the European Section, which had its headquarters at the house. As we have seen, between 1891 and 1895 Besant was preoccupied with the Blavatsky succession, which entailed prolonged journeys abroad. Only when the contest ended with the withdrawal of the American Section from the Society did conditions permit the relations between Leadbeater and Besant to develop. The two became close associates and their particular relationship thrived for many years. In some respects, their relationship was reminiscent of Blavatsky and Olcott's relationship. However, in this case the feminine side (Besant) was responsible for worldly matters, while the male side was in charge of the occult. Besant regarded Leadbeater as Blavatsky's heir in the matter of clairvoyance, with the same magic touch which had enticed her into the Society in the first place. Perhaps she missed this kind of relationship since her mentor's death. In return, she gave Leadbeater legitimacy and recognition, that grew as she herself rose to the leadership of the Theosophical Society.

Their friendship prompted a spurt of writing in Leadbeater. His book, *Invisible Helpers* (a description of invisible entities who guide us and keep us from danger), was published in 1896 – the first of a series of books he would publish in his long Theosophical career. In addition, he engaged in collaborative writing with Besant, based on the esoteric experiments they conducted over the years. They would shut themselves away and go into a trance which lasted for many hours, sometimes entire weekends. In the course of these trances they communicated with the Masters and practised clairvoyance, then dictated to their disciples the visions they had experienced, and these were compiled and published in several books. The most influential was *Thought-Forms*, which appeared in 1901 and portended the future wave of New Age Literature about auras, invisible human bodies and their colours, and the power of thought. The book's main theme, invisible human bodies and their auras, became Leadbeater's main speciality in the coming years.[12]

12. Annie Besant and C.W. Leadbeater, *Thought-Forms* (Wheaton, 1986), first published 1901. This book influenced several artists, such as Piet Mondrian (1872–1944), who was an active Theosophist from 1909 until 1917, and Wassily Kandinsky (1866–1944), who had a copy of its German translation. The latter's biographer claims that the book had an immense influence over Kandinsky, who

After being fostered by Besant as her close associate for several years, Leadbeater's reputation spread beyond England. In 1900–1901 he went on a long lecture tour in the United States, returned to England for a few months, returned to the US in August 1902 and lectured there until February 1905. In May 1905, he went to Australia for the first time, and gave lectures there for several months. In December 1905 he came to Adyar for the annual conference of the Theosophical Society. During these years he published a number of other works which won him a reputation among esoteric circles worldwide, established him as the leading clairvoyant of the Theosophical Society, and as Blavatsky's undisputed successor.

It was at the beginning of 1906, just when it seemed that his position was stronger than ever, that the scandal erupted which threatened to destroy his reputation along with his friendship with Besant. It began in January, when they were both staying in Besant's headquarters in Benares, to which she had returned after the annual conference in Adyar. Besant received a letter from the United States containing grave accusations against Leadbeater, which stunned the two friends like a lightning strike. The writer was the secretary of the ES in the United States, a Chicago Theosophist named Helen Dennis, whose son had been educated by Leadbeater during his lengthy stay in the US. Dennis claimed that Leadbeater had behaved scandalously with the boys in his care, taught them to masturbate with the pretext of occult learning, promised them that the practice would strengthen their sexual prowess, and moreover demanded that they keep it secret. Dennis demanded that Besant investigate these accusations, and promised to keep the matter confidential, for everybody's sake. But soon afterwards the story became public, when a letter attributed to Leadbeater was circulated among the members of the Theosophical Society. Addressed to one of the boys

---

in his paintings tried to reconstruct Leadbeater's esoteric colour perception: Sixten Ringbom, *The Sounding Cosmos: A Study in the Spiritualism of Kandinsky and the Genesis of Abstract Painting* (Helsingfors, 1970), pp. 59-63 , 82-85, 91 f49; Sylvia Cranston, *HPB: The Extraordinary Life and Influence of Helena Blavatsky, Founder of the Modern Theosophical Movement* (New York, 1993), pp. 484-89. In 1902, Leadbeater published another book, entitled *Man Visible and Invisible*, which described in detail the human bodies, accompanied by colourful illustrations, C.W. Leadbeater, *Man Visible and Invisible: Examples of Different Types of Men as Seen by Means of Trained Clairvoyance* (New York, 1909), first published 1902.

he had trained, it was sensational enough to condemn him out of hand.[13]

The accusations levelled at Leadbeater were especially shocking in those days, when the Victorian ethos condemned masturbation as a cause of blindness, insanity and so on. But even in today's sexually permissive climate few parents would be happy to discover that the teacher entrusted with their children's education was secretly giving them sexual instruction. Still, today the charge would probably have been regarded as a borderline case, since there was no suggestion that Leadbeater had had any physical contact with his pupils, and thus could not be accused of actual sexual abuse. But whether Leadbeater was guilty of pedophilia, or was only trying to help his pupils and provide them with a sexual education at a time when the subject was taboo, the scandal was grave enough for Olcott to appoint a commission to investigate the case. The commission, consisting of three leading Theosophical figures – Sinnett, Bertram Keightley and George Mead – met in London in May 1906. Their conclusion was that Leadbeater should be expelled from the Theosophical Society. Olcott offered Leadbeater an honorable exit, in the form of a letter of resignation. Leadbeater accepted, and so the unpleasant affair was at an end – at least formally.[14]

The scandal was extremely painful for Besant. Leadbeater had been her close friend for many years and needed her protection.

---

13. That letter contained an easy to decipher paragraph, which reads as follows: 'If it comes without help, he needs rubbing more often, but not too often or he will not come well. Does this happen when you are asleep? Tell me fully. Glad sensation is so pleasant. Thousand kisses darling', Tillett, *The Elder Brother*, pp. 82–83.

14. Tillet offers an original explanation to the scandal, claiming that Leadbeater was trying to absorb his pupils' sexual energy, thus strengthening his own magical powers: Tillett, *The Elder Brother*, pp. 283–84. This explanation relies on documented magical practices used by other well-known contemporary occultists, such as Aleister Crowley from the Hermetic Order of the Golden Dawn, who approved magical use of sexual energy, Joscelyn Godwin, *The Theosophical Enlightenment* (Albany, 1994), p. 361. Dixon gives another illuminating explanation, in which she recognizes a tight relation in the European religious heritage between heresy and homosexuality, and comprehends Leadbeater's case as an appropriate example. Moreover, she claims that the Theosophical belief in reincarnation contributed to sexual permissiveness, since the same souls incarnate in male and female bodies alike, Joy Dixon, 'Sexology and the Occult: Sexuality and Subjectivity in Theosophy's New Age', *Journal of the History of Sexuality* 7 (1997), 409–33. However, one should notice that when dealing with sexuality, Theosophists tend to preach against sexual permissiveness and favour celibacy.

On the other hand, if he had in fact sexually exploited his pupils, then his claim of spending long periods in the company of the Masters was a lie, as such experience required spiritual and sexual purity. The implication was a death sentence for everything they had written together and for her own reputation as an initiate. At first she kept her distance from Leadbeater, but eventually she set their friendship higher than the protection of her reputation. This choice cost her dearly in the political sphere, as echoes of the scandal continued to reverberate in the race for the leadership of the Theosophical Society. As we have seen, Besant's main rivals for the presidency of the Society in 1907 were Sinnett, Keightley and Mead – the very three who had investigated the Leadbeater affair and decided to expel him from the Society. It is unlikely that their cooperation in the contest was accidental. It is more likely that they resented Besant's friendship with a person whom they saw as a deviant and outright felon. Mead's reach for the presidency of the Society may thus be seen as an attempt to preserve its moral tone. This interpretation is bolstered by the fact that all three men quit the Theosophical Society a short time after Besant's election. It would seem that the new president was regarded as, at best, lacking sound judgment, and, at worst, as tainted with immorality. Subsequent events show that they were not mistaken, at any rate regarding Besant's judgment. Not long after her election as president of the Theosophical Society, Besant fully rehabilitated Leadbeater, and in February 1909 he was back in Adyar and once again at the forefront of the Society's leadership.

Krishnamurti: The Early Years of Apprenticeship

One afternoon in April 1909, a couple of months after his return to Adyar, Leadbeater went down to the beach near the Theosophical Society headquarters. He was accompanied by some of his pupils, among them B.P. Wadia (the future editor of *The Commonweal*), and his young secretary Ernest Wood (1883-1965). That day there were some young Indian boys splashing about in the sea, and Leadbeater suddenly noticed one of them – a 14-year old boy who was swimming about with his brother. Leadbeater, the renowned clairvoyant, saw an exceptional aura surrounding the boy which led him to conclude that he was a reincarnation of a very ancient soul with a unique

Jiddu Krishnamurti, the Theosophical World Teacher, 1935, USA, photograph courtesy of the Krishnamurti Foundation Trust.

potential.¹⁵ Later he decided that the boy, Jiddu Krishnamurti, was an avatar of the Buddhist entity Maitreya. Fifty-five years later Wood recalled that Leadbeater had told him that Krishnamurti would become a great spiritual teacher. 'How great?' he had asked. 'As great as Mrs Besant?' 'Much greater,' Leadbeater had replied.¹⁶

Jiddu Krishnamurti (Jiddu is a caste name) was born on 12 May 1895, in a small village north of Madras. His father, Jiddu Narayaniah, was a poor Brahmin who had graduated from the University of Madras and worked for the Indian Civil Service as a tax collector. The boy's mother, Sanjeevamma, had died in 1905, when he was 10 years old. His father, who had joined the Theosophical Society back in 1882, had been in financial difficulties since his wife's death, and early in 1909 was permitted by Annie Besant to occupy a house near the Society headquarters in Adyar. Besant also gave him clerical work in the Society's office. Narayaniah and his children moved to Adyar on 23 January 1909. The father was kept busy much of the time, leaving the children at a loose end. Two of the boys, Krishnamurti and his younger brother Nityananda (1899–1925), spent much of the time on the beach, where Leadbeater saw them.

Writing to Besant after his discovery of Krishnamurti, Leadbeater stated: '... if we are to have the karma of assisting even indirectly at the bringing up of one whom the Master has used in the past and is waiting to use again, we may at least give him a chance to grow up decently.'¹⁷

What he probably meant was that the conditions of Krishnamurti's life were more meagre than those the European Theosophists could provide. It seems that Narayaniah agreed with him, if only for a while, as he allowed Krishnamurti and Nityananda to study with Leadbeater. In a few months Leadbeater became convinced that Krishnamurti was indeed the next World Teacher. When Besant returned to Adyar from Europe on 27 November 1909, Leadbeater presented to her the long-awaited new World Teacher.¹⁸ Two

---

15. Tillett, *The Elder Brother*, pp. 103–13; Roland Vernon, *Star in the East: Krishnamurti, the Invention of a Messiah* (London, 2000), pp. 1–6.

16. Ernest Wood, 'No Religion Higher than Truth', *The American Theosophist* (December, 1964).

17. Wood, 'No Religion Higher than Truth'; Mary Lutyens, *Krishnamurti: The Years of Awakening* (London, 1975), p. 1; Vernon, *Star in the East*, p. 276 f4.

18. Besant was familiar with Leadbeater's quest for the World Teacher. Three years prior to Krishnamurti's discovery, Leadbeater had announced that another boy, the American Hubert van Hook, was the avatar of Maitreya. Hubert and his mother

months later, on 11 January 1910, Krishnamurti underwent an esoteric initiation ceremony, and henceforth became the focus of the spiritual interest of the Theosophical Society.

Krishnamurti's studies with Leadbeater were marvellously effective, and allowed him to begin shortly to communicate with the Masters. From his teacher he learned that the original name of his first incarnation was Alcyone, and that in the course of his many reincarnations he had been both Krishna and Jesus, as well as Maitreya. His current incarnation soon discovered its goals and abilities. In 1910, soon after his initiation, Krishnamurti published a booklet entitled *At the Feet of the Master*, describing his encounters with the Master Koot-Hoomi. It was written in English, in which he was not yet proficient. Nevertheless, in her introduction to the work, Besant assured readers that it was written exclusively by Krishnamurti and was his first gift to the world.[19] *At the Feet of the Master* described some principles essential for the student of the occult, as conveyed by Koot-Hoomi. In fact, the booklet was a summary of old Theosophical ideas and free from innovation. Still, for those who were expecting the imminent appearance of a new World Teacher, this was the first evidence of Krishnamurti's destiny and showed that the much-awaited Teacher was actually incarnated in the Hindu lad. Besant took pains to encourage this view. In 1912, two years after the publication of *At the Feet of the Master*, she stated that she did not know of any other book in which the Master's instructions were given in such detail.[20]

The cult of Krishnamurti began to be constructed in 1911 by George Arundale, Besant's associate who was teaching at the Central Hindu College in Benares. In honour of the new World Teacher he founded the Order of the Rising Sun – which Besant disbanded the following year, following objections by the Hindu teachers at the College. But the World Teacher cult was not affected. Even before the Order of the Rising Sun was disbanded, on 8 May 1911 (White Lotus Day,

---

travelled to India and reached Adyar in November 1909, but were disappointed to find out that Leadbeater had already discovered another 'messiah'. Nonetheless, both stayed in Adyar and assisted Leadbeater with his esoteric research. In 1919, Hubert van Hook had his revenge, when he publicly accused Leadbeater of sexually abusing him in his childhood: Nethercot, *The Last Four Lives of Annie Besant*, p. 144; Vernon, *Star in the East*, p. 109.

19. Alcyone, *At the Feet of the Master* (Adyar, 1974), pp. v–vi, first published 1910.
20. Annie Besant, *Initiation: The Perfecting of Man* (London, 1912), p. 51.

the anniversary of Blavatsky's death), Besant founded the Order of the Star in the East (henceforth the OSE) in London. It was to be an international order, and membership of the Theosophical Society was not required. Krishnamurti was named head of the OSE, and Arundale was its secretary general who also founded the Order's monthly publication, *Herald of the Star*.

Besant's grandiose plans for Krishnamurti were on a global scale. She believed that the sub-race he was sent to guide was rising far from India, in the United States. The Theosophical jigsaw puzzle was filling up nicely with the discovery that the birthplace of the new World Teacher was India, the cradle of occult lore. But Besant also believed that for the World Teacher to fulfill his destiny he had to acquire a Western education and rhetorical abilities – in other words, receive a proper English upbringing. In April 1911 she travelled with Krishnamurti and his brother Nityananda to London, where the new World Teacher was presented to the members of the Theosophical Society in England. Shortly afterwards she announced the launching of the OSE. The Indian brothers enjoyed the hospitality of Besant's old friends, Ursula Bright and her daughter Esther. In October they returned to India, but only for a short while – in January 1912 they sailed back to England. It would be ten years before Krishnamurti saw his native land again, when he came to Madras in December 1921.

Krishnamurti's second journey to England led to a serious legal dispute which made headlines in the British press. His father Narayaniah had given his consent to the first trip, but he claimed that the second journey was made without his permission. He argued that Besant had betrayed his trust and in effect kidnapped his two sons. He was so incensed that in 1913 he sued Besant. The High Court in Madras found for him, and ordered Besant to return the boys to their father's custody no later than December 1913. Besant resisted and obtained permission to appeal to the judicial commission of the Privy Council in London. The Lord Chancellor, who presided over the Privy Council, was Lord Haldane, Besant's old friend from her Fabian days. The Privy Council considered the appeal and in May 1914 overturned the verdict of the Madras court and decided that Krishnamurti and Nityananda could choose whether to return to their father or remain in Besant's custody.[21]

---

21. Ann Taylor, *Annie Besant: A Biography* (Oxford, 1992), pp. 296-98.

The judicial discussion in Besant's appeal, as reported in the *Times* of London, illustrates the British attitude towards the Empire's Indian subjects. Deviating from its usual antagonistic attitude towards Besant, the paper reported that the boys' father, Narayaniah, had been a devoted Theosophist for some 30 years, and had benefited from free accommodation in Adyar before the Theosophical Society first took any interest in his sons. The final verdict, quoted in full by *The Times*, sharply criticized the father for his original agreement to grant the Theosophical Society custody of his sons. The verdict stated that while there is no difference between the Hindu and the English cultures concerning a father's rights over his children, since Narayaniah had given up his rights in the past, he could not claim them in future.

The implied assumptions in this verdict were plain to see. Ultimately, the boys' father was depicted as a poor native who had benefited from the kindness of the Europeans and from free accommodation. Such a man was not worthy of raising his children whom he had given up previously, even if he had meant it to be temporary, so as to give them a better upbringing than he could possibly give them himself. The verdict dealt masterfully with the evidence that had been confirmed by the supreme court in Madras, and ignored the fact that it was probably Besant who in reality betrayed the father's trust. Haldane's decision to leave the decision to the boys (still under 21) put the father in his place, supposedly out of sincere concern for his sons. In other words, the court thought it unthinkable that, having once experienced the marvels of British education and culture, the boys would wish to return to their miserable earlier existence. In this connection, the boys' advocate, one Kenworthy Brown, noted in the course of the hearing that the expected decision did not take the real facts into account. The boys, he argued, had been the entire time under the powerful influence of Mrs Besant, whose word was law in the Theosophical Society, so that asking them what they wanted was tantamount to asking Mrs Besant; a reasonable enough inference.[22]

The affair concluded successfully for Besant. Henceforth Krishnamurti was in the custody of the Theosophical Society. He and his brother would see their father – who died in 1924 – only once more, when they returned to India in 1921. In effect, Krishnamurti

22. *The Times* (London, 5 May 1914, 6 May 1914, 26 May 1914).

lost his father, and the Theosophical Society became his extended family. From now on he would be subject to the plans made for him by Besant and Leadbeater, who were awaiting the awakening and maturation of the messianic entity incarnated in him, the coming World Teacher.

The Waiting Period

Most members of the Theosophical Society were thrilled by the news of the discovery of Krishnamurti and his initiation and apprenticeship by Theosophical mentors. The story of the World Teacher reinforced their great messianic expectations. The exultation raised the prestige of the Society, for it had been chosen by the Great Brotherhood to foster its emissary on earth. The success of the cult of the World Teacher was shown by the steady increase in the membership of the Theosophical Society, which continued to grow until Krishnamurti quit it. In 1907 the Theosophical Society numbered 13,000 members; in 1911, two years after the discovery of the World Teacher, it reached 16,000; in 1920 it leapt to 36,000, and in 1929 it scaled the heights with 45,098 members active in 1,586 lodges worldwide – a record it never attained again.[23]

Yet some Theosophists thought that the Krishnamurti cult was not to be taken seriously, that it was a fantasy concocted by Leadbeater, who had already been denounced as untrustworthy and a deviant. One of these skeptics was Rudolf Steiner, who had headed the German Section of the Theosophical Society since 1902. His emphatic rejection of the Krishnamurti cult led to a serious rupture in the Society and caused, 18 years after the split with the American Section headed by Judge, the loss of a large number of members.

Rudolf Steiner was born in 1861 in the small Austrian town of Kraljevec (now in Croatia). While still a young boy he became convinced of the reality of the spirit world and that the soul persisted after the death of the body. He was, however, also interested in science. This inclination suited the claims of Theosophy, which always sought to merge science with spiritualism. Steiner first came across Theosophy in 1887, after reading Sinnett's *Esoteric Buddhism*. But unlike Leadbeater, who was captivated by it, Steiner stated that

23. *General Report of the Theosophical Society* (Adyar, 1908, 1912, 1921, 1929).

the book failed to impress him and struck him as inferior. In 1891 he received his doctorate from the German university of Rostock, and in 1897 moved to Berlin. His first contacts with members of the Theosophical Society took place in 1899, when he was invited to lecture to some German Theosophists. At this time he met the Theosophist Marie von Sivers (1867–1948), who became his close friend; they married years later, in 1914. The two attended a Theosophical conference in London in 1902, where Steiner first met Besant, Bertram Keightley and George Mead. He also heard Leadbeater addressing the gathering, but said he retained no particular impression of the man.

Besant enthused over the scholarly mystic, and appointed him secretary general of the German Section, a post he filled until his split with the Theosophical Society. During the 11 years of Steiner's management the Section flourished, and by 1913 could boast 13 lodges throughout Germany. But, as Steiner stated, from 1906 on various developments indicated to him that the Society was losing its way. Although he was willing to overlook the Leadbeater scandal, the discovery of Krishnamurti and the cult created around him were too much for him. While Steiner believed in the transmigration of the soul and in the principle of karma, he thought the idea that Krishnamurti was a reincarnation of Jesus was absurd. His revulsion was rooted in his belief that Jesus was a genuine divine manifestation and a unique figure in human history. Moreover, he believed that original Christianity contained more truth than any other religion before it was corrupted by the ecclesiastic establishment. Indeed, throughout his life Steiner remained sympathetic towards the Catholic faith, which he had come to know as a child (although his father was an atheist). Aside from these considerations, he viewed the OSE as an artificial attempt to create a society within the Society, in a manner that conflicted with Blavatsky's doctrine. He therefore excluded members of the OSE from the German Section. In response, Besant unilaterally ended his charter as the Section's secretary, and in 1913 expelled him from the Theosophical Society.

Steiner's relations with Besant had never been cordial. He stated that their mutual friends, Orsula and Esther Bright, were frequently obliged to mediate between them. He personally preferred the company of Keightley and Mead, who, as we have seen, quit the Society when Besant was elected its president. He disliked the Oriental tendency of Besant's time, in particular the 'Indian exercises' (by which he probably meant yoga and meditation), which she introduced into the esoteric studies of the ES. During his 11 years as head of the German Section, Steiner promoted an alternative course of study to that of Besant's, with the emphasis on education and art. He stated that even during his incumbency as head of the German Section the link between his followers and the global headquarters in Adyar was a formality. His description of his confrontation with Besant suggests that their association would have ended in any case, and the row over Krishnamurti was the pretext for the split rather than its root cause. Yet we must keep in mind that Steiner wrote about it some 12 years after the split. Perhaps if Besant had been more tolerant towards him, he and his followers would have remained in the Theosophical Society.

Steiner's charisma as a teacher and esoteric leader was vindicated soon after his expulsion from the Theosophical Society, when he founded a new movement, the Anthroposophical Society. This movement sought to enhance the study of esoteric lore with the resources of Western philosophy. Some scholars have suggested another, intriguing, interpretation of the clash between Steiner and Besant. Analysing the differences between them in the light of gender criteria, it has been said that Steiner's spiritual thought was essentially masculine, unlike the feminine nature of Theosophy, which was manifested in women holding central positions in its leadership and the large number of female followers. Furthermore, the philosophical contents of Theosophy bore an Oriental character, which the European mind perceived as more feminine than the masculine, rationalist Western philosophy. In this analysis, Steiner offered his followers a serious and more masculine interpretation, which accorded better with the masculine German philosophy than did the one offered by Theosophy.[24]

When the break occurred in 1913, a tide of members followed Steiner out of the Theosophical Society and into his newborn Anthroposophy. Some 2,500 members quit – the majority of the German Theosophists at that time.[25] Indeed, the Theosophical

---

24. Maria Carlson, 'No Religion Higher than Truth': A History of the Theosophical Movement in Russia, 1875–1922 (Princeton, 1993), pp. 33–34.

25. Rudolf Steiner, The Course of My Life (New York, 1951), pp. 99–100, 299–325, first published 1925; Nethercot, The Last Four Lives of Annie Besant, p. 177; Washington, Madame Blavatsky's Baboon, pp. 145–56. For further information on Steiner's teachings, see, Gilbert Childs, Rudolf Steiner: His Life and Work (Edinburgh,

Society in Germany never recovered from this crisis. Beyond the antagonism between Steiner and Besant, the outbreak of the Great War the following year, that severed all contacts between England and Germany, led Besant to identify the enemy country with the forces of evil. It seems that she was not too shaken by the loss of the German Section. Perhaps the far graver loss of the American Section in 1895 had taught her not to fear such crises. Moreover, Krishnamurti's rising popularity attracted thousands of new members year after year. A simple calculation showed that Besant could well afford to lose a few thousand members who opposed her protégé, while far more supporters flocked to her camp.

Just as during the last split, in which she played a key part, Besant was utterly sure of herself and sought to give the membership the impression that all was well. At the Theosophical conference in Stockholm in June 1913, she referred to the crisis with Steiner and called for a respectful attitude towards the Anthroposophists. She stated that although the breakup was due to Steiner's rejection of the idea of a World Teacher, she nevertheless recommended his writings, being convinced that one should read whatever was written by truth-seekers, without being bound to a single line of thought.[26] As she had done during previous crises, Besant depicted herself as the tolerant and positive side in the conflict. In fact, just as she treated Judge in 1895, and Sinnett, Keightley and Mead in 1907, in her clash with Steiner she acted incisively and intolerantly, utterly confident in her rightness and without a hint of compromise.

Besant returned to India soon after the conclusion of the Krishnamurti court case. Before leaving, she entrusted him and Nityananda to the care of Lady Emily Lutyens (1874–1964). The brothers lived at the Lutyens house for the next few years. Emily Lutyens was a relatively new member of the Theosophical Society, having joined in 1910.[27] No doubt her patrician background appealed to both Besant and Leadbeater. Her grandfather was Edward Bulwer-Lytton, the politician, mystic and writer; her father, Edward Robert Bulwer-Lytton had been Viceroy of India between

---

1995); Rudolf Steiner, *The Essentials of Education: Five Lectures Delivered during the Educational Conference of the Waldorf School, Stuttgart, April, 1924* (London, 1948).

26. Annie Besant, 'The Policy of the Theosophical Society', in *Superhuman Men in History and in Religion* (London, 1913), pp. 131-32.

27. Emily Lutyens, *Candles in the Sun* (London, 1957), pp. 13-16.

1880–1884. Her husband was the renowned architect Edwin Lutyens (1869–1944), who in 1912 was appointed the architect of New Delhi, India's new Imperial capital. Lady Emily, a denizen of London's upper classes, made Krishnamurti and his brother part of her family, and proceeded to devote herself to his cult. Her daughter Mary (1908–1999) grew very attached to Krishnamurti, remained close to him even after he quit the Theosophical Society, and later became his biographer.[28]

The First World War, during which Besant's political activity was most intensive, stopped her regular visits to England. As a result, she did not see Krishnamurti for five years – until July 1919. During this time his education was entrusted to Jinarajadasa and Arundale, both of whom spent part of the war in England.

But Besant's plans for the formal education of the World Teacher did not quite succeed. Krishnamurti repeatedly sought admission to English universities, having been rejected by the various colleges of Oxford and Cambridge, as was his brother. Finally in 1918, Nityananda was admitted to London University, whereas Krishnamurti again failed the entrance examinations.[29] The young World Teacher could take comfort from his greatly improved English, which stood him in good stead in the years to come, when he began to commit his ideas to writing. He was also active in the OSE, where the membership was doubtless impatient for the World Teacher to manifest himself. What went on in the young Hindu's mind during those years is not easy to discern. Did he cooperate with his European patrons from humility and lack of confidence in his own judgment? Or did he believe that they were right and that eventually he would undergo the transformation and become a super-human being? The answer is far from clear. As we shall see, Krishnamurti did for some time internalize the Theosophical fantasy and believe in his World Teacher destiny.

In the meantime, in faraway India, Krishnamurti's discoverer and first mentor Leadbeater underwent a metamorphosis of his own. In February 1914, he left Adyar and moved to Sydney, Australia. There about a year later he met an old acquaintance, James Ingall Wedgwood (1883–1951), a young scion of the well-known china

---

28. J. Krishnamurti, *Krishnamurti's Notebook*, with a Forward by Mary Lutyens (New York, 1976), pp. 5–6; Mary Lutyens, *Krishnamurti: The Years of Fulfillment* (London, 1983).

29. Vernon, *Star in the East*, pp. 66–85.

manufacturing family. He had been initiated into Theosophy in 1904 and served as secretary of the English Theosophical Society in 1911–1913. He claimed to be able to communicate with occult powers, and in 1912 founded an esoteric order by name of the Temple of the Rosy Cross, with rites in which messages were received from the Masters. He was also prominently active in the Co-Masonry, the section of the Free Masons which functioned under the aegis of the Theosophical Society.[30]

In 1913 Wedgwood joined an independent church called the Old Catholic Church, which he successfully promoted among the London Theosophists. While visiting Sydney in 1915 he initiated his friend Leadbeater into Co-Masonry, and later persuaded him to join the Old Catholic Church too. Meanwhile, the archbishop of this church, Arnold Harris Mathew (1852–1919), decided to return to the Church of Rome, and urged those of his flock who were members of the Theosophical Society to quit it and declare their allegiance to Rome. Not everyone obeyed this injunction – some preferred to change their leader and chose Wedgwood as their archbishop, in a ceremony that took place in London in February 1916. Wedgwood did not waste much time and upon returning to Australia, in July 1916, he ordained Leadbeater as bishop.[31] And so, more than 30 years after quitting the church, Leadbeater returned to the Christian clergy, though now as the leader of a small church, for which he and Wedgwood augured a glorious future as the church of the World Teacher.

On 6 September 1918 Wedgwood and Leadbeater changed the name of their church to The Liberal Catholic Church. It was associated with the Theosophical Society and prepared its followers for the appearance of the World Teacher. In 1922 Wedgwood was accused of having had sexual relations with one of his junior priests and had to resign all his posts in the Theosophical Society and the Liberal Catholic Church. Although he was rehabilitated in 1924 and regained his position in both organizations, by then Leadbeater had become the archbishop of the church, having succeeded

---

30. Emily Lutyens, who was a member of the Order of Co-Masonry, was one of the first to join Wedgwood's Temple of the Rosy-Cross. In her memoirs she described the Order's ceremonies and ridiculous costumes. The motto of the Order was 'Lux veritatis'. Lutyens reported sarcastically that George Arundale's interpretation to that motto was 'looks very silly': Emily Lutyens, *Candles in the Sun*, p. 39.
31. Tillett, *The Elder Brother*, pp. 166–71.

Wedgwood's position in March 1923.[32] Leadbeater remained in this position until he died in 1934.

Awakening, Denial and Withdrawal

A short time after the sexual scandal surrounding Wedgwood, the faithful of the Liberal Catholic Church in Australia were presented with the World Teacher, Krishnamurti, who arrived in Sydney in April 1922, accompanied by Nityananda and Annie Besant. The brothers had recently concluded a tour of India, their first visit there since 1912. The general tour marked the final stage in the project of the World Teacher, now that he was a young man. From this time until he disbanded his Order in 1929, Krishnamurti travelled around, visiting the Theosophical communities worldwide. Besant used her time in Sydney to deliver five sermons in Leadbeater's church. Presumably her purpose was to create a broad common base with her Christian audience, hence there was a much stronger Christian element to her speeches. Now she focused on the story of Jesus as a practical model for all humanity, shown in five phases – birth, baptism, transfiguration, passion, and ultimate triumph.[33]

Where did Besant place her Hindu protégé on this trajectory? We cannot tell. Before long Krishnamurti himself would describe a process of transfiguration, or even an actual transformation. He remained in Sydney until June, then went on his first trip to the United States, together with Nityananda. Arriving in California – which, as we have seen, was regarded by the Theosophists as the birthplace of the new Aryan sub-race – he settled in the Ojai Valley near San Francisco, staying with the affluent Theosophist Mary Tudor Gray. He remained there until June 1923. He must have taken a fancy to the place, because when Besant visited Ojai in 1926 she bought him a property of 240 acres nearby. Her purpose was to create 'a centre which shall gradually grow into a miniature model of the New Civilisation (of the 6th Sub-race), in which bodies, emotions and minds shall be trained and disciplined in daily life into health, poise and high intelligence.'[34] The Krishnamurti Foundation is still located in Ojai.

32. Tillett, *The Elder Brother*, p. 192.
33. Annie Besant, *Theosophical Christianity* (London, 1922), pp. 8–9, 21–23.
34. Emily Lutyens, *Candles in the Sun*, p. 153.

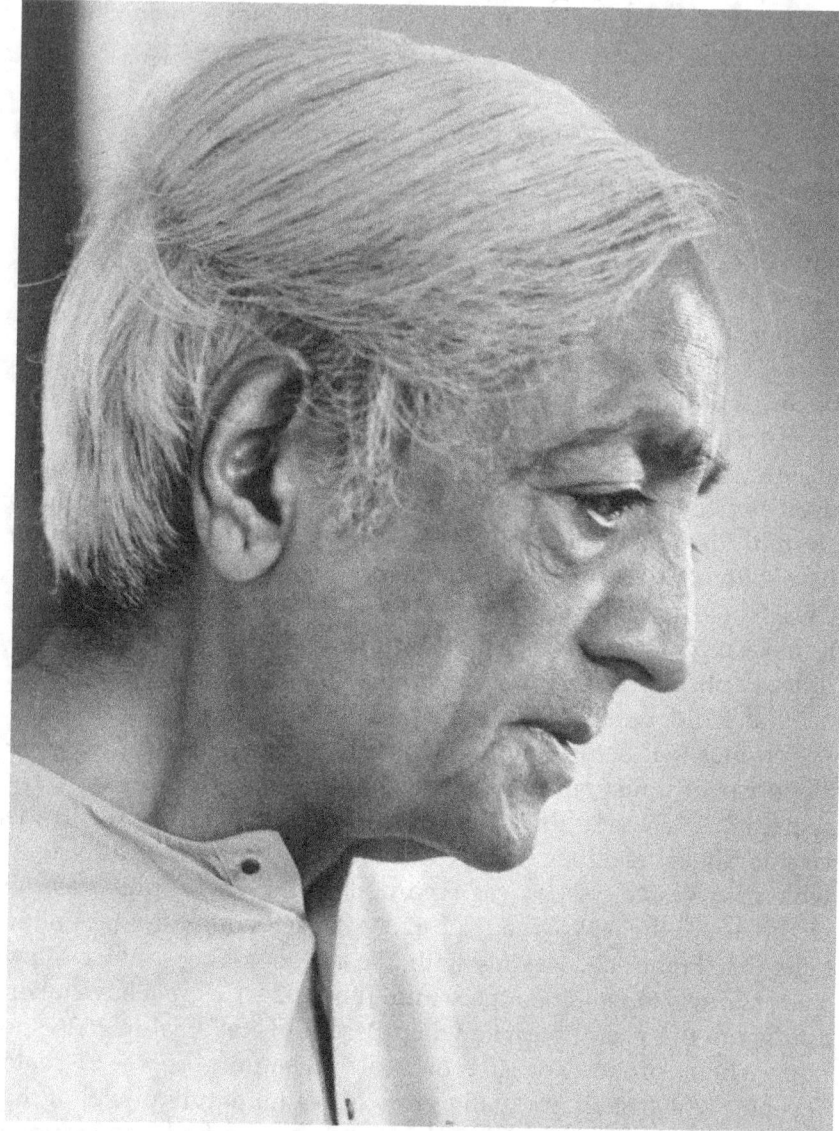

Jiddu Krishnamurti, 1976, New Delhi. Photograph by Sunil Janah, courtesy of the Krishnamurti Foundation Trust.

In 1923, while staying in Ojai, Krishnamurti underwent a mental upheaval in which he experienced repeated visionary trances. Was the World Teacher finally about to enter his designated vehicle? This must have been the question that preoccupied Krishnamurti and his close associates at this time. A book he wrote that year, *The Path*, contained promising indications. *The Path* was an imaginary-moral work about the road that the seeker after Truth must follow. Its messianic quality might have struck cynical readers as delusionary. Krishnamurti expounded on Man's loneliness in the face of eternal death, and about the sacred struggle against meaninglessness which characterizes human existence. Man's ultimate destiny is the recognition that God is inside each one of us. I see this book as proof that Krishnamurti fully believed in his messianic role, at least at this stage of his life. The last passage confirms it:

> I am strong, I no longer falter; the divine spark is burning in me; I have beheld in a waking dream, the Master of all things and I am radiant with His eternal joy. I have gazed into the deep pool of knowledge and many reflections have I beheld. I am the stone in the sacred temple. I am the humble grass that is mown down and trodden upon. I am the tall and stately tree that courts the very heavens. I am the animal that is hunted. I am the criminal that is hated by all. I am the noble that is honoured by all. I am sorrow, pain and fleeting pleasure; the passions and the gratifications; the bitter wrath and the infinite compassion; the sin and the sinner. I am the lover and the very love itself. I am the saint, the adorer, the worshiper and the follower. I am God.[35]

The lyrical style and the belief in his mission would continue to characterize Krishnamurti during the rest of his messianic career. These elements of his personality were expressed in the annual conferences of the OSE in the Netherlands. They were held in Castle Eerde, in the town of Ommen near Arnhem. The castle belonged to a young aristocrat named Philip van Pallandt, who met Krishnamurti in 1921, was captivated by him and gave it to him as a gift, to serve as the world centre of the OSE. Every summer, beginning in 1924, Castle Eerde was the venue of these gatherings, which included open-air activities and sleeping outdoors in tents.

Krishnamurti was the chief speaker at these gatherings. His conversations with his disciples were reproduced and issued as *Ommen Campfire Talks* by the OSE publishing house. These talks certainly suggest that he believed in his mission once the theological course he began to follow with *The Path* matured in 1926, when Krishnamurti called on his followers to find happiness and perfection within themselves by uniting with their indwelling

---

35. J. Krishnamurti, *The Path* (Eerde-Ommen, 1928), p. 35.

divinity.[36] At this stage the element which would dominate his later philosophy, in which he stressed that there is no need for a guide on the way to spiritual awakening, was evolving, although he probably still believed he was the World Teacher.[37]

> Now, when I was a small boy I used to see shri Krishna, with the flute, as He is pictured by the Hindus, because my mother was a devotee of Shri Krishna... When I grew older and met with Bishop Leadbeater and the Theosophical Society, I began to see the Master K.H... Later on, as I grew, I began to see the Lord Maitreya. That was two years ago, and I saw Him then constantly in the form put before me... Now lately, it has been the Buddha whom I have been Seeing, and it has been my delight and my glory to be with Him.

He was saying that even when we are convinced we are seeing divine beings, in reality we are observing imagery supplied by others. Therefore his title of World Teacher was meaningless, except in the sense that he sought to help all human beings.[38]

In the conclusion of the 1927 OSE conference Krishnamurti spoke like a captive of the Theosophical fantasy. He told his followers that although they would disperse to their different countries, '... if you bear that Truth in your heart, if you bear me, who am the end of all search, in your heart, then there will be no separation.'[39]

At this time the sense that the World Teacher was already inhabiting his earthly vehicle and beginning to fulfil his destiny became overwhelming. Krishnamurti changed the name of his order to The Order of the Star, perhaps to indicate that henceforth the star would shine on both East and West. At the end of the summer gathering in Ommen he set out on an extensive lecture tour in India and Europe, and wound up in Ojai, where the first gathering of his American followers, the Ojai Star Camp, took place in May 1928. A little before the gathering, on 15 May, Krishnamurti gave his first public lecture in the United States, in the Hollywood Bowl, before

---

36. J. Krishnamurti, *The Pool of Wisdom* (Ommen Camp Fire Talks, 1926) (Eerde-Ommen, 1928).

37. New books by Krishnamurti continue to be published, posthumously, year after year. A fine example to his philosophical style is 'The Limits of Thought,' J. Krishnamurti and David Bohm, *The Limits of Thought: Discussions* (London, 1999).

38. Krishnamurti, *Who Brings the Truth* (An Address Given at Eerde, 2 August 1927) (Eerde-Ommen, 1928).

39. Krishnamurti, *By What Authority* (Ommen Camp Fire Talks, 1927) (Eerde-Ommen, 1928).

an audience of 1,600. After the gathering he returned to Europe and on 18 and 20 June addressed large audiences in London and Paris. On 27 June he was interviewed on French radio in the broadcasting studio on the Eiffel Tower.[40] By October 1928 the Theosophical mood was so ecstatic, that Besant dismissed the ES and transferred all responsibility for the teaching of occult lore to Krishnamurti.[41]

Although most members of the Theosophical Society were feeling euphoric, some of them, led by George Arundale, acted in the 1920s as an opposition to Besant and the cult of Krishnamurti. This was an essentially political opposition. It is likely that Arundale resented Krishnamurti because he aspired to a higher position in the movement's leadership. This obliged him to prove his superior spirituality and show himself as the masculine alternative to the leadership of the Society, a position which was at this time occupied by Leadbeater. As we have seen, Arundale had been one of Krishnamurti's mentors during the waiting period in England. Later he began to express doubts about Krishnamurti's messianic identity. In 1925 he started to present himself as a religious authority and experience revelations in which he received the blessings and guidance of the Masters. For example, after the death of Nityananda, Krishnamurti's younger brother, Arundale began to transmit messages from him from the next world – this, despite the fact that during Nityananda's illness he had argued that, being the source of the World Teacher's vitality, he could not die.[42] He was also ordained a priest in the Liberal Catholic Church in Holland in July 1925. But being a mere priest did not satisfy him, and a week later Wedgwood made him a bishop, without seeking Leadbeater's approval.[43]

In the coming years Arundale showed himself as a spiritual authority and rising political force, and ultimately achieved his aspiration, when after Besant's death he was elected president of the Theosophical Society.[44] Perhaps it was her awareness of his growing political power that made Besant seek to please him. On 25

40. Emily Lutyens, *Candles in the Sun*, p. 167.
41. The dismissal was only temporary. The ES was reactivated after several months, following Leadbeater's strong objection, Nethercot, *The Last Four Lives of Annie Besant*, p. 410.
42. Emily Lutyens, *Candles in the Sun*, p. 139.
43. Tillett, *The Elder Brother*, pp. 216–17.
44. For an example of his aspiration, see, G.S. Arundale, *Kundalini: An Occult Experience* (Adyar, 1947).

March 1928 she announced the launch of a new missionary project, entitled the World Mother. This referred to an entity which in the past incarnated in the Virgin Mary, and in the coming era would assist the World Teacher. The human vehicle of the World Mother was none other than Arundale's young Hindu wife, Rukmini Devi Arundale, whom he had married in 1920 when she was just 16 years old.[45]

The ecstatic adulation of the World Teacher, lately reinforced by the appearance of a feminine entity, reached a climax in 1928-1929. And it was then that Krishnamurti made the most dramatic decision of his life. On 2 August 1929, at the summer gathering of the Order of the Star in Ommen, and in the presence of Annie Besant, he announced that he was disbanding the Order:

> I maintain that Truth is a pathless land, and that you cannot approach it by any path whatsoever, by any religion, by any sect... Truth, being limitless, unconditioned, unapproachable by any path whatsoever, cannot be organized; nor should any organization be formed to lead or coerce people along any particular path.[46]

In December 1929 he went with Besant to Adyar and took part in the annual Theosophical conference, but early in 1930 he resigned from the Theosophical Society and publicly disavowed his role as the World Teacher.[47]

Besant accepted his decision and continued to believe in his status until the end of her life, presumably from conviction that the road chosen by her protégé formed part of the overall plan of the Great Brotherhood. But probably most Theosophists were profoundly disappointed. Krishnamurti's disavowal of his destiny as World Teacher was an awful blow to many who felt orphaned by the loss of the messiah on whom they had pinned their hopes for so long. Indeed, Krishnamurti's break with the Theosophical Society was the worst crisis in the Society's history. As mentioned before,

---

45. The World Mother project never really took off. However, Rukmini Arundale was celebrated as a social activist and artist. During the 1920s, she studied Ballet in Europe, and soon after her return to India, founded in Madras the famous dance institute, Kalakashetra. She is still very highly regarded in India today. See, for example, the eulogy that marked her 100th birthday, *The Hindu* (Chennai, 16 March 2003).

46. Mary Lutyens, *Krishnamurti: The Years of Awakening*, pp. 272-75.

47. Nethercot, *The Last Four Lives of Annie Besant*, pp. 423-32; Vernon, *Star in the East*, pp. 187-94.

during his long novitiate the membership of Theosophical Society kept growing, and reached a record 45,000 in 1928 – a number it would never reach again. The one who profited from the fiasco was Arundale, who had for some years opposed the cult of the World Teacher, and appeared to have been vindicated. Krishnamurti's withdrawal from Theosophy played into Arundale's hands and paved his way to the presidency of the Society.

In the early 1930s the OSE centre at Ommen was restored to its original owner, Van Pallandt. Krishnamurti's nature camps, which were open to all, continued to take place every summer at Castle Eerde until 1939, but activities at the Ojai centre grew steadily more important.[48] Then came the Second World War and severed the connection between the followers of Krishnamurti and Castle Eerde, which the Nazi occupiers turned into a concentration camp where they held the Jews of Holland before sending them to the death camps in Poland. But Krishnamurti remained a spiritual teacher until his death in 1986. After Besant's death the Ojai centre became his main residence and it continued to flourish for many years. His association with the Theosophical Society was broken for a long time, and he visited the Adyar centre only once, in 1980, after Radha Burnier (1923–) was elected president of the Society. It seems that he regarded all her predecessors as closely identified with the original Theosophical school which he had disowned in 1929.

Conclusions

The story of the World Teacher sheds light on the way the Theosophists generally saw India and the Indians. The relations

---

48. Krishnamurti's circle of admirers in America included Christopher Isherwood (1904–1986), Gerald Heard (1889–1971) and Aldus Huxley (1894–1963). The three left Europe in the late 1930s and worked in Hollywood. Huxley, in particular, became Krishnamurti's disciple, and was heavily influenced by his mentor's ideas, which, in part, had Theosophical origin. This is clearly evidenced in his Perennial Philosophy, Aldus Huxley, *The Perennial Philosophy* (London, 1958), first published 1946; J. Krishnamurti, *The First and Last Freedom* (New York, 1954), Forward by Aldous Huxley, pp. 9–27. Huxley and Isherwood collaborated in the 1940s with Heard, who in 1942 founded the Trabuco College near Los Angeles. All three shared a passion for the occult, and besides their interest in Krishnamurti, were deeply interested in the philosophy of Ramakrishna, Vivekananda's mentor. Accordingly, in 1947 Heard handed Trabuco College to Vivekananda's Vedânta Society, Timothy Miller, *The Quest for Utopia, Vol. 1: 1900–1960* (Syracuse, 1998), pp. 185–88; Vernon, *Star in the East*, pp. 204–207.

between Krishnamurti and Besant seem to reflect these complex relations on a personal level. Just as the Theosophical Society fostered India's national aspirations and played an important part in creating its national-political infrastructure, so Besant treated Krishnamurti, whom she fostered and cultivated from youth. Just as she viewed India as an object to be re-shaped in order to become the light of the world, she subjected Krishnamurti to a long process of formation and education, preparing him for his exalted role. On both levels, the creature turned against its maker. Just as India disowned the Theosophical Society, so did the adult Krishnamurti turn away from Theosophy.

The relations between Besant and Krishnamurti recall the difficult and short-lived relations between Blavatsky and Dayananda Saraswati. Underlying both associations was the Theosophical view of India as a means for the realization of the Society's plans. This view not only failed to acknowledge the distinctive Hindu thought, but practically forced upon it Western and Christian concepts which were alien to its spirit. Blavatsky had erred in presuming to interpret the Hindu scriptures as analogues of Western esoteric thought, but the case of Krishnamurti was much graver in the moral sense, as the Society used dubious methods to advance its messianic plans. The legal battle between Besant and Narayaniah, Krishnamurti's father, exposed the moral price the Society was willing to pay to achieve its purpose. Besant in fact kidnapped the boys, convinced that the aim justified the means.

Yet this may be looking at the moral problem from an anachronistic viewpoint, applying criteria alien to the period in question. We may, however, question Besant's motives and ask if she was not acting out of the kind of racial condescension typical of the time and place. There is no easy answer, but what is clear is that Besant believed she knew best what was right for the young boy, certainly better than his father or he himself. Her behaviour betrayed more than a touch of the patronizing nineteenth century English attitude towards India and her inhabitants. In this sense, the conduct of the Theosophical Society in India in general, and Besant with Krishnamurti in particular, resembled the colonialist attitude as epitomized by Kipling's 'white man's burden'. On the face of it, this may seem an unlikely characterization of a movement which did so much to free India from colonial rule – yet an examination of the Society's history vis-à-vis Krishnamurti supports this diagnosis, revealing the Theosophists as infected with the same malady against which they fought.

The analogy between the cult of Krishnamurti and the Christian religion lends further weight to this conclusion. There is no mistaking the messianic Christian sources of the proclamation of Krishnamurti as the World Teacher. The Theosophical framework did indeed present him as the emissary of the Great Brotherhood, appearing once more in our world in order to move it to a higher evolutionary phase. His birth in India, the cradle of occult lore, was marketed as an exotic detail which attracted public attention, not unlike advance sales promotion. As we have seen, the view of the Orient as the source of esoteria was a regular feature of the Western interest in the occult. Nevertheless, the hopes pinned on the World Teacher drew on deep Christian sources and were invigorated by the long-standing Christian belief in the Second Coming of Christ. There is no doubt that the widespread popularity of the Order of the Star in the East stemmed from its resemblance to this Christian ethos. Thus, behind the cult of the World Teacher was a Western idea clothed in an exotic Indian garment.

Furthermore, the story of Krishnamurti raises another substantial question concerning both the Theosophical theology and the Society's political interests. Belief in the evolutionary process that humanity is undergoing, and in the present time being an important transitionary stage of it, were important elements in Blavatsky's philosophy, and no doubt contributed to the sense of anticipation among the followers. The identification of India as the cradle of esoteric lore led to its becoming the centre of the Theosophical project. The identification of a young Hindu boy as the coming World Teacher completed the picture and enabled the Theosophical Orientalist fantasy to ripen. Choosing a local boy as the person destined to personify the World Teacher seemed a perfect solution to the Theosophical presumption of creating a synthesis between the two currents of the Aryan nation. This presumption, as we have seen, was inspired by Western Orientalist thinking which had little to do with the actual Hindu culture. Thus, the story of Krishnamurti was another expression of this Orientalist fantasy in which many Westerners who first encountered India and her civilization became caught up, from Jones to Max Müller. The idea of a Theosophical synthesis between East and West, culminating in the announcement of a Hindu messiah – whose previous incarnations were Krishna and Jesus – was not dissimilar to the thesis of Max Müller, who sought to link India's ancient Aryans with the Aryans of modern Europe.

The choice of Krishnamurti also entailed a certain political interest, since the Theosophical Society sought to make his cult popular among the Hindus. Local support was essential once Besant entered the hub of India's political activity. It grew all the more urgent after her fall from political power, which left the esoteric project as the Society's central endeavour. The chance of winning the local population's sympathy rested on the freedom from racial prejudice shown by the choice of an Indian as the World Teacher. Nevertheless, the way in which the Theosophists handled Krishnamurti, giving him a Western upbringing, separating him from his country and his family, spoilt the impression and revealed the Society's condescending, essentially Western, outlook. Had the Theosophists sincerely believed that the Hindu culture was superior, or at any rate equal, to that of the West, they would have allowed Krishnamurti to live and be educated in his native land.

A memorial statue, the gardens, Theosophical Society Headquarters, Adyar. Photograph by Isaac Lubelsky.

Had the Theosophical story been written by a Greek tragedian, the ending of the Krishnamurti act would have been a classical catharsis, its moral a denunciation of Western hubris. In the final reckoning, just as India's political establishment disowned Besant and the Theosophical Society, so Krishnamurti disavowed his anticipated mission. The Theosophical Society, having lost its political resources, discovered later that the esoteric alternative likewise ran out with the fiasco of the World Teacher project. The heavy cost of its failure on both fronts, the political and the esoteric, led to a prolonged crisis from which the Society has not recovered to this day.

Postscript

This book has traced the development of the Western thought-process that gave birth to a new image of India during the nineteenth and early twentieth centuries. The crystallization of this image, centred on a view of India as the cradle of spirituality and the Aryan civilization, paralleled the gradual change in the attitude towards India, both among her Western rulers and among their subjects. From the British point of view, the changed image of India permitted a gradual realization of its people's right to independence. Simultaneously, the new image reinforced the national feelings among Indians, whom it encouraged to view themselves as having a history and a culture no less ancient and worthy than those of the West. The effect of this mental change was to bolster the aspiration for national self-determination and to legitimize the struggle for freedom from British colonialism.

I have followed the historical path of the new Indian image and I have attempted to outline the connection between its different phases, which might otherwise be overlooked, especially from the standpoint of our time. The way in which ideas flowed during the Victorian era, alongside the social connections which characterized it, led in the case of India to distinctive results, as ideas which sprang up in the academic sphere were transported wholly into the esoteric field. As I have shown, at this time the Theosophical Society was the outstanding representative of the esoteric field, and came to put into practice the theories of prominent academics, notably Friedrich Max Müller. Thus, a movement whose declared goal was the discovery and study of occult lore became a major contributor to the formation of Indian nationalism.

The Theosophical attitude towards India sprang both from Western condescension, which the leaders of the Society never quite shook off, and from their own particular mentality. Their story was another illustration of the Orientalist fantasy which animated many

Westerners who came in contact with India and her civilization, beginning with Sir William Jones and ending with Max Müller. If the latter created an Aryan vision of a celestial India, based entirely on elements from her ancient literature, the Theosophists dreamed up their own Indian vision based on an imaginary secret doctrine. Distorted echoes of this evolving fantasy would reverberate in Europe for many years – the Nazi adoption of the ancient Hindu symbol of the swastika was but one of them.

But while the Orientalist ideas mainly helped to shape the new image of India, Theosophy carried the Orientalist fantasy into the real world. The doctrine of the Theosophical Society, born from Blavatsky's extraordinary imagination, clearly expressed that fantasy. On Olcott this fantasy had the effect of a mental transformation which happened after his arrival in India. He became a local national figure, without any identity crisis. The quasi-mythical component of Theosophy was most vividly personified in Annie Besant, a rationalist social activist before her conversion to Theosophy, who became a popular leader in India and was totally absorbed by the fantasy of her own creation.

The Theosophical esoteric doctrine remains an influential element in Western culture to this day. To a great extent the phenomenon of the New Age, with its interest in magic, alternative medicine, crystals, reincarnation and the rest, sprang from the Theosophical enterprise in India and in the West. Blavatsky (with her synthesis of various esoteric systems) and Leadbeater (with his focus on auras, reincarnations and chakras) bore much responsibility for the cultural bridging of East and West. In the context of the New Age, the mutual flow of ideas facilitated by this bridge introduced many originally Theosophical ideas into the Western mind. In that sense, although the glory days of the Theosophical Society are long gone, its influence over the modern worldview and the breakdown of the boundaries that used to separate East and West, deserves appreciation.

******

Annie Besant died at her home in Adyar on 20 September 1933, aged 86, after several months of infirmity and dementia. Her longtime associate, Bishop Leadbeater, who had been called to Adyar in view of her failing health, conducted her burial rites and cremation. Some five months later, on 29 February 1934, he himself died in Perth, Australia. Besant's successors in the leadership of the Theosophical Society belonged unmistakably to the political camp of Arundale, who was elected president after her demise. After he died, in 1945, the post went to Jinarajadasa, who remained president until his death in 1953. The elections that year pitted two contenders for the presidency – Arundale's widow, Rukmini, against none other than her own brother, Sri Ram (1889–1973). Sri Ram won, and remained the president until he died. He was succeeded by the British Theosophist John Coats (1906–1979), who had been initiated by Arundale. After his death the post went to Radha Burnier, Sri Ram's daughter, and Rukmini Arundale's niece. It appears that Arundale had won the political contest for the control of the Theosophical Society, with his associates and members of his family, on the Indian side, leading it for the past few decades.

The passing of Besant and Leadbeater ended an era in the history of the Theosophical Society. The glory of much of Besant's leadership was gone for good. Although the Theosophical Society still maintains dozens of lodges worldwide, it no longer has the kind of presence it used to have in the diverse societies in which it is found. The membership has been fairly steady in recent years, ranging between 30,000 and 35,000. The international headquarters in Adyar continues to direct the global Theosophical activities, holds annual conferences and runs a large library.

The somewhat gloomy aspect of the Theosophical centre in England, the country where the Society once enjoyed special prestige among the upper classes, illustrates the passage of time since then. Although located in the prestigious West End of London, the somewhat shabby and overcrowded premises of the English Theosophical Society, at 50 Gloucester Place, must cause veteran Theosophists to feel nostalgic for the past. The extensive library which occupies the second floor contains a rich trove of esoteric literature. In the middle of the floor stands a display cabinet containing some objects which had belonged to Blavatsky and Besant. Among these sacred relics are a hair-clasp of Blavatsky's and a pair of Besant's house-slippers. It is difficult to imagine the grand Theosophical ladies, such as Lady Emily Lutyens or even Besant herself, meeting to discuss esoteric philosophy in such a setting.

The Society's great days are long over, but there is no denying the contribution it made to India's national movement. The history of the Theosophical Society is interwoven with modern Indian history – for a fairly short but significant period. In 1947 Theosophists the world over marked the centenary of Annie Besant's birth. That year, as the culmination of the process which the Theosophical Society helped to advance, India became independent. Had the veteran Theosophical fighter lived to witness that historical moment, she would doubtless have felt that the goal that she and her movement had struggled for through decades had been finally achieved.

Bibliography

Primary Sources

Theosophy

Helena Petrovna Blavatsky

Blavatsky, H.P., *Gems from the East* (London, 1890).
— *Isis Unveiled: A Master-Key to the Mysteries of Ancient and Modern Science and Theology* (2 vols., Pasadena, 1998), first published 1877.
— *Letters to The American Conventions*, republished online by The Theosophical University Press: http://www.theosociety.org/pasadena/hpb-am/hpb-am1.htm
— *The Key to Theosophy* (London, 1938), first published 1889.
— *The Secret Doctrine: The Synthesis of Science, Religion, and Philosophy* (2 vols., Pasadena, 1999), first published 1888.
— *The Voice of the Silence, Being Chosen Fragments from the 'Book of the Golden Precepts'* (Wheaton, 1992), first published 1889.
Some Unpublished Letters of Helena Petrovna Blavatsky (London, 1929).

Henry Steel Olcott

Olcott, Henry Steel, *A Buddhist Catechism* (London, 1882), first published 1880.
— *Old Diary Leaves* (6 vols., Adyar, 1895–1935).

Annie Besant

Besant, Annie, *An Autobiography* (Adyar, 1995), first published 1893.
— *Congress Speeches* (Adyar, 1917).
— *Esoteric Christianity, or the Lesser Mysteries* (London, 1901).
— *Evolution and Occultism* (Adyar, 1913).
— *Giordano Bruno: Theosophy's Apostle in the Sixteenth Century* (Adyar, 1913).
— *How India Wrought for Freedom* (Adyar, 1915).
— *Initiation, The Perfecting of Man* (London, 1912).
— *Super-Human Men in History and Religion* (London, 1913).
— *The Coming Christ* (Chicago, 1927), first published 1910.
— *The Riddle of Life* (London, 1911).
— *The Story of the Great War: Some Lessons from the Mahābhārata for the Use of Hindu Students in the Schools of India* (Adyar, 1927).
— *The Wisdom of the Upanishats* (Adyar, 1907).

— *Theosophical Christianity* (London, 1922).
— *Theosophy and the New Psychology* (London, 1904).

Annie Besant's Secular Pamphlets

Besant, Annie, *Giordano Bruno* (London, 1883).
— *God's Views on Marriage, as Revealed in the Old Testament* (London, 1883).
— *The Gospel of Atheism* (London, 1882).
— *True Basis of Morality* (London, 1882).
— *A Selection of the Social and Political Pamphlets of Annie Besant*, ed. John Saville (New York, 1970).

Besant's Co-Works with Charles Webster Leadbeater

Besant, Annie, and C.W. Leadbeater, *Man, Whence, How and Whither* (Adyar, 1913).
— *Occult Chemistry Investigations*, ed. C. Jinarajadasa (Adyar, 1946).
— *The Book of Occult Chemistry* (Adyar, 1908).
— *Thought-Forms* (Wheaton, 1986), first published 1901.

Charles Webster Leadbeater

Leadbeater, C.W., *How Theosophy Came to Me* (Adyar, 1986), first published 1930.
— *Invisible Helpers* (Adyar, 1952), first published 1896.
— *Man Visible and Invisible: Examples of Different Types of Men as Seen by Means of Trained Clairvoyance* (New York, 1909), first published 1902.
— *The Hidden Side of Things* (2 vols., Adyar, 1913).
— *The Other Side of Death, Scientifically Examined and Carefully Described* (Adyar, 1954), first published 1903.

Jiddu Krishnamurti

Krishnamurti, J., (under the name Alcyone), *At the Feet of the Master* (Adyar, 1974), first published 1910.
— *By What Authority* (Ommen Camp Fire Talks, 1927) (Eerde-Ommen, 1928).
— *Krishnamurti's Notebook*, with a Forward by Mary Lutyens (New York, 1976).
— *The First and Last Freedom* (New York, 1954).
— *The Path* (Eerde-Ommen, 1928).
— *The Pool of Wisdom* (Ommen Camp Fire Talks, 1926) (Eerde-Ommen, 1928).
— *Who Brings the Truth* (An Address given at Eerde, 2 August 1927 (Eerde-Ommen, 1928).

General Theosophical Literature

Arundale, G.S., *Kundalini: An Occult Experience* (Adyar, 1947).
General Report of the Theosophical Society (Adyar, 1908, 1912, 1921, 1929).
Hume, Allan Octavian, (under the name H-X), *Hints on Esoteric Theosophy*, No. 1 (Benares, 1909).
Jinarajadasa, C., *The Message of the Future* (Glasgow, 1916).
Kingsford, Anna, *The Perfect Way in Diet: A Treatise Advocating a Return to the Natural and Ancient Food of Our Race* (London, 1881).

— To the President of the Theosophical Society, Madras (31 October 1883, held at the British Library).
Kingsford, Anna Bonus, and Edward Maitland, *The Perfect Way, or, Finding of Christ* (London, 1882).
— *A Letter Addressed to the Fellows of the London Lodge of the Theosophical Society: by the President and Vice-President of the Lodge, Private and Confidential* (December, 1883, held at the British Library).
Lutyens, Emily, *Candles in the Sun* (London, 1957).
Lutyens, Mary, *Krishnamurti: The Years of Awakening* (London, 1975).
— *Krishnamurti: The Years of Fulfillment* (London, 1983).
The Mahatma Letters, to A.P. Sinnett from the Mahatmas M. & K.H. (Adyar, 1972), first published 1923.
Maitland, Edward, *Remarks and Propositions Suggested by the Perusal of 'Esoteric Buddhism'* (held at the British Library).
Mead, George Robert Stow, *Orpheus* (London, 1965), first published 1896.
— *Pistis Sophia: A Gnostic Miscellany: Being for the Most Part Extracts from the Books of the Savior, to Which are Added Excerpts from Cognate Literature* (London, 1921).
— *Thrice-Greatest Hermes: Being a Translation of the Extant Sermons and Fragments of the Trismegistic Literature with Prolegomena and Notes* (3 vols., London, 1964), first published 1906.
Sinnet, A.P., *Esoteric Buddhism* (London, 1883).
— *The Occult World* (London, 1882), first published 1881.
— *Theosophy and 'Esoteric Buddhism', Some Comments on the Recent Pamphlets by 'the President and Vice-President of the London Lodge, T.S.', and especially on the 'Reply to the Observations of Mr. T. Subba Row'* (For Private Circulation) (March, 1884, held at the British Library).
Wachtmeister, Constance Countess, *Reminiscences of H.P. Blavatsky and The Secret Doctrine* (London, 1893).

Theosophical Newspapers and Periodicals

Lucifer, A Theosophical Magazine (London).
New India (Madras).
The Commonweal: a Journal of National Reform (Adyar).
The Theosophical Review (London).
The Theosophist (Bombay and Madras).

Major Theosophical Websites

Blavatsky Study Center: http://www.blavatskyarchives.com
Blavatsky Net – Theosophy: http://www.blavatsky.net
Theosophical Academy: http://www.theosophicalacademy.iinet.au
Theosophical Society in America: http://www.theosophical.org
Theosophical University Press Online: http://www.theosociety.org/pasadena/tup-onl.htm

Hermetical, Early Theosophical, Occultist and New-Age Literature

Atwood, née South, Mary Anne, *A Suggestive Inquiry into the Hermetic Mystery: With a Dissertation on the More Celebrated of the Alchemical Philosophers, Being an Attempt towards the Recovery of the Ancient Experiment of Nature* (London, 1850).

Bailey, Alice A., *The Destiny of Nations* (Albany, 1968), first published 1949.

— *The Unfinished Autobiography* (London, 1951).

Ballard, Guy Warren, *Ascended Master Discourses* (Chicago, 1937).

Barrett, Francis, *The Lives of Alchemystical Philosophers; With a Critical Catalogue of Books in Occult Chemistry, and a Selection of the Most Celebrated Treatises on the Theory and Practice of the Hermetic Art* (London, 1815).

— *The Magus, or Celestial Intelligencer: Being a Complete System of Occult Philosophy* (London, 1801).

Böhme, Jacob, *Essential Readings*, ed. Robin Waterfield (Wellingborough, 1989).

— *Six Theosophic Points, and other Writings* (Ann Arbor, 1958).

Bruno, Giordano, 'On Magic', in Giordano Bruno, *Cause, Principle and Unity, and Essays on Magic* (Cambridge, 1998), pp. 103–42.

Bulwer-Lytton, Edward, *The Coming Race* (London, 1886), first published 1871.

— *Zanoni* (London, 1853), first published 1842.

Caithness, Countess of, *Old Truths in a New Light, or, an Earnest Endeavour to Reconcile Material Science with Spiritual Science, and with Scripture* (London, 1876).

Cayce, Edgar Evans, *Edgar Cayce on Atlantis* (New York, 1968).

Cervé, W.S., *Lemuria: The Lost Continent of the Pacific* (San Jose, 1931).

Conan Doyle, Arthur, *The History of Spiritualism*, Vol. 2 (London, 1926).

Copenhaver, Brian P., *Hermetica: The Greek Corpus Hermeticum and the Latin Asclepius* (Cambridge, 1992).

Davies, Andrew Jackson, *The Principles of Nature, Her Divine Revelations, and A Voice to Mankind* (3 vols., London, 1847).

Donelly, Ignatius, *Atlantis: The Antediluvian World* (New York, 1973), first published 1882.

— *Ragnarök: The Age of Fire and Gravel* (New York, 1883).

Ficino, Marsilio, *Book of Life* (trans. Charles Boer; Woodstock, 1994), first published 1980.

— *Commentary on Plato's Symposium on Love* (trans. Sears Jayne; Dallas, 1964).

— *Meditations on the Soul: Selected Letters of Marsilio Ficino* (trans. Members of the Language Department of the School of Economic Science, London; Rochester, 1996), first published 1975.

— 'The Soul of Man', in 'Platonic Theology', *Journal of the History of Ideas* (April, 1944), 38–40.

Hardinge Britten, Emma, *Art Magic: or, Mundane, Sub-Mundane and Super-Mundane Spiritism* (New York, 1876).

— *Autobiography*, edited and published by Margaret Wilkinson (her sister and sole relative) (London, 1900).

— *Nineteenth Century Miracles: or, Spirits and Their Work in Every Country of the Earth: A Complete Historical Compendium of the Great Movement Known as 'Modern Spiritualism'* (Manchester, 1883).

Bibliography

Higgins, Godfrey, *Anacalypsis, an Attempt to Draw Aside the Veil of the Saitic Isis; or, An Inquiry Into the Origin of Languages, Nations, and Religions*, Vol. 1 (London, 1833); Vol. 2 (London, 1836).
Hitchcock, Ethan Allen, *Remarks upon Alchemy and the Alchemists, Indicating a Method of Discovering the True Nature of Hermetic Philosophy* (Boston, 1857).
Jennings, Hargrave, *The Indian Religions: or, Results of the Mysterious Buddhism* (London, 1858).
— *The Rosicrucians, their Rites and Mysteries* (London, 1870).
Lévi, Eliphas, *The Book of Splendours* (Wellingborough, 1973), first published in French 1894.
— *The History of Magic* (trans. Edward Waite; Reading, 1982), first published in French 1860.
— *The Mysteries of the Qabalah, or the Occult Agreement of the Two Testaments* (Wellingborough, 1974), first published in French 1920.
— *Transcendental Magic, its Doctrine and Ritual* (trans. Arthur Edward Waite; London, 1995), first published in French 1856.
Moses, William Stainton, *Spirit Teaching* (London, 1894).
Rinpoche, Sogyal, *The Tibetan Book of Living and Dying* (New York, 1993).
Schuré, Edouard, *The Great Initiates, Sketch of the Secret History of Religions* (2 vols., London, 1912), first published in French 1889.
Stead, Estelle W., *Communication with the Next World, the Right and Wrong Methods: A Text-Book Given by William T. Stead from 'Beyond the Veil' through Madame Hyver* (London, 1937).
Steiner, Rudolf, *The Course of my Life* (New York, 1951), first published in German 1925.
— *The Essentials of Education: Five Lectures Delivered During the Educational Conference of the Waldorf School, Stuttgart, April, 1924* (London, 1948).
Swedenborg, Emanuel, *The Universal Human and Soul-Body Interaction* (ed. and trans. George F. Bole; New York, 1984).
Uspenskii, P.D., *In Search of the Miraculous: Fragments of An Unknown Teaching* (New York, 1949).

Friedrich Max Müller

Max Müller, *Auld Lang Syne* (New York, 1898).
— *Auld Lang Syne, Second Series, My Indian Friends* (New York, 1899).
— *Chips from a German Workshop*, Vol. 1: *Essays on the Science of Religion* (Chico, 1985), first published 1867.
— *Chips from a German Workshop*, Vol. 2: *Essays on Mythology, Traditions, and Customs* (New York, 1893), first published 1867.
— *Chips from a German Workshop*, Vol. 3: *Essays on Literature, Biography, and Antiquities* (New York, 1892), first published 1870.
— *Chips from a German Workshop*, Vol. 4: *Essays Chiefly on the Science of Language* (New York, 1895), first published 1875.
— *Contributions to the Science of Mythology* (2 vols., London, 1897).
— 'Esoteric Buddhism', *The Nineteenth Century* (London, May, 1893), 767–88.
— *Hitôpadeśa: Eine alte Indische Fabelsammlung aus dem Sanskrit* (Leipzig, 1844).
— *India: What Can It Teach Us?* (Escondido, 1999), first published 1882.

— *Lectures on the Science of Language*, Vol. 1 (London, 1994), first published 1861.
— *Lectures on the Science of Language*, Vol. 2 (London, 1994), first published 1864.
— *My Autobiography, a Fragment* (New York, 1901).
— *Suggestions for the Assistance of Officers in Learning the Languages of the Seat of War in the East* (London, 1854).
— *The Classification of the Turanian Languages* (London, 1854).
— *The Sacred Books of the East, Vol. 1: the Upanishads* (New York, 1962), first published 1879 and *Vol. 15, the Upanishads, Part 2* (Delhi, 1995), first published 1884.
— *Theosophy or Psychological Religion* (London, 1893).
Life and Religion, An Aftermath from the Writings of the Right Honourable Professor F. Max Müller, ed. Georgina Max Müller (New York, 1905).
The Life and Letters of the Right Honourable Friedrich Max Müller, ed. Georgina Max Müller, (2 vols., New York, 1902).

Philology, Orientalism, Comparative Religion

Albuquerque, Alfonso de, *The Commentaries of the Great Alfonso de Albuquerque, Second Viceroy of India* (4 vols., New York, 1970), first published in Portuguese 1774.
Anquetil-Duperron, Abraham Hyacinthe, *Oupnek'hat, id est, secretum tegendum* (trans. Anquetil-Duperron; Paris, 1801).
— *Zend-Avesta*, Reprint of the 1771 edition (3 vols., New York, 1984).
Arnold, Edwin, *The Light of Asia, or the Great Renunciation (Mahabhinishkramana), Being the Life And Teaching of Gautama, Prince of India and Founder of Buddhism* (London, 1879).
Asiatick Researches, or, Transactions of the Society, Instituted in Bengal, for Inquiring into the History and Antquities, the Arts, Sciences, and Literature, of Asia, vols. 1–7 (London, 1799–1812) and vols. 12–20 (Calcutta, 1788–1836).
The Bhagvat-Geeta (trans. Charles Wilkins; Gainesville, 1959), first published 1785.
'The *Bhagavad Gītā*', trans. K.T. Telang, *The Sacred Books of the East*, ed. F. Max Müller, Vol. viii (Oxford, 1882).
The Bhagavad Gītā, or, The Lord's Song (trans. Annie Besant; London, 1895).
The Bhagavad Gītā (trans. Annie Besant and Bhagavan Das; Adyar, 1950), first published 1905.
Böhtlingk, Otto von, and Rudolph Roth, *Sanskrit-Wörterbuch herausgegeben von der Kaiserlichen Akademie der Wissenschaften* (7 vols., Delhi, 1990), first published 1853–1875.
Bopp, Franz, *A Comparative Grammar of the Sanskrit, Zend, Greek, Latin, Lithuanian, Gothic, German and Slavonic Languages* (trans. principally by Lieutenant Eastwick, conducted through the press by H.H, Wilson; 3 vols., London, 1856), first published in German 1833–1852.
— *Über das Conjugationssystem der Sanskritsprache in Vergleichnung mit jenem der griechischen, lateinischen, persischen und germanischen Sprache* (London, 1995), first published 1816.
Brown, Robert, *Semitic Influence in Hellenic Mythology, with Special Reference to the Recent Mythological Works of F. Max Müller and Andrew Lang* (Oxford, 1898).

Bibliography

Bunsen, Christian Carl Josias von, *Egypt's Place in Universal History: An Historical Investigation* (trans. C.H. Cottrell; 5 vols., London, 1848–1867), first published in German 1845.
— *God in History: or, The Progress of Man's Faith in the Moral Order of the World* (trans. Susanna Winkworth; 3 vols., London, 1868–1870), first published in German 1857.
Burnouf, Eugène, *Legends of Indian Buddhism* (trans. Winifred Stephens; London, 1911), first published in French 1844.
Clarke, James Freeman, *Ten Great Religions: An Essay in Comparative Theology* (Boston, 1871).
Clive, Robert, 'Battle at Calcutta', *Yorke's Hardwicke Papers*, II: 385 (23 February 1757).
Colebrooke, Henry Thomas, *A Grammar of the Sanskrit Language*, Vol. 1 (Calcutta, 1805).
— *Essays on the Religion and Philosophy of the Hindus, by the Late H.T. Colebrooke, Esq.* (New Edition) (London, 1858).
Conway, Moncure Daniel, *Autobiography, Memories and Experiences* (2 vols., Boston, MA, 1905).
— *My Pilgrimage to the Wise Men of the East* (London, 1906).
Darwin, Charles, 'The Descent of Man, and Selection in Relation to Sex', in *The Complete Works of Charles Darwin*, eds Paul H. Barrett and R.B. Freeman, Vol. 21 (London, 1989), first published 1870.
De Sacy, Silvestre, *Principles of General Grammar* (trans. D. Fosdick Jr.; Andover, 1834), first published in French 1799.
Draper, John William, *History of the Conflict between Religion and Science* (New York, 1903), first published 1874.
Emerson, Ralph Waldo, 'Brahma', in *The Complete Works of Ralph Waldo Emerson*, Vol. 9 (New York, 1903), p. 195.
— 'Plato; or, The Philosopher', in 'Representative Men', *The Complete Works of Ralph Waldo Emerson*, Vol. 4 (New York, 1903), pp. 37–79.
— 'Swedenborg: or, The Mystic', *The Complete Works of Ralph Waldo Emerson*, pp. 91–146.
Firishtah, Muhammad Kasim Ibn Hindu Shah, *The History of Hindostan, from the Earliest Account of Time to the Death of Akbar* (trans. A. Dow; 3 vols., London, 1768–1772).
Grimm, Jacob, *Deutsche Grammatik* (4 vols., Göttingen, 1819–1837).
Hitôpadeśa (1787), *Fables and Proverbs from the Sanskrit* (trans. Charles Wilkins; Gainesville, 1968), first published 1787.
Hitôpadeśa of Vishnu Sarman (trans. Sir William Jones; Calcutta, 1851), first published 1807.
Hume, Allan Octavian, *The Game Birds of India, Burmah and Ceylon* (3 vols., Calcutta, 1879–1891).
Johnson, Samuel, *Oriental Religions, and their Relation to Universal Religion: India* (Boston, 1872).
Jones, Sir William, *Institutes of Hindu Law; or, The Ordinances of Menu, According to the Gloss of Culluca, Comprising the Indian System of Duties, Religious and Civil* (trans. Sir W. Jones; Calcutta and London, 1796).

— *The Collected Works of Sir William Jones*, ed. Garland Cannon (13 vols., New York, 1993), first published 1807.

Kālidāsa, *Sacontala: or, The Fatal Ring; An Indian Drama* (trans. Sir W. Jones; Calcutta, 1855), first published 1789.

— *La Reconnaissance de Sakountala, drame sanscrit et pracrit de Calidase* (trans. A.L. Chézy; Paris, 1830).

— *The Mégha Dùta: or, Cloud Messenger* (trans. H.H. Wilson; London, 1814), first published 1813.

King, C.W., *The Gnostics and Their Remains, Ancient and Mediaeval* (London, 1864).

Lang, Andrew, *Blue Fairy Book*, ed. Brian Alderson (New York, 1987), first published 1889.

— *Modern Mythology* (New York, 1968), first published 1897.

— *Myth, Ritual and Religion* (New York, 1968), first published 1887.

Lord, Henry, *A Discovery of the Banian Religion and the Religion of the Persees: A Critical Edition of Two Early English Works on Indian Religions*, ed. Will Sweetman (Lewiston, 1999), first published as *A Display of Two Forraigne Sects in the East Indies: The Sect of the Banians and the Sect of the Persees* (London, 1630).

Macaulay, Thomas Babington, 'Warren Hastings', in *Critical and Historical Essays*, ed. Hugh Trevor-Roper (New York, 1965).

Mansel, Henri Longuevillel, *The Gnostic Heresies of the First and Second Centuries*, ed. J.B. Lightfoot (London, 1875).

Mill, James, *The History of British India* (3 vols., London, 1817).

Mill, James, and Horace Hayman Wilson, *History of British India, from 1805 to 1835* (3 vols., London, 1845–1848).

Monier-Williams, Monier, *An Elementary Grammar of the Sanscrit Language, Partly in the Roman Character, Arranged According to a New Theory, in Reference Especially to the Classical Languages* (London, 1846).

— *Religious Thought and Life in India: Vedism, Brahmanism and Hinduism* (New Delhi, 1974), first published 1883.

Moor, Edward, *The Hindu Pantheon* (London, 1810).

Mosheim, Johan Lorenz von, *An Ecclesiastical History, Antient and Modern, From the Birth of Christ, To the Beginning of the Present Century* (2 vols., London, 1765), first published in German 1755.

Priestley, Joseph, *A History of Early Opinions Concerning Jesus Christ* (4 vols., London, 1786).

Renan, Ernest, *Histoire Générale et Système Comparé des Langues Sémitique* (Paris, 1855).

Roger, Abraham, *Abraham Rogers Offne Thür zu dem verborgenen Heydenthum: oder Warhaftige Vorweisung dess Lebens, und Sittens, samt der Religion und Gottesdienst der Bramines auf der Cust Chormandel, und herumliegenden Ländern* (Nürnberg, 1663), first published in Dutch 1651.

Schlegel, Friedrich von, *The Philosophy of Life, and Philosophy of Language* (trans. A.J.W. Morrison; New York, 1973), first published 1847.

— *Über die Sprache und Weisheit der Indier: ein Beitrag zur Begründung der Alterthumskunde* (London, 1995), first published 1808.

Schopenhauer, Arthur, *The World as Will and Idea* (trans. R.B. Haldane and J. Kemp; 3 vols., London, 1964), first published in German 1818.

Shore, John, Baron Teignmouth, *Memoirs of the Life, Writings and Correspondence of Sir William Jones* (London, 1804).

Tarkapanchanana, Jagannatha, *A Digest of Hindu Law on Contracts and Successions, with a Commentary (the Whole called Vivababhangrnava)* [trans. H.T. Colebrooke; 4 vols., Calcutta, 1798].

Tylor, Edward Burnett, *The Collected Works of Edward Burnett Tylor* (8 vols., London, 1994).

Ward, William, *A View of the History, Literature, and Mythology of the Hindoos: Including a Minute Description of their Manners and Customs, and Translations from Their Principal Works* (Port Washington, 1970), first published 1822.

Wedgwood, Hensleigh, *A Dictionary of English Etymology* (3 vols., London, 1859–1865).

Wilkins, Sir Charles, *A Grammar of the Sanskrit Language* (London, 1808).

Wilson, Horace Hayman, *A Dictionary, Sanscrit and English* (Calcutta, 1819).

— *A Dictionary, Sanskrit and English*, extended and improved from the Second Edition of the Dictionary of H.H.W., together with a Supplement, Grammatical Appendices, and an Index, serving as an English-Sanskrit Vocabulary, by T. Goldstücker (Berlin, 1856).

— *Ariana Antiqua: A Description Account of the Antiquities and Coins of Afghanistan, with a Memoir on the Buildings called Topes*, by C. Masson (London, 1841).

— *Select Specimens of the Theatre of the Hindus* (3 vols., Calcutta, 1826–1827).

— *Sketch of the Religious Sects of the Hindus* (Calcutta, 1846).

Younghusband, Sir Francis, *Wonders of the Himalaya* (London, 1924).

Other Sources

Bacon, Francis, 'New Atlantis', in *The Advancement of Learning and New Atlantis* (Oxford, 1974), pp. 215–47; first published 1627.

Besant, Arthur Digby, *The Besant Pedigree* (London, 1930).

Bradlaugh, Charles, *A Selection of the Political Pamphlets of Charles Bradlaugh*, ed. John Saville (New York, 1970).

Bradlaugh Bonner, Hypatia, *Charles Bradlaugh, A Record of His Life and Work* (2 vols., London, 1902).

— *Humanity's Gain from Unbelief, and Other Selections from the Works of Charles Bradlaugh* (London, 1932), first published 1929.

Edison, Thomas A., *Thomas A. Edison Papers*, republished online by Rutgers University Press, http://edison.rutgers.edu/

Fabian Essays in Socialism, ed. George Bernard Shaw (London, 1889).

Freud, Sigmund, *Psychopathology of Everyday Life* (trans. Anthea Bell; London, 2002), first published in German 1901.

— *The Collected Papers of Sigmund Freud*, ed. Philip Rieff, Vol. 10: Studies in Parapsychology (New York, 1963).

— *The Interpretation of Dreams* (trans. Joyce Crick; Oxford, 1999), first published in German 1899.

— 'The Uncanny', in *The Standard Edition of the Complete Psychological Works of Sigmund Freud*, ed. James Strachey, Vol. 17 (London, 1953), pp. 219–52; first published in German, 1919.

— *Three Essays on the Theory of Sexuality* (trans. James Strachey; London, 1962), first published in German 1905.
Gandhi, M.K., *An Autobiography, or the Story of My Experiments with Truth* (Ahmedabad, 1998), first published 1927.
— *Speeches and Writings* (Madras, 1922).
Homer, *The Iliad* (trans. Andrew Lang, Walter Leaf and Ernest Myers; London, 1914), first published 1883.
Humboldt, Alexander von, *Kosmos: Entwurf einer physischen Weltbeschreibung* (4 vols., Stuttgart, 1845–1858).
Jantsch, Erich, *The Self-Organizing Universe: Scientific and Human Implications of the Emerging Paradigm of Evolution* (Oxford, 1980).
Jung, C.G., 'On Spiritualistic Phenomena', in *Psychology and the Occult* (Princeton, 1977), pp. 92–107; first published in German 1902.
— 'On the Psychology and Pathology of So-Called Occult Phenomena', *Psychology and the Occult* (Princeton, 1977), pp. 6–91: first published in German 1905.
— *Psychology and the East* (Princeton, 1978).
— *The Psychology of Kundalini Yoga: Notes of the Seminar Given in 1932*, ed. Sonu Shamdasani (Princeton, 1996).
Knowlton, Charles, 'The Fruits of Philosophy: An Essay on the Population Question', in S. Chandrasekhar, *'A Dirty Filthy Book': The Writings of Charles Knowlton and Annie Besant on Reproductive Physiology and Birth Control and an Account of the Bradlaugh-Besant Trial* (Berkeley, 1981), pp. 87–147; first published 1832.
Krishnamurti, J., and David Bohm, *The Limits of Thought: Discussions* (London, 1999).
Malthus, T.R., *An Essay on the Principle of Population, and, a Summary View of the Principle of Population*, ed. Anthony Flew (Harmondsworth, 1970), first published 1798.
Marx-Aveling, Eleanor, and Edward Aveling, 'The Woman Question', in *Thoughts on Women And Society*, ed. Joachim Müller and Edith Schotte (New York, 1987), pp. 10–29, first published 1886.
Mozoomdar, P.C., *The Life and Teachings of Keshub Chunder Sen* (Calcutta, 1891).
Nehru, Jawaharlal, *An Autobiography, with Musings on Recent Events in India* (London, 1949), first published 1936.
— *The Discovery of India* (New York, 1946).
Novikoff, Olga, *Russian Memories* (London, 1917).
— *The M.P. for Russia: Reminiscences and Correspondence of Mme. Olga Novikoff*, ed. W.T. Stead (2 vols., London, 1909).
Pearson, Hesketh, *Bernard Shaw, His Life and Personality* (London, 1943), first published 1942.
Pease, Edward Reynolds, *The History of the Fabian Society* (London, 1916).
Plato, *The Timaeus and the Critias or Atlanticus* (trans. Thomas Taylor; New York, 1944).
Podmore, Frank, *Modern Spiritualism: A History and Criticism*, ed. R.A. Gilbert (2 vols., London, 2000), first published 1902.
— *Robert Owen: A Biography* (2 vols., London, 1906).

Bibliography

Prigogine, Ilya, and Isabelle Stengers, *Order Out of Chaos: Man's New Dialogue with Nature* (Toronto, 1984).
Proceedings of the Society for Psychical Research, Vol. 1, 1882–1883 (London, 1883) and Vol. 3, 1884–1885 (London, 1885).
Robertson, J.M., *A History of Freethought: Ancient and Modern, to the Period of the French Revolution* (London, 1936), first published 1899.
— *Did Shakespeare Write Titus Andronicus?* (London, 1905).
— *Pagan Christs: Studies in Comparative Hierology* (London, 1903).
Roy, Rammohun, *The English Works of Raja Rammohun Roy*, ed. Jogendra Chunder Ghose (New Delhi, 1982).
— *The Essential Writings of Raja Rammohan Ray*, ed. Brice Carlisle Robertson (Delhi, 1999).
Saraswati, Dayanand, *The Autobiography of Dayanand Saraswati*, ed. K.C. Yadav (New Delhi, 1978).
Sena, Kesavachandra, *Keshub Chunder Sen's Lectures in India* (2 vols., London, 1901–1904).
Shaw, George Bernard, *An Autobiography*, Vol. 1, 1856–1898 and Vol. 2, 1898–1950: The Playwright Years, Selected from his Writings by Stanley Weintraub (New York, 1969 and 1970).
— *Collected Letters, 1874–1897*, ed. Dan H. Laurence (London, 1965).
— *Essays in Fabian Socialism* (London, 1949), first published 1932.
— *Everybody's Political What's What?* (London, 1944).
Sidgwick, Henry, *A Memoir* (London, 1906).
Silberer, Herbert, *Problems of Mysticism and Its Symbols* (New York, 1917), first published in German 1914.
St. Augustine, *City of God* (New York, 1958).
Thoreau, Henry David, *The Journal of Henry D. Thoreau*, ed. Bradford Torrey and Francis H. Allen (2 vols., New York, 1962).
— *Walden* (Köln, 1996), first published 1854.
Vivekananda, Swami, 'My Plan of Campaign' (Delivered at the Victoria Hall, Madras, 1897), in *The Complete Works of Swami Vivekananda*, Vol. 3: Lectures from Colombo to Almora, republished online by Ramakrishna Mission Center, http://www.ramakrishnavivekananda.info/vivekananda/volume_3_frame.htm
— *The Yogas and Other Works, Including the Chicago Addresses, Jnana-yoga, Bhakti-yoga, Karma-yoga, Raja-yoga, Inspired Talks, and Lectures, Poems and Letters* (New York, 1953).
Wedderburn, Sir William, *Allan Octavian Hume, 'Father of the Indian National Congress', 1829–1912, A Biography*, ed. Edward C. Moulton (New Delhi, 2002), first published 1913.
Yeats, W.B., *Autobiographies* (London, 1973), first published 1955.
— *Later Essays*, ed. William H. O'Donnell (New York, 1994).
— *Memoirs*, ed. Denis Donoghue (London, 1972).
— *The Letters of W.B. Yeats*, ed. Allan Wade (London, 1954).

Newspapers and Periodicals

Journal of the Society for Psychical Research (London).

The Contemporary Review (Oxford).
The Fortnightly Review (London).
The National Reformer (London).
The Nineteenth Century (London).
Our Corner (London).
The Pall Mall Gazette (London).
The Quarterly Review (London).
The Spiritualist (London).
The Times (London).

Secondary Sources

Aarsleff, H., *The Study of Language in England, 1780–1860* (Princeton, 1967).

Akerman, Susanna, *Rose Cross Over the Baltic: The Spread of Rosicrucianism in Northern Europe* (Leiden, 1998).

Arberry, A.J., *Oriental Essays, Portraits of Seven Scholars* (Chippenham, 1997), first published 1960.

Arnstein, Walter L., *The Bradlaugh Case, A Study in Late Victorian Opinion and Politics* (Oxford, 1965).

Art, Science, and History in the Renaissance, ed. Charles S. Singleton (Baltimore, 1968).

Ashton, Rosemary, *Little Germany, Exile and Asylum in Victorian England* (Oxford, 1986).

Asian Religions in America: A Documentary History, ed. Thomas A. Tweed and Stephen Prothero (New York, 1999).

Baldwin, Neil, *Edison, Inventing the Century* (Chicago, 2001), first published 1995.

Bednarowski, Mary Farrell, 'Women in Occult America', in *The Occult in America: New Historical Perspectives*, ed. Howard Kerr and Charles L. Crow (Urbana, 1983).

Berlin, Isaiah, 'The Counter-Enlightenment', in *Against the Current, Essays in the History of Ideas*, ed. Henry Hardy (New York, 1980), pp. 1–24.

Bevir, Mark, *The Logic of the History of Ideas* (Cambridge, 1999).

— 'Annie Besant's Quest for Truth: Christianity, Secularism and New Age Thought', *Journal of Ecclesiastical History* 50 (1999), 62–93.

— 'In Opposition to the Raj: Annie Besant and the Dialectic of Empire', in *History of Political Thought* 19 (1998), 61–77.

— 'The West Turns Eastward: Madame Blavatsky and the Transformation of the Occult Tradition', *Journal of the American Academy of Religion* 62 (1994), 747–67.

— 'Theosophy as a Political Movement', in *Gurus and Their Followers: New Religious Reform Movements in Colonial India*, ed. Antony Copley (Delhi, 2000), pp. 159–79.

Bishop, Peter, *Dreams of Power, Tibetan Buddhism and the Western Imagination* (London, 1993).

Bossy, Joseph, *Giordano Bruno and the Embassy Affair* (London, 1991).

Bowler, Peter J., *The Invention of Progress: The Victorians and the Past* (Oxford, 1989).
Bosch, Lourens P. van den, *Friedrich Max Müller, A Life Devoted to the Humanities* (Leiden, 2002).
— 'Theosophy or Pantheism?: Friedrich Max Müller's Gifford Lectures on Natural Religion', published online by *Here-Now4U Online Magazine*, http://www.here-now4u.de/eng/theosophy_or_pantheism__friedr.htm
Brown, Terence, *The Life of W.B. Yeats: A Critical Biography* (Oxford, 1999).
Brecher, Michael, *Political Leadership in India: an Analysis of Elite Attitudes* (New York, 1969).
Cannon, Garland, *The Life and Mind of Oriental Jones: Sir William Jones, the Father of Modern Linguistics* (Cambridge, 1990).
Cannon, Garland and Kevin R. Brine (eds), *Objects of Enquiry, The Life, Contributions, and Influences of Sir William Jones (1746–1794)* (New York, 1995).
Carlson, Maria, *'No Religion Higher than Truth', A History of the Theosophical Movement in Russia, 1875–1922* (Princeton, 1993).
Chakrabarty, Dipesh, 'Postcoloniality and the Artifice of History: Who Speaks for "Indian" Pasts?', in *The New Historicism Reader*, ed. Harold Veeser (London, 1994), pp. 342–69.
Chaudhuri, Nirad, *Scholar Extraordinary: The Life of Professor the Rt. Hon. Friedrich Max Müller* (London, 1974).
— *Thy Hand, Great Anarch!* (London, 1987).
Childs, Gilbert, *Rudolf Steiner: His Life and Work* (Edinburgh, 1995).
Christians and Missionaries in India: Cross-Cultural Communication Since 1500, with Special Reference to Caste, Conversion, and Colonialism, ed. Robert Eric Frykenberg and Alaine Low (London, 2003).
Cohn, Norman, *Warrant for Genocide, The Myth of the Jewish World-Conspiracy and the Protocols of the Elders of Zion* (London, 1967).
Cole, Margaret, *The Story of Fabian Socialism* (London, 1961).
Congress and the Raj: Facets of the Indian Struggle, 1917–1947, ed. D.A. Low (London, 1977).
Cranston, Sylvia, *HPB: The Extraordinary Life and Influence of Helena Blavatsky, Founder of the Modern Theosophical Movement* (New York, 1993).
Cullingford, Elisabeth Butler, *Gender and History in Yeats's Love Poetry* (Cambridge, 1993).
De Terra, Helmut, *Humboldt: The Life and Times of Alexander von Humboldt, 1769–1859* (New York, 1955).
Dinnage, Rosemary, *Annie Besant* (Middlesex, 1986).
Dixon, Joy, *Divine Feminine: Theosophy and Feminism in England* (Baltimore, 2001).
— 'Sexology and the Occult: Sexuality and Subjectivity in Theosophy's New Age', *Journal of the History of Sexuality* 7 (1997), 409–33.
Eliade, Mircea, *The Sacred and the Profane: The Nature of Religion* (New York, 1959).
Ellmann, Richard, *Yeats: The Man and the Masks* (New York, 1948).
Elswood, Robert S. Jr., 'The American Theosophical Synthesis', in *The Occult in America: New Historical Perspectives*, ed. Howard Kerr and Charles L. Crow (Urbana, 1983), pp. 111–34.

Eyck, Erich, *Gladstone* (London, 1966), first published in Dutch 1938.
Faivre, Antoine, 'Questions of Terminology Proper to the Study of Esoteric Currents in Modern and Contemporary Europe', in *Western Esotericism and the Science of Religion*, ed. Antoine Faivre and Wouter J. Hanegraaf (Leuven, 1998), pp. 1-10.
— *Theosophy, Imagination, Tradition: Studies in Western Esotericism* (Albany, 2000), first published in French 1996.
Fleming, Peter, *Bayonets to Lhasa: The First Full Account of the British Invasion of Tibet in 1904* (London, 1962).
Forster, R.F., *W.B. Yeats: A Life, Vol. 1: The Apprentice Mage, 1865-1914* (Oxford, 1997).
Gal, Allon, Isaac Lubelsky, 'The Disintegration of the British Empire and the Nationalist Cases of India and Israel: a Comparative Analysis', *Israel Affairs*, ed. Efraim Karsh, Vol. 14, No. 2 (London, April 2008), 165-83.
Garin, Eugenio, *Italian Humanism, Philosophy and Civic Life in the Renaissance* (Westport, 1965).
Gatti, Hilary, *Giordano Bruno and Renaissance Science* (New York, 1999).
Godwin, Joscelyn, *Music and the Occult, French Musical Philosophies, 1750-1950* (Rochester, 1995).
— *The Theosophical Enlightenment* (Albany, 1994).
Godwin, Joscelyn, Christian Chanel, and John Patrick Deveney, *The Hermetic Brotherhood of Luxor: Initiatic and Historical Documents of an Order of Practical Occultism* (York Beach, 1995).
Grafton, Anthony, *Forgers and Critics, Creativity and Duplicity in Western Scholarship* (Princeton, 1990).
Hall, Julie, 'The *Saptaparña*: The Meaning and Origins of the Theosophical Septenary Constitution of Man', *Theosophical History*, ed. James Santucci, Vol. XIII, No. 4 (October, 2007), 5-38.
Hammer, Olav, *Claiming Knowledge, Strategies of Epistemology from Theosophy to the New Age* (Leiden, 2001).
Hanegraaff, Wouter, J., *New Age Religion and Western Culture, Esotericism in the Mirror of Secular Thought* (New York, 1998), first published 1996.
Harvey, Christopher, 'Reform and Expansion, 1854-1871', in *The History of the University of Oxford*, Vol. 6, *Nineteenth-Century Oxford, Part 1*, ed. M.G. Brock and M.C. Curtyhoys (Oxford, 1997), pp. 697-730.
Heelas, Paul, *The New Age Movement: The Celebration of the Self and the Sacralization of Modernity* (Oxford, 1996).
Hermeticism and the Renaissance: Intellectual History and the Occult in Early Modern Europe, ed. Ingrid Merkel and Allen G. Debus (London, 1988).
Ingalls, Daniel H.H., 'The Heritage of a Fallible Saint: Annie Besant's Gifts to India', *Proceedings of the American Philosophical Society*, 109 (1965), 85-86.
Inden, Ronald, *Imagining India* (Oxford, 1990).
Irschick, Eugène F., *Politics and Social Conflict in South India: The Non-Brahman Movement and Tamil Separatism, 1916-1929* (Berkeley, 1969).
Israel, Paul, Edison, *A Life of Invention* (New York, 1998).
Jacob, Margaret C., *Living the Enlightenment: Freemasonry and Politics in Eighteenth-Century Europe* (New York, 1991).

Jackson, Carl T., *The Oriental Religions and American Thought: Nineteenth-Century Explorations* (Westport, 1981).
— *Vedânta for the West: The Ramakrishna Movement in the United States* (Bloomington, 1994).
Jankowsky, Kurt R., 'F. Max Müller and the Development of Linguistic Science', *Historiographia Linguistica* (1979), 339-59.
Johnson, Gordon, *Provincial Politics and Indian Nationalism: Bombay and the Indian National Congress, 1880 to 1915* (Cambridge, 1973).
Jordens, J.T.F., *Dayananda Sarasvati, Essays on His Life and Ideas* (New Delhi, 1998).
Kapp, Yvonne, *Eleanor Marx, Vol. 1: Family Life (1855-1883)*, (London, 1972).
Katz, David S., and Richard H. Popkin, *Messianic Revolution* (New York, 1999).
Katz, David S., *The Occult Tradition, from the Renaissance to the Present Day* (London, 2005).
Kejariwal, O.P., *The Asiatic Society of Bengal and the Discovery of India's Past, 1784-1838* (Delhi, 1988).
Kinahan, Frank, *Yeats: Folklore, and Occultism* (London, 1988).
Kopf, David, *British Orientalism and the Bengal Renaissance* (Berkeley, 1969).
Kulke, Herman, and Dietmar Rothermund, *A History of India* (London, 1986).
Kumar, Raj, *Annie Besant's Rise to Power in Indian Politics, 1914-1917* (New Delhi, 1981).
Lawson, Philip, *The East India Company: A History* (London, 1993).
Lehman, Winfred P., *A Reader in Nineteenth-Century Historical Indo-European Linguistics* (Bloomington, 1967).
Lubelsky, Isaac, 'The Star in the East: the Theosophical Perception of the Mystical Orient', ed. Andreas Önnerfors and Dorothe Sommer, *Sheffield Lectures on the History of Freemasonry and Fraternalism, Vol. 1, Freemasonry and Fraternalism in the Middle East* (Sheffield: Sheffield University Press, 2009), 85-108.
Luckhurst, Roger, *The Invention of Telepathy, 1870-1901* (Oxford, 2002).
Ludowyk, E.F.C., *The Modern History of Ceylon* (London, 1966).
MacKay, Carol Hanbery, *Creative Negativity, Four Victorian Exemplars of the Female Quest* (Stanford, 2001).
Martin, Briton, *New India, 1885: British Official Policy and the Emergence of the Indian National Congress* (Berkeley, 1969).
Masuzawa, Tomoko, *In Search of Dreamtime: The Quest for the Origin of Religion* (Chicago, 1993).
McBriar, A.M., *Fabian Socialism and English Politics, 1884-1918* (London, 1962).
Mehrotra, S.R., *The Emergence of the Indian National Congress* (Delhi, 1971).
Miller, Timothy, *The Quest for Utopia, Vol. 1: 1900-1960* (Syracuse, 1998).
Moon, Penderel, *Warren Hastings and British India* (London, 1947).
Mukherjee, S.N., *Sir William Jones: A Study in Eighteenth-Century British Attitudes to India* (Cambridge, 1968).
Nanda, B.R., *Gandhi: Pan-Islamism, Imperialism and Nationalism in India* (New Delhi, 1989).
— *Gokhale: The Indian Moderates and the British Raj* (New Delhi, 1977).
— *Gokhale, Gandhi and the Nehrus: Studies in Indian Nationalism* (London, 1974).
— *The Nehrus: Motilal and Jawaharlal* (London, 1962).

Nethercot, Arthur H., *The First Five Lives of Annie Besant* (Chicago, 1960).
— *The Last Four Lives of Annie Besant* (London, 1963).
Oppenheim, Janet, 'Prophets without Honour? The Odyssey of Annie Besant', *History Today* 39 (1989), 12–18.
— *The Other World: Spiritualism and Psychical Research in England, 1850–1914* (New York, 1985).
Owen, Alex, *The Darkened Room: Women, Power, and Spiritualism in Late Nineteenth-Century England* (London, 1989).
Oxtoby, Willard G. (ed.), *World Religions, Eastern Traditions* (Oxford, 1996).
Prothero, Stephen, *Purified By Fire: A History of Cremation in America* (Berkeley, 2002).
— *The White Buddhist: The Asian Odyssey of Henry Steel Olcott* (Bloomington, 1996).
Pugh, Patricia, *Educate, Agitate, Organize: 100 Years of Fabian Socialism* (London, 1984).
Richards, John F., *The Mughal Empire* (Cambridge, 1993).
Ringbom, Sixten, *The Sounding Cosmos: A Study in the Spiritualism of Kandinsky and the Genesis of Abstract Painting* (Helsingfors, 1970).
Rothermund, Dietmar, *Government, Landlord and Peasant in India, Agrarian Relations Under British Rule* (Wiesbaden, 1978).
— *The German Intellectual Quest for India* (New Delhi, 1986).
— *The Phases of Indian Nationalism and other Essays* (Bombay, 1970).
Said, Edward W., *Orientalism* (New York, 1978).
Santucci, James, 'The Conception of Christ in the Theosophical Tradition', in *Alternative Christs*, ed. Olav Hammer (Cambridge, 2009), pp. 190–211.
Scholem, Gershom Gerhard, *Major Trends in Jewish Mysticism* (Jerusalem, 1941).
Schremp, Gregory, 'The Re-Education of Friedrich Max Müller: Intellectual Appropriation and Epistemological Antinomy in Mid-Victorian Thought', *Man*, New Series, 18 (1983), 90–110.
Schuchard, Marsha Keith, *Restoring the Temple of Vision: Cabalistic Freemasonry and Stuart Culture* (Leiden, 2002).
Schwab, Raymond, *The Oriental Renaissance, Europe's Rediscovery of India and the East, 1680–1880* (New York, 1984), first published in French 1950.
Seager, Richard Hughes, *The World's Parliament of Religions: The East/West Encounter, Chicago, 1893* (Bloomington, 1995).
Secrets of Nature, Astrology and Alchemy in Early Modern Europe, ed. William R. Newman and Anthony Grafton (Cambridge, MA, 2001).
Sharpe, Eric J., *Comparative Religion, A History* (La Salle, 1987).
— *The Universal Gita, Western Images of the Bhagavad Gītā, a Bicentenary Survey* (La Salle, 1985).
Sitaramayya, Bhogaraju Pattabhi, *The History of the Indian National Congress, 1885–1935* (Delhi, 1935).
Stevenson, David, *The Origins of Freemasonry: Scotland's Century, 1590–1710* (Cambridge, 1988).
Streusand, Douglas E., *The Formation of the Mughal Empire* (Delhi, 1999).
Stocking, George Ward, *Race, Culture, and Evolution: Essays in the History of Anthropology* (New York, 1968).
— *Victorian Anthropology* (New York, 1987).
Surette, Leon, *The Birth of Modernism* (Montreal, 1993).

Sweet, Paul R., *Wilhelm von Humboldt: A Biography* (2 vols., Columbus, OH, 1978–1980).
Taylor, Anne, *Annie Besant, A Biography* (Oxford, 1992).
Tillett, Gregory, *The Elder Brother: A Biography of Charles Webster Leadbeater* (London, 1982).
Trautmann, Thomas, *Aryans and British India* (Berkeley, CA, 1997).
Trompf, G.W., 'Macrohistory in Blavatsky, Steiner and Guénon', in *Western Esotericism and the Science of Religion*, ed. Antoine Faivre and Wouter J. Hanegraaff (Leuven, 1998), pp. 269–96.
Tsuzuki, Chushichi, *The Life of Eleanor Marx, 1855–1898: A Socialist Tragedy* (Oxford, 1967).
Tweed, Thomas A., *The American Encounter with Buddhism, 1844–1912: Victorian Culture & the Limits of Dissent* (Chapel Hill, NC, 2000), first published 1992.
Vernon, Roland, *Star in the East: Krishnamurti, the Invention of a Messiah* (London, 2000).
Vickers, Brian, 'Analogy Versus Identity: The Rejection of Occult Symbolism, 1580–1680', in *Occult and Scientific Mentalities in the Renaissance*, ed. Brian Vickers (New York, 1986), pp. 95–163.
Victorian Sages and Cultural Discourse: Renegotiating Gender and Power, ed. Thais E. Morgan (New Brunswick, NJ, 1990).
Wach, Joachim, *Comparative Study of Religion* (New York, 1958).
Waley, S.D., *Edwin Montagu: A Memoir and an Account of His Visits to India* (London, 1964).
Walker, D.P., *Spiritual and Demonic Magic from Ficino to Campanella* (London, 1958).
Walker, Steven F., 'Vivekananda and American Occultism', in *The Occult in America: New Historical Perspectives*, ed. Howard Kerr and Charles L. Crow (Urbana, 1983), pp. 162–76.
Washington, Peter, *Madame Blavatsky's Baboon: A History of the Mystics, Mediums, and Misfits Who Brought Spiritualism to America* (New York, 1995), first published 1993.
Waterman, Adlai E., *The 'Hodgson Report' on Madame Blavatsky, 1885–1960: Re-examination Discredits the Major Charges Against H.P. Blavatsky* (Adyar, 1963).
Weeks, Andrew, *Böhme: An Intellectual Biography of the Seventeenth-Century Philosopher and Mystic* (Albany, 1991).
Weisberger, William R., *Speculative Freemasonry and the Enlightenment: A Study of the Craft in London, Paris, Prague, and Vienna* (New York, 1993).
Whyte, Frederic, *The Life of W.T. Stead* (2 vols., London, 1925).
Wild, Anthony, *The East India Company: Trade and Conquest from 1600* (London, 2000).
Wolpert, Stanley A., *Tilak and Gokhale: Revolution and Reform in the Making of Modern India* (Berkeley, CA, 1962).
Yates, Frances A., *Giordano Bruno and the Hermetic Tradition* (Chicago, 1964).
— *The Rosicrucian Enlightenment* (London, 1972).
Zipes, Jack David, *The Brothers Grimm: From Enchanted Forests to the Modern World* (New York, 1989).

Index

alchemy 165–6
Arundale, George 268–9, 298–9, 311–13, 320
Arundale, Rukmini 269, 312, 320
Aryan
    civilisation, Besant on 281–2
    ideology, basis of 13, 15–16
    language and culture 50–4, 58, 61–2
    myth 34, 266 see also Max Müller, Friedrich
    race and Germany 27
    thought in Theosophist doctrine 126, 129–30, 133–7, 143–6
    vision see Max Müller, Friedrich
Asiatic Society of Bengal, The
    after Jones 21–3
    foundation of 9–11
Asiatic Society, Royal (London) 23
Atlantis 124, 129–31, 143–4, 185–7
Aveling, Edward 202–3, 206–7

Bentham, Jeremy 24
Besant, Annie see also Theosophical Society
    doctrine of see Theosophical doctrine
    and the Esoteric Section see Esoteric Section (ES)
    first tour of India 235–7
    and the Knowlton Trial 198–200
    and the Masters 80–1
    in the National Secular Society 196–7
    personality 190–1
    relationship with Leadbeater 139, 141–5, 291–5
    role in Indian politics 247, 255–7, 261–70, 276–84 see also Gandhi, Mahatma
    and socialism 203–11
    as sucessor to Blavatsky 115–17, 214–16, 220, 222–4
    before the Theosophical Society 193–212
    transition to Theosophy 212–13
    and the World Teacher see Krishnamurti, Jiddu; World Teacher
    at the World's Parliament of Religions 229–30
Bhagavad Gītā 21, 69, 183, 271–2
Biblical historiography 16
Blavatsky, Madame Helena Petrovna
    in comparison with Besant 191–2
    criticisms of 103–4 see also Hodgson Report; SPR
    on Darwin's theory of evolution 123, 130
    disagreement with Olcott 103–4
    final years 214–23
    foundation of the Theosophical Society 82–4
    influences on 147–89
    Isis Unveiled 86–7, 121–6
    Lucifer 114
    The Mahatma Letters 80, 95–6, 109, 250–1
    The Secret Doctrine 115–17, 126–31
    split with Olcott 110
    and Theosophical doctrine 118–31

before the Theosophical Society 77–83
  writing abilities 84, 96
Böhme, Jacob 159–61
Bopp, Franz 30, 30–3, 40
Bradlaugh, Charles 195–201, 204–5, 207–8, 212, 253
Brahmanism 34, 174
British East India Company 3–8, 42
British Empire 19, 65, 145, 278–9
British Theosophical Society (London Lodge of the Theosophical Society) 90–1, 112–14
Bruno, Giordano 124, 133, 153–4, 164
Buddha 14, 136, 142
Buddhism
  esoteric 94–5, 228, 232–4
  Jennings's view of 174
  Sinhalese 101–3
  Tibetan 81
Bulwer-Lytton, Edward, esoteric novels of 167–72
Burrows, Herbert
  commission against Judge 238
  in the ES 218
  political work 210–11
  relationship with Besant 117, 202, 207, 244–5
  with Besant in France 214–15

Cagliostro, Alessandro 158–9
Caithness, Countess of 182–4
Christian mission
  in Ceylon 101–2
  in India 71, 89, 107, 257
Christianity
  Besant's view of 132–4
  Blavatsky's criticisms of 124–5
  and Buddhism 123, 289
  esoteric 132
  Hindu motifs in see Hindu
  history of 53–4, 63, 112, 162
Clive, Robert 4–5
Colebrooke, Henry Thomas 7, 21–4

Darwin, Charles 55–8
de Chézy, Antoine 36–7
Dutch East India Company 3

Edison, Thomas 87, 91

Fabian Society, the 204–9, 212
Ficino, Marsilio 151–4, 162, 164
Freemasonry 155–6, 159, 163, 306
French East India Company 3

Gandhi, Mahatma 270–6, 278, 280, 283–4
Gnosticism 99, 162–3
Gokhale, Gopal Krishna 260–1, 263, 269, 272–3
Grimm, Jakob 30, 32

Hardinge Britten, Emma 183–4
Hastings, Warren 5–7, 11
Hermes Trismegistus 124, 137, 149, 151, 164–5
Hermeticism 149–55
Higgins, Godfrey 178–9
Hindu
  character 69
  culture see Indian culture
  education 258–61
  laws 7–8, 17–18, 22, 46
  motifs in Christianity 34
  mythology 60
  philosophy in Theosophic doctrine 120, 148
  reform 226–7
  scriptures 97, 99, 175
  texts see Bhagavad Gītā; Hitôpadeśa; Meghaduta; Rig Veda; Śākuntalā
  wisdom, Theosophic interpretation of 99
Hinduism
  relationship with theosophy 100, 257–8, 315–16
  Western histories of 172–3, 176
Hitôpadeśa 21, 40
Hodgson Report 107–10, 251
Humboldt, Alexander von 30, 33, 40
Humboldt, Wilhelm von 30, 33
Hume, Allan Octavian 94–5, 107, 109, 248–55

India *see also* British East India
  Company; Indian culture; Moghul
  government
  British rule in 5-7, 21-6
  Christian mission in *see*
    Christian mission
  European attitudes to 38
  histories of *see* Hinduism
  images of 1, 10
  judicial system *see* Hindu laws
  Max Müller on *see* Max Müller,
    Friedrich
  politics of *see* Besant, Annie;
    Gandhi, Mahatma; Indian
    National Congress
  Portuguese trade with 2-3
  role of in occult literature 163,
    181, 183, 185
  role of in Theosophical doctrine
    see Theosophical doctrine
  Theosophical Society in *see*
    Theosophical Society
  theosophist attitude to 313-16
Indian culture
  British attitudes to 7, 66-9
  chronological superiority of 16
  European attitudes to 2-3, 17,
    26, 38, 188
  French attitudes to 35-6
  German attitudes to 26-30
  Jones' attitude to 12, 17, 20
Indian National Congress (INC)
  247-8 *see also* Besant, Annie;
  Gandhi, Mahatma

Jennings, Hargrave 157, 173-4
Jones, Sir William
  and the Asiatic Society 9-11
  career in India 7-20
  and Indian culture *see* Indian
    culture
  and the Indian judicial system
    17-18
  racial theories of *see* racial
    theories
  and the study of Sanskrit 11-14,
    20

Judaism
  Blavatsky's criticisms of 125, 128
  Jennings's view of 174
  Max Müller's view of 52-3
Judge, William Quan 83-4, 220-5,
  229, 235, 237-40

Kingsford, Anna 91, 112-14, 218
Knowlton Trial, the *see* Besant,
  Annie
Krishnamurti, Jiddu 295-305, 307-17

Lang, Andrew 55, 61-2 *see also*
  mythology
Laws of Manu, the 7, 18
Leadbeater, Charles Webster
  biography 286-95, 305-7
  doctrine of 139-45
  and Krishnamurti 297-8
  scandal 293-4
Lévi, Eliphas 180-2
Lutyens, Edwin 305
Lutyens, Emily 304, 306, 320
Lutyens, Mary 305

Macaulay, Thomas Babington 7, 20,
  25, 46-7
magic, history of 164-5, 181
Malthus, Thomas 198
Masters of the Great Brotherhood
  Besant and 214
  Blavatsky and 79-81, 86, 95-6,
    221
  Hume and 250-1
  Judge and 238-9
  Krishnamurti and 298
  Leadbeater and 288-90
Max Müller, Friedrich *see also* racial
  theories; Romanticism
  Aryan vision of (Aryan myth)
    49-53, 68-70, 72-6
  biography 39-48
  criticisms of *see* Darwin; Lang;
    Tylor
  on his predecessors 22-3, 28, 35
  on India 10, 38, 53, 63-72
  on mythology 50-1

and philology 50-2
on religion 30, 34, 53-4
and the *Rig Veda* see *Rig Veda*
and the study of Sanskrit 40
on the Theosophists 100, 230-4
Meghaduta 23
Mead, George 166, 216, 234, 238, 244-5, 294-5
Mesmer, Franz 158
Mill, James 24-5
Mill, John Stuart 24, 206
Moghul government 4-5, 7, 18
Montagu, Edwin 278-280, 282-3
mythology
   Aryan 51
   Besant's view of 133
   Jones' view of 14-15
   Lang's view of 62
   Max Müller's view of (comparative) 50-1, 60
   Tylor's view of 59-60

Napoleon 36-7
New Age movement, Leadbeater's influence on 139, 292, 320

Olcott, Colonel Henry
   and Besant 235-40, 243-4
   with Blavatsky 87-94, 97-101
   in Ceylon *see* the Theosophical Society
   and the foundation of the Theosophical Society 82-4
   and the leadership of the Theosophical Society 219-24
   and Max Müller 230-4
   rift with Blavatsky 110-11, 216
Oriental imagery 10, 30
Orientalist research 11, 15, 36-8

philology
   comparative 50
   as a Natural Science 33
   the Rosetta Stone's effect on 36
   Sanskrit 27, 29, 31-2
   and the study of religion 52, 54

racial theories
   of Blavatsky 130, 144
   of Higgins 178-9
   of Jones 13-16
   of Max Müller 49, 64-5
Roy, Rammohun (Raja) 72, 89, 178
religion *see also* Buddhism; Christianity; Gnosticism; Hinduism; Judaism
   comparative 62, 73
   esoteric 128
   history of 51-4, 86, 136, 178, 184-5
   India as birthplace of 68
   superiority of Indian 93
Rig Veda 41-3, 58
Robertson, John 202-4, 206-7
Romanticism
   of Max Müller 49-50, 60, 65
   in nineteenth century Germany 27, 160
Rosicrucian Fraternity 155-7, 174, 188

Śākuntalā 19, 24, 27, 37
Sanskrit *see also* Jones, Sir William
   Higgins' philological view of 178-9
   Max Müller's philological view of 51, 69
   studies 2-3, 22-32
Saraswati, Dayananda 88-90, 96-100, 127
Schlegel, Friedrich 28-30
Schlegel, Wilhelm 28, 33
Schopenhauer, Arthur 30, 34-5, 70, 122
Shaw, George Bernard 202-7, 210-12
Shore, John 21
Sidgwick, Henry 104, 106-7
Sinnett, Alfred 94-6, 113-14, 245
Society for Psychical Research (SPR) 104-7, 109-10, 205
spiritualism 77-8, 97, 105, 138, 183
Steiner, Rudolf 223-4, 301-4
Swedenborg, Emanuel 159-61

The Theosophist 93
Theosophical doctrine
　Atlantean theory in 124, 130, 143
　Besant's role in 132–8 *see also* World Teacher
　Blavatsky's role in 119–31
　credibility of 118–19
　Egyptian lore in 122
　Leadbeater's role in 139
　new world order 145
　racial origins in 129–30, 135–6, 144
　reincarnation in 142
　role of India in 122–3, 131, 145
　view of other religions 125, 128
Theosophical Society, the
　after Besant 321
　and the Anthroposophical Society 303–4
　under Besant 132, 190–1, 223–4
　in Ceylon 101–3
　connection with India 88–90
　crisis after Krishnamurti 312–13
　Esoteric Section (ES) 216–20
　foundation of 82–4
　and the Hodgson Report *see* Hodgson Report
　in India 91–5, 227, 229 *see also* Besant, Annie; Olcott, Colonel Henry; Saraswati, Dayananda
　Leadbetter's role in *see* Besant, Annie
　leadership after Blavatsky 215, 220–4
　leadership struggles 235, 237–42, 244–5
　and Max Müller *see* Max Müller, Friedrich
　under Olcott 111, 243
　principles of 90
　role in Indian politics 93, 148, 281 *see also* Besant, Annie
　and Saraswati *see* Saraswati, Dayananda
　slow progress of 87–8
　and the World Teacher 285, 298–301, 310–12
　at the World's Parliament of Religions 225, 229
Tilak, Bal Gangadhar 263, 269–70, 276, 280
Tingley, Katherine 224, 240–2
Transcendentalism, American 175–7
Trevelyan, Sir Charles 46
Tylor, Edward Burnett *see also* mythology 55, 59–61

Upanishads 34–5, 70, 181, 233
utilitarian approaches to India 18, 24–5, 46, 257

Vedic literature (*vedas*) 34, 69–70, 86, 96–8 *see also Rig Veda*
Vivekananda 72, 89, 226–8, 313

Wilkins, Charles 2, 8, 21–2
Wilson, Horace Hayman 19, 23–6, 41–3
World Teacher 132–8, 224, 285, 301 *see also* Besant, Annie; Krishnamurti, Jiddu
World's Parliament of Religions 225–30

Yeats, William Butler 217–19

www.ingramcontent.com/pod-product-compliance
Lightning Source LLC
Chambersburg PA
CBHW070749230426
43665CB00017B/2300